WARRIOR WOMEN
AND TRANS WARRIORS

Purdue Studies in Romance Literatures

Editorial Board

Íñigo Sánchez-Llama, Series Editor Beth Gale
Elena Coda   Laura Demaría
Paul B. Dixon

Howard Mancing, Consulting Editor
Floyd Merrell, Consulting Editor
R. Tyler Gabbard-Rocha, Production Editor

Associate Editors

French   *Spanish and Spanish American*
Jeanette Beer   Catherine Connor
Paul Benhamou   Ivy A. Corfis
Willard Bohn   Frederick A. de Armas
Thomas Broden   Edward Friedman
Mary Ann Caws   Charles Ganelin
Allan H. Pasco   David T. Gies
Gerald Prince   Roberto González Echevarría
Roseann Runte   David K. Herzberger
Ursula Tidd   Emily Hicks
                                 Djelal Kadir
Italian   Amy Kaminsky
Fiora A. Bassanese   Lucille Kerr
Peter Carravetta   Howard Mancing
Benjamin Lawton   Floyd Merrell
Franco Masciandaro   Alberto Moreiras
Anthony Julian Tamburri   Randolph D. Pope
                                 Elżbieta Skłodowska
Luso-Brazilian   Marcia Stephenson
Marta Peixoto
Ricardo da Silveira Lobo Sternberg

 volume 92

WARRIOR WOMEN AND TRANS WARRIORS

Performing Masculinities in Twentieth-Century Latin American Literature

Carolina Castellanos Gonella

Purdue University Press
West Lafayette, Indiana

Copyright ©2025 by Purdue University. All rights reserved.

Cataloging-in-Publication Data on file at the Library of Congress.

978-1-61249-980-2 (hardcover)
978-1-61249-981-9 (paperback)
978-1-61249-982-6 (epub)
978-1-61249-983-3 (epdf)

Cover image: "Diadorim" by Mario Cau

Contents

ix Acknowledgments

1 Introduction
- 5 Why "Warrior Women" and "Trans Warriors"?
- 11 Trans Warriors and Warrior Women in Latin American Literary Criticism
- 17 Warrior Women and Trans Warriors as Transgressive Characters
- 23 Trans Warrios and Warrior Women Characters in Latin America
- 30 Thematic Structure

33 Chapter One

The Sartorial Transgressions of Warrior Women and Trans Warriors
- 33 Fashioning Trans Warriors and Warrior Women
- 40 Pintada's Clothed Images
  - 48 Dressing to kill
- 50 Doña Bárbara's Manipulated Images
  - 52 Dressing for Strength
  - 54 Dressing to Seduce
- 58 Diadorim Clothed and Naked
  - 60 Dressing the Masculine Trans*
  - 67 Undressing the Corpse
- 70 Conclusion

73 Chapter Two

Empowered Names, Disempowered Nicknames
- 74 The Name as Proper Noun
- 78 Naming Pintada
  - 81 Dehumanizing Pintada
- 85 Naming Barbarity
  - 89 Demystifying the *Cacica*
- 94 Naming Diadorim
  - 96 Diadorim's Trans(itory) Names
- 102 Conclusion

105 Chapter Three
The Masculinities of Trans Warriors and Warrior Women
112 Pintada's Female Masculinity: Performing the Revolutionary
    113 Masculine Attitude
    114 Masculine Courage
    115 Manipulation
    117 Leadership
    118 Alcohol Consumption
    120 Disempowering the Warrior Women
122 Doña Bárbara's Female Masculinity: Performing the *Cacica*
    123 Dominating Men
    126 The Ideal Masculinity for Civilizing Barbarity
132 Diadorim's Trans* Masculinity: Performing the Hero Warrior
    134 Masculinity of Youth
    137 Masculinity of Adulthood
    140 Sacrifice of the War Hero
142 Conclusion

145 Chapter Four
Warrior Women, Trans Warriors, and Traditional Feminine Characters
    147 Diverse Femininities in *Los de abajo*
        152 Exchanging Women
    156 Mediated Femininities in Doña Bárbara
        161 Mestiza Mother and Daughter
        164 Embodying National Femininities
    165 Sexuality in *Grande sertão: veredas*
        169 Sexually Active Women Characters
        172 The Feminine Fiancée
        176 The Feminine Object
    178 Conclusion

181 **Chapter Five**
Trans Warriors and Warrior Women in Twentieth-Century Latin America
    184 Warrior Women and Trans Warriors in the Mexican Revolution
        188 Changing Images of a Warrior Woman from 1931 to 1960
        192 Controlling Images: The Black Warrior Woman
    204 Women Guerrillas in Latin American Revolutions
    205 Cuban Women Guerrillas of the Late 1950s
    209 Brazilian Women Guerrillas of the 1960s through 1970s
    214 Nicaraguan Women Guerrillas of the 1970s
    220 Latin American Trans Warriors in Revolutionary History
    224 Conclusion

229 **Epilogue**

239 **Notes**

249 **Bibliography**

285 **Index**

Acknowledgments

This book has been a long journey. I am enormously grateful to everyone involved in producing this book at Purdue University Press. Thanks to Joyce L. Detzner, R. Tyler Gabbard-Rocha, and the team at the Purdue Studies in Romance Literatures. I especially want to thank Gwen Kirkpatrick, Spanish editor, whose invaluable feedback and suggestions enhanced my analysis. I am also indebted to the two anonymous readers who provided me with bibliographical references and insights that improved my manuscript.

My doctoral advisor Emanuelle K. F. Oliveira-Monte deserves a special thank you for everything that she has done for me. Not only has she been a great mentor, attentive reader of my dissertation, and professor, she has demonstrated by example how a woman scholar from Latin America can navigate the often-unwelcoming academic environment of the United States. Emanuelle, I do not have the words to express how happy and thankful I am to have you in my life. To Earl E. Fitz, another big thank you for serving on my dissertation committee and for believing in, supporting, and encouraging me to pursue this topic from the beginning. I am also indebted to other professors at the University of Massachusetts Amherst and Vanderbilt University who helped me during the very early stages of this project, including Nina Gerassi-Navarro, Luis A. Marentes, Brooke Ackerly, Jason Borge, Cathy L. Jrade, Jim Lang, and Marshall E. Eakin.

I thank Dickinson College for the support I received to pursue my research. Special thanks to the Research and Development Committee for granting me a Dana Research Assistant, as well as providing me the funds to conduct research and paying for the cover of this book and other book-related costs. I also want to thank my colleagues at Dickinson who supported me throughout the

Acknowledgments

process. I especially thank Marcelo Borges, Elise Bartosik-Vélez, and Mariana Past for their advice, support, and proofreading skills. I am indebted to Margaret Frohlich, Patricia van Leeuwaarde Moonsammy, Erin Díaz, Regina Sweeney, and colleagues in Sharon O'Brien's writing support group. I am also grateful to colleagues in other institutions, Nikolina Dobreva and Giseli Tordin, as well as former students Alex Agiliga, Monica Panigassi Vicentini, and my Dana Research Assistant, Mary Naydan. I also want to thank Mario Cau @mariocau for designing the amazing cover for this book and Jaida Samudra for being my copy editor.

Thanks to my friends Gladys Robalino, Mayra Fortes, Cecília Grespan, Emma Rivera-Rábago, Cecilia Cuesta-Vélez, the late Víctor Vélez, and Douglas Alan Preston. I also thank the late David William Foster not only for his pioneering and inspiring work in gender and sexuality studies in Latin America, but also for being a generous mentor.

A big thank you to my family for their love and support: my mom, grandma, aunts, godparents, cousins, nieces, and nephew. A special thank you to my cousin Angela María and her husband, Alejandro, for their assistance. I thank my uncles, all of whom I miss profoundly. And the last and more important thank you is to Gunnar Feldmann, my husband. Thanks so much for supporting me so I could take time off to write the dissertation and take yearlong sabbaticals. Thank you for listening to all my ideas and encouraging me during all the stages. Your friendship and love have been central to my personal and professional growth.

Carlisle, April 2022

Introduction

The life of Catalina de Eraúso (1592–1650), known as the Lieutenant Nun, is very well-known in Latin American history. Abandoning his early life in a convent in San Sebastián, Spain, he donned masculine clothing, cut his hair short, and set out to live as a man; he then traveled to the New World, where he held various jobs and even became a soldier for the Spanish empire in Chile. Once he disclosed that he had female genitalia, however, he was expected to project the image of a woman and return to convent life. Realizing he would no longer be able retain his independent life as a man if he complied with these social expectations, he travelled to Rome to seek permission to wear masculine clothing. Having obtained permission from the pope, he returned to live in Mexico, where he worked as a mule-driver until his death. Despite his gender identity, biographies of Eraúso consistently emphasize that he was a woman and a nun. His case serves as a touchstone for the topics explored in this book, which explores the diverse gender identities, performances, and involvement in armed combat of real and fictional women and trans* men in Latin America.

Warrior Women and Trans Warriors: Performing Masculinities in Twentieth-Century Latin American Literature reexamines the performances of transgressive warriors in three major novels written in the first part of the twentieth century: *Los de abajo* (1915), *Doña Bárbara* (1929), and *Grande sertão: veredas* (1956). The trans warrior and warrior woman characters in these novels—Pintada, Doña Bárbara, and Diadorim—have usually been critiqued following traditional gender binary tropes by diminishing their empowerment even though they represent important gender transgressions and access to power during armed conflicts. Pintada has either been analyze as being just a "prostitute" (A. Franco 70), as one of the "footloose prostitutes" who embodies a "negative for-

Introduction

ce" in the text (Griffin 66–67), and as corrupt character who does have not have the peasant origins of most of Demetrio's band (J. Franco, *An Introduction* 197). She has also been studied as a strong woman portrayed in a negative light (Arce, *México's* 95; Baker, *Revolutionaries* 104–05; Estrada, *Troubled* 144). Doña Bárbara has been treated as a representation of the dictator who usurped the country/land (Sommer 275–76) or as the embodiment of power (González Echevarría, "Doña Bárbara escribe" 10). She also has been read as an allegory for barbarism and monstrosity that the novel itself ends up undermining, as well as tragic character unable to reconcile her traumatic past with her present (Alonso, *The Spanish* 124–25, 131–32). And Diadorim has been examined as an androgynous figure (Serra 187; Olivieri 44, 47; Payne and Fitz 91; Neitzel 48) or inserted as part of the centuries-old tradition of warrior maidens (*donzelas guerreiras*) who sacrifice themselves for society (Galvão "Ciclo" 25). He has also been considered as a cross-dresser and as a woman with strong masculine traits (Balderston 85–87). While contemporary critics drawing on gender studies have provided complex readings of these characters, their analyses could be enriched by other combinations of intersectionality, gender performance theory, masculinity studies, and especially trans theory. I use such theoretical developments and a close reading of the novels to analyze how performing masculinities and transgressing traditional gender rules allow Pintada, Doña Bárbara, and Diadorim to develop strategies of self-empowerment. I argue that these characters manage to occupy the most-desired position within their contexts, but they are disempowered because of the novels' urge to reestablish and protect a superseded traditional social order.

Pintada, Doña Bárbara, and Diadorim exemplify "trans warrior" and "warrior women" as defined in this book because they are all skilled fighters who gain access to power and leadership roles habitually reserved for cis men in part by appropriating garments and other possessions that typically represent a masculine role or image. Warrior women and trans warriors, whether real or fictional, may be identified by three primary characteristics: masculine appearance and behavior, rejection of traditionally feminine roles, and access to and use of weapons (firearms or knives or daggers). Wielding weapons (especially expertly) transgresses traditional feminine roles because weapons are usually linked to displays of masculine power. If weapons represent the phallus—often constructed as both symbol and origin of power within patriarchal cultures—then accessing and wielding them successfully suggests that warrior women and trans warriors have symbolically obtained the phallus and by extension the power traditionally associated with masculinity. At the same time, trans warrior and warrior woman characters subvert the logic of this power by showing that cis men are not the only people who can be empowered during wartime.

Their masculinization also enables them to secure the most-desirable position in their societies, which in these three novels include being leaders, caciques, or top-notch soldiers. As skilled fighters, they engage in armed conflict and carry out roles usually assigned to heterocissexual men soldiers, revolutionaries, or guerrillas for extended stretches of time: Pintada during the Mexican Revolution, Doña Bárbara during the sometimes-violent struggle for land and power in a region of Venezuela, and Diadorim during regional guerrilla warfare in Brazil. Although these characters are empowered through their access to weapons and by gaining normatively masculine leadership roles, they are then disempowered by disappearing or dying in the end, as each novel strives to reestablish and protect the traditional social order. While trans warriors and warrior women have embodied valid national projects in history—and their presence in these novels showcases the diversities of gender, gender performance, and gender identity in Latin America—their displacement from power demonstrates that discourses of nationalism have been built on the image of cis men heroes.

In his study of women in war, David E. Jones explains that women warriors inherently threaten society because they question gender norms and, as threats, they must be marginalized or silenced (xi–xii). I agree that hegemonic society aims to disempower warriors whose performances demonstrate a level of empowerment within contexts where they are not usually thought to have such potential. According to Gabriela Cano, masculinized females were explicitly rejected during the Mexican Revolution because they disrupted gender norms ("¿Es posible" 19). Their presence was made public with the goal of contrasting it with the passive and feminine *adelita* so that the *adelita* would continue to be the preferred role model (19). Following Cano, I see that the performances of the characters I analyze do not represent a *threat* to the system so much as show that the system is *already* failing. Warrior woman and trans warrior characters are already embedded, empowered, and committing transgressions within a faulty system. As I explain in the next section, by participating in the field of combat, they demonstrate that women and trans* men are not limited to the recognized subservient roles of camp followers, *soldaderas, adelitas,* and other "nobodies" (following B. Christine Arce's usage of the term). They must be disempowered because their transgressions from within reveal the incoherence of the heterocispatriarchal system.

This book endeavors to trace the evolution of gender transgressiveness and identities in Latin American literature by conducting a close reading of novels published over a forty-year span in the first part of the twentieth century, each of which features a trans warrior or warrior woman character. It also adds a recapitulation of testimonies of warrior women in the second part of the twentieth century. One of the characteristics of literary texts is that they last over time and gain new meaning for successive generations of readers. Even if twentieth century authors such as Mariano Azuela and Rómulo Gallegos intended to portray gender transgressive characters in a negative light, Pintada, Doña Bárbara, and Diadorim can be and have been reassessed according to contemporary values and the social contexts of readers who continue to consume their novels today. I find that warrior characters in these novels became increasingly rebellious in their displays of gender identity and transgressions of gender borders as the twentieth century progressed. In contravening gender borders and showing women and trans* men developing mechanisms for empowerment in Latin America, the three novels represent issues that beset all humankind. The trans warrior and warrior women in these novels express the profound human experiences of gender passing, trans identities, and the ongoing struggle to assert empowered identities. The novels analyzed herein thus remain important precisely because they discuss issues, struggles, and transgressions that are still relevant to women and the LGBTQAI+ community.

Below, I provide more complete definitions of "trans warrior" and "warrior woman," compare them with other terms that have been used to describe women's roles during wartime, and discuss the importance of recognizing trans men's and women's participation in combat. The following section positions this book in dialogue with Latin American literary criticism particularly around gender and sexuality studies. I then outline the main theoretical approaches taken in this book, drawing in particular from Judith Butler's gender performance theory, trans theory, intersectionality, and masculinity studies. I clarify how I use both gender performance and trans theory to analyze Latin American literary productions. Next, I summarize the socio-political context of each novel and, lastly, outline the structure of the book.

Why "Warrior Women" and "Trans Warriors"?

Over the past several decades, women have increasingly obtained positions of power in public life, the world of crime, and armed conflicts. Warrior women have also come to occupy a more prominent place in popular culture, including in Hollywood films and television. Demi Moore as Jordan O'Neil in *G.I Jane* (1997), Michelle Yeoh as Yu Shu Lien in *Crouching Tiger, Hidden Dragon* (2000), Angelina Jolie as Lara Croft in *Lara Croft: Tomb Raider* (2001), and Zoe Saldaña as Cataleya Restrepo in *Colombiana* (2011) are some of the actors and roles that immediately come to mind when considering popular representations of skillful women fighters in cinema. Moreover, the depiction of Black women who are warriors in *Black Panther* (2018) is widely credited for having made it a blockbuster movie. The presence of trans warriors remains hidden and barely studied, however, so in this book I focus on Diadorim in order to emphasize their roles and contributions to combat as well.

My analytic focus on gender performance leads me to prefer the noun "woman" as a social category to the adjective and noun "female" as a biological category. With the term "warrior women," I specifically reference transgressions made by (cis and trans*) women who have fighting skills and have been involved in armed combat. I emphasize their importance as well as that of trans* men because the traditional masculine hegemony continues to erase biographies of real warrior women and trans* men from military history. I also use "trans" to mitigate the erasure of the presence of trans* peoples from literature and history. For instance, because most critics have treated Diadorim as a woman character, his gender identity must be addressed rather than effaced; this can be accomplished with "trans warrior." It is therefore imperative to underscore their performances and skills even in literary fiction.

Introduction

Jack Halberstam argues that the term "trans*" (from the 2018 book, *Trans**) is especially appropriate for discussing the broad trans community. Understanding that identity politics are complex, fluid, and vary according to each individual's experiences, Halberstam argues that the trans* experience cannot be reduced to surgical procedures (27). Trans* embraces the full diversity of experiences of trans* peoples because it is more about process than separation.

Trans warriors and warrior women alike break with the normatively disempowered femininity that trans* men and women are expected to embody. In being and behaving 'masculine', warrior women challenge what Virginia Woolf calls the "Angel in the House," the type of woman who "was intensely sympathetic. She was immensely charming. She was utterly unselfish. She excelled in the difficult arts of family life. She sacrificed herself daily … she never had a mind or a wish of her own" (285). Because their conduct opposes the roles dictated by society's somatic categories, trans warriors and warrior women call into question what Raewyn Connell calls "emphasized femininity," a pattern of femininity that subordinates women to men and reproduces the rules of patriarchal culture (*Gender* 184). Warrior women and trans warriors highlight the artificiality of traditional gender roles by ignoring patriarchal rules, obtaining positions of power, and fighting alongside men. Julia Serano argues that trans people do not necessarily perform specific types of femininity or masculinity (47). They can distance themselves from naturalized notions of acceptable gender performances. While recognizing such diversity, I chose to emphasize trans* men's masculinities to elucidate their commonalities with warrior women's performances during times of war. Centering on these performances, this book seeks to dismantle the heterocisnormativity embedded in discourses about masculinities and power in Latin American armed conflicts.

I coin the term "trans warrior" to emphasize the otherwise invisible presence of trans* people in combat without limiting their gender performances and identities. Highlighting the importance of trans* people is also vital because they pay a high price for their "transgressions." Five Latin American countries are on the list of the top six countries with the highest numbers of murders of trans* people in the world, including Brazil, Mexico, Colombia, Venezuela, and Honduras. Brazil holds the global record for having the most killings (in real numbers) of *travestis*, but Honduras has a higher rate of reported murders of trans* people per million inhabitants. In 2016, according to the Trans Murder Monitoring report prepared by the member-based organization Transgender Europe, Brazil had a rate of 4.3 and Honduras 10.4 murders of trans and gender-diverse people per million inhabitants (Balzer and Berredo 14). These statistics also reflect the overall levels violence of each country. Most countries do not provide official statistics on violence against trans* people, so researchers must rely on the work of NGOs, media, and activists. The real numbers may be even higher considering that many of those attacked are not classified as victims of gender violence. Although few trans warrior characters are discussed in this book, the fact that various forms of violence continue to be perpetrated against trans* people pushed me to foreground their presence in Latin American literature not just as victims, but as empowered, resilient heroes.

Not all women and trans* men who confront patriarchy and break gender stereotypes are warriors as I use the term, however. Many characters in Latin American literature have transgressed gender borders and confronted patriarchy in their societies, but they are not considered warriors unless they have done so in combat situations. I have tremendous respect for all women and trans* men and women who have participated in war in any capacity, not only on the frontline. As Miriam Cooke states, the diversity of women's roles in war helps us to reassess war and the narratives around war. I would add that trans warriors' performances also invite such reassessment. Calling all trans* men and women who have been involved but not physically fighting in armed conflicts "warriors" in a metaphoric sense can diminish the roles, skills, and negotiations conducted by those who consistently took up arms. Since this book examines the transgressions of characters who do engage in combat, I establish a divide between warriors and non-warriors in order to identify specific strategies of empowerment.

Many terms have been used to refer to women (and hide trans* men) who have participated in armed conflicts in Latin America. Pintada, Doña Bárbara, and Diadorim belong to the specific traditions of *soldaderas* and soldiers in Mexico, *llaneros* (cowboys) in Venezuela, and *jagunços* (a sort of soldier/criminal) in Brazil, respectively. By contrast, the social categories "warrior woman" and "trans warrior" can be applied throughout Latin America.

Introduction

They embrace similar performances and sources of empowerment in generally bellicose environments, while remaining flexible enough to incorporate the cultural specificities of each context. I also favor these terms over simpler gender-neutral words such as "warrior" and "soldier," place-specific terms such as "*cangaceira*" (used to reference women bandits in Brazil) and "*adelita*," or the more troublesome concepts "warrior maiden," "virago," or "androgynous warrior." Most of these terms are either too general for my purposes or reduce women to sexual categories.

Like the term "warrior," the word "soldier" erases the gender condition unless a modifier is added. "Soldier" is even more problematic than "warrior" because it refers only to fighters who have been officially incorporated into nation-state armies. Until relatively recently and despite some important exceptions, women and trans* men and women did not usually participate in an official way as soldiers in Latin American wars, although they did fill other wartime positions. When warrior women and trans warriors play the (ordinarily cis men's) roles of soldiers or military officers, they confront heterocispatriarchal culture. Trans warriors and warrior women therefore represent transgressions and rebelliousness, while soldiers organized in regulated units within a structured system inherently belong to the system. While the growing number of professional women and trans* men and women soldiers might call into question the future validity of the terms proposed here, for the time being these terms denote alternative possibilities and contexts that continue to escape official discourses. They are also useful for analyzing twentieth-century literature featuring combat settings.

The most widely known words for women who have gone to war, especially in Mexico, are *soldadera* and *adelita*. In her 1990 book, Elizabeth Salas considers *soldadera* has become a descriptor for any bad-mannered, low-status women (34), whereas previously it encompassed numerous activities and professions of women during wartime, including soldier, camp follower, prostitute, and lover. For instance, the actions of the character Jesusa in *Hasta no verte, Jesús mío* (1969) by Elena Poniatowska would seem to demonstrate the *soldadera*'s complexity. Jesusa initially travels with the revolutionary troops to look after her father and the other soldiers, then is forced to marry Pedro, an officer in the Carrancista army. She only enters the arena of armed combat because she accompanies Pedro; after he dies, she steps in as troop leader to save the soldiers and then fights out of necessity. After the fight is over, she steps down from her leadership position, arguing she is not a soldier and she had only been there because she was forced to follow her husband (whom she views with animosity) into combat. Jesusa is obviously more than a camp follower whose main duty is cooking and washing clothes. In the same book, Poniatowska presents another character, the daughter of General Genovevo Blanco, named Lucía. Lucía resembles a trans warrior. Jesusa describes Lucía as behaving just like the men soldiers, as she "jalaba parejo en todo. Cuando ordenaban: '¡Pecho a tierra', ella se tiraba como todos los demás al suelo, y así iba avanzando y disparaba su fusil. Nunca se quedó con la impedimenta" (80). Moreover, Lucía gives orders to the men, checks their aim, trains the cavalry, and assists her father in making plans for attack and defense. This masculine behavior leads Jesusa to opine that Lucía is too *machorra* (butch). In describing her as butch, a word filled with condemnation and rejection, Jesusa speaks to her own ultimate alignment with a traditional gender ideology that places a high value on femininity for women. Despite this embedded ideology, the two characters in Poniatowska's novel illustrate the variety of roles played by women and trans* men in the Revolution.

In her 2017 book, Arce discusses that despite the widespread presence of *soldaderas* participating in war situations in varied ways, they have largely been ignored; they are México's nobodies (*México's* 2). In the few cases where they are not overlooked, they are depicted using simplistic, inflexible terms that limit their complex mutability (27). Despite this historical oblivion, *soldaderas* have received more attention in recent decades. Poniatowska published a book on them, *Las Soldaderas* (1999), and other scholars have analyzed their presence. For instance, Oswaldo Estrada contends that *soldaderas* have been seen as a homogenous group of "passive camp followers" or *adelitas* (*Troubled* 2–3). According to him, for the most part *soldaderas* are still represented in traditional idealized ways, as in *corridos*, or ignored so that their contributions and empowerment are not accounted for (172, 183). Notwithstanding *soldaderas*' complexity, I still consider the term to be loaded with pejorative connotations regarding sexuality and kinship; it is also specific to Mexico. The term "warrior women" (*mulheres guerreiras/mujeres guerreras*) provides a fresh approach to rereading

Introduction

Latin American women's history and literature featuring women characters involved in armed conflict. "Trans warriors" further supports the agenda of rethinking history and literature and it should help critics cease to refer to trans* men such as Zapatista Colonel Amelio Robles Ávila as "*soldaderas.*"

Like *soldadera*, the term *adelita* (also used during the Mexican Revolution) encompasses too many complex roles; it was used to refer to women who were soldiers, lovers of soldiers, nurses, or camp followers. Mexican *corridos* (a folk song genre) often featured an "Adelita" in their titles. The songs depict Adelita as either a soldier's love object or as a brave soldier who nevertheless cries hysterically and prays for the safety of her man (Arce, *México's* 87). According to Arce, the *adelita* concept is permeated with an accusation of ingratitude arising from men's traditional fear of rejection (84). *Adelitas* are often vilified because they can leave and betray men soldiers. Cano provides another reason for the existence of the traditional *adelita* character. She argues that the *adelita* image has lasted a long time because it is the binary match to the image of the stereotypical man revolutionary ("¿Es posible" 13). If taken merely as a companion and conceptual match, the *adelita* concept downplays women's full participation in armed conflict.

Walnice Nogueira Galvão uses the term *donzela guerreira*, or warrior maiden, to describe the cross-dressed woman who goes to war. Her research shows that this character has been present in armed conflicts throughout history and across many cultures. She describes the "warrior maiden" as:

> Filha única ou mais velha, raramente a mais nova, de pai sem filhos homens, corta os cabelos, enverga trajes masculinos, abdica das fraquezas femininas – faceirice, esquivança, medo –, aperta os seios e as ancas, trata seus ferimentos em segredo assim como se banha escondida. Costuma ser descoberta quando, ferida, o corpo é desvendado; e guerreia; e morre. ("Ciclo" 9)

This description suggests that warrior maidens only engage in war when pressed to do so by family circumstances. The centrality of kinship in their lives perpetuates the idea that cross-dressed women only fight out of duty, not desire. The word "maiden" (*donzela*) further implies that these women do not have sexual relations. By having and keeping their virginity, such warriors are able to return home and take back their lives as ordinary women and brides-to-be or they die. That is, after they return from combat, they reinstate the "natural" order. Because the focus on virginity objectifies their bodies and sexuality, the term "warrior maiden" reinforces rather than transgresses heteropatriarchal culture. It also implies that these women are cis; there seems to be no space in the word *donzela* for trans* identities. I do not mean that there have not been gender fluid or non-binary warriors, but that using "maiden" also forecloses the possibility of a trans* identity. In *A donzela-guerreira* (1998), Galvão does acknowledge two different sexual categories of warrior maidens (i.e., the nun and the promiscuous) (32) and explains that some women who went to war were married and had children (47) while others were bossy or autarchic (211–14). She does not develop specific terms to refer to these different types, however.

By advancing the concepts of "warrior women" and "trans warriors" in this book, I accentuate the presence of trans* men and women in war and erase the alleged clear distinction between those who perform femininities and those who perform masculinities. I am able to emphasize warrior qualities along with gender complexities and transgressions. These terms provide a perspective that has mostly not been promulgated in other analyses or references to gender transgressive characters in Latin American literature. By utilizing both terms, I seek to avoid reproducing discourses that treat such characters as simply evil, helpless, backwards, or virginal. In a sense, by transgressing heterocispatriarchal rules, warrior women and trans warriors can resignify what has been considered evil or barbarous. I read such characters, usually vilified, as positive and meaningful models for those who have been for the most part treated as inferior nobodies or simply nonexistent. Understanding them can also give others hope about transgressing conventional gender rules.

Trans Warriors and Warrior Women in Latin American Literary Criticism

Latin America has had an exceptionally long history of warrior women and trans warriors. Women participated in battles of indigenous peoples against European colonizers and later revolutionary movements not only as nurses, messengers, or cooks, but as combatants and leaders. Trans* people and trans warriors were also

Introduction

involved in warfare, but it is more difficult to track their presence, partly because of lack of historical records, but also because gender and gender identity were understood differently in previous centuries. Although they have not occupied the same prominent place in history as cis men warriors, trans warriors and warrior women have been the subject of interviews, biographies, and documentary films. They have also been featured in fictional texts, though many critics have tended to overlook such characters or study them in ways that perpetuate gender binaries. Informed by queer theory, more contemporary critics reassess texts and characters, such as Louise O. Vasvári's work on the warrior maid.

The literary presence of trans warriors and warrior women can be traced back to the Middle Ages (Vasvári 93). A famous ballad, "The Romance of the Warrior Maiden" ("Romance de la doncella guerrera" or "Romance da Donzela-Guerreira"), has been very popular and there are more than one hundred versions of it (Vasvári 94). Their presence also dates back to *Orlando Furioso* by Ludovico Ariosto and *Jerusalem Delivered* by Torquato Tasso (Cândido, *Tese* 120). Theatrical productions of sixteenth century Iberia also included women characters who donned masculine clothing to play warrior roles, although these transgressive characters always restored the social order by putting on women's attire and reasserting their femininity by the end of each play. Warrior women (more than trans warriors) appeared in Latin American literature with increasing frequency throughout the twentieth century, especially in novels set during the Mexican Revolution (1910-1920), and in autobiographies, *testimonios* (testimonials), and interviews about the Cuban (1956) and Nicaraguan (1979) revolutions, as well as guerrilla warfare and drug trafficking. Despite the popularity of warrior woman and trans warrior characters, most literary critics have underplayed their participation in war and ignored, denied, or diminished their complex gender identities. A traditional view of women and trans* men cannot acknowledge that they could fight effectively or otherwise perform the masculinities of combat.

I accentuate the masculine images and behaviors of these characters precisely because their performances allow them to be empowered in a patriarchal world. Pintada has mostly been analyzed as a sex worker or loose woman, although critiques by Arce and Pascale Baker have recognized Pintada's agenda and gender transgression (Arce, *México's* 95; Baker, *Revolutionaries* 104). Still, they do not analyze the full complexity of the character's gender performance and transgression from a race, class, ethnic, and gender intersectional framework as I do. Based on Carlos Monsiváis's reading of Pintada, Arce insists that this character is not constructed as a heroine (95), while Baker refers to her as a *mujer bravía* (untamed woman) and considers her performance to be that of a survivor in the Revolution (98, 102). Reading against the grain of the text makes traditional discourses about Pintada more evident; I use this tactic to analyze her strength. As brave as any man, she seeks to improve her socioeconomic situation not only by manipulating Demetrio, but by becoming a leader and plundering and ransacking houses. Even if she represents corruption, as do other characters in the novel, her intersecting gender, racial, and social transgressions, which would have been "entertaining" for readers at the time the novel was published (Arce, *México's* 95), must be highlighted. Considering the prevalence of *machismo* and sexism and the alarming number of cases of feminicide (*feminicídio/feminicidio*) and domestic violence in Mexico and throughout Latin America, Pintada's strength must be examined as exposing feminicide and as a form of ingenuity that challenges the discourses of subordination of (cis and trans*) women in Latin America.

Meanwhile, many critics have analyzed how the novel *Doña Bárbara* represents the conflict between civilization (democracy, progress, education)—exemplified by the saintly Santos character—and savagery (dictatorship, the backwards state)—demonstrated by Doña Bárbara's monstrous evil. Like Pintada, Doña Bárbara embodies meanings related to corruption and impunity and fights to empower herself. Although she starts out an impoverished *mestiza* orphan (and later is the victim of gang rape), she becomes the *cacica* (woman cacique/political boss) of her region through her own efforts. As Sommer explains, her assumption of dominance goes against the prevailing gender norms of her time (276). Doña Bárbara's capacity for socioeconomic improvement as well as manipulation of others speak to her resilience and resourcefulness in an elitist, white, and traditional society. Her transgression helps us understand how empowerment and gender operate together.

Critical readings of Diadorim in *Grande sertão: veredas* characterize him either as androgynous or a warrior maiden. Some critics conclude that Diadorim's performance is unbelievable because no "woman" could pass so successfully as a man or engage in armed combat so effectively as this character does in the book (Dixon 143; Mac Adam 74). Daniel Balderston notes that critics have emphasized the theme of ambiguity in the novel, but have not discussed it regarding the relationship between Riobaldo, the novel's narrator, and Diadorim (87). By analyzing the relationship between Diadorim and Riobaldo from a queer perspective, Balderston fills this gap. He also acknowledges that as a child Diadorim was a tomboy and even calls him a "mujer guerrera" (86–87, 92). I consider Diadorim to be a trans warrior and the best fighter in the novel.

Written between the 1960s and 1990s, many of these critiques of the three characters represented ideas about gender and sexuality that became contested with the emergence of gender and queer studies. Published in 2004, Balderston's analysis is to my knowledge the first queer reading of *Grande sertão*. I draw on queer, trans, and masculinity theories and more contemporary literary criticism to reassess the role of trans warriors and warrior women characters in Latin American literature and their relevance to contemporary society. Scholarly books such as Judith Butler's *Gender Trouble* (1990) and *Bodies that Matter* (1993), Marjorie Garber's *Vested Interests* (1992), Eve Kosofsky Sedgwick's *Epistemology of the Closet* (1990), and Halberstam's *Female Masculinity* (1998) remain among the foundational works of queer theory to this day. Considering the repercussions her works have had in gender and sexuality studies and transfeminism, I must add to this list Connell's *Gender and Power. Society, the Person and Sexual Politics* (1987) and *Masculinities* (1995). Her books are fundamental to my analyses of trans warriors' and warrior women's transgressive performances.

Since the 1990s, studies on queer and queering Latin America have flourished. Many of them have retrieved the works of authors who identify as members of the LGBTQAI+ community, examined queer topics, and analyzed non-heterosexual and trans* characters in order to highlight other voices, perspectives, and stories in the region. This is evident in pioneering books such as David William Foster's *Latin American Writers on Gay and Lesbian Themes* (1994) and *Sexual Textualities* (1997) and anthologies such as Emilie Bergmann and Paul Julian Smith's *¿Entiendes?* (1995), Balderston and Donna Guy's *Sex and Sexuality in Latin America*

Introduction

(1997), and Sylvia Molloy and Robert McKee Irwin's *Hispanisms and Homosexualities* (1998). More specifically, the books with which *Warrior Women and Trans Warriors* dialogues belong to the field of Latin American masculinities. Rebecca E. Biron's 2000, *Murder and Masculinity: Violent Fictions of Twentieth Century Latin America*, focuses on texts about murders that question traditional images of masculine characters and their relationships with women characters and femininity. Ben. Sifuentes-Jáuregui's 2002 book, *Transvestism, Masculinity, and Latin American Literature*, discusses Spanish American *travestismo* (cross-dressing) of gay and/ or *travesti* characters in major novels such as José Donoso's *El lugar sin límites* and Manuel Puig's *El beso de la mujer araña*. Although there were previous studies of *travestismo* in Latin America, using psychoanalytic theory to understand the complexities of the characters' performances, Sifuentes-Jáuregui brings to the forefront a much-needed discussion of cross-dressing and *travestis* in Latin American literature. I build on his analysis in my discussion of cross-dressing in Chapter 1.

I am also indebted to Irwin's 2003 book, *Mexican Masculinities*, wherein his reading of *Los de abajo* as a homosocial text undoes masculinity as a monolithic concept. Domínguez-Ruvalcaba's 2007 book, *Modernity and the Nation in Mexican Representations of Masculinity*, reads masculinity in a homosocial/homosexual context to inform a discussion of identity politics. I extend his work by looking at how images of machismo and masculinity have displaced other images and how analyzing masculinities allows for new observations of national cultures. Vinodh Venkatesh's 2015 book, *The Body as Capital. Masculinities in Contemporary Latin American Fiction*, connects masculinities with capitalism and commodification of the body in novels of the late-twentieth century. I draw on Venkatesh's use of Connell's theories on masculinities, as well as his concern for Latin American specificities, to frame a theoretical background for analyzing trans* men's and warrior women's performances of local masculinities. Published the same year, Jason Cortés's *Macho Ethics: Masculinity and Self-Representation in Latino-Caribbean Narrative* emphasizes the connection between ethics and masculinity in the Caribbean. His book renders visible the ways in which masculinity and authoritarian machismo function. I build on his questioning of masculinity as an invisible discourse.

Introduction

Arce's *México's Nobodies. The Cultural Legacy of the Soldadera and Afro-Mexican Women*, published in 2017, is perhaps the closest book to mine from an ideological standpoint. While Arce does not engage with masculinities studies, her book rescues from oblivion women characters and women who have been ignored, neglected, or discriminated against in Mexican history. She describes historical *soldaderas* and characters from Mexican ballads (*corridos*), literature, and films, with an emphasis on Black *soldaderas* and Black women singers. Estrada contributes to the same agenda in his 2018 book, *Troubled Memories: Iconic Mexican Women and the Traps of Representation*. Like Arce, Estrada provides a positive and empowering revision of some key characters and figures from Mexican history that have formerly been presented as symbolic of traditional gender roles. As Arce states, every nation and region has depended on keeping women marginalized, so national ideologies, narrations, images, songs, and so on must be revisited if we are to do away with gender inequity (2, 9, 27). This applies even to characters written by men authors. Subjects who do not conform to traditional gender norms must not remain on the periphery, as afterthoughts in literary analyses. By examining the ways in which women and trans* men have been involved in armed combat, interpersonal fights, and power struggles, *Warrior Women and Trans Warriors* rescues their gender performances from oblivion and gives them more visibility in Latin American literature.

All the scholarly books so far mentioned further the discussion of queer and gender studies in Spanish American literature and culture and examine the pervasiveness of masculinity, but, with the exception of Arce and Estrada, do not focus on women characters or trans* men. Mostly gay men authors and/or characters have been analyzed. In *Dude Lit: Mexican Men Writing and Performing Competence, 1955–2012* (2019), Emily Hind observes that in the Mexican intellectual milieu "gay men seem to enjoy greater status than most women" (3). I agree with Hind because, while sexism, homophobia, and transphobia remain pervasive in Latin America, most men enjoy more benefits or privileges than most women, regardless of sexual orientation. By concentrating on two women characters and one trans* man character who queer traditional gender binaries, I expand the fields of Latin American queer and gender studies. I also bring Brazilian literature into the discussion in order to foster a broader regional perspective.

Hind suggests using the term "man writer" whenever a critic focuses entirely on men artists and intellectuals. She also advocates for acknowledging women writers and quoting women critics in order to attain a balance (*Dude* 212). I recognize that, even though I am a cis woman critic, I mostly examine three famous novels written by men writers in this book. However, following Hind's recommendation, I make a point of citing women and trans* authors and critics, and in Chapter 5 I analyze the experiences of women guerrillas as well as two texts authored by women writers (Nellie Campobello and Gioconda Belli). My approach also harmonizes with Domínguez-Ruvalcaba's methodology in his 2016 book, *Translating the Queer: Body Politics and Transnational Conversations*. He states that queer Latin American theory must portray the "uncanny side of the imperial corpus of knowledge" (11). In studying three major novels written by men writers, I critique the "imperial corpus" while at the same time highlighting its "uncanny side" by analyzing women and trans* characters who for the most part have only been examined from a gender binary standpoint. Investigating their performative power and acts of empowerment enriches our understanding of gender transgressions in canonical Latin American literature.

Warrior Women and Trans Warriors as Transgressive Characters

This book adopts Peter Stallybrass and Allon White's definition of the word "transgression" as the act of crossing barriers imposed by hegemonic society. To transgress is an expressive behavior that inverts, contradicts, annuls, or presents an alternative to social codes, values, and cultural norms (17). Unlike Venkatesh, who considers that transgressive bodies are ineffective in producing alternatives to traditional ideologies because they cannot establish a new system outside of patriarchy (154), I perceive value in trans warriors' and warrior women's transgressions. Because bodies are not normally allowed to transgress gender binaries, defiant acts of transgression inherently open up possibilities. The warrior woman and trans warrior characters discussed herein transgress by calling into question social and political values and presenting alternatives within the realm of gender.

Introduction

I analyze their transgressions under the lens of Butler's gender performance theory. Identity is constituted by the repetition of rules which, promoted by hegemonic society, enable and restrict how people understand any individual. Society reinforces binary rules and heteronormativity gives them structure (Butler, *Gender* 185). Gender is thus perpetuated in society through iterative performative practices dictated by an ideal of heterocisnormativity. Gender is not coherent throughout time and place, but is made to appear coherent by conservative traditional practices. Despite the strength of heterocisnormativity and the importance put on the physical body in many societies, individual agency remains theoretically possible as people conduct performances that underscore the artificiality of the hegemonic society (185–87). Such "performativities," as Butler calls them, are not necessarily employed deliberately or consciously and they are not always successful, however (*Bodies* 2). Many theorists have criticized the performativity concept for attributing an excess of willingness to the performing subject, as a sort of voluntarism. That is, it assumes a person is free to decide to switch their performance at any time. Butler did not consider gender performance to be voluntary, however. She clarifies that performativities are constituted by neither deliberate acts nor facts, but by repetitive practices (2).

While sociologists have questioned the applicability of gender performance theory to understanding society, problematizing performativity remains a vital tool in literary studies. I find the concept useful because I see that the behaviors of the three trans warrior and warrior woman characters discussed herein demonstrate the artificial hierarchies of the armed conflict environment within which they take action. Analyzing how these characters adopt specific attitudes and appearances perceived as masculine exposes and defies the established masculinities of their societies. Pintada, Doña Bárbara, and Diadorim each portray a different masculinity, thereby revealing a plurality of possible gender performances attuned to the fact that cis men also develop complex masculinity performances.

While acknowledging the differences between trans studies and Butler's gender performance studies, I find a reconciliation between the two fields in the works of scholars such as Halberstam, J. R. Latham, and Andrea Long Chu. The main criticism from trans theory is that gender performance theory does not consider biology in the determination of a person's gender identity and that trans* people have an innate predisposition for gender. According to Halberstam, Butler has had a major impact on trans and feminist theory in showing that, while all bodies are constrained by gender norms, some bodies break them (*Trans** 122–23). For Halberstam, Butler questions how gender influences human intelligibility (123). That is, gender is a key category necessary for human beings to understand each other. Gender is not performed in isolation because "one does not 'do' one's gender alone" (*Undoing* 1).

Latham's and Chu's work on trans theory further addresses gender as a social construction. In examining medico-legal discourses, Latham argues that the context in which trans men operate constructs their male embodiments because gender is not only a practice (a repetitive performance) but also a narrative that materializes maleness (351–52). That is, the intersection between performance and narrative discourse constructs the subject. Latham adds that "there are a number of organizing strategies trans men use to assemble and enact maleness in sexual practices and relationships" (352). In her book *Females* (2019), Chu takes the relationship between subject and context a step further by arguing that everyone is female—not woman—and everybody hates it (1–2, 11). Gender is thus the result of internalized misogynous stereotypes (35). She also considers social constructionism's reading of gender to be very incomplete because gender is built upon people's interactions (35, 38). That is, gender materializes through the desires of other people (36). She does not deny that each person has their own gender identity so much as expose how gender is constructed in society, which she calls the "sexualization of gender" (36). Gender identity is directly related to how gender is perceived, granted, or interpreted in each social context and interaction.

The Latin American context also facilitates the reconciliation of these theoretical approaches because the debate between trans and gender performance theories that occurred in the global North does not have the same ramifications in Latin American societies where recognition, visibility, and support remain critical to surviving and navigating hostile environments. As José Quiroga explains, visibility is central to producing memory and thereby gaining recognition (13). I do not imply that countries in the global North have resolved all issues, but that different countries in Latin America have different priorities and agendas. For instan-

Introduction

ce, Domínguez-Ruvalcaba considers that queer Latin American theorists and activists focus more on communality and fighting homophobia (*Translating* 118). I agree with Latin American and U.S. critics who argue that queer theory must deal with transphobia, sexism and misogyny, classism, and racism.

Perceptions of the body or how the body is understood in public have different meanings and urgencies in Latin American countries and the global North. Brazilian critic Berenice Bento states that gender is a practice connected to social recognition (*Transviad@s* 108). She sees a body as intrinsically genderless, with gender only being constructed in social interactions. This contradicts some trans theorists, but does call attention to the identity politics and materialization of bodies in Latin America. Gender performance theory can be adapted and used strategically in the region. Accepting the validity of non-traditional gender practices and performances supports socioeconomic and political survival and generates recognition and empathy.

Global North theories on gender performance, masculinities, and trans studies were not produced with Latin American specificities in mind. Even terms such as LGBTQAI+ community and queer, *kuir*, or *cuir* (Portuguese and Spanish phonetic transcriptions of the English term "queer") are not always appropriate to all contexts. There are also significant differences given the complexities of each country in Latin America. According to Domínguez-Ruvalcaba, however, queer theory in Latin America can be enhanced through the use of an intersectional methodology (*Translating* 5). An intersectional methodology grounds my study of Latin American literature, which is solidified by my close reading of the novels examined in this book. I adopt Kimberlé Crenshaw's approach to intersectionality by factoring class, ethnicity, and race into understanding the gender performances of warrior woman and trans warrior characters. Jasbir Puar proposes the concept of "assemblages" to emphasize that intersectionality cannot be a rigid method of examination, and as an invitation to perceive bodies as unstable and positioned in networks of relationships that go beyond identity categories ("I would"). Given the importance of visibility in fighting multiple oppressions, I still find the examination of identity categories within particular Latin American contexts relevant. However, my approach to intersectionality overlaps with Puar's concept in that I highlight differences between trans warrior and warrior woman characters, their varied positionalities, and their relationships with other men and women characters (see Chapters 3 and 4). The detailed examination of different intersections amongst Pintada, Doña Bárbara, and Diadorim elucidate the diversity of warrior women's and trans warriors' experiences.

In examining the diverse performances of the studied characters, I refer to masculinities following Connell's theory that states that hegemonic discourse imposes ideals and establishes a hierarchy in which different masculinities function at different levels of a pyramid. Hegemonic masculinity occupies the top position. Below hegemonic masculinity are subordinated or marginalized masculinities or forms of masculinity that function as accomplices to the top (*Masculinities* 76–81). If the conditions within which hegemonic masculinity is constructed in a particular society change, the role and image of this masculinity changes too. The hegemonic position can be retained or performed regardless of age or gender because it is not predetermined and is always being challenged (76). Following Venkatesh's claim that transnational influences and globalization do not make local gender configurations simply go away (134), I consider the interactions between masculinities and femininities in three regional contexts. Venkatesh also clarifies that masculinities are actually fluid, have specific social histories, and have generated plural interrelational identities (3). I then use Halberstam's claim that, among the variety of masculinities and their hierarchies, one must include those performed by women. That is, someone who identifies as a woman can perform masculinities. To Halberstam's concept, I would add trans* masculinities. These masculinities force the question of how masculinity is discursively constructed as "natural." Additionally, so long as women and trans* people are considered inferior and their bodies are only seen through a reproductive lens, there remains the need to value and emphasize other roles.

I also use Halberstam's revalorization of female masculinity to argue that trans warriors' and warrior women's masculinities challenge the traditional masculine discourse on war in Latin America. If the dominant, decisive, and sacrificing figure of the man hero appears abundantly in art, as Domínguez-Ruvalcaba has demonstrated in Mexico (*Modernity* 13), the presence of warrior women and trans warriors in literature contributes to the complexity of depictions of war heroes. With this dialogue with theory and criticism in mind, I examine all aspects of Pintada's, Doña Bárbara's, and Diadorim's gender complexities. Their characteristics and agendas, whether evil or angelic, do not limit them socially nor are they constrained to the traditional binary roles (i.e., whore vs. virgin) often assigned to women and women characters, including *soldaderas*, in literature.

Based on my close readings and intersectional analyses of these novels, I recommend changing the language used by theorists such as Connell to refer to hegemonic masculinity. As I discuss in Chapter 3, I propose the expression "most-desired position" instead of "hegemonic masculinity" to dismantle traditional perspectives on power and gender dynamics dominated by men. This concept invites us to rethink gender configurations and ongoing transformations in how people function. "Most-desired position" de-masculinizes gender hierarchies, diminishes the myriad connotations and impact of the word "macho," and highlights the fluctuating aspect of gender performances and the particularities of each context in which they occur. At the same time, using it allows me to draw connections with homophobia and fears and anxieties about being gay, as Sifuentes-Jáuregui, Domínguez-Ruvalcaba, and Venkatesh realize are part of Latin American masculinities. (These concerns are most visible in Chapter 4 regarding *Grande sertão*.) The use of "most-desired position" thus avoids perpetuating through flawed labels the false patriarchal order in Latin America, an order that has insisted on remaining unchanged by keeping heterocissexual men in most-desired positions.

While this term may not do away with gender and sex as ontological categories, the goal here is to question the alleged separation (and consequent hierarchy) between femininity and masculinity. They are not exclusive categories, but porous ones informed by each other and in contact with other variables, categories, objects, and affects. The concept of "most-desired position" emphasizes the inherent relationship between masculinities and femininities by demonstrating that traditional gender discourses have been constructed on false exclusions. The literary characters examined in this book contradict the accepted idea that armed conflict is a cis- and men-dominated space. In representing valid alternatives to the traditional hegemonic masculinities embodied by the putative heterocissexual men heroes in the novels, the struggles of these three transgressive characters lead them into their own heroism.

In the 2010 book, *Naciones intelectuales. Las fundaciones de la modernidad literaria mexicana (1917–1959),* Ignacio Sánchez-Prado proposes the concept "intellectual nations" to explain how literary texts can produce alternative projects of nationhood (1). "Intellectual nations" do not necessarily follow the hegemonic system, but suggest other ways to think and to imagine the nation. I extend Sánchez-Prado's conceptualization of "intellectual nation" beyond Mexico to embrace Latin America as an "intellectual region" capable of questioning the myth of cis men exclusivity in war. The historical presence of white cis men in Latin America has been read in ways that dismiss other intellectual regions in which women and trans* characters and women's and trans* masculinities are and have been historically valid—the uncanny side Domínguez-Ruvalcaba asks us to reassess. My analysis of warrior woman and trans warrior characters speaks to changes that have happened and continue to happen in the region, but have largely been erased or ignored because other more pervasive ideas have provided a more traditional or established intellectual national/regional project.

Trans Warrior and Warrior Woman Characters in Latin America

Published in 1915 by the Mexican author Mariano Azuela (1873–1952), *Los de abajo* is considered the most distinguished novel of the Mexican Revolution, although it only became successful after it was published in Mexico City in the newspaper *El Universal* in 1925. This novel tells the story of Demetrio Macías, who joins a band of peasants rising up against the injustices of the government and the regional cacique. After winning several battles against the federal army, the band joins the revolutionary army. In the second part of the novel, Demetrio meets Pintada, a young woman travelling with the revolutionaries. Pintada carries a gun and wears a cartridge belt. She becomes his lover, but spends most of her time ransacking and plundering villages along with the other neophyte revolutionaries. After an innocent, impoverished peasant woman named Camila displaces Pintada as Demetrio's lover, Pintada murders her. Demetrio then commands Pintada to leave. Although a character who appears for only a short time in the novel, Pintada is important as a literary depiction of many of the real women who participated in the Mexican Revolution.

In 1927, as part of his intellectual project to modernize the nation, Venezuelan writer Rómulo Gallegos (1884–1969) traveled to the Venezuelan Plains to find material for what ended up becoming his most celebrated novel, *Doña Bárbara*. Published in 1929, this text attained immediate success, was extremely well-received by literary critics, and became one of the most important Latin American novels of the twentieth century. This work relates the story of Santos Luzardo's (his name combines "saint" with "light") return to Arauca from Caracas to recover his land. In attempting to bring political and economic reform to the region, he confronts a *cacica* named Doña Bárbara (literally "Barbarous"). Doña Bárbara wears masculine attire when she works with her cattle and is capable of castrating a bull. She manipulates the legal system at will and even has her employees murder people. Doña Bárbara makes a play for Santos, who rejects her. Meanwhile, he falls in love with his cousin, Doña Bárbara's disowned daughter Marisela. Doña Bárbara finally leaves the region after recognizing Marisela as her daughter and sole heir. What happens to her remains unknown, although rumors suggest she has either left to travel by boat on the river or died.

Published in 1956, almost thirty years after the Venezuelan novel and forty-one years after the Mexican novel, *Grande sertão: veredas* was written by the Brazilian author João Guimarães Rosa (1908–1967). It enjoyed immediate success in Brazil and literary critics declared it was a Portuguese-language masterpiece. It is still widely considered one of the most important Brazilian—indeed, Latin American and Lusophone—novels. Riobaldo is the main character and narrator of the story. He recounts his life as a *jagunço*, a sort of soldier in the Backlands, including the battles he was in and how he became a leader who ultimately brought armed conflict to an end. Another main character, Diadorim, is Riobaldo's best friend, helper, and guide. They sustain such a close relationship that Riobaldo begins to have romantic feelings for Diadorim, then struggles with the implication that he might be homosexual. After Diadorim dies from wounds sustained while killing their archenemy (Hermógenes), preparing his corpse for burial reveals that he had female genitalia. Riobaldo concludes

Introduction

that Diadorim has been passing as a man soldier. Discovering Diadorim's sex allows Riobaldo to accept his love for Diadorim as "heterosexual."

Gender performances always occur within specific spatial and historical contexts. The context for Pintada's character in *Los de abajo* relates to shifting gender dynamics in Mexico in the mid- to late-nineteenth century and the years preceding the Revolution. According to Anna Macías, the social roles available to unmarried women in Mexican society were modified after liberals came into power in the mid-nineteenth century. Up to 1855, unmarried Mexican women who did not want to marry could become nuns, but this option became limited when the anti-clerical laws favored by liberals prompted the closing of convents. Only after the first school for girls was opened in 1869 did single women have another option, that of becoming teachers (Macías 10). Even then, the number of schools was limited, not everyone had access to or desire for schooling, and compensation for teachers was minimal (8). While there was a growth in the industrial and mining sectors between 1877 and 1910, the great geographical displacement that resulted from the introduction of the railroad system as well as the previously-mentioned restricted opportunities turned more low-income women either to domestic service or sex work (12).

The contexts for Gallegos's and Guimarães Rosa's novels are similarly rooted in gender dynamics from colonial times through the nineteenth and early twentieth centuries. The legal status of women in Venezuela did not change much during the nineteenth century. While independence fights and constant revolts influenced women's movements throughout the century, the perpetuation of colonial law reproduced women's traditional status (Díaz, *Female* 5, 9). Throughout the continent, new nations retained a European legal system that saw only (cis) white men owning property as legitimate citizens (5). Only men who paid taxes or were members of the upper classes could vote, which preserved the integrity of the colonial system. Arlene J. Díaz argues that women in Caracas did not ask for political rights because they were more interested in obtaining legal protection in domestic relationships (*Female* 6).

White women from the upper classes, who were the minority, were able to obtain some autonomy in Brazil during the nineteenth century, however. Feminist movements supported civil rights legislation that improved the situation for unmarried white

Introduction

women, particularly those from privileged socioeconomic classes. For example, such women became allowed to administer their own assets and businesses (Hahner, "Feminism" 80). During the second half of the century, their access to political and economic rights then became limited by a Positivist ideology that assumed women belonged in the domestic sphere (91).

In Mexico, the tension between such progressive movements and conservative gender values framed the gender context preceding the Revolution. The publication of the monthly magazine *La mujer mexicana* in 1904 marked the start of an incipient feminist movement despite strong opposition (Macías 13, 16). The advent of the Revolution allowed for more freedom for women, as engaging directly or indirectly in the fight for independence shaped their participation in political life a century earlier. According to Macías, low-income women from rural and urban areas alike were caught up in the armed conflict and so had no choice but to become actively involved in the revolutionary struggle (25). The story of the Camila character in Azuela's text suggests how poor, rural women might have participated in the Revolution. The novel does not explain the origins of Pintada's involvement in the Revolutionary atmosphere, however, only her socioeconomic objectives for joining Demetrio's band (analyzed in Chapters 1 and 2). Pintada's presence provides evidence of the tension between conservative values and progressive ideologies that was present during the Revolution. She shows that women could be protagonists outside the domestic sphere and that sex workers could empower themselves socioeconomically in the midst of the fight.

Unlike Mexico, the early twentieth-century Venezuelan government put limits on women's social mobility. It suppressed social changes of the late nineteenth century that could have provided legal protection to Venezuelan women (Díaz, *Female* 20). Even in 1904, when Venezuela became one of the first countries in Latin America to promulgate a law that allowed people to divorce and remarry (235), it continued to promote traditional gender roles. Women who followed the ideal of femininity constructed by the elite class, which romanticized women's domestic power, tended to be favored in divorce cases (20, 208). It was not until 1916 that women were allowed to freely manage any assets they had acquired through their own skills or professional activities (238). Venezuelan women's rights and the organization of women's movements (whether feminist or not) continued to be limited throughout the almost thirty years of Juan Vicente Gómez's dictatorship (1908–1936), which aimed to silence all its intellectual and political opponents (Gallegos Ortiz 144; Mijares 148–49). Venezuelan feminist movements stagnated compared to those that developed in countries such as Argentina, Brazil, Chile, México, and Uruguay, which had already organized conferences on women's issues by the early 1900s (F. Miller 72). Similar movements would only be established in Venezuela after the end of Gómez's dictatorship (Díaz, *Female* 241).

Doña Bárbara reflects a new Venezuelan context in which women had gained legal rights while still being expected to reproduce traditional images of femininity. In a way, Doña Bárbara's power represents a sort of hyperbolic example for women who went to court over their rights. Her manipulation of attributes of femininity shows how reproducing certain traditional images could be translated into personal, economic, and social advantages. Because she also manipulates the law at will, Doña Bárbara's presence in the novel points out the vulnerability of a system that, although intended to reinforce women's oppression, could be subverted by clever and deceitful women such as herself.

In Brazil, the challenge to women's *status quo* became greater and took on a more public tone in the first decades of the twentieth century (Besse 2). Industrialization continued to support the rights of women, at least for those from privileged socioeconomic classes and white. According to June E. Hahner, women's movements in the early part of the twentieth century did not take the lead because other social issues were deemed more important ("Feminism" 94–95). That situation changed during the second decade of the century along with the development of the industrial sector in Rio de Janeiro and São Paulo, which resulted in the growth of the middle class and emergence of a small urban working class (Eakin, *Brazil* 40). As Susan K. Besse explains, (white) women who lived in urban areas and had higher incomes took advantage of these changes to increase their participation in social spheres (2). Middle- and upper-class urban (white) women became consumers, studied in schools and universities, and held professions that had previously been denied them (2). Like their Mexican counterparts, Brazilian white women formed feminist organizations and demanded more judicial and civil rights (2).

Introduction

In 1932, Brazilian women obtained the right to vote, making Brazil the third Latin American country to pass such a law (after Uruguay and Ecuador). Sonia E. Alvarez does not consider obtaining the right to vote to have had much impact. Just as Anastasio Somoza García did in Nicaragua, Fulgencio Batista in Cuba, and Rafael Trujillo in the Dominican Republic, the dictatorial government of Getúlio Vargas legislated most of the reforms recommended by women's movements of the 1930s and 1940s only on paper, without implementing them (Alvarez 20). The right to vote barely affected most Brazilian women's lives, only middle- and upper-class urban (white) women profited from suffrage, and women remained absent from positions of political leadership (Alvarez 20; Bassanezi 608; Hahner, "Feminism" 102). *Grande sertão* was thus published in a social context similar to that of *Los de abajo* and *Doña Bárbara*: a traditional society still rejecting modifications to women's rights and condemning any transgressions to domestic roles.

Diadorim's gender transgression nevertheless builds on the work of women's and feminist movements and on historical narratives of cross-dressing and trans* identities. While *travestis*, transsexuals, transgenders, and trans* people have existed throughout Latin American history, their public presence has been tightly controlled. Article 379 of the 1890 Brazilian penal code forbade concealing one's sex and using clothing incorrectly in public (J. Green, *Beyond* 22). During Vargas's authoritarian government, *Estado novo* (1935–1945), strict regulations were enforced and the body was a site of constant state surveillance and organization. It was not until the 1970s that the presence of *travestis* became more obvious in large cities such as Rio (245–46). Rights for the LGBTQAI+ community were only publicly pursued in the early 1980s toward the end of the right-wing military dictatorship and then in the late 1980s and early 1990s because of the spread of the HIV virus. Despite the slow start, these claims to rights have continued into the twenty-first century. Sex-correction surgeries began to be regulated in 1997 and the National Health System (SUS) started conducting such surgeries in 2008, although only in five hospitals in the entire country. The 2008 decree establishing sex-reassignment surgeries only included procedures for trans women; trans men were not included until 2013 (Ávila, *Transmasculinidades* 25). People seeking these surgeries are put on long waiting lists because hospitals still do not have sufficient resources and personnel to conduct more than two per month. A major victory was achieved in 2018, when trans* people became allowed to change their legal names without having first undergone surgery.

Despite the lack of resources and long time it has taken to enact inclusive legislation, Brazil has still been more progressive than many other Latin American countries. In 2008, Mexico City began allowing trans people to change their legal names, but they needed legal and medical support to do it and it was an expensive process. In 2014, Mexico City approved the Gender Identity law, so that people seeking to obtain the right to be recognized by their gender did not have to go to a judge or administrator (León Ortiz 127–28). In 2020, the states of Sinaloa, Nayarit, Michoacán, and Coahuila had also implemented this law. In Venezuela, the right to identity is theoretically protected by the 1999 Constitution, but because there are no specific laws for trans* people, they do not really have the right to change their legal name or access other rights (Balzán 12, 16).

If the broad context for all three novels is a Latin America just beginning to develop movements to include women's rights and later the rights of the LGBTQAI+ community, the general literary context for my discussion of transgressive characters in *Los de abajo*, *Doña Bárbara*, and *Grande sertão: veredas* is the literary movement known as Regionalism. Latin American Regionalist literature includes any text set in a specific area within a country or nation and that faithfully reproduces the geographical, social, human, and historical characteristics of that region (Miguel-Pereira 179). The novels discussed in this book are situated in three specific regions: Jalisco and Zacatecas in Mexico, the Araucan Plains in Venezuela, and the Backlands in Brazil. In Latin America, regionalist literature in one form or another has existed since before the nineteenth century and has continued as an important movement throughout the twentieth and into the twenty-first centuries. Earl E. Fitz even claims that this movement not only pertains to Latin America, but to the entire New World ("Regionalism" 170). These three novels are therefore major works within a major literary movement of the entire American continent (although *Los de abajo* has mainly been analyzed as a novel of the Mexican Revolution). The transgressive performances conducted by trans* warriors and warrior women in twentieth-century Latin American novels speak to the local and transnational relevance of regionalist literature.

Introduction

Thematic Structure

This book takes a thematic approach to analyzing gender rebelliousness and strategies of empowerment amongst trans warriors and warrior women. The first four chapters center on *Los de abajo*, *Doña Bárbara*, and *Grande sertão: veredas*, while Chapter 5 examines other Latin American texts, including novels, films, and testimonials that include trans warrior and warrior woman characters. This chapter complements the others by discussing how gender transgressions no longer necessarily implicated masculinization in the second half of the twentieth century.

Chapter 1 draws on fashion theory to analyze transgressive use of clothing. I argue that donning masculine clothing is the first empowerment strategy of the warrior woman and trans warrior characters. The works of Roland Barthes, Elizabeth Wilson, Joanne Entwistle, and Regina A. Root et al. support my argument that clothes have a performative power because they represent a second skin that rearticulates each character's position in their social contexts. I employ Sylvia Molloy's concept of "posing" to explore temporal gender practices. I also use Halberstam's definition of visual "passing" to highlight the unnaturalness of gender rules. Through the transgressive use of clothes, trans warriors and warrior women carry out a performativity that rearticulates their social role, thus making visible and questioning dominant hierarchies of class, race, ethnicity, and culture.

Bearing in mind Shimizu Akiko's criticism of Butler's performativity as putting too much emphasis on only the visible aspects of performance (3), my analysis moves beyond the performative use of clothing. The second chapter examines the names and nicknames of the characters in the novels. I discuss Claude Lévi-Strauss's and Butler's theories to reveal how hegemonic ideologies regulate social and gender matters through names and naming. I complement this framework with Louis Althusser's concept of interpellation to explain the relationships between trans warriors and warrior women's names and their social contexts, histories, and gender dynamics. While full names often suggest empowerment, nicknames reveal attempts to disempower the characters by labeling their transgressions irrelevant.

Chapter 3 centers on masculinity theories and continues the discussion on empowerment and disempowerment. Keeping in mind Sifuentes-Jáuregui's declaration that gender analyses of Latin America must include context, I examine how trans warriors and warrior women interact and compete with cis men characters in the particular socio-historical contexts depicted in the novels. Drawing on the works of Stefan Dudink, Karen Hagemann, and John Horne, I also explore the association of masculinities in war with the emergence of nation-states. I contend that trans warriors and warrior women manage to achieve the most-desired position in war contexts. Their inevitable disempowerment by being killed off or disappeared then highlights the traditional patriarchal ideology embedded in these novels.

Following Quiroga's argument in 2000 that identity emerges based on networks of relationships (17), the fourth chapter explores the relationships between warrior women and trans warrior characters with other men and women characters in the novels. The gender dynamics in their interactions reveal whose bodies and which performances are accepted in society, whether there is any fear or anxiety regarding homosexuality, and how transgressions to the norm are constrained. Theories on femininity, erotic triangles, and kinship relations are examined in light of the interactions between the characters in the novels. I propose that the performances of the warrior women and trans warrior expose and resist patriarchal culture and men homosocial domination. They also show how other women characters reproduce traditional feminine roles and how men characters reproduce men's domination. Studies by Gayle Rubin, Luce Irigaray, and Sedgwick inform the theory in this chapter.

Chapter 5 broadens my analysis to include other texts. The first section discusses transgressive warriors of the Mexican Revolution, including Petra/Pedro Ruiz and characters in *Cartucho* and *La negra Angustias* (The Black Woman Angustias). The first text was written by a woman, Nellie Campobello, and the latter has a Black warrior woman as protagonist, which allows me to address misogynoirism. The second section examines women guerrillas in the Cuban and Sandinista Revolutions and in revolutionary movements in Brazil to trace changes in gender roles and equity. It includes testimonials, films, and novels featuring fictional and historical women. I am aware that this selection privileges warrior women over trans warriors. My goal in this section is to demonstrate how visible women became in the second part of the twentieth century, while trans* men continued to be erased or ignored.

Introduction

To mitigate this erasure, I trace their presence by including discussions of LGBTQAI+ movements in Brazil, Cuba, and Nicaragua.

The Conclusion focuses on overall strategies of empowerment that have been adopted by trans warriors and warrior women to rearticulate their role in society and access positions of power. These strategies were modified and adapted to new contexts through time. Such mutability attests to the continued presence of representations of trans warriors and warrior women as alternatives to the traditional war heroes of Latin American literature, that is, heterocissexual men. Warrior women and trans warriors embody original alternatives that speak to the gender and sexuality diversities in societies that are still deeply permeated by heterocispatriarchal values.

Chapter One

The Sartorial Transgressions of Warrior Women and Trans Warriors

Dressing is a performance that has the power to disrupt traditional gender discourses. When women and trans* men embedded in heteronormative patriarchies don clothing usually reserved for cis men, they distance themselves from their supposed biological condition (i.e., female sex), disrupt the trust others place in such natural(ized) knowledge, and introduce diverse gender performances into the public sphere. Transgressively changing clothes likewise allows fictional trans* men and women to escape oppressive and constraining social roles. Exchanging feminine for masculine attire enables warrior woman and trans warrior characters to circulate freely outside the household and access elements of power otherwise denied them. For example, the character Pintada from *Los de abajo* uses clothing to overcome gender, race, and class hierarchies. Doña Bárbara in *Doña Bárbara* manipulates her attire to project whichever gender image—masculine or feminine—will enable her to obtain the most power in the given circumstances. While Diadorim in *Grande sertão: veredas* is not as focused on personal empowerment as the other two characters, his clothing and behavior nevertheless transgress societal expectations to establish a trans* identity. These three warrior characters thus use clothing to undermine the normative subjugation of the feminine to the masculine. Drawing on contemporary fashion and queer theory, the next section outlines the main concepts used in this chapter to explain their sartorial transgressions.

Fashioning Trans Warriors and Warrior Women

Aside from providing protection from the elements, clothing encodes distinctions of gender, class, race, religion, profession, and other social groups within different cultures. Fashion theorists generally agree that dress has represented different forms of social organization throughout Western history. Clothing has certainly been a means of classification and order since the European Middle Ages, when conventions of dress separated people into distinct classes and cultures (Barthes 65; Garber 21, 25; Roche 4). Of all possible social distinctions, Joanne Entwistle and Elizabeth Wilson consider gender "the most crucial feature of dress, the aspect of identity most clearly and consistently articulated by clothes" ("Introduction" 5). Since at least the seventeenth century, dress codes have established roles for and made visible the social barriers that divided men and women (E. Wilson 117). In addition to marking non-binary variables such as class, ethnicity, or race, clothing often reinforces an assumed binary gender division by marking each subject as a member of either one of only two genders. Such a gender separation became less obvious during the twentieth century as garments previously considered men's became unisex, many women began dressing like "men" in Western societies, and fashion trends blurred traditional gender divisions in other ways.

Clothing is an artificial skin covering the body's living skin. Clothing hides and veils, exhibits and unveils the body. Besides distinguishing amongst different social groups, dress thus "marks the boundary between self and other, individual and society" (Entwistle, "The Dressed" 37). People combine a variety of garments and other objects such as jewelry to produce a visual statement (Kaiser 6). However, according to Ana María Díaz Marcos, the second skin of clothing also integrates the body within culture ("Un ángel" 33). The visibility of this second skin enables the person wearing it to be understood, recognized, and codified as a subject in the public sphere. In articulating and rearticulating the subject's position, dress simultaneously communicates one's identity and fits one into one's culture (Geczy and Karaminas 20).

Clothes acquire and communicate meaning within specific social contexts by deviating from or reinforcing social rules. In historical contexts of war in Latin America, dress reproduced heterocisnormative rules by constantly reinforcing the assumed sex/gender binary. Wearing clothing that aligns one's biological sex with one's gendered role prevents confusion from arising that might threaten society's logic. Clothes reproduce a naturalized knowledge that associates certain garments with a guarantee of the genitalia and other sex features of the body they cover (Butler,

Gender xxii–iv). In establishing this correspondence, the heterocisnormative system continues to be sustained.

Nevertheless, according to Judith Butler, the very necessity to thus continually reinforce heterocisnormativity highlights the system's ultimate inefficacy and opens the possibility for questioning hegemonic rules. If clothes functioning as a second skin articulate a subject in culture, I argue that the transgressive use of clothes rearticulates the same subject's expected position. Transgressing sartorial norms allows the subject to renegotiate their position in the public sphere. Adam Geczy and Vicki Karaminas term this renegotiation "queer style." Queer style reflects a more continuous relationship between the naked body and clothing than does straight style because it does not aim to cover the body and obey the compulsory heterocisnormativity embedded in clothing codes (7). Clothing becomes more than just a divider between private and public spheres: it represents or even becomes one's "skin."

Louis Althusser's theory of rituals of ideological recognition is particularly helpful for analyzing the ways in which trans warriors and warrior women transgress Western sartorial norms to disrupt traditional notions of gender, ethnicity, and class. His theory complements the social process approach currently favored in fashion theory. Rituals of ideological recognition guarantee to others that we are concrete and unmistakable subjects ("Ideología" 140) and also affirm that people are autonomous from society but capable of identifying other members of society (147). Dressing oneself may be considered a ritual of ideological recognition in Althusser's terms because people put on clothes in acknowledgment of naturalized gender. At the same time, people expect to read society's heteronormative rules in the garments and bodies of other people. Their expectations are part of the ritual of recognition that reinforces each subject's interpellation vis-a-vis hegemonic ideology.

Clothing rituals not only recognize but assist in constructing a dominant masculine ideology. According to Lynne Segal, traditional masculinity is considered superior because it operates by exclusion: to be masculine is to be neither feminine nor gay, that is, not "infected" with what is considered inferior (*Slow Motion* x). This masculinity discourse tends to reinforce heteronormative relations. Warrior women's and trans warriors' performances of masculinities do not reinforce heterocisnormativity, however. Rather, they

Chapter One

permit the possibility of greater gender (and power) variability than implied in the normative binary ideology. In his analysis of queer Latin America, Héctor Domínguez-Ruvalcaba affirms that the logic of transvestism "distrust[s]" the discourse of what is authentic and natural (*Translating* 138). That is, "transvestism" undermines societal rituals of ideological recognition. As practiced through dressing and other rituals of ideological recognition, masculinity and femininity are not separable phenomena (Connell, *Masculinities* 36, 44, 72–75). Furthermore, since masculinity and femininity share a history and social context and intersect with other aspects of identity, any ambivalence about gender cannot be separated from other identity ambivalences (Kaiser 44).

Dressing also negotiates social position and power relations (Kaiser 1). For example, in Latin America, masculine men of any "race" (recognized by skin color) tend to hold higher social status or claim more prestigious roles than women who have the same skin color. By wearing gender-marked garments transgressively, warrior women such as Pintada and Doña Bárbara improve their positions within hierarchies of class, race, and public power. By dressing to resemble men and display masculinity, trans warriors and warrior women rewrite social norms and rearticulate the possible roles for female-sexed people in society. That they do so within the context of war is even more significant because they demonstrate their ability to attain power within an especially men-dominated space.

Four theoretical concepts are deployed in this chapter to elucidate the power of transgressive dress amongst warrior woman and trans warrior characters, although not all of them are equally important for each character: cross-dressing, passing, the dandy's technique, and posing. By going against gendered sartorial rules, cross-dressing inherently challenges hegemonic expectations of femininity and masculinity. Within the binary system, cross-dressing refers to using elements of the clothing of the "opposite" gender in order to project the image of that other gender. The cross-dresser questions the rituals of recognition that are supposed to affirm the identity and integrity of subjects in society. Indeed, the cross-dresser is seldom recognized or acknowledged as a subject because they threaten the binary logic of established gender categories. Marjorie Garber argues that the figure of the cross-dresser represents a third "gender," so cross-dressing constitutes a "category crisis" (11). Because their performance cannot be neatly separated into two genders, the cross-dresser not only undermines the stability of the binary gender scheme, they also call into question the stability of a third gender (11). Where the androgynes tend to consolidate the binary, when they are seen as a combination of the two traditional genders, the cross-dresser's performance of gender demonstrates its contingency. The figure of the cross-dresser is neither masculine nor feminine nor androgynous. Femininity and masculinity are never "well-" defined because the cross-dresser does not allow one to predominate over the other. Ben. Sifuentes-Jáuregui takes this even further by arguing that transvestism not only disrupts any notion of gender (*Transvestism* 2), it "inaugurates an epistemological shift that locates, defines, performs, and erases the fundamental dichotomy: Self/Other" (4).

Literary critics and cultural studies scholars of Latin America have investigated the specificities of cross-dressing in the region, but have focused primarily on transvestism. I prefer the term "cross-dressing" to "transvestism" because it is more apt for exploring the gender performances of the specific warrior woman and trans warrior characters examined in this book. The cross-dresser's transgression invites us to see gender as a complex performance that need not conform to specific rules or categories. In the cross-dressing performance, gender is subjected to diverse representations and identities. The plurality of the cross-dresser is also connected to power dynamics. For example, Diadorim being trans* is manipulated by Riobaldo in *Grande sertão*. While I take into account Sifuentes-Jáuregui's analysis, the performances of warrior women and trans warrior do not carry the same meanings as the *travesti* identities he investigates. For instance, a major difference is that in his study the majority of drag performers are (and are perceived as) gay (*Transvestism* 47), while Pintada and Doña Bárbara are heterosexual, although Doña Bárbara is suspected at times of not being so (this relates to the history of cross-dressers and *travestis* alike).

Considering the trans* concept and Diadorim's performance in the *Grande sertão*, I do not analyze him as a *travesti*. Dora Silva Santana has demonstrated the importance of the *travesti* concept in that it denies imposed narrow definitions of womanhood while capturing a racist history of exclusion and violence (low-income Black *travestis* are often incarcerated, beaten, or assassinated in

Brazil) (213). However, Diadorim never identifies himself as such and does not have any connection to the resilient *travesti* community. He is better understood as a trans warrior because, like the two warrior women characters, he empowers himself under adverse war circumstances by assuming the mantle of a soldier's masculinity.

More pertinently, warrior woman and trans warrior characters are able to improve their situation and empower themselves precisely because being considered a man or deploying a powerful masculinity is socially prestigious. Their acquisition of power and improvement of social status only holds up to a certain point, however. Masculine or masculinized trans warrior and warrior woman characters are (eventually) seen as inconvenient usurpers and competitors. The temporary empowerment warrior woman and trans warrior characters obtain through donning cis men's dressing is evidence that clothing helps construct a subjectivity by mediating between the body and the rules of language and social institutions (Cavallaro and Warwick 3).

By covering the private body and projecting a self-representation in the public sphere, clothes create images that connect individuals to stable identities. In other words, clothes can allow the subject to rearticulate their role in society, that is, to pass. In the U.S., passing has been usually applied to racial identification, like in Nella Larsen's novel. In contemporary gender and sexuality studies, passing is a gender identification strategy. According to Jack Halberstam, it is a narrative in which a self effectively conceals another type of self (*Female* 21). Diadorim's performance exemplifies this strategy of establishing a gender identity of masculinity. Similar to the act of cross-dressing, gender passing for warrior women and trans warriors empowers them by disrupting the gender norms established by the rules of heterosexuality. Like cross-dressing, passing goes beyond such gender rules to involve other elements of identity, such as class. It occurs with Pintada, who attempts to pass into a different social class by obtaining and using clothing of upper-class women. Halberstam adds that the passing self may correspond to one's identity (*Female* 21), but Julia Serano argues that for trans people, passing is being misgendered. That is, it takes place when trans people are categorized in the gender with which they do not identify (179). When trans peoples are finally identified with their gender, they are not passing (180).

In Halberstam's discussion of representations of transgenderism, he uses "passing" to refer specifically to visual veracity, which he states must be complemented with haptic perception and a narrative of continual transition (*Trans** 96). This last sense of "passing" applies to Diadorim's self-representation in his performance of masculinities when he is young and as an adult. He is identified as a man most of the time and his performance enables him to pass as the most skilled warrior amongst the *jagunços* (see Chapters 2 and 3).

The challenge to sartorial and traditional identity rules can also be seen in the techniques of the nineteenth century dandy, as explained by Roland Barthes. The dandy modifies the details of his attire to distinguish himself from others. By playing with his attire and presenting it with an attitude of care, the dandy calls into question rigid concepts of gender and class (*The Language* 66–67). According to Barthes, the detail, such as the knot of a cravat or the material of a shirt, was a new aesthetic category for men's clothing (66). Although the dandy's gender performance did not constitute cross-dressing as such, the adjustments he made to his clothing transgressed social categories. Similarly, warrior women such as Pintada and Doña Bárbara challenge gender categories by manipulating the details of their attire even when they are donning their most "feminine" clothing.

Finally, "posing" is a temporal practice closely related to performance politics in that it suggests the subject chooses to represent their self in an oppositional manner that does not accord with societal expectations (Molloy 184). Such posturing is neither banal nor superficial, according to Sylvia Molloy. Posing instead provides evidence that constructions of identity—that is, the performative (visible) features of identity—cannot be clearly defined and are therefore artificial (187). By questioning the social reproduction of models of gender, posing subverts the formulations and divisions of gender. Posing offers new strategies for gender performance, new ways to play with sexual identities, and new modes of self-identification (187). Both Diadorim and Doña Bárbara perform masculinities as well as pose in the most-desired positions of their social contexts.

The sartorial transgression that each trans warrior and warrior woman character carries out signals how clothes and their manipulation are able to rearticulate their role in their societies. Just as

Chapter One

Sifuentes-Jáuregui finds that transvestism's questioning of masculinity enables gender differences to occur (*Transvestism* 23), the cross-dressing of warrior women and trans warriors allows for new social spaces to open up: Pintada's performance challenges norms of class and gender, Doña Bárbara's questions gender dichotomies, and Diadorim's subverts traditional gender categories. To explore these themes, I begin by analyzing Pintada's transgressive use of clothing, because *Los de abajo* was the first of the three novels to be published.

Pintada's Clothed Images

As mentioned in the Introduction, several critics have tended to revile Pintada as a force for evil or dismiss her as a mere sex worker rather than treat her as a leader. More recent critiques informed by gender studies, such as those by Pascale Baker, B. Christine Arce, and Oswaldo Estrada, have analyzed Pintada under a more gender-progressive lens and recognized the strength of the character in a men-dominated atmosphere. Baker sees Pintada as masculine in that she leads looting expeditions, does not submit to any man character, and survives without being punished (*Revolutionaries* 97, 101–02). Furthermore, according to Baker, Azuela developed the prototype of the adventurer in the Pintada character, an opportunist who came to represent a negative future for Mexico (104). Arce does not discuss Pintada's race, although she does mention the character's class. She argues that, as the first in a line of *cucarachas* (cockroaches), Pintada has agency, but she is rendered undesirable as a woman because having any power means she fails to embody a traditional femininity (*México's* 94–95). Finally, Estrada describes Pintada as a "loose woman" who murders Camila only in order to preserve her position as Demetrio's lover (*Troubled* 143). He indicates, however, that portraying women characters like this during the Revolution was part of a larger scheme of disappearing women from armed conflict (144).

While Baker, Arce, and Estrada highlight important gender aspects of the character, I see that analyzing Pintada requires reading the intersection of gender, race, and class. Pintada's strategic use of clothing and other objects attached to her body not only illustrate the complexity of that intersection but call all these social categories into question. Her clothed images are transgressive in that they suggest a doubling of antithetical opposites: lower versus upper class, feminine versus masculine, and sexual being versus warrior. Pintada plays several roles in *Los de abajo*. She is a lover (of Demetrio), an assassin (of Camila), and a would-be leader in that she gives orders, instigates plunder expeditions, and provides and manipulates information to other characters. Her attire symbolizes these various roles by simultaneously representing her as a feminine woman of indigenous, *mestizo* and/or Black ancestry embedded in a masculine environment and being poor and fighting in a revolutionary band to improve her socioeconomic standing.

Pintada's attire is described in two places within the novel. The first instance occurs inside a house that serves as a roadside inn:

> La Pintada apareció de pronto en medio de la sala, luciendo un espléndido traje de seda de riquísimos encajes.—¡No más las medias se te olvidaron!—exclamó el güero Margarito desternillándose de risa. La muchacha de la Codorniz prorrumpió también en carcajadas. Pero a la Pintada nada se le dio; hizo una mueca de indiferencia, se tiró a la alfombra y con los propios pies hizo saltar las zapatillas de raso blanco, moviendo muy a gusto los dedos desnudos, entumecidos por la opresión del calzado, y dijo:—¡Epa, tú, Pancracio! ... Anda a traerme unas medias azules de mis «avances». ([Cátedra] 153)

As this text demonstrates, the elegant dress that differentiates Pintada from all the men characters is not her primary transgression, rather, it is her lack of stockings to complete the outfit. Although she distinguishes herself from the rest of the band by donning an elegant dress, Güero Margarito's ridicule brings her back to the level of the band. The ridicule (and her kicking off her satin slippers) suggests that Pintada is incapable of successfully passing as an upper-class white woman. Just as the luxuriousness of her dress is made irrelevant by the lack of appropriate stockings, so her representation of a rich white woman is shown to be incomplete and hence false. Likewise, sitting on the carpet flouts social conventions and further suggests that Pintada's social, economic, and cultural class supersedes any of the symbolic power of the dress. Herbert Spencer, who was also a fashion studies pioneer, argued in 1892 that fashion "derived from the habits and appearance exhibited by those in power" (28). In this sense, Pintada seems to be imitating members of a socially and racially privileged class by wearing a splendid lace dress and white satin shoes. Normally she could not afford to buy such clothes: the tightness of the shoes reveals that this apparel was not made for her. She has only been able to acquire fine clothing by stealing it during revolutionary raids.

I propose that Pintada's sartorial behavior is not a case of class imitation, but of appropriation—theft—of status symbols. The dress she wears does not *resemble* an elegant dress—it is in itself elegant. But appropriating such attire does not turn Pintada into an upper-class white woman. She does not even project a "false" or "incomplete" image of such a woman. Rather, by not wearing stockings and sitting on the floor, Pintada demonstrates that she is not interested in passing as an upper class "other." I here use "other" to explain that Pintada rejects upper-class people in much the same way as poor/low-income and non-white people have been excluded. That is, she treats them as an undesirable other. Following Gayatri Spivak's definition of "othering," Pintada seems to subvert classist discourses. She does not even pretend temporarily to be a rich white woman to amuse her comrades. Instead, she stamps her recently acquired attire with her personal character. Pintada's appropriation of some elements of the attire of a woman from a privileged social class and white skin color is thus transgressive rather than imitative. Following Molloy's understanding, this is an example of posing as a way of disrupting social categories.

However, the fact that the white satin slippers do not fit Pintada's feet implies that she is not transforming her body to fit all the markers of the feminine, white, upper class. She may have stolen them, but she does not fully reappropriate these upper-class objects. Her transgressive use of clothes, in conjunction with her agenda to improve her status, constitutes a performativity that reveals the racist and classist hierarchies of her society. Pintada's dressing behavior represents the desires of the oppressed social and non-white classes, particularly the country people, who rose up during the Mexican Revolution in an attempt to improve their social and economic conditions. Her disinterest in imitating the upper classes combined with her use of force to appropriate expensive objects extends to all of the country people depicted in the novel.

Similar to Pintada, the rural poor had no opportunity to improve their socioeconomic standing other than by plundering the wealthy during the Revolution. Indeed, their lack of socioeconomic mobility in Mexico is a major theme of Azuela's text. The title of the novel, *Los de abajo* (lit. "those from below," usually translated as "The Underdogs"), reminds us that those from below can never become those from above. Arce found this to be the case in her analysis of real and fictional *soldaderas* who have been considered "nobodies" despite their important presence in the Revolution and contributions to Mexico (*México's* 8). As a poor woman of indigenous, *mestizo* and/or Black background, Pintada is such a nobody. She is treated as an Other who must disappear from the national discourse, because at the time the presence of masculine women of color would have made military officials to feel embarrassed (8–9). By dismissing such women as nobodies, Arce goes on to argue, the Mexican state projected an image that preserved the PRI (Political Revolutionary Party) in power until 2000 (9). Like the women, most of the underdogs in Azuela's novel happen to be men of indigenous, *mestizo* and/or Black origin. Of the members of Demetrio's band, only Luis Cervantes—who is white, not from the countryside, and a member of a privileged socioeconomic class—survives and profits from the Revolution. Even when they appropriate elegant attire, the other underdogs cannot be turned into "fat cats."

It is important to note that Pintada is not wearing an outfit intended either for the battlefield or to ride a horse. Even though her silk dress and laces are not usually combined with cartridge belts and guns, in the context of the Revolution, there is no reason not to wear such an outfit. There were no dress codes for upper-class women involved in war in Mexico. With her appropriation, Pintada thus creates her own unique style. According to Arce, Chicana artist Nao Bustamante found a photograph that depicted a battalion of women wearing late-Edwardian dresses amongst the revolutionary photographs in the archives of the University of California Riverside (*México's* 273–74). The striking difference between this photograph and typical *soldadera* images from the Revolution prompted Bustamante to design a series of military outfits for *soldaderas* for her 2015 installation "Soldadera" (274). I mention Bustamante's work here in order to observe that the Revolution allowed women like Pintada to develop, appropriate, invent, reappropriate, use, reuse, disregard, and improvise clothing in the middle of ongoing armed conflict.

Chapter One

Pintada's attire is described for the second time when the band of revolutionaries leaves the city:

> Muy ufana, lucía vestido de seda y grandes arracadas de oro; el azul pálido del talle acentuaba el tinte aceitunado de su rostro y las manchas cobrizas de la avería. Perniabierta, su falda se remangaba hasta la rodilla y se veían sus medias deslavadas y con muchos agujeros. Llevaba revólver al pecho y una cartuchera cruzada sobre la cabeza de la silla. (160)

Her appearance here presents what I call "double images." The description of her poorly washed stockings full of runs suggests she is careless about her dress, which I see as her disinterest in projecting a middle or upper-class image of decency. However, the luxuriousness of her dress and earrings projects an image of wealth and pride. This second doubled image is gendered. Although she is not passing as a man, Pintada is projecting simultaneous feminine and masculine images. Her appropriated dress and earrings are that of a feminine woman, while her cartridge belt, gun, and habit of riding astride instead of side-saddle are signs of a masculine warrior. (Her appropriation of the weapons of war is discussed in Chapter 3.) She thus continues to develop her own visible style. This conjoining of femininity and masculinity can also be understood as a consequence of Pintada's association with the hegemonic masculine milieu of war, as Gustavo Casasola said occurred for many women in the Mexican Revolution.

During the Revolution, Casasola problematized the role of women in war when he wrote that if "la soldadera empuña la carabina a la hora de la acción decisiva, la gloria es para el soldado, para el oficial y para el jefe" ("La soldadera" 720). His words elucidate why some of the most famous images in this conflict are of men such as Pancho Villa and his Dorados. Casasola also describes how the women who accompanied the columns masculinized their appearances and behaviors. He wrote that they must "vestir como hombre y conducirse como hombre; ir a caballo, como todos, resistir las caminatas y a la ahora de la acción demostrar con el arma en la mano que no es una soldadera, sino un soldado" (720). Such physical masculinization characterizes warrior women and trans* men in men-dominated spheres because, in order to demonstrate that they are equal to men, they must act and look like cis men. Still, Casasola suggests that the most authentic *soldadera* is one who does not lose her feminine role as woman, wife, mother, or even victim (720). Traditional ideologies persist even when women confirm their skills and masculinities in war.

Another major cross-dressing character from novels of the Mexican Revolution is Angustias, the protagonist in Francisco Rojas González's novel *La negra Angustias* (1944). Angustias is a young Black woman who comes from a poor background. She runs away from home after murdering a man that has been sexually harassing her. Trading on her Black father's history as a famous bandit, she becomes a Zapatista colonel. Angustias dons men's clothing by wearing suits meant for *charros* (skilled traditional horsemen in Mexico). Just as Pintada does when she wears an elegant dress along with stockings full of runs, Angustias stamps her own agenda onto her desirable attire. For example, she removes an image of the Christ of Chalma from her hat and replaces it with one of the Virgin of Guadalupe (104). In making the substitution, she makes it clear that she does not identify with the religious figure of a "white" man, but with that of a *mestiza*. Still, as a Black woman in the Revolution, Angustias is not allowed to participate in the national discourse of the Revolution. Her husband, who treats her as a lover rather than as his official wife, collects for himself all the monetary benefits she accrued from having participated in the war as a Zapatista colonel. While, as Arce argues, her complex image indicates the presence of high-ranking women in the Revolution, her ultimate fate shows that she too is a nobody. (I analyze Angustias's masculine *charro* outfits in detail in Chapter 5.)

The Zapatista Colonel Amelio Robles Ávila (1889–1984) provides another example of the marginalization of some performances of masculinities during the Revolution. Robles, who was born female-sexed, changed his image to enter the masculine atmosphere of the Mexican Revolution by ceasing to wear feminine clothing and adopting the masculine name "Amelio." He continued wearing masculine clothes and behaving like a man after the war was over. According to historian Gabriela Cano, Robles was neither transsexual nor a butch lesbian, but a transgendered male whose gender performance included poses, gestures, attitudes, and clothing ("Unconcealable" 37). While his performance illustrates the power and importance of trans* masculinity, trans* identities, and cross-dressing, various journalists, academics, and writers throughout the twentieth century projected their own ideologies or political platforms onto his body by refusing to see Robles as a man or trans* man. As Cano asserts, their imposed meanings signal the invisibility and fragility of the trans* person who must negotiate a place in the world while continuing to be represented or misrepresented by others ("Amélio" 150). Robles's identity has been treated as a sort of *tabula rasa* in which meanings are placed on him that he cannot control. For instance, in 1989, a museum in his honor was opened in his hometown under a female name (Amelia Robles). Because the Secretariat of Women of the State of Guerrero sponsored the museum as a way to celebrate the participation of women warriors in the Revolution, Robles's gender identification was not taken into consideration (Cano, "Unconcealable" 49).

Politics and ideologies have a great impact on representations of trans* people, trans warriors, and even warrior women; no matter what the context, the voice of the trans* person is most of the time neither heard nor respected. Chilean author, Diamela Eltit, provides another example of how Robles's body and performance continued to be misinterpreted even in the late-twentieth century, when discourses that aimed to emphasize the (forgotten) presence of women in the Revolution did so by ignoring trans* men. In 1991, Eltit wrote about Robles's masculine image as deceitful or surprising with the goal of questioning traditional notions on gender, but in doing so her text reproduces transphobic themes. For instance, Eltit seems to accuse Robles of not being in solidarity with women's social conditions and choosing the blood of the war over the one from menstrual cycles (176). It seems Eltit is nostalgic of the woman that does not exist because of the trans* man (175–76). While Eltit aims to expose the weight social codes have on how people interact with each other in society, her nostalgia ends ups reinforcing traditional ideas on gender. She only discusses two genders, essentializes womanhood, and argues that Robles's transgression makes him complicit with power structures and traditional masculinity.

These topics can be related to what Julia Serrano defined as "cissexism," now more commonly called cisgenderism. Cisgenderism is obvious throughout Eltit's reading of Robles's body and performance. While I recognize that Eltit wrote before the development of trans theory, her words build on the Secretariat's action by ignoring the existence of trans* people and disregarding Robles's self-positioning, gender identity, and social agenda. Besides overlooking Robles's desires, aims, and profits, Eltit makes him an accomplice to the dominant and traditional oppressive discourse of white men's masculinity. In Eltit's reading, it would seem Robles does not challenge such conventions. Robles is thus disempowered and his gender identity, transgression, and relentless struggle to be considered a man are all erased and he is inserted as just another subordinate in the dominant power structure.

If Pintada's strategic use of clothing in *Los de abajo* demonstrates the presence of warrior women, the character of Camila represents another type of woman involved in the Revolution. She plays the role of the feminine lover, one of the roles Casasola considered as representing the authentic *soldadera*. Camila is also of indigenous, *mestizo* and/or Black descent, but she does not resemble Pintada in appearance or behavior and only gets caught up in the Revolution through becoming Demetrio's lover. She is a poor peasant from the little village where the revolutionaries stay while Demetrio is recovering from battle wounds. She falls in love with Luis Cervantes, who initially rejects her. Once Demetrio expresses his desire for her, Cervantes convinces her to run away with him, then hands her over to Demetrio. She becomes his sexual partner against her will. Throughout the novel, Camila is portrayed as a submissive and selfless woman representative of one of the many women who were stolen from their homes during the Revolution.

Camila's clothing highlights her lack of economic means, cultural background, and failed attempt to become Cervantes's fiancée: "Y en el fondo de guijas lavadas se reprodujo con su blusa amarilla de cintas verdes, sus enaguas blancas sin almidonar, lamida la cabeza y estiradas las cejas y la frente; tal como se había ataviado para gustar a Luis" (119–20). Camila's blouse and underskirt are traditional clothes that mark her as a member of a specific class and culture. By dressing to please Cervantes, her behavior reinforces the subordination of women to men in a patriarchal society. In contrast, Pintada dresses for herself and her non-traditional clothes represent a form of agency and a complex manifestation of feminine transgression into a masculine environment.

Pintada's double image and use of contrasting garments construct her performance of class, gender, and even racial status. Although she projects the image of an upper-class woman with her stolen dress, because the shoes do not fit and the only stockings

Chapter One

she has are full of runs, she is still a poor woman. Moreover, she is simultaneously a woman and a warrior with a gun. While traditionally masculine elements in her dress emphasize her agency and gender transgression, traditionally feminine elements signal her social status (her lack of stockings) and her hopes, wishes, or agenda (her elegant dress). While the seeming doublings of Pintada's attire suggest that what she hopes to achieve (class and money) and what she is able to achieve (dress) remain inevitably separate, they are actually intertwined within the imagery of the novel. Her doubled image distorts normative gender bifurcations and adds complexity to status categories otherwise seen as exclusive.

If cross-dressing, as Sifuentes-Jáuregui states, is a "desire that seeks recognition" (*Transvestism* 118), Pintada's dressing strategies call attention both to herself and her empowerment. For instance, Pintada has "stains" on her face that are signs of a sexually transmitted disease. Critics have argued that those stains imply that she is a sex worker. However, the elegance of the stolen dress adds dimension to her facial stains and racial status. By partially projecting an upper-class image with her dress, she challenges the assumed requirements for being a member of a certain class. That is, her performance calls into question classism and racism. Her proud (*ufana*) attitude also contrasts with the "bad" (i.e., not gender normative) posture she exhibits by riding her horse astride rather than side-saddle as was considered proper for "decent" women. Her dress contrasts with the gun and cartridge belt. Her sartorial transgressions and doubled image position her at the forefront of the band. She is there to be recognized.

While Pintada appears just as physically decadent and morally corrupt as the other underdog characters, she does distinguish herself by appropriating an elegant dress, which (temporarily) rearticulates her socioeconomic position, challenges perceptions of her racial status, and demonstrates her autonomy. Her stockings add another dimension to this already transgressive use of clothing.

Dressing to Kill

The item of Pintada's clothing that appears most frequently in the novel is her stockings. The torn blue stockings are used to symbolize her low social status, femininity, and sensuality at different points in the book. They cover and uncover Pintada's character, economic status, and even race, as their blue color hides the dark skin of her legs, a racialized indicator of low income. Stockings seem to be a private or personal item of attire, an apparently insignificant feminine piece of clothing that is often fetishized. Pintada's stockings are more than a second skin allowing Pintada to perform traditional femininity and social class, however. As Dani Cavallaro and Alexandra Warwick argue, "The power of dress to threaten boundaries (between self and non-self, the individual and the collective, discipline and transgression) is emphasized by items of clothing such as masks and veils, which epitomize duplicity and the co-existence of concealment and revelation, presence and absence" (*Fashioning* xxi).

Pintada's stockings are a sort of veil that conceals her capacity for violence. After Demetrio tells Pintada to leave the band, she attacks and kills Camila, her rival for Demetrio's affection: "Y todo fue en un abrir y cerrar de ojos, se inclinó, sacó una hoja aguda y brillante de entre la media y la pierna y se lanzó sobre Camila" (183). Whereas the absence of "good" stockings (i.e., without any runs) signals Pintada's low economic status, the presence of "bad" stockings (i.e., torn and dirty), which she uses to conceal a weapon, veils her intention to take action on her own behalf. The concealing power of the stockings actually allows Pintada to exercise agency and subvert the rules of her society by killing the one character that embodies the objectification of women in patriarchal societies.

Critics such as Clive Griffin have interpreted Pintada simply as evil because she murders the innocent, good Camila, but by killing Camila, Pintada demonstrates that it is possible to rebel against the patriarchal power represented by Demetrio. I do not deny she is a murderer and that her victim was the most helpless character in her context—an easy prey—, but Pintada's action can be read as having another meaning. Even though killing Camila may be deemed "evil" and results in Pintada being "othered" and expelled from the band, Pintada's actions, like her dress, challenge and transgress the normative behavioral borders of gender and class. Thus, while Pintada performs "evil" actions, she is not just an "evil" character. Instead, by representing the social and financial desires of a marginalized lover and poor woman of indigenous, *mestizo*, and/or Black descent, Pintada's posing and transgressive doubling both expose and interrogate her society's rules.

Chapter One

This transgression is also present in Rómulo Gallegos's novel in the character of Doña Bárbara. Like Pintada, Doña Bárbara's clothing calls into question the underlying structure of patriarchal society. Using queer and fashion theories to supplement Sharon Magnarelli's, Stephen Henighan's, and Jorge J. Barrueto's feminist and postcolonial approaches to the novel, the next section offers a new interpretation of Doña Bárbara's character by focusing on her transgressive social and sartorial strategies.

Doña Bárbara's Manipulated Images

Critics have most commonly interpreted Gallegos's novel as a representation of the conflict between civilization and barbarity. Within this dialectic, Doña Bárbara, labeled backward and savage, is usually said to represent the side of barbarity. Critics such as Sturgis E. Leavitt and Victorien Lavou Zoungbo have explained Doña Bárbara's presumed symbolic identification with barbarity by arguing that Gallegos wrote the novel to promote a progressive ideology. For example, Leavitt considers Doña Bárbara an incoherent character because her appearance (including her clothing) changes along with her attitude toward Santos Luzardo over the course of the novel (118–19). He sees such supposed incoherence as representing obstruction to progress in Venezuela.

Although agreeing that Doña Bárbara is a metonym for barbarity and backwardness (discussed further in Chapter 2), Magnarelli, Henighan, and Barrueto read Doña Bárbara's character in less negative terms. Magnarelli, for example, argues that she is a strong character able to challenge traditional norms that are represented as "civilized" ("Woman" 12–16). Along the lines of critics such as Carlos Alonso, Roberto González Echevarría, Doris Sommer, and others, Barrueto suggests that Doña Bárbara has to be erased or expelled from society precisely because she represents racial, gendered, and cultural othernesses that do not fit with Gallegos's ideology (185–86, 191). (Doña Bárbara's disempowerment is analyzed in Chapters 2 and 3.) Henighan addresses gender in arguing that Doña Bárbara and Santos both represent deviations from traditional constructions of gender identity (29). In order to correct these deviations, Doña Bárbara is made to construct a more feminine image, and Santos a more masculine one, as the novel progresses (44).

D. L. Shaw has argued that Doña Bárbara's change from a more masculine to a more feminine appearance reflects a moral progression as she attempts to redeem herself from her past actions over the course of the story (*Gallegos* 46–47). Doña Bárbara's gender performances are not chronologically progressive, however. I must highlight that she does not transform herself from a hyper-masculine to a hyper-feminine figure as the novel progresses. The episode in which her sensual femininity is most emphasized occurs in the middle of the novel, only a few pages after she has been portrayed as masculine or butch. She is depicted wearing more neutral and less seductive attire at the end of the novel. Her alternating projections of feminine and masculine images are thus far from incoherent. They empower her and enable her to attain a higher socioeconomic station in life.

Doña Bárbara dynamically represents herself as masculine, semi-feminine, or ultra-feminine depending on the context and her interests. Her attire is directly connected to her intentions: to work, to please, to win, and to redeem her sins. She cleverly manipulates her clothing to project varied images of herself, sometimes as a beautiful bewitcher of men, other times as a butch *mujerona* (big woman), *llanera* (cowgirl), or *cacica* (woman cacique). She wears pants under a skirt while working alongside the laborers on the cattle ranch and carrying out the tasks of a *llanero*. When she is at home dining or with her lover Balbino, she wears a simple dress that covers her body. She wears more feminine and revealing clothing during her encounters with Santos, whom she seeks to seduce and dominate. In her ability to alternate between projecting a traditional image of feminine womanhood and performing a butch woman who is more *llanero* than the *llaneros*, Doña Bárbara subverts the biases that inform both gender roles and obtains power for herself.

Doña Bárbara has also been linked with the Plains, especially in the 1954 prologue, when Gallegos describes her as "¿Bella entonces, también, como la llanura? (*Doña* 5). Gallegos describes the Plains in feminine terms: "[t]ierra abierta y tendida" (55), but according to Henighan, Doña Bárbara is not represented as a particularly feminine character (34). He considers her such a strong, masculine presence in the book that she fits better into a discourse of gender ambivalence. Such a discourse does not structure her character, however. Rather, as a warrior woman fighting to distinguish herself simultaneously as a mainstay of power in Arauca and a beautiful woman, I argue that she represents a manipulation of rituals of ideological recognition. By adapting how she clothes her body to suit specific circumstances, she simultaneously transgresses and ratifies hegemonic categories of masculinity and femininity.

Dressing for Strength

The extradiegetic narrator of the novel characterizes Doña Bárbara's most masculine style of dress as disgusting. Doña Bárbara is described as an "amazona repugnante de pantalones hombrunos hasta los tobillos bajo la falda recogida al arzón, lazo en mano" (111). Her attire is repellant because it transgresses the sartorial limits of the two normative genders: a woman's skirt is inherently incompatible with men's pants. She does not incarnate an ideal of masculinity; instead, the inappropriate combination of a feminine element (skirt) with the doubly masculine element ("pantalones hombrunos," mannish pants) results in her being pejoratively labeled an Amazon.

The Spanish word "*amazona*" is not necessarily derogatory, since it traditionally refers to upper-class horsewomen who ride side-saddle while wearing skirts (rather than riding astride a horse wearing pants). Doña Bárbara is no ordinary horsewoman, however. She wears masculine clothes when she is behaving like a man and working as a *llanero*: "Durante las jornadas se entregaba a una actividad febril...lazo en mano detrás del ganado altamireño que paciese por sus sabanas, insultando a los peones por el menor descuido y destrozándole los ijares a la bestia con las espuelas" (111–12). By breaking with the rituals of ideological recognition related to upper-class white women, Doña Bárbara's sartorial performance opposes the social expectations based on sex, and thus, as Sifuentes-Jáuregui explains, any notion of gender (2).

The term "*amazona*" used in this context likely references the warrior women known as Amazons in Greek mythology. In Book IV of *The Histories*, Herodotus described Amazons as wearing the same clothes as men (273). According to David E. Jones, for the ancient Greeks Amazons wore "long trousers, midthigh-length coats, leather boots, and Phrygian hats" (6). Doña Bárbara's attire is similar to that of Herodotus's Amazons and, like the Amazons, she calls into question binary gender categories. Nevertheless, Amazons have been presented throughout history primarily as slender, beautiful women with well-developed muscles and perky breasts, frequently wearing push-up corsets and skimpy tunics to emphasize their traditional femininity (Wilde 4). The contrast between these two images of the Amazon—the feminized warrior versus the one who wears masculine clothing—represents an attempt to balance rampant masculinity and strength with visibly feminine sexual attributes. Amazons were thus reimagined as feminine women rather than as monstrosities or members of a socially unregulated, divergent gender. The twentieth-century literary and artistic emphases on the female attributes of Amazon women's bodies may have been intended to quell suspicions of lesbianism, since, as Garber explains, cross-dressing is historically linked to discourses on and fears of homosexuality (4).

Each culture shapes the body according to its own rules, giving it significance by both decorating and hiding it (Entwistle and Wilson 4). By associating Doña Bárbara with the Amazons, the text implicitly contrasts the femininity revealed in the exposure of the Amazons' bodies with the concealment of Doña Bárbara's body within layers of clothes. If she revealed her female-sexed body, it would confirm her position within the social hegemon. By covering her physical attributes, she becomes a sexual enigma. Veiling the visible markings of her sex challenges the prevailing gender structure. She is then denounced as repulsive because her gender and sexual orientation cannot be easily identified by her costume. If cross-dressing is a pursuit of recognition (again following Sifuentes-Jáuregui), it seems Doña Bárbara plays with clothing to seek acknowledgement, but only when it is strategic for her to do so. That is, her cross-dressing is not permanent and does not occupy all spaces, as it is dependent on changing contexts and audiences.

Doña Bárbara repeatedly wears double-layered clothing to establish her masculine power as a *llanero* and *cacica*. This manipulation of her attire allows her to consolidate a place in the masculine and patriarchal context of Venezuelan Plains society. Her mannishness is a form of social resistance that demonstrates the artificiality of the roles that would be traditionally assigned to her as a poor orphan, *mestiza*, and indigene. The visibility of wearing mannish pants while working as a *llanero* permits Doña Bárbara

Chapter One

to rearticulate her gender and social role in society. Doña Bárbara's performance as an expert *llanero* is ratified through highly symbolic actions, including castrating a bull and dictating the law in Arauca. In line with Butler's concept of performativity, Doña Bárbara's gender performance challenges the alleged selective nature of the hegemonic masculine sphere of the Venezuelan Plains by depicting it as a space in which the masculine does not exclude the feminine. Her *llanero* performance demonstrates that the most-desired position is not solely a men's prerogative and that masculinity and femininity can coexist in the same subject. (See Chapter 3 for more on her performance of most-desired positions.)

This coexistence is further represented in the clothing Doña Bárbara wears at home with her lover Balbino, usually a "sencilla bata blanca, cerrada hasta el cuello y con mangas que le cubrían completamente los brazos, que era el máximo de feminidad que se consentía en el traje" (62). This clothing lacks the embellishments that would normally mark traditional femininity. Like her work clothes, the dress covers rather than displays her body and conceals or at least underplays her identity as a female-sexed person. The adoption of this semi-feminine dress distances her from presenting a purely masculine image. The dress worn in private with her lover covers up her reputedly "butch" appearance that is supposedly accentuated by her mannish style of clothing worn at work. It diminishes her exaggerated masculinity without emphasizing her feminine features. By veiling and modifying her physical body, the dress establishes an even more complex character than is suggested by the double-image of the skirt worn over pants. The dress worn at home reshapes the masculine image she has already articulated for society.

Dressing to Seduce

Doña Bárbara's image is further complicated by her adoption of very feminine attire in some contexts. She sometimes wears clothing that reveals rather than conceals her body, highlights her feminine beauty, and emphasizes her sexuality. The clothing she wears to the rodeo, where she intends to seduce Santos but ends up falling in love with him, is described as follows: "Llevaba un pañuelo azul de seda anudado al cuello, con las puntas sobre el escote de la blusa; usaba una falda amazona, y hasta el sombrero 'pelodeguama', típico del llanero, única prenda masculina en su atavío, llevábalo con cierta gracia femenil" (117). This attire is extremely feminine. The femininity of her tailored skirt and blouse is reinforced by Doña Bárbara's attitude. She behaves like a traditional upper-class woman at the rodeo, riding side-saddle and supervising work from a distance (117, 119). Here, the word "amazon" lacks negative connotations; it is merely an adjective describing the type of skirt and saddle worn by horsewomen. Even possibly masculine elements of her image are not treated as suspicious or negative by the novel's narrator in this scene.

Two elements of her attire—the scarf (bandana) and the hat—have exceptional performative power. Scarves and hats are the kinds of sartorial details employed by the dandy. According to Barthes, such details permit the dandy to distance himself from the masses in a uniform society (67). Doña Bárbara, however, uses such details to distance herself from the less uniform, more mannish image that had so disgusted Santos earlier (117). The scarf and hat express her desire to be accepted as a feminine woman. The scarf does so by highlighting her outfit's feminine delicacy. The tips of the scarf located in her cleavage draw attention to her breasts. This is the first time the text alludes to this corporeal mark and thus confirms a correspondence between her sex and gender.

Even when Doña Bárbara apparently obeys society's sartorial gender rules, she is actually manipulating hegemonic gender images. Her manipulations uncover the artificiality of constructed social codes. For example, the single traditional masculine element—the *llanero* hat—in her attire at the rodeo is worn gracefully and only emphasizes the femininity of her entire image. The masculine hat is not transgressive in this scene, but it does suggest that clothes and their accessories are inherently gender neutral, since any item can be used to invoke femininity or masculinity. As Barthes argues, "the vestimentary 'detail' is no longer a concrete object here, no matter how minute; it is a way, often subtly indirect, of destroying or 'deforming' clothing, or removing it from all sense of value as soon as a value becomes a shared one" (67). By changing the social value of the masculine hat and combining it with the feminine scarf, the total image Doña Bárbara presents subverts ordinary social parameters.

Doña Bárbara's attire is not sufficient to transform her from a masculine to feminine figure. Her body (cleavage) is exposed, but she must do more to be perceived as feminine. She does this by changing how she rides her horse: "[f]inalmente, montaba a mujeriegas, cosa que no acostumbraba en el trabajo, y todo esto hacía olvidar a la famosa marimacho" (117). By changing her physical posture on the horse, she alters her masculine attitude into a feminine pose. This feminine pose is revealed even more clearly when she greets Santos at the rodeo: "Ella avanzó a tenderle la mano con una sonrisa alevosa y él hizo un gesto de extrañeza; era casi otra mujer muy distinta de aquella, de desagradable aspecto hombruno, que días antes había visto por primera vez en la Jefatura Civil" (117). In this quote, the narrator underscores Santos's reaction to Doña Bárbara's transformed behavior and appearance: Santos cannot reconcile her femininity at the rodeo with her previous butch image. His shock provides evidence that her feminine pose is successful. It seems to eradicate any suspicion on Santos's part that Doña Bárbara's power makes her a monstrous masculine woman or lesbian.

Given her earlier butch masculinity, Doña Bárbara's performance of femininity at the rodeo at first seems paradoxical. She is not merely drifting between traditional gender categories, however. Following Molloy's analysis of posing, both costumed performances are moves to acquire and maintain economic and social power. Each manipulation of her appearance is strategically intended to expand her realm. She first presents the mannish image of an expert *llanero*, then develops the pose of a more feminine but powerful *cacica*. Having seduced and dispossessed Lorenzo Barquero from his land and become *cacica*, her feminine pose at the rodeo thus demonstrates her ability to transgress and then question social barriers. Being able to occupy multiple positions is inherently transgressive; when doing so rewrites roles, it has the potential to be subversive. By alternating between a traditional image of feminine womanhood and a butch woman who is more *llanero* than the cis men *llaneros*, Doña Bárbara subverts the biases that inform both gender roles and obtains power for herself.

Instead of a *travesti* or cross-dresser, Doña Bárbara is a kind of *poseur*, to use Molloy's term. The *poseur* controls visibility by exaggerating their appearance to provoke a reading or understanding of the pose by society (185). Doña Bárbara compels Santos to pay attention to her, to look *at her* at the rodeo. Doña Bárbara's disparate images coincide within his gaze and he is forced to search for an answer to explain these alternate images and her identity. Santos's gaze is what Henri Lefebvre calls the explanatory look of the social text. Doña Bárbara manipulates him and other men observers (*llaneros*) by deliberately projecting the desired image of femininity. As the narrator explains, "No podía escapársele a Santos que la feminidad que ahora ostentaba tenía por objeto producirle una impresión agradable; mas, por muy prevenido que estuviese, no pudo menos de admirarla" (117). Encountering Santos's gaze—that of the educated man—at the rodeo then exaggerates and confirms her construction of femininity.

Each pose thus demonstrates an attempt to acquire different kinds of power: men's or masculine powers of land ownership and physical labor and women's or feminine powers of attraction and temptation. Her attempts are not altogether successful. When Doña Bárbara subverts her earlier butch image to assert her power as a seductress, she actually ends up subordinated to the patriarchy. At the rodeo Santos lassos a rebellious bull and proves himself a true *llanero*. The feminine Doña Bárbara begins to fall in love with him following this performance of most-desired masculinity. Henighan argues that the rodeo establishes masculinity in Santos and femininity in Doña Bárbara (37). I see this point in that the rodeo re-establishes the accepted hierarchical order. By lassoing the bull, Santos demonstrates that he has the power to lasso Doña Bárbara and tame her masculinity. Although she tries to acquire power through seduction, his masculine, upper class, educated, and white *llanero* performance is more powerful.

While her love for Santos indeed transforms Doña Bárbara morally, as Shaw argues, she never submits to the role of selfless, woman-in-love as her daughter Marisela does. She only portrays herself as feminine in an attempt to dominate and win over Santos. She uses clothes manipulatively throughout the novel to try to get what she wants. As Barthes argues is typical of the dandy, Doña Bárbara's clothing is always crafted to achieve her goals. If she does not look butch or mannish, she might not command respect from her workers. Likewise, if she does not manipulate her attire to appear more feminine, she cannot hope to dominate men such as Lorenzo and Santos.

To summarize, her ability to manipulate her image according to circumstance and context throughout the novel is a form of power in itself, one that allows her to free herself from the social expectations usually applied to her sex. As a warrior woman, Doña Bárbara is always conscious of playing a role. She is aware that she must transform her image to rearticulate her social position. She subverts society's rules in order to gain something for herself. Her performances make it evident that gender roles are not immutable biological facts but flexible social constructions. Her performances take her from marginality to empowerment. Even when taking advantage of the norms of femininity, Doña Bárbara, who started life as a poor, orphaned, abused *mestiza*, challenges the classist, racist, and sexist structures of her society (explained further in Chapter 3).

In performing gender, Pintada and Doña Bárbara are motivated by similar desires to improve their socioeconomic positions. Diadorim's sartorial transgressions differ from those of Pintada and Doña Bárbara because he has different reasons for his gender performances. He wears men's clothes and projects a masculine image because he intends to be seen (pass) as a man, a *jagunço*, and a warrior. Guimarães Rosa's novel is thus more transgressive in terms of gender than the earlier two novels because it includes a trans* character whose performance breaks naturalized associations between sex, gender, and sexuality.

Diadorim Clothed and Naked

Traditional ideologies of gender have greatly influenced critical interpretations of the Diadorim character in *Grande sertão: veredas*. Most critics have focused on his biological sex, which is revealed only at the end of the novel after he has died in combat. They react conservatively to a gender performance that challenges the hegemonic gender binary. Ignoring the character's gender performance and basing their interpretations exclusively on the sex of his corpse reproduces patriarchal rules and perpetuates binary divisions. Alfred Mac Adam finds it so inconceivable that a "woman" could be a warrior or *jagunço* that he questions the entire credibility of the novel (74). He considers Diadorim's gender performance impossible because he believes that no female-sexed individual could have the physical prowess to fight in combat or pass as a man in the field of war. He has no problem suspending disbelief when it comes to topics other than gender, however. For example, he does not question the novel's credibility when it proposes the existence of the devil. Mac Adam thus ignores Diadorim's gender performance and the possibility of breaking with the gender binary.

Unlike Mac Adam, Walnice Nogueira Galvão accepts that a person with female sex can fight effectively and pass as a man, and even emphasizes the historical presence of women in war through the figure of the warrior maid (*donzela guerreira*). The warrior maid is an acceptable figure because she only transgresses temporarily and only when authorized by a patriarchal figure. Ormindo Pires Filho's similar argument that a tyrannical father must have imposed masculine clothing on Diadorim lacks textual evidence: the novel never mentions any such occurrence. Such interpretations also fail to recognize that Diadorim's father is an active *jagunço* leader, not an old man unable to go to war himself. Meanwhile, critics who consider Diadorim an androgynous figure explain gender as comprised of three possibilities: woman, man, and androgyne. This tripartite division loses the richness of Diadorim's gender performance. Adding a simple third category to the usual male/female dyad does not question the system itself, but rather complements, closes, even ratifies it. Analyzing Diadorim using androgyny as a concept in which two opposites reunite neglects the plurality of gender performances and complexity of human nature. Rather than recognize trans* identities, it reduces his transgression to a single possibility, a union of supposed opposites.

In sum, earlier critics have understood Diadorim's sex as either implausible, plausible because it lies within a tradition of (temporarily) cross-dressing daughters, or fixed within a system of gender binaries. I read Diadorim from a different standpoint. As a trans warrior, he questions the very logic upon which gender identity is based. His performance not only limits and shapes discourses on masculinities, as Domínguez-Ruvalcaba explains is the implication of the cross-dressed male (37), but accomplishes the same for discourses on femininities. As Susan Stryker explains, transgendered phenomena call into question the category of "woman" and challenge gender inequalities (7). I treat Diadorim's performance as that of a trans warrior, because, unlike the more specific term "trans male warrior," "trans warrior" puts no limits on the variety of possible trans* performances and is thus more inclusive of trans* people.

Before discussing Diadorim's clothing, I must address two major elements of the novel that have influenced critical perceptions

Chapter One

of his performance of masculinity. The first is that Diadorim is perceived only through Riobaldo's memory of him. As the narrator, Riobaldo has the power to manipulate stories and events precisely because of his privilege; he controls the (writing) phallus as he subdues other characters to his perspective. He mediates the reader's access to the character of Diadorim. His recollections of Diadorim are couched in mystery and homoeroticism. The second is that the revelation of the biological sex of Diadorim's corpse comes as a surprise to the reader. This disclosure is a major plot twist in the novel. Riobaldo manipulates the narrative to include the reader in the unfolding of the plot. He plays with his intended reader by presenting Diadorim as enigmatic. By repeatedly addressing his reader with phrases such as "[o] senhor por ora mal me entende, se é que no fim me entenderá" (156), Riobaldo avoids mentioning Diadorim's sex, creates suspense, and keeps the reader interested in the plot.

This narrative strategy is different from those employed in the two other novels under discussion. In each of the other two texts, the narrator is extradiegetic and the warrior woman character is identified from the beginning as in the category of "woman." By contrast, Diadorim is until the end identified as a woman in the novel. Even though Riobaldo's discourse of love for Diadorim seems to treat him as a woman and a short prolepsis on page 207 associates him with a dead woman, Diadorim's female sex is only revealed when his corpse is going to be shrouded. I argue that the narrative ploy of exposing the sex of Diadorim only after he is dead leads the reader to question dichotomous gender roles and identities within the heterocisnormative system.

Dressing the Masculine Trans*

Trans* identities are not limited to particular orientations or experiences. As Stephen Whittle argues, anyone who does not fit the gender role assigned at birth or who challenges the two gender categories can claim a trans identity (xi). Trans studies rethink the position, agency, agenda, embodiments, subjectivities, and gender identities of the trans* community. Trans* identities, based on both biology and social parameters, allow us to understand how society functions and to question cis privileges. Trans theory claims that both trans women and trans* men have an innate predisposition for gender, which can manifest in the diverse performances and embodiments of femininities or masculinities.

Diadorim's masculinity is grounded in his performance and clothing. Riobaldo even describes Diadorim's physical beauty in terms of his masculine garments: "Guardei os olhos, meio momento, na beleza dele, guapo tão aposto – surgindo sempre com o jaleco, que ele tirava nunca, e com as calças de vaqueiro, em couro de veado macho, curtido com aroeira-brava e campestre" (191). His clothes are masculine and he projects a man's image. That his leather cowboy pants are made from the hide of a male deer (buckskin) further ratifies the masculinity of his clothes. I suggest he is trans* because he identifies as a man, his clothes show him as a man, he performs masculinities, and is never depicted in feminine clothing or associated with femininity.

Diadorim's transgressive use of clothes and gender performance signal a category crisis similar to Garber's interpretation of the cross-dresser (11). The cross-dresser demonstrates that gender boundaries are porous, overlapping, and intersect with class, race, and religion (16). Diadorim's performance might also be seen as a drag enactment. Butler argues that going in drag highlights the artificiality of the gender binary and reminds us that reality is not as fixed as is generally assumed (*Gender* xxiii–iv). The hyperbolic gender enactment of drag challenges the rigidity of the gender categories themselves (186–87). Diadorim's gender performance can thus be interpreted as enacting a drag performance, specifically that of the drag king. Halberstam contends that a drag king is a woman who usually wears a costume that openly portrays a man and who carries out a theatrical performance in that costume (*Female* 232). However, Diadorim's cross-dressing is not a drag performance. His clothes are not mere costume and his gender performance is not temporary.

In the Northeast of Brazil in the first half of the twentieth century, the clothing of women and men involved in armed conflicts was very important. The clothing worn by *jagunçxs* and *cangaceirxs* (a type of bandit) was meant to endure the rough conditions of the region. Virgulino Ferreira da Silva (1898?–1938), better known as Lampião, was the most famous twentieth-century *cangaceiro* from that region. Women who participated in his groups were known as *cangaceiras*. Although both Diadorim and the *cangaceiras* participated in armed fights, they are different. *Cangaceiras* carried

Chapter One

weapons and wore practical clothing, but they dressed as women, while Diadorim dresses as a man.

Lampião's group was the first to allow the participation of women, but only on the condition that they be married to one of his men. In some of the bands he led, whenever a man died, the widow was forced to choose another husband among the *cangaceiros* (Araújo, *Lampião* 127). Some widows were not allowed to leave because they knew the secrets of the group (127). One of the most celebrated *cangaceiras* is Sérgia Ribeiro da Silva (1915–1994), known as Dadá. She was the partner of Cristino Gomes da Silva Cleto (1907–1940), also called Corisco, who headed an important *cangaceiro* group under Lampião's leadership. According to interviews Dadá gave to Antônio Amaury Correia de Araújo, the women in these groups wore two different types of clothing. One was a civilian outfit that they used when they knew they were not going to be attacked by the police and the other was worn to enter the Backlands. The latter attire had to remain comfortable while carrying bags and other accessories during long walks in scorching sunlight or heavy rains (*Lampião* 106). The Backlands dress was made out of strong cloth, fell below the knee, and was long-sleeved. Women used gloves of the same thick cloth to protect themselves from thorns (106) and wore strong espadrille shoes (107). Women would also wear expensive jewelry if their partner was an important member of the group (107). *Cangaceiras* carried guns, a cartridge belt, a dagger, and a hat (109). Their hat, according to Mariana von Hartenthal, was an industrialized felt hat that was very different from the half-moon shaped hat made iconic by *cangaceiros*.

The men in the group knew how to use sewing machines and were in charge of making their bags and other parts of their outfit (Araújo, *Lampião* 104). Since Dadá had learned to sew at an early age, she adorned her own outfit by adding stylish, colorful cloth flowers to the bags and straps (104). Her attention to detail resembles that of the dandy. Such adornments, according to Araújo, became the trademark of the *cangaceirxs* even though they were only used between 1932 and 1940 (*Lampião* 105). It is clear that *cangaceiras* paid attention to the way they looked, their femininity, and took care of their appearance, as their photographs demonstrate (Câmara et al. 214). Such details added distinction to all of the *cangaceirxs*' outfit, but they already stood out as unusual for their social context in Brazil.

The testimonial of Ilda Ribeiro de Souza, known as Sila, the wife of Zé Sereno (José Ribeiro Filho), confirms the unique position of the *cangaceiras*. In her testimonial, Sila explains that when she entered the band, she only wore dresses until Neném, the wife of Luís Pedro, gave her culottes to wear and then Zé Sereno gave her cloth to sew her own outfit (*Angicos* 28). Sila also describes slightly different clothing that sounds more like a uniform than merely pragmatic attire for the Backlands. She says she carried a green bag and wore a green dress that ended in culottes instead of a skirt and that her twisted-brim hat, a present of her husband, was encrusted with medals (30). She adds that women wore underpants but no bras, while men did not use any underwear (38). Sila also states that gender roles in her band were clear: men did the cooking and women sewed clothing, bags, and other necessities (30). It is evident that not all bands had the same gender roles and images but, despite this gendered division of labor, *cangaceiras* enjoyed freedoms denied to other women. They smoked in public and wore pants (*culottes*) at a time when other women did not (49). Such historical facts also give more emphasis to Diadorim's gender transgressions. He does not look like women in the Northeast, not even as *cangaceiras*. I observe that Diadorim's ongoing use of clothes constitutes visual gender passing, as Halberstam defines this concept. Diadorim's masculine garments (hat, vest, cowboy pants) not only help him build a masculine subjectivity (i.e., the image of a "he"), they enable him to perform his trans* masculine identity in the sphere of war.

Cangaceiras are fascinating figures that remain alive in the Brazilian imaginary. In 1993, writer Francisco Dantas published the novel *Os desvalidos*, which includes the story of Maria Melona. She is the wife of the narrator's uncle Filipe, and she ends up as a *cangaceiro* in Lampião's group. Known as Zé Queixada, she carries a dagger and a rifle, wears pants, and changes her appearance to look "homem macho" (105). She even asks the narrator not to reveal her gender, although later on she is allowed to live as a woman in the band. One of the most recent literary examples of the *cangaceiras* is Newton Moreno's 2019 musical *As cangaceiras, guerreiras do sertão* in which a *cangaceira* leaves the band because she discovers her son is alive; other women end up joining her in order to pursue their own goals.

The success of Diadorim's visual passing is supported in *Grande sertão* in numerous ways. Diadorim's masculinity and maleness are established also in Riobaldo's memories of meeting Diadorim when they were not yet fourteen years old. Using garments and other objects linked to the sphere of men, Diadorim appears to be a white boy; he has since always been seen as a white man. Diadorim is still passing as a man when Riobaldo joins his group to fight, and he remains a man even when Riobaldo admits to being in love with him. Daniel Balderston considers the use of masculine pronouns as evidence that Diadorim's masculinity is actually what seduces Riobaldo, not some sort of hidden femininity (67–68). In fact, Riobaldo's descriptions of Diadorim's beautiful eyes, hands, and arms resemble a traditional discourse that treats women as objects of desire. Indeed, Riobaldo is putting Diadorim into a passive position, as an object rather than subject, but this discourse does not necessarily place Diadorim in the feminine sphere.

Diadorim is different from other *jagunços* because of his hygiene. He takes care of his appearance and takes baths alone and in the dark (161). Instead of suggesting he follows the conventions of warrior maids who hid their sex, I see that bathing alone in the dark is perceived by Riobaldo as idiosyncratic behavior that triggers superstitious beliefs (161). Riobaldo connects bathing in the dark to his doubts about Diadorim. He wonders if Diadorim is an angel or a demon whose evil will tempt him into homosexuality. This homophobia emerges because Riobaldo cannot reconcile his feelings of love for Diadorim with his identity as a *jagunço* and he is horrified at the thought that he might be gay. For Balderston, Riobaldo's fear of his love for Diadorim is a reference to what Eve Kosofsky Sedgwick calls "homosexual panic" (94). Balderston proposes that Riobaldo fears Diadorim's deviance will mark him as abnormal as well (94). I agree with this reading but take it further in considering the context of the Backlands. *Jagunços* were expected to be very macho heterosexuals. In this context, loving Diadorim would mean that Riobaldo cannot be a real *jagunço*. This is especially problematic because being a *jagunço* is his preferred profession and the only cultural space in which he feels he truly belongs. Belonging is a major theme in the novel; as an orphan and the illegitimate son of a rancher, belonging amongst the *ja-*

gunços is of utmost importance to Riobaldo. But if he is found out to be gay, he will be cast out once again from society.

Critics have linked the history and performances of queer Latin American men to homophobia. Domínguez-Ruvalcaba considers undoing homophobia to be the main target for the LGBTQAI+ community in Latin America. As a western imposition, homophobia has permeated all bodies (*Translating* 152). Riobaldo's homophobia is so pervasive that it relates gender identity to another main theme: the fight between good and evil. Riobaldo's horror of gay love (which for him coincides with being gay) and his identification of Diadorim with the trope of the devil represent this struggle. However, Riobaldo's traditional homophobic associations between homosexuality, the devil, and evil are complicated by Diadorim's performance as a loyal friend and outstanding warrior. Diadorim's behavior raises questions about the simplicity of these associations and renders Riobaldo's homophobia incoherent. As Domínguez-Ruvalcaba suggests, trans-dressing "depowers" the system upon which homophobia is built (*Translating* 150).

Within the logic of the novel, however, Riobaldo's "problem" of homosexuality is resolved by the revelation that Diadorim is biologically female. Balderston argues that the discovery of Diadorim's sex represents a gesture toward traditional gender norms in the text. It erases the possibility of homosexuality and downplays the homoerotic desire between the two main characters (85–86). The uncovering of Diadorim's sex is not just a gesture to hegemonic tradition, however. The loss or absence of clothes signals Diadorim's trans* identity. The discovery of Diadorim's dead, naked body therefore opens the heterocisnormative discourse in the text to question. Undressing Diadorim's masculinity to reveal female genitalia speaks to issues of trans* empowerment, problems with binary gender categories, and the presence and value of trans* identities.

Another trans warrior character appears in the novel *Duerme* (Sleep) (1994) by the Mexican woman author Carmen Boullosa. The protagonist is Claire Fleurcy, a French orphan who grew up dressed as a man in the middle of war and was taught how to fight. He escapes the sexual and labor exploitation he had been enduring since his mother died, by joining a pirate ship as a man sailor. He travels to Mexico City, where he is drugged and forced to impersonate a Count who is condemned to be hung. However, just

Chapter One

before Claire is hung in the Count's place, an indigenous woman, doña Inés, gives him water that makes him immortal provided he remains in the proximity of Mexico City—doña Inés had discovered his trans* status. Claire survives being hung and, after that, he ends up becoming a soldier in order to protect the viceroy in New Spain. He cannot continue fighting because his lies are uncovered and he has to flee the city. He is then sleeping somewhere outside Mexico City waiting to be reawakened. His friend, Pedro, unable to wake him up, decides to write a story in which Claire becomes a revolutionary leader who defeats the Spanish crown.

Claire is trans* because he identifies as a man; his cross-dressing constitutes a permanent part of his identity. Recognizing that he prefers a man's appearance, he rejects feminine clothing. Even though he did not don the outfit of the Count voluntarily, it provides him with the desired socioeconomic and gendered image of a rich man: "por fin soy rico, un Caballero, un Noble, de Buena Cuna. Es mi consuelo morir siendo lo que siempre quise ser en vida" (26). Clothes officially make him the man (from the socioeconomic class) he wants to be. They allow him to break with the normative rituals of ideological recognition to fulfill his own desires. Still, he is constantly misgendered as a woman by other characters in the novel.

Also like Diadorim, Claire does not develop a complete sexual or love relationship with any other character. At one point in the story, while he is recovering from wounds sustained in battle, a woman named Afrodita caresses his genitalia. Claire is surprised, but does not respond and they do not engage in a sexual act (114). He only admits to being jealous when he later sees Afrodita and his friend Pedro sleeping naked together on a bed (116). His lack of a sexual relationship with Pedro somewhat resembles Diadorim and Riobaldo's story, although at the end of the novel Pedro says that they do have sex once he manages to wake "her" (Claire) up (140). Still, neither of the trans* characters in the two novels fully engage in sentimental or sexual relationships. The impossibility of their establishing a family or community represents the barrenness of their societies. In the end, trans warriors are social outcasts: Claire because he never has a love relationship and is left sleeping in order to survive; Diadorim because he is killed. While Claire's non-decaying body is waiting to be taken back to Mexico City so he can be reawakened, Diadorim's corpse is appropriated by

Riobaldo. As I explain next, Diadorim's performance does not end with his tragic death and the subsequent manipulation of his body. His corpse is as much evidence of his life and experience as it is of his heterocisnormative society.

Undressing the Corpse

In accordance with Lefebvre's ideas, the body is a social text. A living body is different from a corpse, however, because the dead subject is stripped of agency and agenda. A naked corpse displaces associations between the person (behaviors, attitudes, biography) and the rituals of ideological recognition located on their physical body. Diadorim's sex is uncovered only after he has lost agency over his body: "Que Diadorim era o corpo de uma mulher, moça perfeita ... Estarreci. A dôr não pode mais do que a surpresa. A côice d'arma, de coronha. Ela era" (615; ellipsis in the original). It comes as a revelation that the masculine person Riobaldo has known and loved does not correspond to the dead body before him because it is the body of a white woman. Riobaldo's first reaction is to discursively separate the living person from the dead body because he cannot match Diadorim's gender performance to the evidence of his biological sex.

He refers to Diadorim using the feminine pronouns "her" and "she" only after he discovers that his best friend and love object has female genitalia, that is, when Diadorim's corpse is about to be shrouded for burial: "Ela era" (615); "[e]la tinha amor em mim" (616); "dela lembrados quando tinha sido menina" (620); and "o amor, e a pessoa dela, mesma, ela tinha me negado" (621). The use of feminine pronouns would seem to ratify Diadorim's sex and gender and Diadorim's and Riobaldo's heterosexuality, but the narrator interweaves masculine pronouns in referring to Diadorim on the same pages: "[e]nterrem separado" (616); "a saudade dele" (621); "nele imaginar" (621). Balderston analyzes the pronouns Riobaldo uses to refer to Diadorim after his death to conclude that, even after Diadorim's death, Riobaldo continues loving him as a man (64–65, 71). I agree with Balderston that Riobaldo experiences same-sex desire and with Adélia Bezerra de Meneses that the relationship between Diadorim and Riobaldo is homoerotic (51). The use of masculine pronouns signals that the gender performances of the living can override the sex categories of the

Chapter One

dead. The corpse thus certifies that gender roles do not necessarily correspond to the binary division of genders.

For Maria Amália Johnson, however, Diadorim's corpse is a redeeming female Christ-figure that reconciles Riobaldo to his love for Diadorim (17). Jonson overlooks the fact that nothing in the discovery of the corpse explains Diadorim's intentions or motivations. Instead, it only clarifies the narrator's intentions. The corpse is the only concrete evidence that Diadorim ever existed. Riobaldo uses the fact of the sex of the corpse to erase Diadorim's history as a *jagunço* and emphasize his own importance as a *jagunço* leader. Diadorim's displacement is also represented in where he is buried. Riobaldo initially wants to bury him where nobody can find him, but then leaves him in a grave in the Paredão cemetery in the Backlands (616). By taking Diadorim's cadaver to the cemetery, Riobaldo symbolically returns his friend to the social conventions of the patriarchal, hegemonic, Christian society Diadorim refused in life. Diadorim's actions and decisions disappear along with Riobaldo's feelings for another man.

Furthermore, it could be argued that the sex of the corpse proves that Riobaldo was not in love with a man and is instead an astute man capable of perceiving the truth about a veiled woman. The reinterpretation of Diadorim's gender and life afforded by the corpse reduces his character to the roles middle and upper-class women are supposed to fill in patriarchal societies: perpetuating the family by having children and perpetuating the culture by supporting men. In death, Diadorim is fit into deep cultural scripts. He loses his masculinity and becomes a beautiful white cis young girl who was in love with the properly heterosexual Riobaldo. By turning Diadorim from a "he" into a "she," the corpse in Riobaldo's narration reproduces the system's heterocisnormativity and buries Diadorim's successful performance as a masculine trans warrior. Riobaldo's discursive correlation between sex and gender undercuts Diadorim's gender transgressions, eliminates trans* identities, and reasserts the rules of the heteropatriarchal hegemony. At the same time, and despite Riobaldo's discursive manipulations, the unveiling of Diadorim in the discovery of his corpse challenges those rules. Without clothes to perform with, a naked corpse erases the meanings that adhere to the body of a subject, especially a dressed body. The revelation of Diadorim's sex, coupled with Riobaldo's references to his dead body as "she," points out to the reader that a body perceived as feminine or female is considered passive in patriarchal society. The corpse's sex annuls the agency, wishes, fears, and goals of the embodied character.

Another trans* character in Brazilian literature who challenges the rules of society with their corpse is Ana Maria in *Uma mulher diferente* (A Different Woman) (1968) by Cassandra Rios. This novel reconstructs the life and murder of the *travesti* Ana Maria who would only uncover her genitalia or her identity as a *travesti* to men after having sex with them. She also asks to be treated as a woman and that people use feminine adjectives when referring to her (123). When the genitalia of her corpse are revealed to the public after she is murdered, the men who desired her and those with whom she had sexual relationships are "outed" as gay or their sexual orientation/identity is brought into doubt. Ana Maria's *travestismo*, as well as Diadorim's trans* status, both provide evidence that the body is the main evidence. I propose that it is the naked corpse, the dead body that has been stripped of clothing, that is the final arbiter of sexual orientation and gender identity in Latin American literature. Diadorim's corpse is reread by Riobaldo and included forcefully in retaining heterocisnormativity. When Diadorim's complex character is made to be a woman by the fact of having female genitalia and breasts, I argue that the novel makes evident that the hegemonic concept of sex is based only on the visible physical body—external reproductive organs and breasts. It does not include hormones, gonads, chromosomes, and internal reproductive organs. Additionally, it also reveals that hegemonic gender categories are constructed solely on the basis of dead (as inactive) sex. Personal identities, meaningful practices, or active performances are made irrelevant.

The reactions of Riobaldo (and many literary critics) to Diadorim's corpse lend support to Butler's theory of gender performance, which proposes that gender is the constant practice of body rules imposed by the hegemonic society. Based on my reading of Latin American literature, I would add to this theory that gender implies a living, active body, that is, a dressed body. The dressed body remains extremely important because clothing is a key element in rituals of ideological recognition. The characters' clothing, along with other aspects of their performances and behaviors, construct their perceived or visual genders on a daily basis, including for those who fall in love with them. Ana Maria is a woman and Diadorim is a man, but without clothing they are misgendered and other characters' sexual orientations are questioned.

Conclusion

Warrior women and trans warriors confront heteropatriarchal societies with gender performances that transgress hegemonic divisions of gender, race, social class, and culture. Their gender performances make use of clothing as a second skin to pose, pass, and project their "real" gendered skin (while failing to hide their skin color). Trans warriors and warrior women appropriate clothes in order to appropriate spaces within the predominantly masculine spheres of armed conflict in Latin America. Their presence in combat alongside men soldiers challenges the social function and exclusivity of these spheres.

Pintada attempts to ascend the social hierarchy by stealing and wearing an elegant dress and other signs of wealth. She does not wear the dress according to upper-class white conventions, however. She wears it with dirty, torn stockings. This attire challenges the logic of the hierarchy and allows her to question the patriarchal and class norms of her society and her own role as a woman in the Revolution. Doña Bárbara dons a variety of outfits to manipulate her image. She dresses like a *cacica,* a butch or mannish woman, to access the masculine power bestowed on the *llanero* and on the landowning caciques. She also projects a sensual, feminine image to access the traditional women's power of sexual attractiveness. Her performances destabilize traditional social and gender roles, even those she has established for herself. Clothes are an inherent part of Diadorim's trans* identity. He not only dresses in a masculine fashion, he is an upper-class white man, *jagunço,* and warrior. Only undressing his corpse turns him into a white cis woman. If sartorial rules enable a gendered body to be recognized (i.e., labeled and accepted) within a cultural context (Entwistle, "The Dressed" 33), then unclothed nakedness brings the social body into question. Any difference between the clothed alive body and the dead naked body generates an unacceptable image that unsettles observers who are ideologically bound within heteronormative society. They then adopt pathological discourses to *explain* any performances of masculinity (such as Diadorim's) that do not accord with biological sex.

The Sartorial Transgressions

An interpellated society moves to protect itself by producing naturalizing discourses and pathologizing anyone, including most trans warriors and warrior women, who do not abide by its sartorial conventions. The emphasis some critics have placed on Diadorim's dead biological sex is part of a discourse that considers as a defect or error that which is not typically seen or done. It is a language that treats the transgression as a deviation, as a mistake in order to neutralize or diminish its power. The logic of the patriarchy demands that Diadorim be *explained* as pathological so that his gender performance stops representing a challenge or threat to society. This is the same discourse that *explains* Doña Bárbara as a repellent Amazon, an evil and backward indigenous woman who only pretended to be as powerful as a masculine white man. It is the same discourse that *explains* Pintada is a mere brown "prostitute," so her non-sexual attempts to improve her life may be ignored. Such interpretations of these characters do not consider the possibility that warrior women's and trans warriors' gender transgressions might be deliberate strategies of empowerment. These *explanations* ultimately fail to understand these characters, since even if the characters are obliterated by death or disappear from the story, their transgressions and achievements are left behind and questions about them are left unanswered.

In *The Will to Knowledge* (1976), the first volume of the *History of the Sexuality*, Michel Foucault argues that since the mid-nineteenth century the body has been a matter of concern for the bourgeoisie. The bourgeoisie are determined to regulate the body by crafting their own version of sexuality and shaping specific bodies to conform to a binary gender ideology (150–51). Pintada, Doña Bárbara, and Diadorim resist marking, covering, or clothing their bodies according to those inherited bourgeois standards of gender and sex. Trans warriors and warrior women oppose the regulated body by adopting a variety of sartorial strategies. They pose, cross-dress, use the techniques of a dandy, and pass. Their dynamic sartorial manipulations enable them to negotiate their socio-economic positions.

Chapter Two

Empowered Names, Disempowered Nicknames

Names concretize how a person is incorporated into a specific society and social role. Names and nicknames signal the extent of empowerment of trans warrior and warrior woman characters, as well as attempts to disempower them, in Latin American literature. Naming such characters reflects perceptions of their social, economic, and cultural statuses, as well as of their gender performances and the scope of their agency. This chapter therefore examines two aspects of the power dynamics of naming. I first argue that feminine and masculine categories and roles in heterocispatriarchal societies are transgressed or rejected when trans warrior and warrior woman characters' names do not match their gender performances. I then show how such transgressions are normalized by the creation of nicknames, as nicknames label and thus naturalize characters' transgressive attitudes. In particular, my discussion of nicknames complements the argument in the previous chapter regarding how the characters must be explained in order to be non-threatening.

I use the words "names" and "nicknames" to refer to a wide variety of appellations, including proper nouns, family names, last names, and qualifying adjectives, both derogatory and complimentary. Specifically, "nickname" alludes to appellations (*apelativo*) that do not necessarily imply intimacy or affect between characters, but do signal power plays and often pejorative labeling. The first section of this chapter explains my theoretical approach to contextualizing the names and nicknames of warrior women and trans warrior characters. The remainder of the chapter dialogues with literary criticism by addressing the names, nicknames, and other appellations given to trans warrior and warrior woman characters in *Los de abajo*, *Doña Bárbara*, and *Grande sertão: veredas*.

I argue that gender is clearly connoted in the various nicknames given to Pintada. Her nicknames reflect disempowerment for her failure to portray a traditional image of womanhood. The nicknames also constitute a critique of poor *mestiza* women in Mexican society. Similarly, while Doña Bárbara's name signals her capacity to empower herself, her nicknames marginalize her in terms of gender, race, ethnicity, and social class. She is a transgressive character who questions her heterocispatriarchal society, so her gender performance becomes marked as negative by the derogatory nicknames given to her by the novel's narrator. Diadorim's different names also highlight his gender identity and transgressive performance of masculinity. They are suggestive of a complex relationship with Riobaldo and reflect his disempowerment when Riobaldo asserts himself as the superior warrior.

The Name as Proper Noun

That personal appellations carry social meaning now seems obvious, but it has been much debated throughout the history of Western philosophy. As early as the fourth century B.C.E., the nature of the name was addressed in Plato's Socratic dialog titled *Cratylus*. Cratylus argues that every name carries an essence of its own, while his interlocutor, Hermogenes, says that names merely designate the conventions of tradition. In the same century, Aristotle extended the discussion in the second chapter of *Poetics* by arguing that a name is a composite sound without inherent meaning (*Poética* 75). Aristotle's conclusion prevailed in Western philosophy well into the nineteenth century (Summerell 369–70).

Most philosophers treated the proper name as an indicator void of meaning until French anthropologist Claude Lévi-Strauss supplied a different argument in the mid-twentieth century. Lévi-Strauss recognized that names have intrinsic meaning and function as classifiers. In *The Savage Mind*, he described how the proper name has been treated in different societies. Since each culture establishes its own rules for marking objects (i.e., naming people and things), there is a vital step between the act of signification and the act of indicating (215). Names are produced based on unique systems of classification and the relationships between categories and social, economic, and historical variables (215). Like Lévi-Strauss, U.S. philosopher Saul Kripke addressed the social import of proper names in *Naming and Necessity*. He argued that each name makes several references and thus a variety of implications adheres to any name. The meanings of a name depend on us, on other people in our social community, and on the history of the name, since "[i]t is by following such a history that one gets to the reference" (95). The meaning of any proper name cannot be delimited, because names do not have intrinsic essences; names can only be understood as having histories (76).

In *Bodies that Matter*, Judith Butler built on the arguments of Lévi-Strauss, Kripke, and other thinkers by emphasizing gender differences in the acts of naming and being named. I follow Butler's approach because it underscores dynamics relevant to warrior women's and trans warriors' performances. In addition, she criticized social philosophers who had treated proper names as identity markers without intrinsic gender and sexual content. Examining the social dynamics in which subjects are inscribed through their names, Butler noted that "the social pact which confers legitimacy on the name remains uninterrogated for its masculinism and heterosexual privilege" (*Bodies* 154). Names continue to operate within heterocispatriarchal conditions in which privilege is traditionally granted to masculine, heterosexual (also white, upper-class) men. The referential function of the proper name thus has repercussions for feminine, female, and trans* subjects. The name is not a meaningless label. Rather, the name as label retains strong social and historical meanings involving sexuality, identity, and perceived limitations on the sexed body.

Although all names delimit the subject, the family name has an even more specific function because it places a subject within a role in kinship relations. Using Lacan's terms, Butler argued that the family name positions the subject within the Symbolic Realm. This is an idealized field of relations structured by sanctions and taboos such as Lacan's Law of the Father and the incest prohibition (*Bodies* 72). According to the Law of the Father, a subject accepts the Name of the Father (i.e., rules of the hegemony) by repressing the desire for the mother (Dor 106–07). Accepting or being interpellated by society's conventions (i.e., by following the Law of the Father) results in individuals being marked and demarcated in terms of sexual and gender categories. Butler observed that "[t]he name as patronym does not only bear the law, but institutes the law" (*Bodies* 154). Because subjects obey the Symbolic order, each time they give and secure the family name (almost always a patronym), they reiterate the heterocispatriarchal structures of the law.

Subjects are visible only to the degree society accepts them and grants them social roles defined by gender and other attributes. As Butler explains, "[t]he name, as part of a social pact and, indeed, a social system of signs, overrides the tenuousness of imaginary identification and confers on it a social durability and legitimacy" (*Bodies* 152). Family names, given names, and nicknames position the subject as a member of society. They delimit the subject according to the conventions of their social context, but also provide them with a form of identification and social legitimacy. In her book about João Guimarães Rosa's narrative, Ana Maria Machado emulates Butler's argument when she explains that full legal names represent official discourses. She compares different names to Guimarães Rosa's distinction between *estórias* (stories) and *histórias* (histories) (39). Machado suggests that eponyms and nicknames are like *estórias*, while full legal names including patronyms are like *histórias*. If the name on a baptismal record is the name accepted by hegemonic society, it is also the historical name, a name that reflects official history. A nickname or pseudonym such as "Diadorim" then becomes the name of an *estória* about an unofficial account of war or unsanctioned feelings of love.

The act of naming is as important as the names themselves for analyzing trans warriors' and warrior women's strategies of empowerment. In *Excitable Speech*, Butler discusses what happens the moment a subject is named. Although she focuses on pejorative naming involved in hate speech, her discussion is relevant for understanding the disempowerment of warrior women and trans warriors. Her argument that hate speech "reinvokes the position of domination, and reconsolidates it at the moment of utterance" and operates as a "site for the mechanical and predictable reproduction of power" can be extrapolated to the names applied to trans warriors and warrior women (17). When an offensive name is uttered, it reinforces the speaker's position of domination and the subject's subordination. The original name given to a subject already marks their place in a gendered binary; the moment other people insult or name them otherwise reinforces their position within hegemonic racial, ethnic, and economic social structures.

Empowered Names, Disempowered Nicknames

Following Louis Althusser, Butler notes that interpellative marks (such as names) do more than merely describe or reinforce hegemonic conventions. The interpellative mark inaugurates a reality. The goal of interpellation is to constitute the subject's social surroundings and thereby establish control over the subject. Names aim to keep the interpellated subject in a state of subjection. The names and nicknames given to trans warriors and warrior women simultaneously locate them within hegemonic norms and reject or ridicule them for failing to follow such norms. Heterocispatriarchal law is invoked every moment warrior women and trans warriors are rejected or ridiculed for their transgressions, such as when Pintada is called a devil or a *chinche* (bedbug) for failing to perform a properly feminine role as a sex worker.

However, interpellation is an iterative practice in which the subject constantly creates themselves and other people create them based on hegemonic parameters of gender, race, and class (*Excitable* 33). Since names are just as interpellated as the people who conduct the act of naming, neither names nor naming actions accurately represent subjects' identities. Since names follow social conventions, they cannot explain who the subjects are or have been or what they have accomplished. Still, the name retains discursive power because of its historicity. As Butler explains, "the sedimentation of its usages … become part of the very name … [it's] a repetition that congeals, that gives the name its force" (*Excitable* 36). The discourse that precedes the name also conditions it and gives it strength.

Subjective agency remains possible, however, because historicity does not preclude new meanings being attributed to the name. Speech is never completely under control and even an insult can open up the possibility of counter-attack (*Excitable* 11–15). People who speak offensively, such as by using derogatory nicknames, imagine they have the support of the hegemony and thus power of their own. This is a fallacy because speech fails when the values embedded in hegemonic structures differ from those held by the insulted subject. Thus, examining the offensive names given to trans warriors and warrior women allows me to elucidate the ideologies embedded in the novels and how they produce the possibility of a counter discourse. The many names attributed to these characters in twentieth-century Latin American novels generated spaces for agency and subversion.

Chapter Two

Naming Pintada

As Oswaldo Estrada notes, the contributions of almost all the women involved in the Revolution are still overlooked (*Troubled* 172). Their names, words, actions, and dates of birth and death have been dismissed as irrelevant (172). The story of the warrior woman character in *Los de abajo* is only slightly different. She does have a name, but it is only a single name and it is neither an ordinary personal name nor a family name. It is instead a nickname as laden with significance as the absence of a full name for this character. The name "Pintada" references ways in which the character embodies cultural changes that occurred during the Mexican Revolution, while other appellations used to refer to this character in the novel locate her at the margins of Mexican society. From this marginalized position, her gender performance challenges the structures of the heterocispatriarchy within which she is embedded.

"Pintada" literally means "painted female." Although it carries some of the same connotations as the English phrase "painted lady," the implications of this name are more complex and subtle. Being painted suggests that something false or fake, a reproduction, covers or paints over the original subject. Perhaps the reader cannot see the real Pintada because she is painted over. The nickname may function as a mask or disguise to render Pintada anonymous, thereby allowing her to represent other women and women's roles during the Mexican Revolution. This is suggested in Max Parra's interpretation of the name as a reference to a specific kind of paint: "war paint" (29). Naming a character "Pintada" thus underscores the atmosphere of war in which the novel takes place, as well as Pintada's personal fight to survive. B. Christine Arce also observes Pintada's talent for war and indicates that her nickname demonstrates bravery (*México's* 93–94). She adds, however, that given the character's lack of a "proper name," her "authority is a mere pathetic simulacrum of male potency and honor" (94). While I agree with Arce that the lack of a family name exposes the belief that potency and honor can only be attributed to people conforming to the heterocispatriarchy, I do not consider Pintada's authority to be simply an emulation of the patriarchy. Instead, my analysis of how the novel simultaneously demonstrates and downplays this character's scope of action and importance reveals Pintada's real strength. I examine her nicknames to understand how the heroism I see in her is diminished in the novel. They are evidence of the urge to ignore the non-traditional gender configurations and performances that were already taking place during the Revolution.

At a talk given at the Colegio Nacional de México in 1945, Mariano Azuela provided a simpler derivation for the name of this character. He said he based Pintada on Colonel Maximiano Hernández's real-life partner, who was "una chica prieta, muy pintada de la boca, ojos y carrillos" (*Los de abajo* [ALLCA] 285). Indeed, when Pintada first appears in the novel, the narrator describes her as "[u]na muchacha de carrillos teñidos de carmín" (*Los de abajo* [Cátedra] 146). The character's name is a direct reference to her heavy use of cosmetics. The name "Pintada" thus has two functions in the novel: to indicate the character and describe her physical appearance. Such an explanation is not as straightforward or value-neutral as it appears, however. Using cosmetics, especially rouge, had been condemned during the nineteenth century in the British Empire (Angeloglou 97). Catholic Mexico reproduced Victorian ideals by rejecting cosmetics, although their use was gradually permitted there and in the U.S. Nevertheless, rouge continued to be associated with sex work even in the 1900s (Angeloglou 113).

In "La aparición del subsuelo" (1983), Carlos Monsiváis proposes that the Pintada character signals a cultural revolution. She represents the possibility of women taking on new roles in war, including as *soldaderas,* as just one aspect of many rapid changes taking place after Porfirio Diaz's presidency (1876–1911) in Mexico (36). Monsiváis reveals that the cultural revolution was not so much in opposition to Victorian aesthetics, but to the moral code established by the Porfiriato (Porfirio Diaz's government). Cosmetic use and new concepts of beauty were included in these changes. Although conservative sectors of Mexican society continued to condemn cosmetics, they became increasingly popular amongst Mexican women after the end of the Revolution.

Pintada is not the only woman character described as wearing makeup in Azuela's novel. At the beginning of the second part of the novel, the narrator describes a scene in which Demetrio and his men are in a crowded restaurant. Some young women wearing makeup enter the restaurant: "cuando con las hembras norteñas de caras oscuras y cenicientas se revuelven jovencitas *pintarrajeadas* de los suburbios de la ciudad" ([Cátedra] 149, italics mine). The word "pintarrajeadas" is derogatory. In recalling Porfiriato beauty ideals and condemning the use of paint (i.e., cosmetics), it indicates intolerance toward the changes in feminine appearance that were occurring at the time. The narrator differentiates females (*hembras*) from the north who have a dark skin tone from the young and almost ridiculously painted women from the suburbs. This suggests that cosmetics were gaining popularity in urban areas, but not in rural northern Mexico. Because Pintada uses cosmetics, but arrives with "females" from the north, she is positioned between and combines characteristics of both types of women—she is simultaneously a *pintarrajeada* and a *hembra*.

The novel's conservativism in regard to women is demonstrated by superseding a warrior woman character's full, legal name with a nickname referencing her scandalous use of cosmetics. Pintada's personal or birth name is never revealed. It is overridden or annulled by her use of cosmetics. Just as the cosmetics hide her true face, Pintada's name caricaturizes her and renders the real Pintada missing and unimportant. Arce states that Pintada is depicted as belonging to the *cucaracha* kind to symbolize the discourse of the "corruption of traditional womanhood" (*México's* 95). I concur with Arce, but I see other dimensions in Pintada's performance and her diminishment. By forefronting paintedness as her single most important quality and denying her legal or formal names, Pintada is removed from the familial atmosphere and heterocispatriarchal kin relationships. Her nickname also labels as negative her personal agency in exploiting her sexuality to win Demetrio, the leader of the revolutionary band. By erasing other names and being known only by a pejorative nickname, the novelist avoids giving her credit for personal empowerment. According to Estrada, women in the Revolution were "almost always mentioned in passing or in a slim footnote" (*Troubled* 142). Pintada's lack of name indicates such a situation. In this sense, in the novel she is meant to be a nobody, to use Arce's term, because her lack of name and patronymic erases her from the annals of the Revolution (*México's* 8).

Her marginality is only reinforced by the portrayal of her love affair with Demetrio as if she were just a sex worker. As his lover, she never manages to supplant Demetrio's wife or acquire any other socially acceptable status. She instead ends up displaced as

Empowered Names, Disempowered Nicknames

Demetrio's lover by Camila (who has a proper first name) and is then relegated to ever more marginal and negative roles by Demetrio's band. In *Soldaderas in the Mexican Military*, Elizabeth Salas argues that in choosing to call the woman warrior in his novel "Pintada," Azuela demonstrates contempt for all women involved in the Mexican Revolution (85). While I agree with Salas that Azuela shows contempt toward women involved in the Revolution, I disagree that his contempt applies to all of the women. Since he describes another major woman character—the unpainted innocent Camila—in favorable terms, Azuela's prejudice only seems directed at warrior women, that is, women who behave as equals to men, carry guns, and are masculine, empowered, skilled fighters.

Not only is the woman warrior character relegated to a lesser social status by the nickname "Pintada," she is also dehumanized by it. Dehumanization occurs in two ways in *Los de abajo*: first, by not providing patronymics, and, second, by labeling characters as animals or supernatural beings. I next address these two points.

Dehumanizing Pintada

If Pintada embodies a cultural revolution, as Monsiváis suggests, what does her lack of a full legal name imply? Pascale Baker proposes that "female characters become projections of male anxieties" in the novel (*Revolutionaries* 100). I agree with Baker that the actions conducted by Pintada demonstrate an anxiety towards her empowerment. Moreover, Pintada's lack of a patronymic shows that she is not a productive member of her heterocispatriarchal society and thus does not have rights. By only having a nickname, Pintada represents a variety of women—the nobodies—who were involved in the Mexican Revolution. Their multi-faceted roles in the war cannot be easily explained without calling into question heterocispatriarchy, so their names have been erased from history.

The use of nicknames for marginalized characters in Mexico develops other unofficial or marginal spaces in the Revolution. The revolutionary environment brought to the forefront not only those from below, the underdogs (*los de abajo*) such as Demetrio Macías and Anastacio Montañez (who have legal names), but even those below the underdogs (*los de más abajo*) such as Meco, Manteca, Codorniz, and Pintada, none of whom have proper names. Such

81

Chapter Two

members of society seem unworthy of having patronymics in the novel. Furthermore, the nicknames and other appellations these characters are given suggest that they are not completely physically human. As with all insulting monikers, they are intended to be unflattering. In the novel, each nickname refers to animals (e.g., *codorniz* [quail]), food (e.g., *manteca* [lard]), or aspects of physical appearance or personality (e.g., *pintada* [painted], *meco* (native Mexican). These nicknames are naked descriptions of their environment. Azuela does not describe the heroism or beauty of these characters, but reifies and animalizes them.

In part this is because Azuela is not interested in providing a romantic or idealized version of the Mexican Revolution. Taking up arms against injustice corrupts characters with and without patronyms. Demetrio becomes more concerned about having a woman than fighting, while his men become dedicated to plundering villages. Even the ideologue, Luis Cervantes, buys a fourteen-year-old girl to take as his fiancée and ransacks other people's homes. The novel lays bare a vision in which revolutionaries are not just heroes, but can also be animals and corrupt rebels who obey no laws and have no ethics. Having a proper legal name is not enough to differentiate among such characters operating in a corrupt atmosphere. Having a family name only makes a difference for one character, Cervantes, the only member of the band to survive and profit from the Revolution, probably because his last name accords him higher socioeconomic status and prestige. Pintada, meanwhile, is treated more or less the same as the *adelitas* described by Gabriela Cano, in the sense that they too lack family names, regional origins, and political affiliations ("¿Es posible" 13–14). Pintada and the *adelitas* are conceived as peripheral beings rather than active participants in political and social change.

Although Pintada is on the same social level as the other dehumanized characters, being a warrior woman marginalizes her even further. Members of Demetrio's band treat her as an animal and label her with dehumanizing epithets such as *chinche* (lit. bedbug, fig. "pain in the neck"), *sierpe* (viper), and devil *(diabla/o)*. Güero Margarito twice refers to Pintada as a devil. The first time occurs when Margarito and Pintada meet Demetrio for the first time and Margarito tells Pintada "–¡*Diablo* de Pintada tan lista! ... ¡Ya quieres estrenar general! ... " (147; ellipsis in the original, italics mine). The second time occurs after Pintada finds a beautiful mare on her own: "–¡Yo no sé qué carga esta *diabla* de Pintada que siempre nos gana los mejores «avances»! –clamó el güero Margarito–. Así la verán desde que se nos juntó en Tierra Blanca" (156; italics mine). Both times, Pintada is labeled a devil because she is an astute woman who wants to improve her socioeconomic position either by winning Demetrio or possessing a valuable animal. That she goes after Demetrio, who has recently acquired an elevated military title (i.e., General) traditionally reserved for men, denotes that Pintada is looking for prestige by joining herself to a man of high economic and social rank. Use of the word *diabla* demonizes Pintada's astuteness even as it seems to praise it, however. It also conveys Margarito's envy. Margarito does not like Pintada getting close to Demetrio. His envy is clearer the second time he utters the word "devil," when Pintada has acquired better spoils of war than he has. Pintada is envied for being smarter than the men because she appropriates elements that traditionally symbolize masculine power: the phallus. Even female horses are seen as powerful animals associated with war. Pintada's success calls into question the cleverness of the other band members and, consequently, the validity of traditional masculinities in the Mexican Revolution.

The tendency to demonize and dehumanize Pintada worsens as the novel progresses and the men characters change their attitudes toward her. Cervantes later asks Demetrio, "¿y por qué se *aguanta* a esa *sierpe* de la Pintada?" (167; italics mine). Pintada is here portrayed as a viper (*sierpe*) that bothers men who have to put up with (*aguantar*) her anyway. By refusing to behave either as a traditional wife or as a submissive, selfless camp follower, she does not fulfill the men's ideal of proper womanhood. In addition, she rivals the men when it comes to ransacking villages. Indeed, as I discuss in the next chapter, Pintada is actually the person who teaches the men about war plunder.

Despite Pintada's intelligence and skills, men mainly view her as a sexual object. For example, when the band is in Tipatitlán, a widower asks for food for his nine children. Meco tells him that the band could sell Pintada to him at purchase cost (179–80). While this dialogue seems to be an attempt to place her within the heterocispatriarchal kinship system—as a wife for the widower—, Meco's comment is treated as merely a joke because Pintada does not submit herself to this traditional role. It nevertheless indicates that the men see Pintada as an object available for transfer. Later, Pancracio comments that whenever Pintada sees a man, she gets ready to attack (180). That is, from Pancracio's perspective, Pintada's main goal is to find a man, as if she looked forward to being exchanged.

Both Pancracio's and Meco's belittling comments represent attempts to subdue Pintada to the rules of heterocispatriarchy. However, they also signal her (unfeminine) independence from those rules. Another animalistic appellation applied to Pintada registers the men's displeasure at her independence. When she is expelled from Demetrio's group, Güero Margarito exclaims, "–¡Ah, qué bueno! ... ¡Hasta que se me despegó esta *chinche*! ... " (183; ellipsis in original, italics mine). The men characters do not want to see Pintada as independent: they name her a bloodsucking louse, a parasite they must rid themselves of. That they compare her to such a small insect—bedbugs are only four or five millimeters long—is further evidence of how they reduce her importance.

The names Pintada is called illustrate how her character opposes the traditional image of the stolen woman as represented by Camila. They also mark her diminishment as time passes in the novel. She starts out as a devil, becomes a viper, and finally becomes no more important than a bedbug. After being called a bedbug, she disappears from the story and is not named again. This discursive disappearance indicates that transgressive women could not occupy space within the heterocispatriarchal environment of revolutionary Mexico. Transgressive characters in other Latin American novels are also made to disappear. When Iracema, the main character in Brazilian author José de Alencar's 1865 eponymous novel, transgresses barriers and questions social norms, she is likewise ignored, devalued, and eventually obliterated by finally giving up and dying. Iracema has to make way for a homosocial culture in which men, whether white, indigenous, or racially mixed, always have priority.

By accessing phallic/power symbols, such as the mare and the general, and using them to her own advantage, Pintada performs gender approximately as men are traditionally expected to do. Unlike empowered men, however, Pintada's success results in her debilitation. She is mocked and dehumanized by animalistic nicknames because her transgressive performance calls into question the logic of her social system. As Butler argues, negative appellations re-invoke societal rules and sustain the interpellation of the system. Although the insults make Pintada's agency as a warrior woman more visible, they also foretell her rejection from the band.

Naming Barbarity

Unlike Pintada, Doña Bárbara is a lead character in Rómulo Gallegos's novel, but like Pintada, she is a warrior woman who gains power and transgresses gender norms. She does not access power by partnering with a military man, as Pintada does; instead, she becomes a sort of military person herself—a *cacica*. As with Pintada, the appellations assigned to Doña Bárbara signal her deviation from traditional feminine roles and represent her as "evil." Also like Pintada, Doña Bárbara is ultimately disempowered and made to disappear.

Doña Bárbara's name is a direct reference to savagery or barbarity (lit. *bárbara*), as Gallegos himself explains in a prologue to the 1954 edition of the novel. He explicitly links her character to the barbarity of the Venezuelan Plains: "¿Y devoradora de hombres, no es cierto? –pregunté con la emoción de un hallazgo, pues habiendo mujer simbolizadora de aquella naturaleza bravía ya había novela" (5). In addition to representing the savagery of nature and the Plains society, some critics linked the title of the novel to the political context in which it is set (5). One of several implications of the name "Doña Bárbara," according to Doris Sommer, is its reference to the barbaric dictatorship of General Juan Vicente Gómez, who ruled from 1908 until 1935. He was infamous for incarcerating, torturing, and murdering politicians and intellectuals who opposed him. Other literary critics have brought in Domingo Faustino Sarmiento's distinction between civilization and barbarity (E. Johnson 456; Galaos 301; Morínigo 91; Osorio 22). Adapted from European ideas, this discourse aims to eradicate backwardness, barbarity, and lack of civilized culture. Doña Bárbara's name, in this discussion, represents a backwards, uncivilized past that must be overcome. In a way, she thus embodies the Latin American countries that have aimed to be inserted as part of the Western civilization tradition while remaining perceived by traditional European discourses as "uncivilized."

Because the discussion around barbarity in the novel has been pervasive, analyzing this topic in Doña Bárbara's names and nicknames allows me to analyze how the character is both constructed and demystified. First of all, her name is not merely or only "Bárbara," it is modified by the honorific "Doña," a form of address indicating authority and respect. According to Machado, it marks age and class, including ownership of property (6). It also assigns the subject to a particular social group (6). Furthermore, the Mondragones brothers refer to Doña Bárbara as "*la señora*" (Mrs.) (61), another honorific that signifies their relative socioeconomic status and that they work for her. Santos uses the same term when they are at court because he sees her as a landowner (100–01). These instances provide evidence that Doña Bárbara's high socioeconomic status is recognized and respected by men characters in the book.

Alfonso González argues that Gallegos combined "*doña*" with "Bárbara" to construct a dominating barbarity: "The name Doña Bárbara is composed of two parts: *doña* from L. *domina*(*m*) and *Bárbara*. The implication is that barbarism *dominates*, is master of the plains" (41, italics in original). Here, land ownership, as evidenced by the Doña and *la señora* honorifics, is elevated to the level of owning the *llanos*. This connection leads González to relate the character to the *caciquismo* phenomenon, which refers to a socioeconomic and political system commonly found throughout rural Latin America. The cacique is a sort of supreme leader who controls a particular region. In Doña Bárbara's case, I argue that an orphaned, poor, indigenous, non-white warrior woman generates her own *caciquismo*. Her control of the region is therefore socially revolutionary.

Moreover, her name suggests that her *caciquismo* is revolutionary because it is foreign to the region. "Bárbara" derives from a word of Greek origin that designated non-Greeks, that is, foreigners. She was not born where the action occurs, as the novel's narrator explains: "¡De más allá del CUNAVICHE, de más allá del Cinaruco, de más allá del Meta! ... De allá vino la trágica guaricha" (21, emphasis in the original). Doña Bárbara's transgressive warrior-ness, woman-led *caciquismo*, and her brutality as a ruler are unfamiliar to the people who live in the Araucan Plains. Following the heterocispatriarchal ideology of the novel, the people treat her as a foreigner, not as a *llanera* (woman cowboy), and describe her *caciquismo* as barbarous and unnatural. Doña Bárbara is also unnatural and subversive because she obtains power normally exclusive to heterosexual, masculine cis men such as Santos. Victorien Lavou Zoungbo goes further into her subversiveness by arguing that "[d]oña Bárbara invierte la tradicional división del trabajo sexual en la cual la Mujer tiene siempre que ser el objeto (pasivo) del deseo del Varón" (213). With this inversion, Doña Bárbara transgresses gender limits and empowers herself. Her foreignness and unnaturalness justify the reversion back to the natural order via Santos's eventual takeover of the *caciquismo*.

In addition to Bárbara and Doña Bárbara, the character is called "Barbarita" in one chapter titled "La devoradora de hombres." Usually translated as "The Ogress," the title of this chapter literally means "eater of men." In it, the narrator describes Doña Bárbara's childhood as Barbarita (little Bárbara). Stripped of a formal mode of address (i.e., Doña), the diminutive form of her name infantilizes her and gives her an air of innocence that is later contrasted with her being gang raped. Just after she falls in love for the first time while working in a pirogue, three of the crewmen rape Barbarita. She is then rescued by Eustaquio, leaves the pirogue, and later sets herself up as a *cacica* going by the adult name Doña Bárbara. The change in names signals the character's progression in socioeconomic status. The contrast between the diminutive form of her name and her adult name also suggests a pejorative evaluation of her empowerment. Although diminutives vary according to time, context, and other variables, she is never called "Doña Barbarita," which would be a name more fitted to a benevolent, non-threatening matriarch or even a paternalistic boss. She is never given that privilege. This evaluation is one of the reasons why I consider her a *cacica* and not a matriarch.

Doña Bárbara's lack of a patronym is significant. Because she was born of the rape of an indigenous woman by a "white adventurer" (21), she does not have a legal surname and does not enjoy the social status of being somebody's daughter. For Sharon Magnarelli, the absence of a paternal name indicates that Doña Bárbara has no legally sanctioned relations with men at all, so "she defies the concept of property which is basic to Western society. Her lack of a surname reflects her lack of a possessor" ("Woman" 15). As an adult, Doña Bárbara continues to challenge heterocispatriarchal law by refusing to create a surname or adopt a man's name through marriage. Like Pintada, Doña Bárbara is not considered valuable because she has no kin relations.

In rejecting a patronym, Magnarelli argues that Doña Bárbara "defies what is defined as culture and must therefore be personified as the enemy to that civilization, as is nature" ("Woman" 16). Her refusal to surrender to civilization is evident in the ways others formally address her as Doña. Doña implies that instead of being owned by a man, she owns herself and others. Doña Bárbara thus defies and subverts the concept of woman as property, and even uses it to her advantage. Both the form of address and her proper name reveal Doña Bárbara's empowerment, but her claim to ownership as *cacica* is disqualified by her being a barbarous foreigner.

Another character who manipulates her form of address and proper name is Maria Moura in *Memorial de Maria Moura* (Maria Moura's Memorial), a novel published in 1992 by Brazilian woman author Rachel de Queiroz (1910–2003). At 17 years old, Maria Moura becomes an orphan and then runs away (after burning down the house where she lives) because she does not want to be forced to marry one of her cousins. After escaping, Maria masculinizes her appearance and behavior. She then becomes the successful leader of a group of *capangas* (thieves) in the Backlands of Brazil, mostly constituted by those of her subordinates who ran away with her. Her traditional image as a young orphan woman is also transformed by her changing her name. Immediately after cutting her hair off, Maria tells her subordinates "[a]gora se acabou a Sinhazinha do Limoeiro. Quem está aqui é a Maria Moura, chefe de vocês," (84). Previously, she was known as "sinhazinha," the word enslaved people used to refer to the daughters of the master. As I explain somewhere else, using "Maria Moura" instead of "sinhazinha" marks Maria's adoption of a full legal name for her new life style ("Mulheres" 119–20). Having a full name and holding a position as boss erases her earlier image as a *sinhazinha*, the little daughter of a landowner (120). A *sinhazinha* is a childish, dependent, and domestic figure. Still, using her family name implies that Maria does not cease being the daughter of the landowner. Keeping the patronym means that she continues to put herself in a socioeconomically powerful class, although in doing so she creates tension with her transgression (120).

It is in this tension—between being transgressive and traditional—that Maria manages to empower herself as a young orphan in a traditional society. She uses the structures of her society to climb up the hierarchy. Like Doña Bárbara, Maria's men even begin to call her "dona Moura." As for Doña Bárbara, the honorific *dona* represents the respect due to her. However, unlike the Venezuelan warrior woman, the honorific refers to her paternal name (Moura), not her given name (Maria). She thus claims access to traditional power and hierarchy. Moreover, despite facing many challenges, Maria sustains her position of power until the end of the novel, when she decides to go to war and risk everything. This historical novel, written by a woman author at the end of the twentieth century, thus illustrates the autonomy, power, and gender dynamics of warrior women. It also challenges the heterocispatriarchal stereotypes that Gallegos's novel looks to restitute.

Demystifying the *Cacica*

Throughout the novel, Doña Bárbara is referred to with a variety of nicknames and other appellations, including *cacica* (woman cacique or regional boss), *mujerona* (big woman), *mestiza* (mixed race), *guaricha* (young and single native woman; prostitute), *barragana* (concubine), *mujer indomable* (untamable woman), *devoradora de hombres* (devourer of men, man-eater), *dañera* (destroyer), *bruja* (witch), *embrujadora de hombres* (bewitcher of men), *hija de los ríos* (daughter of the rivers), and *esfinge de la sabana* (sphinx of the savannah). Most of these largely pejorative nicknames represent attempts to label and define Doña Bárbara, but taken together they confirm the complexity of her character. Their usage indicates a need to stabilize her image within the hegemony, even as she continues to transform over the course of the novel.

Doña Bárbara is most often called a *mujerona* (big woman). Use of the word "*mujerona*" to describe her physical appearance suggests that she is a tall, corpulent woman. Alberto Blasi argues that it also references her age (forty years old) and thus has pejorative connotations (72). The word may also reflect the butch image she projects by wearing mannish clothes. Overall, the term highlights her masculine personality and performance, as do other nicknames applied to her. As Stephen Henighan notes, "[d]oña Bárbara, the 'marimacho' [butch or macho woman] (Gallegos 95) and 'devoradora de hombres' (82), defies bourgeois ideals of feminine appearance and behavior" (32). Doña Bárbara's transgressions go beyond gender, as she defies expectations of how she should behave and look as a *cacica*, a term that would be applied to an upper-class, feminine, submissive, Catholic, domestic, cis woman.

The abundance of epithets and variety of their nuances present contradictions in how Doña Bárbara is viewed. For instance, despite her butch or macho appearance, Doña Bárbara's sexuality as a heterosexual woman is an important part of her character. Being mannish (*hombruna*) seems to contradict being a man-eater, a sexual devourer of men. Looking like a heterosexual man or a butch lesbian opposes the ordinarily feminine image of heterocissexual promiscuity embedded in the term "man-eater." Note that the term "man-eater" dredges up fear of the *vagina dentata* and the danger of women in general. By simultaneously rejecting the feminine and destroying men with her female sexuality, Doña Bárbara threatens the binary logic of gender that is the basis for heterocispatriarchy. She is not only dangerous to men, she is dangerous to her entire society.

Doña Bárbara has no family, is from poor origins, and belongs to an indigenous culture. Nevertheless, this single, non-virgin, *mestiza*, indigenous woman achieves a powerful position as *cacica*. When she takes over the ranch, she changes its name to "El Miedo" (the fear), asserting her ability to dominate the region and sending the clear message that she is to be feared. Such actions undermine the heterocispatriarchal and classist hierarchies of her society. The danger to society represented by her character is evident in Venezuelan history. Arlene J. Díaz argues that nineteenth century Venezuelan men rhetorically represented women in the allegoric figure of Liberty (*Female* 13). As Díaz argues, "[i]n paintings and in metaphoric language, the message was that both Liberty and Woman had to be closely controlled and guided because otherwise they could lead to corruption and disorder" (13). Indeed, lack of supervision and control leads Doña Bárbara into corruption and disorder in Gallegos's novel. The traumatic gang rape she experienced also relates to the lack of supervision and how she ended up being corrupted. Doña Bárbara's power must be deconstructed and she (or her land) must be brought back under men's authority. Her wild, barbarous image must be domesticated, made submissive, and reconstructed as that of a traditional woman.

Santos—a white, masculine man born to become *llanero* by virtue of his family connections—is the enlightened man who must supervise and suppress her freedom. Regarding their opposing roles in the novel, Magnarelli observes that, "throughout the text, the very adjectives which are complimentary and laudatory when applied to him [Santos] are intended as disparaging when applied to her. Obviously, then, the power of the word rests not in the term itself but rather in the supplementation which inevitably accompanies it" ("Woman" 15). The novel's double standard is revealed in that only the subject who is sexed male (Santos) is permitted to be correctly and properly manly or mannish. This double standard highlights the hegemonic gender binary entrenched in the novel.

The contradictory appellations given to Doña Bárbara likewise serve to reinforce the heterocispatriarchal hegemony. The epithet "the sphinx of the savanna" (*la esfinge de la sabana*) is a case in point. Donald L. Shaw argues that the phrase unifies different aspects of her character, since the sphinx combines "feminine beauty and cunning with animal strength and savagery" (*Gallegos* 72). "La esfinge de la sabana" is the title of a chapter in which Balbino appears not to understand Doña Bárbara's motivations, and so is a comment on Doña Bárbara's inscrutability. The novel's narrator states that "[e]n efecto, la superioridad de aquella mujer, su dominio sobre los demás y el temor que inspiraba parecían radicar especialmente en su saber callar y esperar" (63). As Shaw points out, the sphinx Doña Bárbara is an enigma; she represents an order that her society cannot apprehend. Her mysteriousness enables her to dominate others.

However, a contradiction emerges in the paragraph that follows the preceding quote:

> La leyenda de aquel poder sobrenatural que la asistía, haciendo imposible, por procedimientos misteriosos, que nadie le quitase una res o una bestia, era quizás invención de la bellaquería de sus mayordomos-amantes que habían hecho sus negocios fraudulentos con la hacienda de ella, pues, sumamente supersticiosa como era, por creerse asistida, en realidad, de aquellos poderes, se descuidaba y se dejaba robar. (63)

Even though the extradiegetic narrator equivocates by inserting a "maybe" (*quizás*), this passage states that her foremen, who are robbing her, actually created her powers by tapping her extreme superstitiousness. Two distinct images of Doña Bárbara oppose each other in this quote. One is of an observant, quiet, patient, even wise woman and the other is of a superstitious and gullible woman. Having earlier constructed a strong version of her character, the narrator then deconstructs her actions and suggests that she is actually powerless, weak, and stupid.

Blasi claims that this passage in the novel functions to rationalize the character in that it "tiende a anular el mismo estereotipo mitográfico que el capítulo pretende construir" (73). For this critic, also, the annulment of the *cacica* myth produces a return to the theme of ambiguity, to playing down all of the "señales maravillosas" (wonderful signs) of the character (73). I argue that this deconstruction of her power does not indicate ambiguity regarding the character so much as it exposes the ideological manipulations of the novel. The passage implies that Doña Bárbara is not the evil, conniving barbarian suggested by her name, and thus not as dangerous or as untouchably powerful as she at first seems. By reframing her as a stupid and gullible fool, the narrator demonstrates that Santos's power and prestige are not really threatened or permanently usurped by Doña Bárbara. The heterocispatriarchal ideology is reasserted. This turnabout is seen in each of the three novels: whenever a trans warrior's or warrior woman's behavior demonstrates flaws in a hegemonic system, she or he must be disempowered.

A similar upset of her power occurs when Doña Bárbara visits San Fernando. There the narrator explains that the stories in circulation around Doña Bárbara are products of fantasy:

> Ya, al saberse que estaba en la población, habían comenzado a rebullir los comentarios de siempre y a ser contadas, una vez más, las mil historias de sus amores y crímenes, muchas de ellas pura invención de la fantasía popular, a través de cuyas ponderaciones la mujerona adquiría caracteres de heroína sombría, pero al mismo tiempo fascinadora como si la fiereza bajo la cual se la representaba, más que odio y repulsa, tradujera una íntima devoción de sus paisanos. (234)

By clarifying that her legend is a popular fiction or folklore, the narrator unwrites and demystifies the earlier image of a woman of almost legendary power (i.e., man eater, *mujerona*, sphinx, *cacica*). He deconstructs her image by showing it had been manipulated. This demystification of her character is reinforced by implying that Doña Bárbara became *cacica* by chance, not through her own hard work and acumen. This demystification further signals that the warrior woman's strength and power—that allowed her to seize the ranch and extend her properties—are not valued by society.

Undoing and unwriting her strength as a mannish, barbarous, man-eating, woman boss is problematic in that it leaves the reader with doubts, however. This may be why Blasi speaks of ambiguity and Sturgis E. Leavitt argues that her character lacks coherence (118–19). However, it is not the character who is incoherent: it is the narrator who is dealing with her in an incoherent way. At first she is depicted as a strong, vigorous woman with supernatural powers who can manipulate men and the law as she pleases. Later the narrator deliberately reveals a completely different image of her as stupid, gullible, and easily manipulated. Gallegos intended his novel to promote "civilization" in the Plains, so Doña Bárbara's claim to power must be deconstructed. If Doña Bárbara were truly a strong contender for *caciquismo*, she would hinder the civilizing of the Plains and her barbarity would resist the "progress" that Santos embodies. Her strength and power had to be erased so they would not undermine the heterocispatriarchy. Only then can Santos fulfill the ideal gender role as a man leader, representing *caciquismo* and dominating the Plains.

When discussing how men's traditional rhetoric functions to sustain the heterocispatriarchy, it is important to note that Gallegos edited his novel twice. Shaw examined the differences between the two editions of the novel. He asserts that in the second one, Gallegos presents Doña Bárbara's actions as unpremeditated rather than planned ("More About" 212). Shaw believes these modifications were intended to soften Doña Bárbara's negative image (210). It could also be argued that the supposed ambiguities or incoherence of Doña Bárbara's character emerged because of the rewrite, as Gallegos attempted to change the depiction of this warrior woman from perverse and evil to stupid, gullible, superstitious, and disorganized. The revisions do not soften so much as unwrite and demystify Doña Bárbara as a barbarous, mannish landowner and thus make her innocuous to heterocispatriarchal society. Once she is shown to be powerless, the barbarity she represents need not be feared. Any power she obtains is made to seem fragile and unreal.

Despite the rhetorical deconstruction of Doña Bárbara's power through pejorative nicknames and other descriptions, the honorific Doña and other appellations such as *mujerona* and *hombruna* continue to highlight her masculinity, strength, and empowerment—her warrior-ness. Even if the novel is intended to support the hegemonic ideology, it does include a woman character who empowers herself within a heterocispatriarchal space. Doña Bárbara obtains power normally reserved for cis men characters who perform gender according to the rules of masculinity dictated by their social context. Indeed, as I demonstrate in the next chapter, the strength of Doña Bárbara's performance as *llanero* cannot be discursively deconstructed by the novel's narrator.

Naming Diadorim

Guimarães Rosa's texts are known for their linguistic innovativeness, including the elaborate and creative use of names and nicknames. As in Gallegos's novel, the narrator of *Grande sertão: veredas* applies nicknames to the trans warrior character that reveal issues of gender and class. In this section, I summarize some of the critical analyses of Diadorim's names that relate to gender performance and his complex relationship with Riobaldo. I argue that the appellations given to Diadorim demonstrate empowerment while simultaneously differentiating him from Riobaldo.

One of the first and most quoted literary critiques of *Grande sertão* is Augusto de Campos's 1959 analysis of names in the novel. He outlined two main ideas that continue to pervade analyses of Diadorim's name: the presence of the devil and a discourse on androgyny. Noting the repetition of certain phonemes such as the first /d/ in "Diadorim" leads de Campos to connect this character with both god (*deus*) and the devil (*diabo*). De Campos also observes that Riobaldo refers to the devil as *diá*, which constitutes the first three letters of Diadorim's name (61). He argues that Riobaldo's discursive association between Diadorim and the devil reflects his horror of homosexuality (61). Additionally, de Campos notices that the suffix "-im" is frequently attached to both feminine and masculine words in the novel. He suggests that the use of this suffix in Diadorim's name implies gender imprecision, that Diadorim exists between the masculine and the feminine and is therefore an androgyne (62–63). This latter argument is relevant to my analysis here.

In 1970, Antonio Cândido suggested that Diadorim's name is constituted by an almost imperceptible and reversible "gliding" between the masculine and the feminine ("Ser" 61). According to Cândido, the glide is in the phonetic habits of rural men who glide from "(Deodoro) à Deodorina à Deadorina à Diadorina à Diadorim à (Deodorinho)" (61). This phonetic gliding leads this critic to argue that Diadorim is an androgynous character. This conclusion is also problematic because, as argued in the previous chapter, if the androgyne unites the two "poles" of masculinity and femininity in a sort of static third gender it does not call into question hegemonic gender categories. Diadorim is a more transgressive character than being an androgyne would suggest. Indeed, if Diadorim can be seen as a masculine name, as de Campos argues, it allows more room for a performance of masculinity and being trans*.

In the 1983 book *Logos and the Word*, Stephanie Merrim discusses Diadorim's name without remaining trapped in binary dichotomies. Like the previous two critics, she examines the eponym, the proper name that semantically describes its referent. For Merrim, Diadorim's name refers to god and the devil and the masculine and the feminine all at the same time (25). She also claims the name provokes permutations such as *davidiva*, Dindurinh, and Deodorina, or partial variations such as Diá and Di (38). Both types of permutations are found on other words in the text due to the "interchangeability" of the novel. "Interchangeability" means that what is separated into fragments can be reunited into a whole and what is a whole can be divided into fragments, as occurs throughout this text (38). Interchangeability allows for multiple perspectives to be developed in the novel. The interchangeability of the eponym "Diadorim" represents the complexity of a trans warrior character who cannot be reduced to the category "androgyne." The ambiguity of the name suggests that a proper name does not have to directly reference gender. An eponym can challenge the ideological need to "gender" people in rituals of recognition. If, as Butler argues, to have a name is to be placed in a binary gender category, then Diadorim's name challenges this placement. The names and nicknames with which he is labeled do not reduce him to fit into traditional gender conventions.

Critics have also seen the name "Diadorim" as originating from the feminine "Deodorina" because that is the name Riobaldo discovers on Diadorim's baptismal certificate after his friend's death. However, I argue that because the woman's name appears in the novel only after the character's death, "Diadorim" does not derive

95

from "Deodorina." Rather the opposite: "Deodorina" derives from "Diadorim." Furthermore, "Deodorina" neither represents the character nor describes his behavior in the novel. It is a derivative form intended to assist Riobaldo's desire to understand Diadorim. He is desperately searching to explain his friend's past, but the name he discovers only references his genitalia at the time of birth, not his gender identity. The discovery of the baptismal record is Riobaldo's attempt to label and explain away Diadorim's gender performance, his empowerment, embodiment, sexual orientation, and identity. I consider that his attempt fails, as the similarity between the two names connects us to discourses on trans* identities and invites us to see gender as fluid and changing.

Diadorim's Trans(itory) Names

The many names and nicknames given to Diadorim, such as Reinaldo, *Dindurinh, menino* (boy), and *delicado* (delicate one) further contribute to the construction of Diadorim's gender performance and identity. Through nicknaming, Riobaldo (the narrator and protagonist of the story) discloses different facets of their relationship. Diadorim is alternately cast as a casual friend, guide, warrior, intimate friend, and object of love. Such manipulative appellations indicate how both Riobaldo and Diadorim are constructed: Riobaldo's character is seen to grow and mature, while Diadorim remains static (although always more responsible than Riobaldo). Nonetheless, they are similar in that they are both *jagunços* of about the same age, their fathers are distant figures, and neither of them has a mother. Accordingly, Diadorim is a figure with which Riobaldo compares himself. For instance, as a teenager or as a new *jagunço*, he underscores his inferiority because he has not reached Diadorim's level or skills. His superiority appears only when he becomes a *jagunço* leader, which makes him Diadorim's boss.

The first time the two characters meet, Riobaldo calls Diadorim *menino* (teenage boy), *menino moucinho* (little boy), *Menino-Moço* (young boy), and *Menino do Porto* (boy from the harbor) because he does not yet know Diadorim's name. Riobaldo indicates that the birth name is unimportant: "[n]em sabia o nome dele. Mas não carecia. Dele nunca me esqueci, depois, tantos anos todos" (125). Diadorim's name is less important than Riobaldo's memories of him. The nickname "*menino*" becomes a referent to both the person and the encounter. "*Menino*" avoids the class labels that come with many eponyms and patronyms, while depicting Diadorim's air of innocence and masculine performance. Machado considers the appellation *menino* a proper noun because it is one of the "muitos exemplos de termos de referência à condição ou à idade que passam a ser empregados como Nomes próprios pelos personagens de Guimarães Rosa" (37–38). It is a manipulative term because it describes the character's gender and youthfulness, but I see that it diminishes Diadorim's important role as Riobaldo's guide. Even as a boy, Diadorim is a trans warrior, however. He makes decisions, demonstrates bravery, and invites Riobaldo to emulate him, so the real *menino* should be Riobaldo.

"Reinaldo" is Diadorim's official name in the *jagunço* world. This name contains the roots *rei*, meaning "king" (from the German *ragan*, "advice") and *wald*, meaning "to govern or to dominate" (J. Santos 119). The name thus refers to a leader who governs through providing good advice. Critics such as Machado and Julia Conceição Fonseca Santos connect this meaning to the fact that Diadorim is the son of the main *jagunço* leader, Joca Ramiro. Machado argues first that the name "Reinaldo" provides stability to a young character who does not have a proper name. Second, the name echoes Riobaldo's name, as Diadorim himself says: "'—Riobaldo ... Reinaldo ... '—de repente, ele deixou isto em dizer:—'Dão par, os nomes de nós dois ... '" (160; ellipsis in the original).

Machado finally notes that the name "Reinaldo" is only used in the context of war. "Reinaldo" is established as his war name when Diadorim confesses that it is not his real name: "Escuta: eu não me chamo *Reinaldo*, de verdade. Este é nome apelativo, inventado por necessidade minha, carece de você não me perguntar por quê. Tenho meus fados" (171). This supposed explanation clarifies nothing, but creates mystery, complicity, and solidarity between the two characters. The revelation also transforms "Reinaldo" into a transitory name, a sort of mask that Diadorim assumes with those who are not close to him. Meanwhile, "Diadorim" becomes the name used in his intimate relationship with Riobaldo. The proximity between both characters helps to construct Riobaldo's relationship with Diadorim as homoerotic and even gay.

"Diadorim" does not function independently of the names "*menino*" and "Reinaldo." All his various names function like

Chapter Two

clothing to conceal his female-sexed body and permit a masculine identity and behavior. They represent different facets of the character while hiding the social role he "should" be performing according to heterocispatriarchal rules. Furthermore, the changing names reflect changes in Riobaldo's life along with the growth of their friendship. All three names appear in succession paralleling Riobaldo's development as a character. *Menino* frames the teenage friend who tells Riobaldo to overcome his fears, Reinaldo is the warrior who helps Riobaldo become a *jagunço,* and Diadorim is an intimate friend of the *jagunço* leader Riobaldo. If "Reinaldo" as a name is representative of war, then its displacement by the name "Diadorim" diminishes his role as a warrior. This permits the other warrior (Riobaldo) to mature and become a leader.

Jon S. Vincent argues that Diadorim's names are similar to Riobaldo's names and nicknames (i.e., teacher, Tatarana, and Urutú-Branco) in that they change depending on the roles the characters are playing: "[t]he masculine name she [Diadorim] uses with the group is Reinaldo, suggesting counseling and governing functions, the name known only to Riobaldo is Diadorim, and her real name is Maria Deodorina da Fé Bettancourt Marins ('Mary' and 'Faith' being the two most suggestive components)" (81). I do not agree that Diadorim's names fluctuate with the public or social roles he enacts. Even during battle, Riobaldo does not refer to Diadorim as Reinaldo. "Reinaldo" is only used to refer to Diadorim as Riobaldo's warrior guide earlier in the novel. Diadorim does not explain why he uses that name and asks Riobaldo not to question him about it (171). Later in the novel, "Deodorina" is only proof of Riobaldo's heterosexuality; it does not signal a new social role for Diadorim.

While Riobaldo is seen as the *jagunço* leader who brings peace to the Backlands, Diadorim is actually the great warrior who ends the fight. In the final battle against Hermógenes, Diadorim demonstrates that he has better judgment and combat skills than Riobaldo. Even as Riobaldo loses consciousness, Diadorim goes on to defeat the enemy. Despite Diadorim's abilities, Riobaldo as narrator focuses less on his heroism and more on his death and the discovery of his female sex. The transitoriness represented in the names *menino* and Reinaldo is thus also seen in the name "Diadorim." With the death of the character and Riobaldo's heterocisnormative search for a female past, Diadorim's name also becomes a temporary mask to be replaced by the full proper name "Maria Deodorina da Fé Bettancourt Marins."

Riobaldo's attempt to find proof of Diadorim's sex or people who knew him as a woman or girl is heterocisnormative, heterosexist, and transphobic because it aims to explain Diadorim through his sex and sanction Riobaldo's heterosexuality. After his death, Riobaldo also does not respect Diadorim's preferred name. The written, legal baptismal name (Deodorina) represents a level of knowledge that Riobaldo did not have with his beloved friend. It then becomes the public name that allows Riobaldo to narrate his story and account for his "confusing" feelings. "Deodorina" becomes the real and proper name because it presents both characters as heterocissexuals.

While the revelation of Diadorim's sex and baptismal name empowers Riobaldo by affirming his masculine heterosexuality that is the basis for his *jagunço-ness*, it disempowers Diadorim as a trans warrior. His complex gender performance is ignored and his character reduced to the shape of his genitalia. Just as naming reduces Pintada to an animal and unwrites Doña Bárbara's masculine power, it turns Diadorim, the great man hero and warrior, into a dead cis woman, a female corpse. Diadorim's changing names thus represent the narrator Riobaldo's efforts to erase and explain away Diadorim's transgressions in order to establish himself as the heterocissexual warrior leader.

Despite this attempt at heterocisnormativity, it must be stressed that the name "Diadorim" prevails over the name "Deodorina" for multiple reasons. First, the baptismal name and the sex of the cadaver are the only evidence provided of Diadorim's femaleness. As I argued in the previous chapter, these revelations do not explain Diadorim, they only generate more questions. Second, "Diadorim" is the most important name because of its complexity and affirmation of an intimate friendship. Third, since the name "Deodorina" only appears toward the end of the novel, it never replaces Diadorim's name. While Riobaldo's heteronormative search seems to treat "Diadorim" as a transitory name, Riobaldo cannot override his friend's successful gender performance. At the end of the novel, Riobaldo still refers to his friend as Diadorim, not Deodorina.

In addition to providing evidence that Diadorim was female-sexed at birth, the baptismal record reveals his family surnames.

According to Santos, these patronyms designate qualities Diadorim inherited from his father (much as the name Reinaldo does) (119–20). The family names emplace Diadorim as part of an upper-class warrior family from the Backlands. As Machado notes, "[o]s títulos e os sobrenomes em enumeração ficam reservados à classe dominante, às autoridades, aos proprietários de terra e gado, aos chefes políticos influentes, a 'gente melhor' das cidades" (43). Unlike the other two warrior women characters, Diadorim has a specific social status predicated on his position within a kinship network. However, Diadorim rejects his birthright by creating names other than those imposed by his heterocispatriarchal society. By never revealing his family names (only Riobaldo knows his father's identity), Diadorim refuses to distinguish himself from other *jagunços* in terms of class. By taking masculine or at least ambiguous eponyms, he is not perceived as a feminine object of exchange, and can pass as just another *jagunço*.

In addition to the proper names just discussed, Diadorim is given two informal appellations. First, one *jagunço* calls him *delicado* (delicate) because of his fine features and physical beauty. Diadorim reacts by beating up and subduing the man who insulted his masculinity and strength. His reaction is the socially "proper" way to defend his reputation and *jagunço-ness*. For Kathrin Holzermayr Rosenfield, *jagunço* honor "não suporta nenhuma "contaminação" do lado feminino, materno e vital da existência" (*Desenveredando* 271). The *jagunços* perceive any hint of femininity as weakness. Traditional masculinity excludes femininity, so commenting that Diadorim is "delicate" constitutes an insult. Diadorim has to demonstrate that he is not delicate and weak (i.e., feminine), but brutal and strong (i.e., masculine) as expected of warriors such as the *jagunços*. As previously explained, insults create the possibility of agency. This is evident here when Diadorim retaliates with a display of warrior capabilities and thus invalidates the insult. I return to this episode in the next chapter.

Second, when Riobaldo accidentally calls him "Diadorim" in front of two of his men, one of the men hears his name as "Dindurinh." Like the descriptor "delicate," this distortion of his name feminizes Diadorim. Riobaldo responds to the mistaken apprehension by defending Diadorim's bravery: "Me franzi. – O Reinaldo é valente como mais valente, sertanejo supro. E danado jagunço ... Falei mais alto. – Danado ... – repeti" (583; ellipsis and

Empowered Names, Disempowered Nicknames

emphasis in the original). Both these temporary appellations are insulting because they question *jagunço* virility. Riobaldo's reaction (Diadorim is not present in this scene) affirms the compulsory heterosexuality and masculinity of the *jagunço*. Riobaldo's heterosexuality is secured by his assertion that his closest friend is very brave. Both Diadorim and Riobaldo's reactions work to confirm Diadorim's successful performance of masculinity.

In sum, Diadorim's names and nicknames do not track a progression from the masculine to the feminine over the course of the novel. Rather, they emphasize stages in Riobaldo's journey: the transition from puberty to adolescence (*menino*), becoming a jagunço (Reinaldo), being masculine (delicate; Dindurinh), and becoming intimate friends (Diadorim). The transitions, even rites of passage, between the names are signaled by variants on Diadorim's name such as Diá and Di. In Merrim's terms, the interchangeability of Diadorim's diverse names and nicknames show that the world is in constant transformation (as Machado also notes).

If names indicate gender essentialisms, the moment that contradictory names cohabit with one another, as in Diadorim's, Pintada's, and Doña Bárbara's cases, gender essentialism is challenged. The plurality of names and what they represent signal the complexity of warrior women's and trans warrior' performances and that gender is neither exclusive nor binary. Diadorim's names coupled with his abilities demonstrate, first, that sex does not determine gender performance. The offspring of a great *jagunço* and landowner performs as a *jagunço*, not *jagunça*. Second, the juxtaposition of names indicates that a female-sexed character can perform roles traditionally assigned to male-sexed characters. Regardless of age, they can be braver and more heroic than male-sexed teenagers.

The plurality of names also denotes the impossibility of finding just one definition or label for Diadorim. If names normally function to differentiate subjects, in this novel they lose this capacity because Diadorim's names and nicknames are constantly changing or being challenged. This character cannot be approached from only one perspective. That Guimarães Rosa has his characters change names situationally demonstrates that the name does not designate a unique and exclusive characteristic, but an ongoing process of mutation of the linguistic sign (Machado 27). Diadorim's name therefore represents a constant transgression or

Chapter Two

avoidance of normative limits dictated by society. Theoretically, to be nameless is to be no one, while to have a name is to be identified and categorized, usually on the basis of class, family, gender, sex, and so on. The many names Diadorim assumes, or is given, sidestep simplistic categories and show up the porosity of social divisions and trans* processes. Jack Halberstam uses the term "trans*" to signal the complexity of the transitioning process and how trans* people cannot be located in a ready-made category or position. Instead, trans* is a fluid process and each experience is different and personal. Diadorim's names thus expose a complex trans* process, as he is a *menino*, a public warrior, and a close friend. At the same time, because Riobaldo narrates the novel, Diadorim's names and nicknames reveal how trans* warriors' diverse experiences are simplified or even erased.

Conclusion

The interpellation and connotations of names and nicknames provide evidence of the social values transgressed by trans warrior and warrior woman characters. Because they challenge and attempt to reconfigure social hierarchies, they are labeled with pejoratives such as mannish, witch, viper, or devil. Even "delicate" becomes an insult when meant to undermine their strength. Such linguistic marks aim to pathologize warrior women and trans warriors and prevent them from changing society. Negative labels attempt to render their transgressions unimportant and make it seem that faults and cracks in the system are not dangerous.

Pintada's name indicates that the traditional roles of women and concerns about their appearance were being renovated during the time of the Mexican Revolution. To be *pintada* (painted) was to be part of a group of socially and economically transgressive women who interrupted the masculine atmospheres of the Porfiriato and armed combat. At the same time, being *pintada* was evaluated negatively and Pintada is dehumanized, reduced, and expelled from society because she does not fulfill normative roles. In Gallegos's novel, Doña Bárbara's names and nicknames likewise highlight her transgressions in a society in which being masculine and a *llanero* requires being a cisgender man. The nicknames demonstrate her ability to perform masculinity in order to gain power. At the same time, they undermine her power as a *cacica* because she cannot represent a valid alternative to the (male) cacique that Santos represents. Finally, the complex name "Diadorim" suggests the character's gender performance is so rich that he cannot be readily categorized. His many other names denote changing power relations, however, since Riobaldo does not accept that the better warrior is female-sexed. Diadorim's names also indicate different facets, stages, and levels of intimacy with Riobaldo. They specify the complexity of the world and demonstrate that it is impossible to divide it into two exclusive categories.

A complex relationship occurs between the name as signifier and the subject as signified. Names attempt to mark warrior women and trans warriors as members of a particular gender, but a single name cannot transmit all the complexities of these characters. Other names and nicknames emerge to represent different perspectives and old and new values. Trans warriors and warrior women are named again whenever their performances resist labels and transgress gender norms. Renaming reinvokes the values of a society. Renaming produces a discourse to explain the existence of warrior women and trans warriors (i.e., Amazon, Deodorina) and devalue them (i.e., viper, *mujerona*). Renaming diminishes the threat of their transgressions and new gender proposals to the logic of the hegemony. Renaming trans warriors and warrior women inserts them into traditional views of good or bad women as a way of domesticating their transgressions and annulling their agency and empowerment.

The transgressive gender performances that Pintada, Doña Bárbara, and Diadorim execute and the power plays that surround them are also illustrated in their relationships with and behaviors towards men characters in the novels. Like heterocissexual men, warrior women and trans warriors manage to occupy the place of most-desired position, but unlike heterocissexual men, they therefore have to be displaced and disempowered. This is the topic of the following chapter.

Chapter Three

The Masculinities of Trans Warriors and Warrior Women

In the 1980s and 1990s, scholarly studies on Latin American masculinities were conducted following a feminist framework that aimed to understand gender oppression (Gutmann "Introduction" 5). In subsequent years, the development of masculinity studies as well as gender and sexuality studies influenced how masculinities were researched and understood. In the early twentieth-first century, the work done by scholars, such as Sylvia Molloy, Rebecca E. Biron, Ben. Sifuentes-Jáuregui, Robert Irwin, Héctor Domínguez-Ruvalcaba, Maja Horn, Guillermo Núñez Noriega, Vinodh Venkatesh, and Jason Cortés, among others, discussed the ways in which masculinist discourses and men-dominated spaces have been challenged, reformulated and appropriated by homoerotic discourses and in the inclusion of gay and queer characters in literature. Anthologies such as *Changing Men and Masculinities in Latin America* (2003), *Entre hombres: masculinidades del siglo XIX en América* (2010), and *Modern Argentine Masculinities* (2013) have further expanded studies of masculinities in men in Latin America. If the development of the field has included the analysis of relationships between men and women (Gutmann, "Introduction" 6), class and ethnic intersections (Viveros Vigoya 36–37), as well as using sexuality studies and queer theory frameworks, women and trans* masculinities still remain understudied.

While in general women and trans* people have been denied space within narrowly defined masculinity discourses in war, I see that trans warriors and warrior women have managed to gain access to such spaces and discourses. They do so not only by performing different types of masculinities, but also by having their masculine attributes recognized by others. In a discussion of recognition theory, Paddy McQueen explains that mutual interaction is how humans make sense of themselves and others (5). In fact, he argues that being recognized often involves a new set of struggles because the subject cannot always predict or control the effects of the recognition (4). In the previous two chapters, I described some of the rituals of ideological recognition such as dressing and naming that provide opportunities for the existence of warrior women and trans warriors to be acknowledged by society. In this chapter I discuss how trans warriors and women warrior characters are also recognized when they interact with men characters in novels. By competing with men characters and refusing to inhabit submissive roles ordinarily granted to women and trans* men by the heterocispatriarchy, the characters I analyze present as strong a performance of masculinity as is necessitated by the masculine environments within which they act, including the context of war.

The trope of the war hero is part of a masculinity discourse linked to nationalist ideology. Although love for the homeland had already been evident in medieval epics, asking citizens to love their homeland during the French Revolution implied they must love the State. The French Revolution thus signaled the beginning of political modernity. In "Masculinity in Politics and War in the Age of Democratic Revolutions," Stefan Dudink and Karen Hagemann argue that the Revolution simultaneously inaugurated a new discourse on masculinity as people, especially men, became seen as resources for sovereignty and the self-determination of the nation (6). Masculinity was integrated into the construction of the nation-state in its myths of self-sacrificing heroes. By fighting for national independence, the stories of such masculine war heroes came to stand for the state itself.

While such masculinity discourses generally coincide with the emergence of political and military modernities, Dudink and Hagemann note that the relationship between nationalism and masculinity has not been homogenous (6). Men from diverse social backgrounds have inscribed themselves in nation-state armies in different ways. However, although "[v]alour, sacrifice, and martyrdom were of course not male prerogatives" (Horne 28), these heroic virtues ended up only associated with the heterosexual man (27–28). Discourses of heroic nationalism have almost always excluded women and trans* men along with any men who did not identify with the kinds of masculinity related to combat. Only certain types of men were expected to risk their lives on behalf of the State or their homeland and only the most masculine soldiers or martyrs would be commemorated.

The heroic virtues were also present in Latin America. For example, according to Domínguez-Ruvalcaba, Mexican paintings of the romantic period always depicted men as dominant, decisive, self-sacrificing heroes (*Modernity* 13). Domínguez-Ruvalcaba argues that modern masculinity in Mexico is a mixed of western gender norms and colonial and postcolonial processes (2). While strongly influenced by European standards, Mexico (and by extension Latin America) imitated, simulated, reproduced, and reappropriated these discourses to fit nationalistic projects. Sifuentes-Jáuregui discusses the masculinistic discourse that permeates national identities in Latin America and considers the highly gendered Latin American subject to be "almost always masculine, male, and heteronormative" (*Transvestism* 10). Such nationalist discourses have usually favored a very specific type of most-desired position. Even if the idea that a nation has only one explicit type of masculinity remains to be problematized, as Cortés argues (12), existing gendered constructions of the national subject imply that warrior women's and trans warriors' performances demonstrate that there are many possible masculinities in each nation and throughout Latin America. Emphasizing these other masculinities sheds light on an intellectual region that proposes gendered roles, embodiments, and identities of the kind that have previously been dismissed.

For the most part, canonical Latin American regionalist novels of the early to mid-twentieth century do not permit even temporarily transgressive warrior woman and trans warrior characters to embody the images and ideals of the nation during times of armed conflict. Only heterocissexual men warriors such as *llaneros* and *jagunços* were thought to be masculine enough to behave heroically in combat and thus symbolize a promising future. This type of man character is seen in a major regionalist novel, *Don Segundo Sombra*, published in 1924 by the Argentinian man writer Ricardo Güiraldes. Although this novel is not set in a context of armed combat, it still illustrates how the masculinity of the main character becomes central to the development of the nation. The narrator of the novel, Fabio, represents a successful mixture of urban cosmopolitanism, civilization, and education with rural masculin-

Chapter Three

ity. Fabio begins as an apprentice to a *gaucho,* a sort of cowboy or *llanero,* in Argentina's lowland area known as the Pampa. He receives a European education and becomes a wealthy landowner. Fabio thus resembles Santos, the white *llanero* who becomes cacique in *Doña Bárbara,* and up to a point Riobaldo, the orphan boy who becomes leader of the *jagunços* and a landowner in *Grande sertão: veredas.* An autobiographical text published around the same time as *Don Segundo* presents the same type of masculinity. In *El* águila *y la serpiente* (The Eagle and the Snake) (1928), Mexican author Martín Luis Guzmán depicts his life and how he becomes one of the major ideologues of the Mexican Revolution. While interacting with some of the major leaders of the Revolution, his position as an intellectual evokes the idea that his ideas are the ones bringing civilization to Mexico. Women are not part of his narrative, however. As Domínguez-Ruvalcaba points out, Guzmán's text recounts revolutionary history and the birth of the nation as developing out of contact between men bodies (*Modernity* 57). He mentions a *güera Carrasco* who accompanies the *güero Carrasco,* but does so only to demonstrate the greater visibility of the *güero* (*El águila* 109).

Fictional and historic characters who are men, such as Fabio, Santos, Riobaldo, and Guzmán, were seen to effect a dialectic reconciliation between two cultures or geographic areas that had traditionally been perceived as opposites. Women characters were occasionally able to represent this reconciliation, as is seen in *O quinze* (1930) by Rachel de Queiroz. The protagonist of *O quinze* is upper class, single, white, and behaves autonomously. Unlike trans warrior and warrior woman characters, she does not perform or affirm any masculinity, however. By working as a teacher and adopting a child, her character suggests that women can be independent from men without losing their femininity. Unlike the series of novels dealing with the topic of *mestizaje/mestiçagem,* Queiroz's novel implies that upper-class white women could embody positive values and promote progress in Latin America in the 1920s and 1930s, but only to the degree that they remained feminine and reproduced the ideological role of motherhood. Pintada, Doña Bárbara, and Diadorim break this ideology.

The discourses that came to embody the ideologies of the emerging nation-states of Latin America all referenced masculine heroism. Even when she seems to pervert womanhood, a masculinized woman can be permitted to behave heroically because virility is the goal of the revolutionary state (Domínguez-Ruvalcaba, *Modernity* 40). However, such heroism is always temporary. While it is true that trans warriors and warrior women appeared and achieved prominence during times of armed combat, especially during wars of independence, once the conflicts were over, heterocisnormative ideals of femininity and masculinity were once again enforced. People who were not perceived as sufficiently masculine because of their sexuality, gender performance, embodiment, identity or orientation, or socioeconomic status were no longer seen as the stuff of heroes. Tensions and negotiations concerning definitions of masculinity nevertheless provided openings for women and trans* men to access power in combat situations. Trans* men and women (and men who did not fit the traditional masculine standards) went to war and thereby challenged the presumed correspondences between gender, class, or race and the heroic virtues of valor, sacrifice, and martyrdom.

While there is no inherent reason for women or trans* men to present themselves as masculine if they are going to participate in combat, the modern association between men and war made masculinity a required characteristic of heroism and thus of trans warriors and warrior women. Teresa Corneja and Manuela Tinoco (fighting for the independence of Gran Colombia in nineteenth century) and Petra/Pedro Ruiz and Maria de la Luz Espinosa Barrera de Yautepec (fighting in the Mexican Revolution in the twentieth century) often cross-dressed or otherwise behaved like men in order to enlist as soldiers and obtain authority within the contexts of revolution. Hegemonic discourses in Mexico pressured warrior women and trans* men to abandon their man's attire and return to their earlier habits of femininity after the Revolution was over. However, it has been documented that some soldiers such as the Zapatista Colonel Amelio Robles Ávila continued wearing masculine clothes and behaving like a man after the war. His strategies of empowerment were similar to Diadorim's performance in *Grande sertão*. Also like the Diadorim character, Colonel Robles embodied the ideals of the macho revolutionary soldier, in that he was "courageous and daring, capable of responding to aggression immediately and violently, and skilled in handling arms and horses. His romantic relationships with women conformed to conventional models and reproduced the gender polarity of feminine and masculine roles" (Cano, "Unconcealable" 40). Robles's masculinity was neither subaltern nor marginalized, but instead constituted the most-desired position of the Mexican revolutionary.

His gender performance was quite complex. Robles's performance is transgressive in that it subverts the assumed subordination of women, trans* men, and subaltern masculinities during warfare. Robles's position as a men veteran of the Revolution is thus transgressive by any standard of heterocisnormative society. According to Cano, while it seems to subvert gender categories, it also strengthens the heteronormativity of the war context ("Unconcealable" 42). That is, Robles did not change the rules of masculinity and patriarchy, but reproduced them in his behaviors and relationships. However, I see that asking the trans* person or character to alter the patriarchy can be a strategy to return to cisgenderism. Critics ignore how gender identification (and visual passing) is embedded in the continuous hegemonic tension between cisgenderism and heterosexism.

It is in this space of constant negotiation conducted by the trans* community that I highlight the masculinities of the trans warrior and warrior woman characters analyzed in this book. Venkatesh explains that it is inaccurate to treat homosexual or queer men merely as subordinate to heterosexual men; rather, these masculinities decenter the traditional ones that are essential to sustaining the patriarchy (46). I agree with Venkatesh that masculinities are in fluid dialogue with the larger gender schemes of Latin America (57). My reading is also similar to Venkatesh's because I do not consider all masculinities to be subordinated to the types displayed by heterocissexual men. Trans warriors and warrior women are not just co-conspirators in hegemonic discourses and their masculinities do not merely comply with traditional gender hierarchies. As demonstrated in this chapter, when warrior woman and trans warrior characters—representing people whose masculinities are typically underrated—locate their masculinities in the most-desired positions of their contexts, they are actually hijacking traditional systems.

The marginality and subordination of women and trans* men have been reinforced throughout Latin American war history. The possibility that women and trans* masculinities might reach the peak of a masculine hierarchy is revolutionary. The stories of trans warrior and warrior woman characters discussed in this book reflect this issue. It is in their interaction and competition with men characters that they achieve socially prestigious positions, although they do so in different ways: Pintada gives orders and behaves like the men in her band; Doña Bárbara is a proficient *llanero* and *cacica* who manipulates the law; and Diadorim is an expert *jagunço* recognized as the best warrior amongst his peers. Each character enacts the most-desired position possible within contexts of conflict in Mexico, the Araucan Plains of Venezuela, and the Brazilian Backlands. Pintada, Doña Bárbara, and Diadorim not only interact with men as equals, they compete with them for the most-desired social positions that are normally reserved for masculine cis men.

To display most-desired positions, trans warriors and warrior women appropriate some of the characteristics of the war hero, such as bravery and sacrifice. They also wield phallic weapons such as knives effectively. Knives are often associated with vengeance, death, and sacrifice. Knives are also accessible objects, since they can be found in every kitchen. They stop being household implements and become weapons—daggers—when trans warriors and warrior women pick them up and use them to defend themselves or attack others. In the hands of a warrior woman and trans warrior, the phallic knife thus symbolizes departure from home and patriarchal rule. At the same time, trans* men and women have historically been denied swords, which are the traditional symbol of the warrior.

Warrior women and trans warriors demonstrating such qualities as bravery and fighting skills make it obvious that the discourse on masculine heroism and phallic objects is an artificial construction. As analyzed below, Pintada develops five strategies for empowering herself in her interactions with men characters in *Los de abajo,* but her strategies put her into a disempowered position and she disappears from the story. Doña Bárbara's masculinity and capacity for holding the reins of power are revealed in her relationships with men characters, but her performance of masculinity must be downplayed. Finally, in *Grande sertão*, Diadorim's masculinity is called into question by men characters at two specific moments, each of which showcases the most-desired position of masculinity in the context of armed conflict. The fact that the achievements of Pintada, Doña Bárbara, and Diadorim result in their being rejected and marginalized shows that the social contexts of the novels are permeated with heterocispatriarchal values. The disempowerments and erasures of these otherwise successful characters bring into view the underlying gender ideologies of these canonical Latin American novels. Even where masculinities are fluid, there remains resistance to allowing different masculinities to exist.

Pintada's Female Masculinity: Performing the Revolutionary

Irwin argues that the Mexican Revolution and indeed all wars are homosocial, homoerotic, gay spaces because they consist solely of men soldiers and masculinities. While wartime contexts are highly diverse, his main point is to note the wide variety of masculinities, including the gay fantasy, in the men's homosocial atmosphere of *Los de abajo* ("*Los de abajo*" 78). His analysis elucidates important issues of gender and sexuality, to which I contribute by foregrounding Pintada's masculinity in Azuela's novel.

Pintada's performance of masculinity is embedded in the power plays and gender dynamics of a band of Mexican revolutionaries. Clive Griffin, who produced one of the first thorough critical accounts of the Pintada character, argues that her behavior is more masculine than feminine throughout the scenes in which she appears in the novel. He considers behaviors such as shaking hands, drinking alcohol, and insulting others to be masculine (66). He also mentions her indifference to danger and even "her appearance as a revolutionary—she does not maintain feminine decorum by riding sidesaddle, but '*pierniabierta*' (151), at the same time a manly and a suggestive posture, and carries the revolutionary's typical cartridge belt and revolver" (66–67). Griffin seems to view Pintada's performance as negative, however. While I follow Griffin's list of masculine attributes and even add two more (i.e., leadership and manipulation of information) in order to understand Pintada's masculine gender performance, I explain how Pintada's performance avoids reproducing the gender binary. Even though the novel itself diminishes women who gain authority and enjoy drinking, Pintada's performance enriches our perspective on women involved in the Revolution.

I read Pintada's performance of masculinity as a means of empowerment and an attempt to improve her socioeconomic position. In the atmosphere of the revolutionary band dominated by

The Masculinities of Trans Warriors and Warrior Women

men, Pintada must stress her masculine qualities if she wants to be considered more than a camp follower and achieve class mobility. Unlike Colonel Robles Ávila, she is not a man, but she does try to achieve the status of a powerful person. She accomplishes this through five strategies of empowerment: exhibiting a masculine attitude, displaying courage, manipulating information to her own ends, demonstrating leadership abilities, and consuming alcohol as the men. These five strategies are apparent throughout her interactions with characters such as Demetrio (whom she wants to win over), Güero Margarito (whom she defends), and Pancracio (whom she gives orders). Although none of these characters sanction her entrance into their midst, by competing with them on their terms, Pintada establishes herself as a member of their group.

Masculine Attitude

Pintada's first strategy of empowerment involves demonstrating a masculine attitude of strength and superiority. As Pascale Baker explains, this attitude is made palpable from the first moment she enters the story (*Revolutionaries* 102). Meeting Demetrio for the first time, "Y tendió su mano hacia Demetrio y lo estrechó con fuerza varonil" ([Cátedra] 148). Pintada is no shy woman behaving in a traditionally feminine manner. The virile strength (*fuerza varonil*) of her handshake suggests a masculine attitude of personal autonomy and equality with men. Pintada greets Demetrio so boldly that he actually backs down from their first encounter: "[S]e miraron cara a cara como dos perros desconocidos que se olfatean con desconfianza. Demetrio no pudo sostener la mirada furiosamente provocativa de la muchacha y bajó los ojos" (147). Still, I see that more than being equal, Pintada positions herself as superior. Throughout the rest of the narrative, Pintada's angry outbursts and the directness and brusqueness with which she takes action break with the hegemonic standards of feminine behavior of her time.

Considering her context and status as a nobody, or a subaltern, Pintada uses what she has at hand not only to survive spaces dominated by men during war but to thrive in them. Baker observes that Pintada is not a simple follower of men; she excels at looting and even challenges Demetrio to kill her (*Revolutionaries* 101). As a result of her active transgression of normative gender rules, Baker considers Pintada's performance to constitute "gender as survival"

Chapter Three

(*Revolutionaries* 102). While the expression "gender as survival" aims to explain the character's ingenuity, I do not use it because it undermines the possibility of Pintada having her own agenda— she is more than surviving the Revolution because she thrives by looting and leading the band. The survival trope also ignores how Pintada challenges norms of femininity and masculinity.

Another example of Pintada's lack of normative femininity comes later in the story, when she fails to be perturbed by obscenities (148). She also fails to exhibit subordinate femininity and instead asserts an attitude of superiority over other members of the band. She orders some of them about as if they were servants, telling Pancracio, for example, to find her stockings or fetch alfalfa for her mare. The men are often discomfited by her masculine attitude. Demetrio drops his eyes rather than meet her as an equal. That they cannot tolerate her audacity implies that she is pursuing her own agenda as an independent agent.

When she boldly shakes hands with Demetrio, the person holding the highest military rank, Pintada's agenda becomes obvious to another member of the band, Güero Margarito, who comments: "Diablo de Pintada tan lista! ... ¡Ya te quieres estrenar general! ... " (147). Pintada is more alert and makes decisions with greater agility than Margarito. Later, he emulates her by joining Demetrio's band. Far from imitating men, then, men imitate this warrior woman's "masculine" behavior. Once accepted into the band, Pintada continues to reinforce her masculine attitude by accompanying the men wherever they go: "A las diez de la noche, Luis Cervantes bostezó muy aburrido y dijo adiós al güero Margarito y a la Pintada, que bebían sin descanso en una banca de la plaza" (164). She neither separates nor isolates herself from Demetrio's band. In another scene, "Demetrio, la Pintada y el güero Margarito habían dejado afuera sus caballos; pero los demás oficiales se habían metido brutalmente con todo y cabalgaduras" (169–70). As a member of the group, Pintada continually interacts with its officers, even accompanying them into brutal conflict, and takes on the same roles as her men peers.

Masculine Courage

Pintada's second strategy of empowerment is displaying courage in a traditional masculine way. This tactic mainly appears in scenes with Güero Margarito, who relies on her bravery to enhance his own confidence. Pintada exhibits bravery in a scene in which Margarito dares her not to move just before he shoots at his own reflection in a mirror: "La bala había pasado rozando los cabellos de la Pintada, que ni pestañeó siquiera" (157). Other critics have analyzed this scene as foreshadowing Margarito's later suicide (Murad 551), but it also showcases Pintada's courage. She is not intimidated by dangerous situations.

This scene establishes the relationship between the two characters and shows how they acquire prominence within the band. Margarito is able to project an image of himself as irreverent and fearless, while Pintada demonstrates that she is as brave as any other member of the band. Her calm in the face of danger is almost theatrical: refusing even to blink sustains a pose of bravery. This level of control and courage enables her to display the most-desired position of the Mexican revolutionary.

Pintada's physical courage and willingness to fight are also demonstrated in scenes in which she confronts the leader of the band much as would a man. She is the only character who ever directly confronts Demetrio. For example, at one point she prevents Demetrio from having sex with another woman (Cervantes's fiancée):

> La Pintada metió la pierna entre las de él, hizo palanca y Demetrio cayó de largo, fuera
> del cuarto.
> Se levantó furioso.
> —¡Auxilio! ... ¡Auxilio! ... ¡Que me mata! ...
> La Pintada cogía vigorosamente la muñeca de Demetrio y desviaba el cañón de su
> Pistola. (157)

This scene demonstrates her physical strength and courage. It also provides an example of her capacity to manipulate others when she prevents Demetrio from having sex with another woman and uses her strength to avoid being shot. Such manipulations are part of another strategy of empowerment.

Manipulation

Pintada's third strategy of empowerment involves manipulating information to achieve dominance within the band. In a 1975 essay entitled "The Purveyor of Truth," Jacques Derrida discusses the importance of controlling information to influence others and argues that holding information is a form of power traditionally based on the disempowerment of women. However, since information can shift from person to person, it need not be necessarily embedded in a circular chain of signifiers that keeps women separated from power (201). Anyone has the potential to take control of the dissemination of information (analogic to the phallus). Derrida's discussion of disseminative power allows one to see that, even though she is a woman, Pintada may be able to occupy a position of (masculine) power by controlling the phallus (information). She controls access to information in order to affect situations and other characters. For example, at one point she tells the other members of the band that they need not spend the night at an inn because, as revolutionary soldiers, they can choose any house to sleep in (149–50). Porfirio Sánchez argues that, in telling the men characters in the band that they can steal from others and live however they like because they are revolutionaries, Pintada represents material imperialism (183). Indeed, Pintada and the men in the band all profit from looting people's houses. By telling her peers how to behave, Pintada advances an agenda beyond obtaining material wealth, however. Her manipulations enable her to acquire a position of prominence in the band; she becomes a sort of guide to the men.

Pintada not only controls information, she knows how to disseminate it effectively. Griffin points out that the ability of Cervantes, the upper-class member of Demetrio's band, to communicate with the band is inferior to Pintada's. Cervantes's elegant language is unintelligible to the underdogs (*los de abajo*), while everyone understands her (67). I would add that she is not only intelligible but persuasive because she represents their wishes and desires. Because Pintada speaks the language of people who, like her, want to improve their socio-economic status, her discourse is welcomed and reproduced by those with which she interacts. D. Bradley indicates that "[i]n an action which recalls Hecate's ancient power of granting all gifts to men, La Pintada leads the rebels in their looting, urging them to see the Revolution as an opportunity to seize all" (99). This declaration transforms her from camp follower into their guide and leader, at least during raids. Thus, being aware of what occurs in the environment during the Revolution and being able to communicate privileged information effectively allows Pintada to achieve an important position in the band.

Leadership

Pintada's fourth strategy of empowerment, leadership, derives from the previous tactics. Her attitude of superiority and strength, combined with courage and control over information about her surroundings, enables Pintada not only to give orders, but also have them obeyed. She takes on a leadership role by directing the plundering of villages. Critics have considered her involvement in raiding and looting people's homes as indicative of the decadence and corruption of Demetrio's band. Griffin notes that the actions of Pintada and Margarito represent the worst excesses of the Revolution, which resulted in the corruption of innocent, honest peasants (67). While Griffin offers a valid point, I see that Pintada's corruption is a form of leadership that originates from her ability to recognize and seize opportunities provided by the chaotic atmosphere of the Mexican Revolution to improve her economic condition.

Baker argues that Pintada finds a place in an atmosphere in which women are unwelcome by imitating the conduct of her men counterparts ("In Search" 730–31; *Revolutionaries* 101–02). This critic suggests that there is not enough evidence in the novel to determine if Pintada's behavior is learned or innate (*Revolutionaries* 102). As I mentioned in Chapter 2, B. Christine Arce considers Pintada's power to be mostly imitative (*México's* 94). I complicate their critiques by pointing out that all performances of authority are simulacra, since the "real" references—to men's potency and honor—have been constructed so that only certain privileged heterocissexual men can access the most-desired positions of authority. This is one of the most significant differences in both my reading of Pintada (and characters like her) and readings by Baker and Arce: her behavior is not a mere imitation. Trans warrior and warrior woman characters are resourceful, transgressive, and strategic in positioning themselves in positions of authority. At the same time, the ways in which these characters have been downplayed demonstrates the heterocispatriarchal agenda to preserve a false order—the very simulacrum of authority.

By leading the plundering, Pintada inverts material values: people with possessions lose them while looters become owners of wealth. She and her bandmates acquire more empowered positions via this inversion, which might be more precisely characterized as reappropriation in that obtaining particular possessions associated with economic power alters the social image of their new owner (e.g., the dress Pintada dons, discussed in Chapter 1). Parra argues that Pintada "embodies the drive to overturn the usual social hierarchies, the immediate, unstoppable, and abrupt desire for the redistribution of wealth. Her actions are consonant with the struggle for power" (42–43). As leader of the looting raids, Pintada exemplifies the wishes of the poor to invert oppressive social and economic hierarchies. She is a nobody trying to be a somebody by appropriating material objects.

Pintada's leadership strategy provides her with gender empowerment in addition to socioeconomic empowerment. Specifically, leading the plundering allows her to (briefly) occupy a most-desired position in the revolutionary band. Her leadership role challenges traditional images of women in war and demonstrates that she is not merely a sex worker or a lover. The position is temporary, however, and eventually becomes undone by her fifth performance of masculinity: drinking alcohol.

Alcohol Consumption

Pintada's last strategy of empowerment involves consuming alcohol as an equal with the men in her band. Griffin considers her ability to drink as much alcohol as the men as a form of masculine behavior. Griffin's comment is rooted in the assumption that women do not ordinarily drink alcohol, or at least not as much as men do. I see Pintada's alcohol consumption as a social activity. By interacting with the men characters in the social sphere of drinking, she reveals that she is their equal and has the same attitude as her bandmates. She does not need to compete with them by drinking more alcohol than they do; drinking alcohol with them in itself demonstrates that there are no differences between her and the other members of the group.

Nevertheless, the men's attitudes to this aspect of her performance points to a double standard in the novel. When Pintada is with the men as an equal member of the band or even one of their leaders, she is permitted to drink as much as they do without being denigrated. Once she is no longer considered a member of the group, however, she is made to seem ridiculous. The men characters tire of her company because they envy her success at plundering and Demetrio becomes exasperated because she annoys Camila. Demetrio then expels Pintada from the band. When she reacts angrily by insulting everyone, he calls her *borracha* (drunk). Expelling Pintada and calling her *borracha* evokes the Mexican folk song (*corrido*) "La cucaracha": according to Arce this *corrido* is about an impudent drunken sex worker (*México's* 92). Initially a means of belonging and self-empowerment, the consumption of alcohol ends up signaling Pintada's disempowerment and dehumanization. Her revenge is to kill Camila.

Another warrior woman character who is treated as a *borracha* is depicted in Agustín Yáñez's novel, *Al filo del agua* (The Edge of the Storm) (1947). The novel is set in a sad, isolated town inhabited by very devout people. The story occurs during the Porfiriato, a time in which Catholic priests held tremendous power over village people, including the power to repress their sexuality. María, the niece of a priest, is one of the main characters. Unmarried and bored with her life, she and another woman (a widow) leave town to join the Revolution (at the finale of the story). The novel suggests that widows and single women joined the fight to escape the repressive social environment controlled by Catholic authorities. By leaving behind the black dress she used to wear, joining the revolutionaries, acquiring masculine elements such as a cartridge belt and rifle, and possibly drinking alcohol, María breaks with her previous image of modest, feminine sobriety. While her break with tradition demonstrates a commitment to national freedom and determination to achieve personal autonomy, the town demonizes her for becoming a warrior woman. The townspeople condemn any women who join the Revolution as "perdidas" [loose women] or "malvadas" [evil women] (239), which is similar to Elena Garro's novel about the Cristero War *Los recuerdos del porvenir* (Recollections of Things to Come) (1963). In the final scene of *Al filo*, gossiping townspeople imagine that María "también gritaba <¡Viva Madero!> como *borracha*, y que se iba a pelear por la justicia de los pobres; que llevaba cananas y carabina; que se quitó el vestido negro" (240; italics mine). Calling her a drunk and a loose woman diminishes the possibility that she is choosing to participate in the Revolution for moral or idealistic reasons.

Chapter Three

Disempowering the Warrior Woman

Pintada cannot continue being a leader of men; her superiority must be undermined to restore the naturalized order of gendered power. The disempowerment of warrior woman and trans warrior characters is often is linked to their transgressive behavior within the logic of the texts within which they appear. In Pintada's case, disempowerment is linked to transgressive consumption of alcohol. Her disempowerment also develops out of other characters' envy of her success, powers of manipulation, and leadership qualities. Having overcome various obstacles to leadership with her performance of masculinity to achieve a most-desired position, new obstacles arise for Pintada. She must continue to defend her position of power against the same men with whom she interacts and allies herself. After she is expelled from the band, the men cease to perceive her as a strong, rational, and persuasive person with valuable ideas. Even though she speaks everyone's language and can drink as much alcohol as any man, any complaint or rebelliousness on her part can now be ignored as coming from an incoherent drunk.

Pintada is the only character in the novel whose empowerment is not sufficient to secure her a place within the group. Once she loses her space in the group, the men devalue her (call her a drunk), lose interest in her sexual appeal (there are no more lustful comments), and treat her as a burden. In ethical terms, Pintada is no better nor worse than the other members of the band. Like Margarito, she assassinates innocent people (i.e., Camila). Like Cervantes, she lies and deceives people. Like Demetrio, she gets drunk and fails to adhere to the ideals of the Revolution. Yet she is the only member of the band exposed to public ridicule when she is expelled from the band: "Los soldados reían divertidísimos" (183). Regardless of how evil or cruel the other members of the band are, they are not mocked in such a way in the novel because, unlike Pintada, they do not challenge gender norms and hierarchy.

Although Pintada loses her position of leadership and everything else she has achieved, I observe that she retains masculine strength and courage. As a warrior woman, she demonstrates that she knows how to defend herself even after she has been expelled from masculine society. For example, she fights to save herself after Demetrio orders that she be put to death for having killed Camila: "[d]os soldados se arrojaron sobre la Pintada que, esgrimiendo el puñal, no les permitió tocarla" (183). Her skills as a fighter corroborate that her role in society is not merely sexual. By defending herself with a dagger, Pintada shows that she has appropriated another element of phallic power. As noted earlier, the knife symbolically represents the phallus in many cultures. Drawing the dagger again allows Pintada to occupy a locus of power (or at least self-sufficiency) for a moment, but then she abdicates this position: "se adelantó, entregó su arma, irguió el pecho y dejó caer los brazos" (183). In the end, Pintada relinquishes her power to Demetrio and even asks him to kill her. She chooses visible disempowerment. She poses surrender. Demetrio does not kill Pintada, however; he simply tells her to leave. Chris Harris argues that killing her would acknowledge her equality to men (661). That is, Demetrio does not kill her because of her inferior gender status. I add a different perspective that allows for two readings of her actions. In asking him to kill her, Pintada is continuing to demonstrate manipulative and masculine tactics. Either she is displaying heroic courage or she is cleverly manipulating Demetrio to her own ends. On the one hand, it takes courage to lay down her weapon and present herself as willing to die. On the other, it requires social acumen to challenge a man to break the social taboo of killing a woman. By voluntarily surrendering the power of the phallus and putting herself back into the position of submissive womanhood, Pintada manipulates the rules of patriarchal society in order to survive. As Baker points out, not only does Pintada go unpunished for assassinating Camila, she survives the Revolution ("In Search" 726).

In Pintada's case, a cis woman occupying a most-desired position challenges the structures of patriarchal society. Warrior women and trans warriors who reveal the artificiality of the masculinities pyramid must be displaced from their positions of power. While she survives physically, surrendering her power ultimately marginalizes her and she disappears from the narrative. She cannot retain her position of power because she cannot change the underlying patriarchal rules and gender categories of her society. Because Doña Bárbara, discussed next, is more adept at manipulating the rules, she establishes a stronger position and maintains her power for a longer period of time than does Pintada.

Chapter Three

Doña Bárbara's Female Masculinity: Performing the *Cacica*

Studying how Doña Bárbara interacts with men characters in performing masculinity provides insight on the functioning of masculinities discourses in early-twentieth-century Venezuela. Before analyzing Doña Bárbara's interactions with men characters, I must emphasize that in addition to her clothing (discussed in Chapter 1), Doña Bárbara's masculinity is associated with four qualities in the context of the novel: *llanero* skills, use of weapons, bitter affect, and hatred of maternity. I see that these characteristics reveal different aspects of the social context of the Venezuelan Plains and of Doña Bárbara's claim to power as *cacica*. Nonetheless, her access to power is fraught, as I propose that she is represented as the undesired *mestiza* in the novel. I also argue that the diversity of masculinities implied by Doña Bárbara's leadership and power as *cacica* is lost once Santos becomes the cacique.

Doña Bárbara's masculinity is first of all displayed by her ability to work right alongside men. She is a skilled *llanero* who gives other *llaneros* orders: "[D]irigía personalmente las peonadas, manejaba el lazo y derribaba un toro en plena sabana como el más hábil de sus vaqueros…" (29). By lassoing, knocking down, taming, and castrating cattle, she not only fulfills all the requirements of being a *llanero*, she demonstrates that she is one of the most accomplished *llaneros* in the area. Her skills are so well-developed that Carmelito, one of Santos's employees, comments rather admiringly about her manliness: "Lo que pasa es que esa mujer es de pelo en pecho, como tienen que serlo todos los que pretenden hacerse respetar en esta tierra" (52). Doña Bárbara does not really have hair on her chest, but her capacity to conduct extremely difficult work requiring great skill enables her to project the kind of virile image that most commands respect in the area. She is not imitating these skills in an attempt to pass as a *llanero*, she is an outstanding *llanero* in her own right. She thus represents a type of most-desired position within her social environment.

Doña Bárbara's performance of masculinity is further strengthened by her use of weapons. She is described as "…no se quitaba de la cintura la lanza y el revólver, ni los cargaba encima sólo para intimidar" (29). Carrying a dagger and a gun allows Doña Bárbara to threaten others or inspire fear in them, just as Pintada does

The Masculinities of Trans Warriors and Warrior Women

when she brandishes her knife. Wielding these two elements of phallic power confirms her masculine authority.

Doña Bárbara's bitter affect signals another kind of masculine strength or toughness, albeit one engendered by trauma. After being raped by a gang of men, Doña Bárbara does not fall apart. Instead, the narrator declares, she hardens herself until "[y]a sólo rencores podía abrigar en su pecho y nada la complacía tanto como el espectáculo del varón debatiéndose entre las garras de las fuerzas destructoras" (24–25). Negative affect such as bitterness, hatred, or the desire for revenge has the power to lead subjects to destroy themselves or find creative ways to achieve success (Ahmed 201). Doña Bárbara is not destroyed following the violent rape, but instead channels her feelings into establishing a dominant position in patriarchal society, a place wherein she will no longer be vulnerable. From this position of safety and power, she then enjoys watching men obey her orders and law.

Her embittered masculine affect correlates to her despising maternity. She views pregnancy as a sign that a man has won the war against women: "un hijo en sus entrañas era para ella una victoria del macho" (26). Although she did give birth to a daughter, she does not care for her. Doña Bárbara's refusal to reproduce the traditional feminine role of motherhood is treated as masculine and even monstrous by the novel's narrator. Her rejection of the submissive role signified by maternity is denigrated in the novel because it subverts the normative gender binary and, by extension, hegemonic social values.

Dominating Men

These four aspects of Doña Bárbara's complex performance of masculinity are revealed even further in her interactions with men characters. The primary characteristic that contributes to Doña Bárbara's performance of *cacica* is her socioeconomic position. Owning the most land, having the most money, and making the law (creating rules and enforcing punishment) allows her to dominate the region and embody another of the most-desired positions available in the Araucan and Venezuelan social context: that of cacique. As *cacica*, Doña Bárbara claims a superior social position over most of the men with whom she interacts. Her performance

Chapter Three

of masculinity is most fully manifested when she interacts with subordinate men such as Lorenzo, Balbino, Melquíades, Mister Danger, and her employees. The reactions of such men to her dominant status validate her performance and position of power throughout the novel. I propose that her interactions with them also expose the complexity of the masculine hierarchy of the Venezuelan Plains in the early twentieth century.

The main characters subordinated to Doña Bárbara are her employees, the *llaneros* at El Miedo. They respect her because of her power, strength, and the fact that, as noted above, as "ella también sabía, y mucho mejor que Luzardo, enlazar un toro y castrarlo en plena sabana" (124). They also fear her because they believe she has the powers of a witch. For example, she claims that she sees Santos's image in a glass of water she is about to drink. The narrator notes that this is a way of manipulating her employees: "[e]ra, en efecto, una de las innumerables trácalas de que solía valerse doña Bárbara para administrar su fama de bruja y el temor que con ello inspiraba a los demás" (46). Balbino, one of her employees who is ignorant about her religion and traditions, believes her, but Melquíades, another one of her employees, does not. Melquíades knows about indigenous culture and religion and, according to the narrator, can see she is lying. The narrator aligns with Melquíades in discounting her supernatural abilities.

By showing how she manipulates her image of power, the narrator suggests that her authority is not as hegemonic as it seems at the beginning of the novel. While Doña Bárbara seems to dominate her employees as successfully as any man cacique, her feudal relationship with them is characterized by power conflict (Lavou Zoungbo 215). As Victorien Lavou Zoungbo argues, although Doña Bárbara successfully establishes a hierarchy with herself at the top of the pyramid, her subordinates undermine rather than support her position of power. Since she considers them expendable, her employees seem to feel no compunction about robbing and betraying her. The hierarchy she establishes is more complicated than it would be for a man cacique, since some of those she dominates consider themselves her equal (i.e., as her lover or accomplice). The logic of patriarchy does not permit a woman to remain in possession of a traditional cacique power system.

Doña Bárbara not only controls men financially and through fear, she also uses sex to dominate them. In early twentieth century in Latin America, having sex out of wedlock disempowered women, even when sex was forced on them (e.g., the gang-rape of Doña Bárbara). However, Doña Bárbara subverts the traditional gender connotations associated with sex by using sex to empower herself while disempowering men. Her beauty and sexuality enable her to manipulate men such as Balbino and give them a false sense of privilege. Allowing his masculinity to be subordinated to her by becoming her lover does not much benefit Balbino. In fact, she makes him go work for Santos because she needs an "instrumento suyo en el campo enemigo" (29). Even though Balbino is ostensibly independent from Doña Bárbara because he conducts side-jobs such as stealing cattle and assassinating Carmelito, his performance of masculinity is subordinated to hers. She has her other men kill him, then continues to use him after his death by claiming he was responsible for Melquíades's murder. Balbino is thus subordinated to Doña Bárbara throughout the novel.

Melquíades is another of Doña Bárbara's expendable employees. Initially, she acknowledges him as her most loyal man, but she subordinates his valuable masculinity by turning him into her accomplice. She has him steal cattle and then sends him to kill Santos. Even though he fails to do so and is instead killed by Santos's employee, Pajarote, Melquíades represents another weapon in Doña Bárbara's arsenal of intimidation.

Mister Danger benefits more from his relationship with Doña Bárbara than do her employees such as Balbino and Melquíades. Mister Danger becomes her accomplice by keeping her assassination of Colonel Apolinar a secret. Mister Danger is not depicted as Doña Bárbara's superior or enemy; rather, she rewards him with a piece of land. Because this character is given an English name ("Mister Danger") in the original text, he is thought to represent U.S. imperialism and exploitation of the Venezuelan Plains by the U.S. Nevertheless, he does not threaten her power because, even though he is white like Santos, his agenda is not to civilize the Plains but to take advantage of whatever situation arises. I see that his imperialistic masculinity, in collusion with hers, reveals the complexity of the hierarchy of masculinities that appear in the novel.

The character of Lorenzo Barquero shows a subordinated masculinity that should have been located at the top of the gender hierarchy of Plains society. He is a landowner whose masculinity, like Balbino's, becomes subordinated to Doña Bárbara's following their sexual relationship. His weakness contrasts with her strong image as Doña Bárbara inverts their traditional roles, first by taking his land and then by setting herself up as an independent, powerful *cacica*. Meanwhile, he takes on the role of parent because Doña Bárbara does not care about their daughter, Marisela. Lorenzo's death, presumably because of alcoholism, and Doña Bárbara's accusation that Balbino murdered Melquíades effectively eliminates "the 'ex-hombres' whose sexual submissiveness to Doña Bárbara has constructed their gender identities in terms of troubling (from the narrator's point of view), non-conventional masculinities" (Henighan 42).

Maria Moura, the warrior woman character in Rachel de Queiroz's novel *Memorial de Maria Moura*, follows a similar strategy to Doña Bárbara but takes things even further when it comes to sustaining her autonomous power. When her lover, a man named Cirilo, brags about his influence over her, she ends their sexual-romantic relationship and then has him murdered. When his bragging puts her in a subordinate position and destroys her image as a powerful *capanga* (Backlands bandit) leader, Moura does not allow her carefully constructed position of power to disappear by giving way to the person she loves. Instead, she retains her sexual autonomy and empowerment as a warrior woman, albeit a criminal one. By contrast, Doña Bárbara's power is undone by her complex relationship with the one man she is unable to dominate, the saint-like Santos. Although Lorenzo and Santos seem to share many characteristics (both are educated urbanites from the upper classes and both are white *llaneros* from the same family), she is unable to seduce and take advantage of Santos as she does Lorenzo, Apolinar, and Balbino. Instead, Santos "tames" her and she changes herself to please him. In the end, Santos's idealized masculinity negates her masculinity as a woman warrior.

The Ideal Masculinity for Civilizing Barbarity

Doña Bárbara's love object does not perform a most-desired position, but embodies an idealized masculinity as an upper class, handsome, white, virile, *llanero*, and heterocissexual man. Santos's masculine skills, displayed when he tames a wild horse at the *doma*, prove he is a "true man" (Magnarelli, "Woman" 15). Santos's masculinity is superior to that of the other men with whom Doña Bárbara interacts because he does not have "ni la sensualidad repugnante que desde el primer momento vio en las miradas de Lorenzo Barquero, ni la masculinidad brutal de los otros, y al hacer esta comparación se avergonzaba de haberse entregado a amantes torpes y groseros, cuando en el mundo había otros como aquél, que no podían ser perturbados con la primera sonrisa que se les dirigiera" (127). The masculinities of Doña Bárbara's lovers are derided as brutal, repulsively sensual, or weak. Since Santos is the only character Doña Bárbara cannot treat as an inferior, she grows to admire and eventually fall in love with him.

Love is portrayed in traditional terms in Gallegos's novel: a gender transgressive woman in love surrenders herself to her love object, a heterocissexual man, and thus loses her own undesirable masculinity. According to the narrator, true love makes Doña Bárbara feel the need to give herself to Santos and belong to him (126). However, Claudette Rosegreen-Williams argues that Doña Bárbara's romantic affection for Santos is not a true feeling of love, but that she "is immediately attracted to Santos because she recognizes a superior power in him, his machismo. She feels an awe which, though it might translate into an affirmation of the superiority of civilization, is expressed as her perception of his superiority as male" (293). Moreover, love in the novel is constructed in terms of superiority and domination versus submission, which correlates to unequal gender and socioeconomic positions.

In this context, masculinity is positive only as long as it describes (cis) men. As Magnarelli shows, the adjectives such as masculine and virile that are used to praise Santos seem absurd when applied to Doña Bárbara. In obedience to the hegemonic expectations of gender behavior, Santos complements his image as a civilized and educated man with that of the macho *llanero*, while "it is doña Bárbara's skill at the *doma* which makes her most suspect" (Magnarelli, "Woman" 15). This correspondence between sex and gender expectations explains why Doña Bárbara's performance of masculinity is devalued and made to represent backwardness, deviation, and barbarity in the novel.

Doña Bárbara's deviancy is further represented by the gender and racial transgressions of her physical appearance, of which the narrator continually reminds the reader. The narrator describes her as a woman whose beauty enables her to intimidate and manipulate men. Her beauty is rendered a kind of dangerous strength: "el imponente aspecto del marimacho le imprimía un sello original a su hermosura: algo de salvaje, bello y terrible a la vez" (29). While her powerful butch image is so beautiful that it must be admired, it is also transgressive, and so is devalued according to the heterocispatriarchal standard of the time. I contend that Doña Bárbara's beauty is not only perceived negatively because of its seductiveness, it is seen as a threat because of its gender-transgressiveness. The butch aspects of her appearance do not undermine her physical beauty. The intersection of two spaces that traditionally must be separated (beauty and gender transgression) turns out to be appealing and attractive. Therefore, her physical attractiveness must be evaluated as negative, even monstrous, within the novel so that her character does not confound the rules that separate binary genders and sexual orientations. Once she is treated as a monster, she no longer represents a temptation to men, and thus ceases to threaten the heterocispatriarchy.

An even more "monstrous" aspect of Doña Bárbara's character is that she is *mestiza*, a product of racial mixing. According to Rosegreen-Williams, Gallegos's perspective on race stemmed from the nineteenth century (281). She argues that "it is not fortuitous that Gallegos has made his prime symbol of barbarism specifically *mestiza*, for by so doing, he has established that race, as much as environment, is the determinant of barbarism, and more specifically that barbarism is to be directly attributed to the Indian heritage" (282–83). Gallegos articulates a racist ideology to construct a thesis about civilization versus barbarity in which barbarity (including people of mixed racial ancestry) must be made to disappear or be marginalized (283). This racist ideology, which I explain next, united with a patriarchal vision of gender, explains why Doña Bárbara's performance of masculinity is depicted so negatively in the novel and why she falls in love with Santos and gives away her power.

Even if Doña Bárbara is rejected because of her gender transgressions, as I have been arguing, she is also excluded because her transgressive performance intersects with variables such as ethnicity, religion, class, skin color, and family origin. I emphasize the intersection of gender with race and ethnicity because it stems from Venezuela's politics of immigration and Gallegos's own social context. In the nineteenth century, Latin American countries such as Venezuela began favoring European immigration as a way to li-

The Masculinities of Trans Warriors and Warrior Women

terally "whiten" the population, either by increasing the number of Europeans or by promoting interracial marriage. This concept of whitening through immigration originated in traditional aesthetic ideals and scientific racism developed in nineteenth century in Europe and the United States. Ever since Venezuela became an independent nation in the early nineteenth century, the topic of European immigration has been central to discussions about populating large territories, even though Venezuela received a small number of European immigrants compared to Argentina and Brazil. For instance, during Antonio Guzmán Blanco's administrations (1873–77, 1879–84, and 1886–88), immigration politics consistently aimed to whiten the entire Venezuelan population and increase the proportion of whites in the population. Intellectuals and Venezuelan elites also supported European immigration with the specific purpose of promoting interracial marriages. These elites believed that, over time, interracial marriage would lead to the eradication of indigenous, Black, and *mestizo* populations and other undesirable ethnic and racial groups. According to their prognostics, in a few generations or centuries, the entire population would become white (Wright 2, 54). At that time, they did not know about gene pools or the relationship between genotype and phenotype with regard to skin color; they simply assumed the superiority and endurance of a "white" race.

If miscegenation (*mestizaje/mestiçagem*) aimed to develop a more European society in terms of skin color, the whitening agenda also comprised cultural values and traditions linked to Europe. In 1929, the same year *Doña Bárbara* was published, Venezuelan intellectual Laureano Vallenilla Lanz used the expression "social race" to refer to diverse nationalities that comprised Spanish American countries (Wright 83). According to Winthrop R. Wright, Vallenilla Lanz implied that it was culture and not race that would decide the future of a nation (83). In this sense, the idea of "social race" seemed to give priority to values that had no relationship to skin colors. However, because the cultures of white Europe were sought and respected, racism was reproduced.

I see in Vallenilla Lanz's concept an example of an important factor in Doña Bárbara's exclusion in Gallegos's novel. She characterizes an undesired culture because she represents a specific notion of *mestizaje*. Although the man who raped her mother was white, he does not participate in her life and does not play the role of father to her (21). Her mother and an old Baniba native named Eustaquio raised Doña Bárbara, so in cultural and ethnic terms, she is more indigenous than European. Throughout the novel, she holds on to her indigenous religion, cultural practices, and worldview. Even though she climbs the socioeconomic and power ladder, is physically beautiful according to traditional European standards, and is a key political and economic player in the Arauca region, her *mestizaje* status remains undesirable. Unlike her daughter Marisela, the preferred *mestiza* in the novel, Doña Bárbara never embodies the evolved miscegenated stage that Venezuelan elites desired for their country (Marisela discussed further in the next chapter).

While Doña Bárbara does become a warrior woman and achieves most-desired positions in her society, the results of her performance show that racist patriarchal rules are always exerted to return such individuals to their lower place in the hierarchy. The logic of the novel requires that Doña Bárbara lose her masculine power so that Santos can project himself as the kind of masculine heterocissexual man meant to civilize Venezuela's Plains. Just as the Plains are tamed by civilized values in the novel, she is tamed by Santos and her love is laid out in terms of possession and submission. Her transformation becomes evident when the narrator says that Doña Bárbara wants to belong to Santos just like "las reses que llevaban grabado a fuego en los costillares el hierro altamireño" (126), even though earlier she had claimed to be disgusted by the idea of any man calling her his woman (26).

This conservative gesture is augmented by the fact that Santos's masculine image is neither new nor transgressive. He symbolically represents all the values of the traditional upper class. The novel disguises this conservative ideology by presenting Santos as something better than just another cacique like Lorenzo. Although he shares many demographic characteristics with Lorenzo, he never falls for the "barbarity" represented by the loving Doña Bárbara. Instead, by reuniting the divided land and promising to bring progress to the Araucan Plains, Santos stops Doña Bárbara's cheating and murdering and ends her *cacica* power. He thus represents the idealized hegemonic white upper-class masculinity of the Plains cacique—a role that Doña Bárbara is not permitted to fully embody because of her female sex, skin color, origins, and beliefs. As the novel progresses, the narrator makes Doña Bárbara come to represent the socially approved role of submissive, good womanhood, the desired image of all the other women characters in the novel.

Only an enlightened man such as Santos, who has the mission of civilizing barbarity, can provoke such a "positive" change in Doña Bárbara. Santos's ideal masculinity is merely hypothetical, however. The novel ends with the promise that he will bring civilization to the Plains, but he is not depicted actually doing so. In a way, Doña Bárbara's masculinity must disappear or be marginalized so that the civilizing of the Plains can begin. Doña Bárbara's performance of masculinity comes to an end along with her disempowerment and her transgressive subversion of the masculine hierarchy is erased while Santos is empowered.

Although the narrator devalues Doña Bárbara's performance of masculinity, I highlight one aspect cannot be deconstructed: she remains an expert *llanero*. Since her *llanero* skills cannot be denied, she has to choose to relinquish them. Doña Bárbara must sacrifice her masculinity. She even says she wants to be different: "– Seré otra mujer – decíase una y otra vez. Ya estoy cansada de mí misma y quiero ser otra y conocer otra vida" (197). That is, she still knows how to lasso a horse or castrate a bull, but she chooses not to once she has been "tamed" by Santos. Her new image draws closer to that of Marisela (her daughter, whom Santos loves). The warrior woman character must lose her masculinity in order for "modern" Venezuelan society to develop. The rebellious, masculine woman warrior must subdue herself to the "superior" man just as all women must submit to the rules of patriarchal society and all non-white peoples must submit to European dominance.

As in *Los de abajo*, the warrior woman character is disempowered and then disappears from the narrative. Instead of being expelled from masculine society as Pintada was, Doña Bárbara leaves voluntarily. The ending of the novel implies that she goes on living, but at the margins of society, perhaps in a bog or on a river. Even when a warrior woman willingly subdues herself to social conventions, she cannot reinsert herself into normative society. She must withdraw from the center to make way for new generations of women who, ironically, continue to embody traditional values. After this usurping, indigenous, butch, *mestiza cacica* disappears, Santos and Marisela are united and they rebuild the old ranch (Altamira). The plurality of masculinities (subordinated landowners, lover accomplices, expendable employees) made possible under the *cacica*'s regime is reduced again to a simple pyramid of a white dominant man (Santos) and his obedient subordinates (employees on the ranch). Diverse masculinities, including Doña Bárbara's transgressive masculinity, are completely erased by the end of the novel.

A similar process of erasure of diversity occurs in *Grande sertão*. I argue that many forms of masculinity seem to be in evidence until the man protagonist, Riobaldo, establishes himself as the great bearer of the most-desired position. The effort he must exert to assert his dominance suggests that the presence of a trans warrior character (Diadorim) threatens his positioning.

Diadorim's Trans* Masculinity: Performing the Hero Warrior

Diadorim's performance of various masculinities in *Grande sertão*, including the most-desired one of being the greatest *jagunço* or warrior, indicates the non-exclusive nature of gender dynamics. Backlands literature treats *jagunços* as heroic descendants of medieval knights, modern day Robin Hoods that bring justice to the area, while other depictions dismiss *jagunços* as bandits that threaten the social order. Antonio Cândido explains that the *jagunços* in Guimarães Rosa's novel are socially positioned within lineages of war and adopt medieval standards of courage and bravery in following their leaders into armed combat (*Tese* 119). They are warriors hired by a "Colonel" rather than ordinary "bandits" (as the term *jagunço* is sometimes translated into English): "Mas o jagunço de Guimarães Rosa não é salteador; é um tipo híbrido entre capanga e homem-de-guerra. O verbo que os personagens empregam para descrever a sua atividade é 'guerrear,' qualificando-se a si mesmos de guerreiros" (119). In this way, the *jagunço*'s role is to fight, to be a warrior; Diadorim fulfills this role perfectly.

Fighting skills not only make *jagunços* warriors, they confer dignity on them: "[s]er jagunço torna-se, além de uma condição normal no mundo-sertão (onde 'a vontade se forma mais forte que o poder do lugar'), uma opção de comportamento, definindo um certo estado do ser naquele espaço" (Cândido, "Ser jagunço" 66). To be a *jagunço* is to have a masculine life defined by clear rules of hierarchy. Diadorim's performance challenges this traditional view of masculinity and of cis men in the *jagunço* world. Additionally, this trans warrior character emphasizes the positive aspect of the *jagunços* by aligning himself with justice and ethical values. Vera Lúcia Andrade argues that *jagunços* follow a code of honor (law) that differs from that of the government (496). Diadorim not only follows this code of honor, he pushes Riobaldo to follow it as well.

Diadorim's superior fighting ability locates him in the most-desired position of the *jagunço* world depicted in the novel, just as Doña Bárbara's skills do in the *llanero* world. According to Riobaldo, Diadorim is one of the greatest warriors in the Brazilian Backlands: "Eh, ele sabia ser homem terrível. Suspa! O senhor viu onça: boca de lado e lado, raivável, pelos filhos? Viu rusgo de touro no alto campo, brabejando; cobra jararacussú emendando sete botes estalados; bando dôido de queixadas se passantes, dando febre no mato? E o senhor não viu o Reinaldo guerrear!" (174). Other men characters perceive Diadorim as a man largely because his conduct fulfills the requirements of being a *jagunço* in their world.

Riobaldo seems to focus on describing Diadorim's masculine behavior (i.e., physical courage and ferocity) to compensate for his rather feminine features, which normatively indicate weakness. *Jagunço* constructions of masculinity conform to a gender discourse strongly opposed to women and gay men. Sifuentes-Jáuregui states that the Latin American cultural imaginary treats gay men merely as bodies playing the women's role (*Transvestism* 47). Gay men are seen as feminine and effeminacy in men is read as femininity. Among the *jagunços*, any association between men and femininity or effeminacy is considered inappropriate or wrong; this presents a problem for Diadorim. At first glance, he does not appear strong or masculine enough to do men's work: "Um ou dois, dos homens, não achavam nele jeito de macheza, ainda mais que pensavam que ele era novato" (175). Diadorim's slight stature, age, and delicate features leave his masculinity open to being challenged by any of the men with whom he interacts. My analysis of Diadorim's performance in this section thus focuses on how he demonstrates that he is more masculine and stronger than the men characters with whom he interacts and who attempt to undermine his masculinity.

Two episodes in which Diadorim's masculinity is challenged reveal the complexity of his gender performance. In each situation, he is forced to assert his masculinity or confirm his reputation as a macho *jagunço*. For Domínguez-Ruvalcaba, following Octavio Paz, the macho is the one who dominates other men and employs violence (*Translating* 90). In his analysis of the emergence of the figure of the *nordestino* (man from the Northeast) in Brazil in the 1930s, Durval Muniz de Albuquerque Júnior argues that the entrance of the modernization project, as evidenced in changes in gender roles and the decadence of the agrarian elite, was perceived by intellectuals as a feminization of the region and, hence, as a masculinity crisis (204, 226). Intellectuals responded to the crisis by emphasizing the "masculine" characteristics of the *nordestino* in order to affirm the region's positive values in the national scenario. The virility of the *nordestino* then became his most distinguishable feature (217). Masculinity was associated to defeating other men in a competition of wits or strength (220). This is how Diadorim acts in order to assert his identity. In defending his masculine heterosexuality, he performs different masculinities, including posing as a feminine gay man while being seen as a masculine heterosexual man. His strategies reveal that masculinity is not a uniform discourse independent of femininity and thus challenge the binary gender division of patriarchal culture.

Masculinity of Youth

The first affront to Diadorim's masculine heterosexuality occurs when he and Riobaldo meet for the first time. They are not yet fourteen years old when Diadorim invites Riobaldo to accompany him on a canoe ride on the river. While they take a break from rowing to rest on the bank, a young mulatto man (around 18–20 years old) passes by and asks them what they are doing; he then makes an obscene gesture implying they were having sex (124). Confronted with this accusation, Riobaldo answers that they are not doing anything dirty (*sujice*). Diadorim responds differently, as Riobaldo remembers: "Mas, o que eu menos esperava, ouvi a bonita voz do menino dizer: – 'Você, meu nego? Está certo, chega aqui …' A fala, o jeito dele, imitavam de mulher … " (124). When the young man approaches them, Diadorim avenges the insult to their adolescent masculine heterosexuality by pressing the point of a small knife into his thigh.

Several images emerge in this first affront to Diadorim's masculinity: he is seen as a masculine heterocissexual adolescent by Riobaldo, he is seen as a gay (homosexual) youth by the stranger, and he temporarily poses as an effeminate gay man. Cutting another (taller, older, and Black) man with a knife confirms Diadorim's masculinity, since violence and courage are considered antithetical to homosexuality and femininity/effeminacy in his society. That Diadorim can imitate some of the characteristics of femininity traditionally associated with women in patriarchal societies does not mean Diadorim is projecting the image of a woman. His posing never leads Riobaldo to doubt Diadorim's gender and gender identity. Diadorim only mimics the voice and behavior of a feminine woman as part of his temporary pose as a weak, effeminate gay man. As Sylvia Molloy argues, the highly visible tactic of posing creates a space for agency, which in this episode requires avenging an affront against his heterosexual masculinity. I argue that Diadorim's pose creates a space for agency in that it puts the accuser off guard and draws him within reach of retaliation. Diadorim reaffirms his masculinity and heterosexuality in this very theatrical way in order to dissipate any doubt about his masculinity. By posing as an effeminate young man, allowing the accuser to get closer, and then attacking him with a knife, Diadorim ratifies his own and Riobaldo's masculinity and heterosexuality.

Subverting the accusation of homosexuality here blurs traditional gender barriers. Like Pintada and Doña Bárbara, Diadorim wields a phallic element—a knife—to restore his dignity and confirm his masculine reputation. Rosenfield argues that Diadorim's knife symbolizes repression of sexual eroticism (as a woman) and valuing of the destruction of war (as a man), and thus reflects his ambivalence as a "man/woman" character (382). I take a different position. When warrior women and trans warriors such as Diadorim and Pintada successfully manipulate phallic weapons such as knives, it does not represent repression of their sexuality, but rather their abilities to access traditional masculine power. In Diadorim's case, wielding the knife facilitates his seamless identification as a masculine heterosexual man. Whereas posing is visible and temporary, his visual passing is a permanent strategy that must remain invisible. He is not the cross-dresser or *travesti* who seeks visibility and recognition. Diadorim's visual passing must not be recognized or discovered if he is to be considered man and occupy the most-desired position.

Diadorim is dressed in masculine attire and is performing heterosexual masculinity when he suddenly changes his voice and gestures to pose briefly as an effeminate gay man. I suggest that his manipulation indicates agency. He deliberately changes how his body and sexual orientation are perceived to suit his needs in the moment, while following the social conventions of masculinity. Diadorim's manipulations and posing call into question the idea of identity as inherently self-sufficient, recognizable, and stable. They also indicate the lack of stability of gender categories in the Backlands. In order to find a space of power and respect, Diadorim must modify his appearance and gender performance. The necessity to pose and manipulate reveals that the performance and identity of the masculine heterosexual *jagunço* is constantly under challenge.

This episode exposes different aspects of the masculine heterosexuality expected of men in the Backlands. After cutting the young man with his knife, Diadorim tells Riobaldo: "Carece de ter coragem. Carece de ter muita coragem" (124–25). Diadorim is giving Riobaldo a lesson on how to behave courageously: to face fear and confront challenges to their heterosexuality and masculinity. As Benedito Nunes argues, "é Diadorim menino quem introduz Riobaldo no mundo maravilhoso e áspero do sertão" (159). Adair de Aguiar Neitzel follows Nunes in stating that "É Diadorim quem viabiliza a entrada de Riobaldo no mundo masculino no qual a coragem é o atributo de maior valor" (52). While I agree with Neitzel and Nunes that Diadorim facilitates Riobaldo's entrance into a masculine social sphere, Diadorim is not just teaching Riobaldo how to be courageous, he is demonstrating how to establish and defend masculinity and heterosexuality. These skills are required for appropriate functioning in the heteropatriarchal masculinity of the *jagunço* world. At this key moment, Diadorim becomes Riobaldo's guide and protector and begins to initiate Riobaldo into the *jagunço* world. This episode thus represents a rite of passage for the two adolescent characters in their development into masculine, heterosexual, adult men. At the same time, this early affront to their heterosexual masculinity lays the groundwork for the homoerotic tension between Diadorim and Riobaldo that underlies the entire novel.

Despite the love that Riobaldo eventually develops for Diadorim, I emphasize that Diadorim's responses to challenges to his heterosexual masculinity are linked to the homophobic and racist discourses of the Brazilian Backlands. The young man who insults the two boys is constantly referred to as "mulatto" (124), while

Riobaldo and Diadorim are white. The young man also seems at least interested in having sex with other men. Diadorim's violent response to him makes it clear that gay/queer men of color (or men of color who have sex with men) are not considered desirable and are certainly not considered sufficiently masculine in the Brazilian Backlands of the times. Since *jagunços* discriminate on the basis of gender, sexuality, and race, for Diadorim to become one of them requires that he consistently identify as a white, masculine, heterocissexual man.

Even though Diadorim perpetuates the homophobia and racism of his social context, his own trans* masculinity is inherently subversive. He even tells Riobaldo at the end of the canoe trip that he feels unlike other men: "Sou diferente de todo o mundo. Meu pai disse que eu careço de ser diferente, muito diferente" (125). Many critics have argued that this comment reveals that Diadorim's gender identity is at odds with his biological sex. I find it more revealing that this character talks about his feeling of difference. I argue that his performance is not intended to blend him in with other men, but so he can stand out as different, even superior, to them. His situation is different from that of cross-dressers (as defined by Sifuentes-Jáuregui) because Diadorim does not seek recognition as a *travesti*. Instead, his performance aims to achieve the most-desired position of masculinity. In this sense, his performance is more like those of Pintada and Doña Bárbara, in that they also seek to be visibly noticed.

Masculinity of Adulthood

Although Riobaldo does not yet know it, Diadorim is the offspring of the greatest *jagunço* leader in the Backlands, Joca Ramiro. Diadorim's sense of masculinity is hereditary in that he must sustain the reputation of his family name. His performance of emphasized masculinity is confirmed the second time his heterosexuality is questioned, after he has grown to adulthood. The second affront occurs when two *jagunço* brothers call Diadorim "delicate" (*delicado*) and make fun of him because he does not appear macho (175). Since he is provoked in front of witnesses, the moment becomes a test of his adult virility. During the fight instigated by the insults, Diadorim conducts the performance of the most skilled *jagunço*:

Chapter Three

> Aquilo lufou! De rempe, tudo foi um ao e um cão, mas, o que havia de haver, eu já sabia ... Oap!: o assoprado de um refugão, e Diadorim entrava de encontro no Fancho-Bode, arrumou mão nele, meteu um sopapo:—um safano nas queixadas e uma so-barbarda – e calçou o pé, se fez em fúria. Deu como Fancho-Bode todo no chão, e já se curvou em cima: e o punhal parou a ponta diantinho da goela do dito. (175–76)

In this episode, Diadorim and Riobaldo are surrounded by fellow *jagunços*. Diadorim cannot resort to feminine strategies to restore his honor in the context of war. During hand-to-hand combat, he must not use distraction, manipulation, or temporary feminine/effeminate poses as he did in the earlier episode. Instead, the adult Diadorim reacts angrily and with immediate violence to the challenge to his masculinity.

Fighting is the exaggerated pose of the heterosexual masculine warrior. Fighting emphasizes the masculinity of the *jagunço* just as lassoing horses and castrating bulls are required skills of the masculine *llanero*. Fighting skills alone signal the successful performance of masculinity amongst the *jagunços*, all of whom must constantly reaffirm themselves in the Backlands during war. To prove his adult masculinity and his right to live amongst the heterosexual *jagunços* in the Backlands, Diadorim must demonstrate excellent fighting skills. His masculine courage is further demonstrated by his prowess in close hand-to-hand combat, rather than fighting at a distance (i.e., with swords or pistols). As Riobaldo says, "[h]omem é rosto a rosto; jagunço também: é no quem-com-quem" (176). Diadorim reinforces the patriarchal discourse on masculinity by hitting one of the men who insulted him, knocking him down, and finally threatening him with a dagger. Once again, Diadorim uses a phallic instrument to corroborate his access to masculine power and his ability to dominate other men. Rosenfield notes that "[a] valentia de Diadorim—sempre suspensa entre a virtude respeitável e o virtuosismo invejável—está constantemente apoiada no manejo da faca" (*Desenveredando* 382). Unlike in the earlier episode, he does not actually cut his opponent with a knife. All he has to do to reestablish his masculinity is to threaten his opponent, show that he could kill the man if he wished. He is sufficiently skilled as a warrior that he can defeat an enemy without taking his life or hurting him.

The Masculinities of Trans Warriors and Warrior Women

After Diadorim orders Fancho Bode to get up, he says it was a "brincadeira" (joke): "Oxente! Homem tu é, mano-velho, patrício!" (176). Fancho Bode now perceives Diadorim as fully a man. Diadorim's performance of a traditional emphasized masculinity thus aims for the most-admired masculinity in the *jagunço* world, that of being the best fighter. The pose of excessive, virile, heterosexual, and white masculinity is necessary to erase any signs of homosexuality, weakness, or femininity/effeminacy. To be *jagunço* is to prove one's masculinity with violence, to be the "macho" described by Domínguez-Ruvalcaba (*Translating* 90).

Diadorim's strategy of passing as the most masculine is so successful that he indeed obtains the most-desired position of his context. Unfortunately, Riobaldo also wants to embody that position of power, so Diadorim's success puts him into competition with his friend. When *jagunço* leader Medeiro Vaz is dying he looks at Riobaldo to select him as the new leader (95). When Diadorim confirms this, Riobaldo initially says that he is not interested and Diadorim then asks to be the leader (96). When it seems everyone had accepted Diadorim, Riobaldo disagrees, "era que eu não podia aceitar aquela transformação: negócio de para sempre receber mando dele, doendo de Diadorim ser meu chefe, nhem, hem? Nulo que eu ia estuchar" (98). While Riobaldo does not want to be in charge, he also does not want to be subordinated to his best friend. Hierarchies in the *jagunço* world are very important (V. Andrade 497). This is not an issue of Diadorim not being suited for the position of boss. Rather, if Diadorim becomes leader, Riobaldo cannot keep competing with him and demonstrating his own growth and value as a *jagunço*. Riobaldo then manipulates the situation by naming another man as leader.

After this incident, Diadorim continues to interact with Riobaldo as an equal, while Riobaldo increasingly competes with him and becomes more ambitious. Later on in the novel, when two other leaders get together, João Goanhá and Ze Bebelo, Riobaldo immediately asks who is going to be the new leader. The tone in which Riobaldo repeatedly asks this question goes beyond naïve inquiry (451–53). He is actually demanding to become the new head *jagunço*. He even kills two men that oppose his position. Diadorim supports Riobaldo by being the first to stand next to him (452). This time around Riobaldo does want the power and

Chapter Three

position and does not allow anyone else to be nominated. Moreover, he removes the power from the two leaders who are still alive. The violence with which Riobaldo acts imposes his power over the group and does not allow any room for Diadorim to become a leader. Nonetheless, the best warrior in the novel is Diadorim and his death is that of a war hero.

Sacrifice of the War Hero

Diadorim wields his knife/dagger again in his last battle, when he fights Hermógenes, who had betrayed and murdered his father. To avenge this death, Diadorim fights with a knife: "A faca a faca, eles se cortaram até os suspensórios ... *O diabo na rua, no meio do redemunho* ... Assim, ah—mirei e vi—o claro claramente: aí Diadorim cravar e sangrar o Hermógenes ... Ah," (611; ellipsis and italics in the original). By killing Hermógenes, Diadorim ends that combat and the war Hermógenes had triggered. During this final combat Riobaldo, who is witnessing the fight, fails to muster the strength to shoot his rifle and passes out when Diadorim is on the brink of death (610–12). Although Riobaldo is the leader, the final and decisive hand-to-hand combat is carried out by Diadorim. I propose that Riobaldo's lack of involvement in the fight along with Diadorim's use of the phallic weapon and his honorable reasons for fighting confirm Diadorim as the greatest warrior. He is the war hero.

As an element of patriarchal masculine culture, the knife is a double-edged weapon: it both empowers and disempowers Diadorim. Not only does Diadorim use a knife as a weapon with which to fight in combat, affirm his masculinity, and kill a terrible enemy, he is himself killed by a knife, when he dies from knife wounds sustained during the fight with Hermógenes. He loses all agency by being killed and he is symbolically castrated by having the knife-phallus taken away from his corpse by Riobaldo. After discovering his sex, Riobaldo does not give him the burial of a hero. Instead, Diadorim's corpse is dressed in women's clothes and buried in the cemetery (616) (see Chapter 1). Dressed in feminine attire, Diadorim ceases to be the masculine war hero who gave his own life to end the war. Discourses that celebrate the war hero and masculine sacrifice are here displaced because, in patriarchal cultures, war heroes can only be remembered if they have male

The Masculinities of Trans Warriors and Warrior Women

genitalia. The magnificence of Diadorim's heroism is clothed and thereby diminished. The heterocissexual men's world of *jagunços* is thus preserved and all of Diadorim's diverse performances, including posing and manipulating, are erased.

Diadorim's anonymous burial contrasts with the presumed death of one of the protagonists in João Ubaldo Ribeiro's novel *Viva o povo brasileiro* (1984) (An Invincible Memory). Maria da Fé, a Black warrior woman, starts out with access to a good education and having received full support from her grandfather, but changes her life path after witnessing the murder of her mother. She then allies with subalterns by joining the *Milicianos do povo* (People's Militia) to fight for Black people's rights. Through her wisdom and analytic skills, she eventually becomes the leader of the group. Her dedication to fighting on behalf of common Black people results in her image being projected as that of a saint and she becomes a hero to marginalized, disenfranchised people. In contrast to Diadorim, Maria da Fé's heroism continues to exist beyond her (presumed) death. According to her son, she goes out on a boat and disappears without a trace; no debris from the boat is ever found (606). Because her corpse is never recovered and there is no body to be buried or rot in a cemetery, her disappearance actually transforms her into a legendary hero. The way in which people remember her is not linked to a corpse, so her complex performance is never reduced to the genitalia of a dead body. Maria da Fé remains famous for her feats and sacrifices; her public acts, image, and story become a concrete legacy.

In a way, the body of the trans warrior in the 1950s novel is left in the hands of the narrator, whose agenda is to promote himself as the great warrior. The power of the word, of the narration, attempts to erase the war performance of the trans warrior. In contrast, thirty years later, in the novel of the 1980s, the body of the Black warrior woman is never found, but her memory and feats remain. The power of the word, of the manipulation of the discourse in this novel, cannot undo her actions and importance. The narrator cannot relegate her legacy to a lesser priority than the narration itself, as is the case with Riobado and his narration of Diadorim's war achievements in *Grande sertão*.

Despite Diadorim's disempowerment, the narrator can no more erase his skills as a warrior than Doña Bárbara's skills as a *llanero* can be effaced. Riobaldo never reaches Diadorim's level of

Chapter Three

fighting skill and Diadorim exits the novel by dying as a hero, not by being marginalized or expelled from society like Pintada and Doña Bárbara.

Conclusion

The successes or failures of trans warriors and warrior women's performances of masculinities are made evident in their relationships with other masculine characters. Their interactions with men characters elucidate the diverse strategies they use to place themselves in positions of power. Analyzing these relationships and interactions thus reveals the power dynamics of their social contexts, forms of empowerment and disempowerment, and the intersection of gender with other hierarchical social constructions such as race, class, kinship, and ethnicity. Gender construction is thus linked to the particularities of masculinities in each historical moment and place: the Mexican Revolution in Jalisco and Zacatecas, conflict in Venezuela's Araucan Plains, and war in the Brazilian Backlands. Warrior women's and trans warriors' masculinity performances demonstrate their ability to achieve most-desired positions in each context, while at the same time undermining hegemonic discourses on masculinity and signaling their permeability with non-hegemonic masculinities and femininities.

Phallic weapons such as the dagger or knife are major components of masculinity performances. Pintada confirms her fighting skills by wielding a knife, Doña Bárbara only needs to display her dagger to intimidate men, and Diadorim uses a dagger to defend his masculinity and avenge his father's death. Using knives and daggers enables warrior women and trans warrior characters to ratify their autonomy, individuality, and masculinity. Regardless of their sex, manipulating symbolic phalluses (i.e., information, knives) enables these characters to retain and exhibit traditional masculine power within their patriarchal societies. Pintada's empowered masculinity enables her to become a temporary leader of a band of men warriors (would-be revolutionaries who turn into mere marauders). Doña Bárbara's masculinity allows her to occupy two positions of hegemonic masculinity, as *llanero* and cacique. Diadorim's trans masculinity also achieves one of the most-admired positions for his context, that of being the best *jagunço* and even war hero.

The Masculinities of Trans Warriors and Warrior Women

In his analysis of José Donoso's novel *El lugar sin límites* (Hell Has No Limits) (1966), Sifuentes-Jáuregui contends that the cross-dresser becomes the ideal of womanliness (111). While Donoso's text takes place in a different context from the three novels I examine, I see that trans warrior and warrior woman characters do not necessarily deploy ideal performances of masculinity in any of these contexts. That is, there is neither a single ideal of manliness nor womanliness, since any such ideals and positions are necessarily connected to socioeconomic class, race, and ethnicity. That Pintada, Doña Bárbara, and Diadorim all deploy different most-desired positions contributes to problematizing and diversifying the idea that only one hegemonic masculinity can exist.

Since colonial times and especially in the nineteenth century, outlaws and bandits embodied national virtues in Latin America. In representing masculine heroism in Latin America, Pintada, Doña Bárbara, and Diadorim demonstrate they can also embody national discourses. I propose that these characters are able to occupy social positions normatively attributed to heterocissexual men. Depending on the context these men have been white, upper class, and educated. Trans warriors and warrior women open other possibilities for rereading and understanding Latin American nationalism. They undo the extremely men-dominated, *machista* discourse that has traditionally been portrayed or chosen as the national ideal.

Despite their performances of masculinities, warrior women and trans warriors are disempowered and marginalized within novels in order to reassert the hegemonic structures of power in their societies. Pintada's disempowerment in *Los de abajo* not only punishes her gender transgressiveness, it demonstrates that class and racial mobilities were unattainable during the Mexican Revolution. The marginalization of the Doña Bárbara character also punishes her transgressive power and reestablishes the traditional, idealized, white, and upper-class masculinity of the Venezuelan plains. Even though she is the title character of the novel, the text's goal is to unwrite her importance and marginalize her so that Santos's masculinity can be placed in a most-desired position. Diadorim's fight to the death in *Grande sertão* simultaneously confirms the image of the masculine, heterosexual *jagunço* while removing Diadorim's agency, trans identity, and posing. The disempowerment and erasure of all three characters indicate a turn

Chapter Three

to the past in each novel. Traditional structures regarding gender and performance are recovered whenever warrior women and trans warriors are expelled, disappear, or die. I see that their transgressions and achievements are not always interpreted as altering the hegemonic structures and patriarchal rules of their societies.

The characters' abilities to empower themselves, however temporarily, nevertheless show that specific bodies (sex, race) and social statuses (class, ethnicity) are not required to obtain most-desired positions. In the following chapter, I analyze how traditional femininities are reserved for non-transgressive women characters in Latin America. I discuss these women characters and their interactions with Pintada, Doña Bárbara, and Diadorim.

Chapter Four

Warrior Women, Trans Warriors, and Traditional Feminine Characters

One of the most widely known discourses on traditional femininity in Latin America is known as *marianismo,* a term originally applied to the perpetuation of patriarchal culture by women in catholic Latin American societies, which are devoted to the Virgin Mary. According to Evelyn P. Stevens's article (1973), *marianismo* refers to the ideal woman as a morally superior demigoddess whose spiritual strength pleases men. Abnegation, humility, and sacrifice are characteristic of *marianismo* (127). While Stevens recognizes that not all women in Latin America behave according to these standards, and her analysis does not reflect changes that have occurred since the 1970s, *marianismo* still permeates many Latin American societies. The woman characters who do not enter the masculine arena of combat in *Los de abajo, Doña Bárbara,* and *Grande sertão: veredas* represent the values embedded in *marianismo,* either through the roles they play or the ways in which they are treated by main characters. By contrast, the trans warrior and warrior woman characters in these novels of the first half of the twentieth century disobey the *marianismo* ideal by challenging the domestic roles and spaces into which they have initially been relegated by their genitalia. This chapter aims to debunk accomplice femininities (i.e., *marianismo*) and reveal who benefits from them.

In *This Sex Which Is Not One,* philosopher Luce Irigaray explains how assumptions of binary sexuality marginalize women from power. For Irigaray, all binary pairs function through exclusion: that is, they exclude any possibilities that might undermine the dichotomy (29). Irigaray argues that Western philosophical thought has been constructed around the male organ, taking the erect phallus as its primary object of attention. Women's sexuality has then been explained based on masculine norms (23). The phallocentric social imaginary does not truly know the woman or her pleasure (25). Such social lack of understanding results in artificial definitions of womanhood being assigned to women, treating women as a unified category, and barring women from power (30). Susan Brownmiller further explains that normative femininity is a "nostalgic tradition of imposed limitations" (14). Having a female biology is insufficient to be considered feminine, since femininity always requires more (15); at the same time, refusing to project femininity is to ignore men (15) and, hence, heterocisnormativity.

The gender performances of trans warrior and warrior woman characters make instances of performed femininity by other characters that much more obvious. While terms such as "hegemonic or dominant femininities," "subordinated femininities," and "pariah or oppositional femininities," (Charlebois 41) have been used to compare how femininities function, I do not adopt these terms. Social contexts and the characters or participants must be taken into account when examining whether and how any femininities may be reproducing the heterocispatriarchy. For example, while some femininities can be empowering for members of underrepresented groups, femininities performed by cis, white, upper-class women banking on their social privilege do not necessarily challenge hierarchies. Thus, instead of seeing women's gender performances as limited by femininities, I prefer to center on specific gender practices and most-desired positions that simultaneously highlight and break with traditional binaries in Latin America.

In order to underscore the problem of men's privilege, I also consider how the man protagonist in each novel determines what kinds of relationships cis woman/trans characters are permitted to have. In *The Elementary Structures of Kinship* (1949), Claude Lévi-Strauss states that the most precious object of exchange in kinship systems is the woman (*Las estructuras* 91). He explains that the exchange of economic objects provides a vehicle for development of social goods such as potency, power, sympathy, status, and emotion (93). The transfer of a woman from one man to another thus signifies that women are highly valued. Gayle Rubin takes Lévi-Strauss's argument a step further in "The Traffic in Women: Notes on the 'Political Economy' of Sex." Rubin notes that social discourses that treat women as valuable objects of exchange at least have the advantage of overcoming biological determinisms (175). However, Rubin points out that Lévi-Strauss neglects many aspects of what is transferred along with women in kinship exchanges, including sexual access, genealogies, familial names, rights, and other people (i.e., children). Societies that treat women as objects of exchange tend to develop fixed gender binaries that suppress the natural similarities between men and women. While both men and women are constrained by such binary schemes, Rubin argues that women suffer more from them than men.

In *Between Men* (1985), Eve Kosofsky Sedgwick argues that the erotic triangles that arise when two men compete for one woman maintain and reproduce men's domination. I draw on Sedgwick and Rubin in order to underscore how warrior woman and trans warrior characters challenge the structures in which cis men benefit from exchanging women. I see that the man protagonist in each of the three novels analyzed here places himself in a triangle with a trans warrior or warrior woman character and a significant woman character. Within these relationship triangles, the transgressive warrior characters are supposed to compete with a normative woman character for the man protagonist: Pintada versus Camila, Doña Bárbara versus Marisela, and Diadorim versus Otacília. Even though the gender identity of the characters may have changed because cis men have less presence in the triangles, I contend that in the analyzed novels the dynamics of power continue to perpetuate traditional systems of privilege. Two ostensibly woman characters competing for a man character reproduces the heterocispatriarchy just as much as the erotic bonds Sedgwick analyzes.

I am aware that these theories were produced over thirty years ago and not necessarily for Latin American contexts, yet they remain useful for uncovering how men characters retain the greatest advantages at the expense of trans* and woman characters. I argue that warrior woman and trans warrior characters expose how heterocissexual men support men's domination by exchanging trans* and woman characters. At the same time, these characters resist the traffic in women (and trans* men) and avoid the control of men. In some cases—as in *Los de abajo*—they even undo such domination.

Diverse Femininities in *Los de abajo*

Of the many cis woman characters in Mariano Azuela's novel, including Demetrio's wife, Camila and other women from her village, Codorniz's girl, and Cervantes's fiancée, only Pintada consistently transgresses traditional feminine roles. She embodies new ways of empowerment for women and a critique of traditional feminine roles. In this section, I compare these characters and analyze how Pintada's performance as an independent warrior woman casts a light on the other characters' relative submissiveness to cis men. I also analyze how men characters perpetuate men's domination and how Pintada defies them. This shows that man characters benefit from the exchange of women, but cannot gain anything from Pintada. Her performance and behavior illustrate the ways in which the heterocispatriarchal society operated within the Revolution as women became disposable objects of exchange. I also analyze the intersecting racism, classism, and sexism complicit in the behaviors and attitudes of the man characters.

Pintada interacts primarily with the major woman character called Camila. Camila is like Pintada in that both are poor and not white: Pintada is described as dark with olive skin and Camila as having a bronze complexion. But that is where their similarities end. According to Elizabeth Salas, Camila is characterized as a maternal, submissive, good camp follower, while Pintada is depicted as an Amazon with few positive characteristics (85). Pascale Baker positions them as rivals (*Revolutionaries* 19), with Camila being the "naive soldadera" (98) and Pintada the active "soldada" (100). Such rivalry is supported by Camila replacing Pintada as Demetrio's lover. B. Christine Arce also opposes them against each other in seeing Camila as Pintada's "nemesis" (*México's* 93). I contend that reading Pintada and Camila as diametric opposites only perpetuates historical men's privilege, however. Both Pintada and Camila can be contrasted with Demetrio's wife, the only socially sanctioned spouse in the novel. Thus, these two diverse characters represent different social critiques.

Camila portrays the *marianismo* ideal. Unlike Pintada, she has a family and social identity and an attachment to a specific place. Although her father is absent from the story, she lives with her mother in a small village, where she carries out domestic chores. Within the village, Camila is the good daughter, which means obeying her mother Señá (Ma'am) Agapita. Camila is dependent upon her mother, who mainly asserts authority over her in an attempt to ensure that Camila follows the rules of the patriarchal system. For instance, after Demetrio's band has left the village, Señá Agapita beats Camila to try to make her forget Cervantes, with whom she has fallen in love. Such submissiveness and kinship ties are absent from the Pintada character. Furthermore, Pintada does not seem to belong to any particular place. While Camila is associated with the sierra, the same place from which the original members of Demetrio's band came, Pintada just roams around Mexico with the revolutionaries. Camila's submissiveness and shared background mean she is able to obtain a place in the band, which Pintada cannot do. This is made evident in the novel when Pintada fails in her attempts to attract Demetrio, while Camila's passivity draws his attention. Demetrio is never comfortable with Pintada because she does not have a clear social identity; she is a woman without a family, conventional biography, and, as Clive Griffin states, origins in the sierra (66). She is also fearless and a leader.

As discussed in earlier chapters, Camila approximates the ideal of the Angel in the House, while Pintada resembles a corrupt, masculine libertine. Woman characters are commonly opposed along these lines in literary works written by men. Sandra Gilbert and Susan Gubar contend that women characters have been depicted as either angels or monsters throughout the history of literature written by men ("Toward" 17). Treating Camila and Pintada as rivals thus reproduces a heterocispatriarchal culture that reduces women to two simple types. A similar binary is found in the images of two women who are embedded in the history of Mexico: the Virgin of Guadalupe, which refers to the apparitions of Virgin Mary in Mexico City in 1531, and Malinche (Malintzi), the indigenous woman who translated for the Spanish invaders and became conquistador Hernán Cortés's lover. Because of her initial innocence, Camila would seem to represent the Virgin, while Pintada would be Malinche in *Los de abajo*. However, Camila and Pintada are more complex characters than such binary associations imply. For instance, while Camila's submissiveness and dependence can be related to the Virgin, her position as an object of exchange amongst men can also be linked to Malinche. As narrated by Bernal Díaz del Castillo, Malinche (Doña Marina) was sold by her mother and the man who purchased her then gave her as a present to Hernán Cortés. The idea that a woman can be exchanged or presented to a man is replicated in Camila's story, but not in Pintada's. It should also be noted that, although Malinche was treated as an object of exchange, like Pintada she had

Chapter Four

her own agenda and ended up playing an important role in the Conquest of México, as Norma Alarcón discusses.

Comparing Camila to two other woman characters in the novel shows that she also has a limited space of autonomy, though not as much agency as Pintada. These other two women characters are referred to only as "Cervantes's fiancée" and "Codorniz's girl." Although they are unnamed and only appear briefly in scenes of plunder and celebration in the second half of the novel, they represent important women presences in the Revolution. Both these two characters seem to be much younger than the autonomous Pintada, even though she is also described as a girl (*muchacha*). Cervantes's fiancée is fourteen and Codorniz's girl is only twelve years old. Neither adolescent participates in raids along with the band, although Codorniz's girl tears out illustrations from a book and laughs when Pintada wears her elegant dress (152–53). Their youthful femininity is represented by their docility in the novel, while Camila is shown to have an agenda of her own. Her agency is first visible in her decision to escape the authority of her mother by running away with Cervantes. Her second autonomous decision is to remain with Demetrio even though it means submitting herself to a new set of patriarchal rules under the supervision of a man. She refuses to obey any other member of the band. She keeps herself distant from Cervantes, criticizes Güero Margarito, and disobeys Pintada's commands. In exchanging her mother's authority for Demetrio's, Camila rearticulates her feminine role in a new social context in order to recover stability and obtain a space of privilege as Demetrio's lover. Even after becoming part of the band, Camila does not get involved in raiding villages. She never transgresses rules to empower herself as Pintada does. Her agency is in selecting the life of a General's lover within the patriarchal Revolution while criticizing the revolutionaries with whom she lives.

Pintada and Camila represent different critiques of the Revolution. Camila joins two men named Solís and Valderrama in criticizing other members of the band for being corrupt and mistreating people. Camila complains to Demetrio about the cruelty and violence of some of the band's members (Salas 85). Her complaints demonstrate that she is not a stereotypical camp follower. It is worth remembering that, while Azuela based Pintada on a real-life woman of the Revolution, Camila and his other women characters were products of his imagination. Azuela uses

Camila as a fictitious woman character to criticize the excesses of the revolutionaries and the failure of the Revolution to fundamentally alter an oppressive social system, while the character based on a real person (Pintada) reflects changes in women's roles that Azuela might have considered negative. The imagined women characters share an innocent air and they all perform traditional feminine roles, whether socially sanctioned (e.g., the generous village women who tend the men's wounds) or unsanctioned (e.g., unmarried sexual partners such as Cervantes's fiancée, Codorniz's girl, and Camila as Demetrio's lover). Since the fictional women characters perpetuate traditional binary gender roles, only Pintada can be read as a critique of the traditional social roles available to women in Mexico.

Camila and Pintada can be compared to another woman character who becomes involved with a revolutionary soldier. Partially set during the Mexican Revolution, the novel by Laura Esquivel, *Como agua para chocolate* (Like Water for Chocolate) (1989) includes a warrior woman named Gertrudis in a side story to the main plot. Like Camila, Gertrudis runs away with a *Villista* captain, but she is not depicted as a camp follower or *adelita*. Instead, she achieves the rank of General through her consistent demonstration of fighting prowess (180). Her character thus illustrates the greater potential for achievement amongst women who joined the Revolution compared to women who stayed home. In this way, her story is different from both Pintada's and Camila's. Still, I must note that when she first runs away from home, her mother hears a rumor that she has become a sex worker (58). When Gertrudis returns to visit her family years later, she never mentions having worked in a brothel and only talks about her tenacity on the battlefield (180–81). Her attempt to establish her warrior status is somewhat undone by her returning home married to the man with whom she first ran away, however. She even explains that she and Juan, also now a General, had separated but restarted their relationship when they met again a year later (180). The depiction of Gertrudis as a spouse signals that her accomplishments and position have been blessed by the appropriate social apparatus. In a sense, she is only allowed a role in the military because she is the spouse of a General. Portraying warrior women as sex workers, married, or following patriarchal norms in other ways attempts to put transgressive characters back into the realm of conventionality.

Chapter Four

Exchanging Women

Camila and Pintada have been analyzed as opposites because they seem to compete with each other for Demetrio. D. Bradley conducts a mythological reading of Demetrio and "his" women to show that Camila and Pintada both revolve around Demetrio as sexual partners. I see Demetrio's preference for Camila over Pintada as suggesting that just one man has the power to determine the social positions of women even in the context of a revolutionary band. Demetrio also shapes the relationship between Pintada and Camila, a relationship made more complex by Cervantes's interference and the different ways the two women enter the band. Pintada joins the group of revolutionaries under her own initiative, while Camila is deceived into leaving her village to follow the band. Cervantes pretends to love Camila and promises her marriage in order to convince her to run away with him, but his actual intention is to provide Demetrio with a sex partner.

The triangle composed of Camila, Pintada, and Demetrio modifies the one formed by Camila, Cervantes, and Demetrio. Drawing on Sedgwick's analysis of erotic triangles, I see that Cervantes and Demetrio are not rivals for Camila. They perpetuate men's dominance not by competing for one woman, but instead by helping each other at the expense of that woman. That is, one man (Cervantes) uses a woman (Camila) to serve and curry favor from another man (Demetrio). Robert Irwin argues that the relationship between Cervantes and Demetrio is what matters most in the Camila—Demetrio—Cervantes triangle (*Mexican* 128). While I agree with Irwin that the homosocial bond between Demetrio and Cervantes is stronger than the heterosexual bond either of them have with Camila, it is still important to examine their relationship with this woman character. The ways in which trans* people and women are manipulated and controlled by heterocissexual men are erased when only homosocial relationships formed around men's dominance are analyzed. Furthermore, such analyses fail to expose a creation of a second triangle (Pintada—Camila—Demetrio) that forces women to fight each other over one man. That is, focusing exclusively on men's homosociality contributes to traditional discourses in which men or man characters only interact with each other in a social vacuum, rendering women and trans* people nonexistent.

Neither Camila nor her family benefit from the exchange between the two men in the Camila—Demetrio—Cervantes triangle, as would have occurred in a traditional kinship transaction such as marriage. Any empowerment or profit that Camila (or her mother) might have obtained from Camila's sexual bond with Demetrio is instead transferred to a third party, Cervantes. Furthermore, this exchange is inherently temporary. Camila is presented by Cervantes to Demetrio as a sex object to be used while he is away from his wife. She is not considered even as valuable as a wife. Cervantes's gift of Camila to Demetrio does not uphold the social values implicated in sanctioned exchanges of women amongst men. The exchange highlights a heterocispatriarchal system in which women were valued only for their sexuality, which could only be transferred and used by (alleged) heterocissexual men. This represents a critique of the Mexican Revolution, during which traditional relationships broke down and women became ever more seen as exchangeable goods, a sort of loot.

The descriptions of "Cervantes's fiancée" and "Codorniz's girl" further illustrate how women can be exchanged between men for short periods of time. Both these characters behave submissively toward men. They never give voice to opinions of their own and they do not have any names or nicknames suggestive of individuality. Their identities are summed up as objects that belong to men: "Cervantes's fiancée" is a translation of *la novia de Cervantes* and "Codorniz' girl" is a translation of *la chiquilla de la Codorniz*. Such appellatives reduce teenage girls to exchangeable and temporary goods in the patriarchal society of the Mexican Revolution. Their position as objects of exchange is supported by Pintada's observation that Cervantes "found" his fiancée by purchasing her from two other revolutionaries named Meco and Manteca (158). The vulnerability and objectification of the girl is further reinforced by descriptions of her physical beauty: "sus grandes ojos azules… su piel era fresca y suave como un pétalo de rosa; sus cabellos rubios" ([Cátedra] 154). In conforming to the traditional European standards of beauty, her blond hair and blue eyes render her an even more valuable object to be owned by men. Indeed, all the men in the band—including Demetrio—desire and covet her. The fact that she is purchased and then men compete to be the first to rape her makes it clear that a virgin girl who appears most European exhibits the preferred femininity of women.

Chapter Four

That Cervantes's fiancée is considered the most-desirable woman provides evidence of how racism, sexism, and classism intersect in the novel. Descriptions of other women characters illustrate this intersection. For example, when Demetrio sees Camila for the first time, the narrator describes her as "la muchacha era de rostro muy vulgar, pero en su voz había mucha dulzura" (89). The racism revealed by the word "vulgar" here is made even more overt with how Cervantes sees Camila. She looks like a "especie de mono enchomitado, de tez broncínea, dientes de marfil, pies anchos y chatos" (101). While different degrees of discrimination are implied in these remarks, the hierarchy of physical attractiveness is obviously racist: those who do not appear traditionally European are denigrated and considered less desirable and beautiful than those (such as Cervantes's fiancée) who do.

As a white cis man and the only member of the band who is from the upper class, the character of Cervantes establishes the intersection of race-sex-class in the novel. First, he buys a young (minor) woman who fulfills European standards of beauty and publicly introduces her as his "fiancée." Although she ends up being raped by another white man, her physical appearance sanctions the possibility that she could have become a wife. Then Cervantes deceives another young woman (Camila) and convinces her to elope with him to serve his personal interests in currying favor with Demetrio. Camila can never become his fiancée because he had selected her to be the lover of another man. Furthermore, Camilla cannot be considered for the role of a real fiancée to Cervantes because she is indigenous, *mestiza*, mixed, and/or Black.

The fact that Cervantes gifts Camila to Demetrio also suggests a racial division predicated on the assumption that non-white women are only meant for non-white men. Just as a white character—Güero Margarito—rapes Cervantes's white fiancée, Demetrio rapes Camila. This racism is further reinforced in Cervantes's view of Camila as a "monkey." While Demetrio focuses on her face, Cervantes highlights Camila's skin color, teeth, feet, and overall physical appearance. While the descriptions of Camila in the novel illustrate the different perspectives of these two men characters, they are similar in revealing that men characters are the ones who judge the physical beauty of women. The quotes likewise demonstrate that only the upper-class man in the band has the power to determine the gender and sexual roles of women characters (deceiving Camila results in Pintada being displaced as Demetrio's sex partner); this perpetrates racist, sexist, and classist hierarchies in the novel.

Pintada resists being exchanged and thus breaks the hierarchical system. She does so by uncovering information, destroying Cervantes's hierarchies, using her sexuality to empower herself, and helping other women to escape. For example, she locks Cervantes's "fiancée" in a bedroom to protect her when all the men are trying to have sex with her (raping her). She even fights with Demetrio to prevent him from having sex with Cervantes's fiancée. Before Cervantes can marry the girl or have sex with her, Pintada finds out that Güero Margarito had raped her and she helps the girl escape Güero (159). By outsmarting and mocking Cervantes, Pintada's actions go beyond putting an end to the exchange of other women; they undo a discriminatory hierarchy. Unlike the two nameless, non-revolutionary adolescent girls, Pintada is never an object of exchange and does not belong to anyone. As a warrior woman, she instead presents a strong rebuttal to the image of docile femininity. Even though Pintada does not care about protecting Cervantes's fiancée from rape, and is only trying to eliminate any rivals for Demetrio, Pintada's actions in the novel expand notions of women's roles and opportunities during the Revolution. Meanwhile, the teenage girls remain void of agency. Their presence as sexual playthings for the men in the band demonstrates a climate of corruption and lack of government or family protection of minors during revolutionary times. Even though critics have emphasized Pintada's evilness and corruption, she is far from the most corrupt character in this context.

Camila's decisions provide evidence of how docile, feminine characters can be used to reproduce cis men's power. Pintada initially offers to help Camila return to her village, but Camila does not accept her help because she fears her mother will kill her for having run away with Cervantes. Camila decides not to return to the role of obedient daughter, but remain in the band as Demetrio's obedient lover because "ya le voy cobrando voluntá" (171). Her words suggest that she has overcome the trauma of Cervantes's trickery and subsequent rape by Demetrio rather quickly. Previously, she considered Demetrio "despicable" (109), but now she likes him. In the chauvinistic ideology of this novel, having sex with a real revolutionary transforms Camila. Her acquiescence perpetuates the centrality of homosocial relationships among men.

Both Camila and Pintada use sexuality to achieve their own goals, but unlike Camila, Pintada does not reproduce traditional rules governing sexual relationships. Chris Harris argues that Pintada's use of conventional sex appeal replicates an emphasized femininity (664). However, an emphasized femininity is usually compliant with hegemonic masculinity (Connell and Messerschmidt 848), which Pintada is not. She instead uses her sexuality and strength strategically to win Demetrio as a lover and empower herself, while refusing the conventional lover role. By contrast, Camila quickly adopts a traditional feminine position as camp follower in order to survive.

Pintada is far more transgressive than compliant. Her social, racial, and gender transgressions expose how men characters exchange women of color and white women as part of their racist, sexual, and classist hierarchical system. She resists such transactions with her independence. Finally, she undoes the relationship triangles and social hierarchies by murdering Camila. She thus eliminates the object that has been exchanged only for the benefit of cis men and compels the men to take her seriously. Indeed, they stop laughing and making fun of her after she kills Camila. Since killing is a homosocial act among men, Pintada thereby also transgresses normative gender roles. By assassinating the leader's lover, she obtains some respect for herself, stops the exchange of nonwhite women, and destroys the erotic triangles. Her actions shake the very foundation of the band and even the Revolution itself.

Mediated Femininities in *Doña Bárbara*

As in Azuela's novel, men determine the relationships amongst the women characters in Gallegos's text. However, this novel involves only a few women characters as it is set in the highly masculinized space of *llaneros* working in the plains. The two major women characters, Doña Bárbara and her daughter Marisela, are superficially similar in that both are *mestizas* and neither had strong parental figures. Doña Bárbara is an orphan and Marisela, rejected at birth by Doña Bárbara, was raised only by her father, a man portrayed as weak and lacking authority. In this section, I compare Marisela and Doña Bárbara and analyze how Santos modifies the relationship between these two characters. I argue that Santos's intervention in the relationship between the two women characters prevents Marisela from becoming a *cacica*. His intervention also reveals another aspect of the racist ideology in the novel, which is that Marisela is constructed as superior because she is the preferred *mestiza*.

Marisela and Doña Bárbara do not develop a relationship until the last chapter of the second section of the three-part novel. The scene in which they first interact demonstrates the contrasts in their behavior and their lack of emotional attachment to each other. In this scene, Marisela goes to Doña Bárbara's house to retrieve some rope that Juan Primito had used to measure Santos, as it was going to be used for witchcraft. Marisela had heard a rumor that Doña Bárbara kept the rope because she was planning to use it to put a spell on Santos. Marisela challenges Doña Bárbara and they begin to fight: "La muchacha se defendió, debatiéndose bajo la presión de aquellas manos hombrunas, que ya le desgarraban la blusa, desnudándole el pecho virginal" (172). This episode lightly depicts the customary literary trope of the good woman character (i.e., a virginal woman) opposing an evil, gender-transgressive character (i.e., a powerful woman with man-like hands). The relationship triangle becomes evident when Santos steps in to prevent their fight from escalating. His intervention suggests that he will ultimately determine the trajectory of their relationship, much as Demetrio shaped Pintada and Camila's relationship in *Los de abajo*.

Stephen Henighan argues that this fight scene highlights Doña Bárbara's "peripheral femininity" in comparison with Marisela's passive femininity (41), but I observe more nuance to this scene. Doña Bárbara is not just marginally feminine, she is described as masculine. Furthermore, as Sharon Magnarelli explains, Doña Bárbara is simultaneously victim and victimizer ("Woman" 6). Meanwhile, Marisela is not entirely without agency, since she is willing to fight in pursuit of her goals. She displays an agenda by abandoning the household space to which Santos had consigned her and penetrating another woman's space. Although it is her love for Santos that leads her to confront her mother for the first time, she is the aggressor in this scene. She trespasses on Doña Bárbara's property and then attacks her. Marisela only becomes a victim when Doña Bárbara, with her mannish hands, physically overpowers her. This turnabout in power works to erase Marisela's culpability in the fight and results in her portrayal as an innocent, feminine woman in contrast to Doña Bárbara's masculinity. Santos further dismantles Marisela's autonomy by scolding her for acting upon *supercherías* (superstition). By rationalizing her actions and protecting her from Doña Bárbara, Santos limits the scope of Marisela's autonomy and prevents mother and daughter from continuing interacting with each other.

Santos's intervention shows that, although the Marisela character is defined and limited by her femininity, she does not go through life unprotected. Being embedded by kinship into the patriarchal system shields her from attack (Magnarelli, "Woman" 16). This feminine cis woman character inhabits several kinship positions over the course of the novel, each of which offers her protection. Initially, as a daughter, her father looks after her. Then she acquires social and sexual functions within the patriarchy by being acknowledged as part of Santos's family, as his cousin and later fiancée. Finally, she becomes Doña Bárbara's heir and acquires the protection of wealth. When Santos takes Marisela and her father to live with him, he prevents Mister Danger from raping Marisela. I propose that his paternalistic protection enables her to avoid repeating the tragedy of Doña Bárbara's past, that is, her being raped by a gang of men. Doris Sommer argues that the ways in which white men disenfranchised, violated, and exterminated indigenous communities in Venezuela are represented by Doña Bárbara's truncated education and being gang raped, as well as in the murder of her first love (284). Marisela, thanks to Santos, does not repeat this traumatic episode and subsequent story. After her gang rape, Doña Bárbara refuses to follow the rules designated to women in the heterocispatriarchal system.

The fact that Marisela is embedded in a protective family is not enough to render her a good woman, however. She must first be given a traditional European education so she can embody feminine ideals. According to Sommer, Marisela being "corrected" by Santos also comes from Venezuela's "whitening" project (277). For example, early in their relationship, Santos chides Marisela for not being a good daughter to her father, Lorenzo. The procedure of disempowering an agentive woman character is further evident in Santos's corrections of Marisela's speech patterns and manners. She ceases to behave autonomously as soon as she begins following his instructions. Even when Marisela later explains to Santos that he did not kill Melquíades, the narrator emphasizes that her logical deductions are only a product of her having been educated by Santos (229). I see that only after he sees her suffering on her father's behalf and she demonstrates a willingness to accept his instruction does Santos begin to think of her as a love object and take her as his fiancée and future wife. She gains value in society as Santos molds her image to fit the accepted feminine role of the upper class, but in becoming his malleable object, she ceases to be a subject in her own right.

Just as Doña Bárbara's agency is unwritten by her disappearance (discussed in Chapter 2), Santos's influence over Marisela signals a denial of female agency (Rosegreen-Williams 292). Claudette Rosegreen-Williams argues that Santos's authority over Marisela is Gallegos's main depiction of male supremacy in the novel (291). Santos appreciates Marisela only for her potential to become civilized and adapt to patriarchal norms. I observe the inverse operating in the character of Doña Bárbara. She is never valued because she represents a usurpation of traditional power in her refusal to reproduce the role of a happy, good, submissive domestic woman. In following Santos's instructions, Marisela portrays a femininity that collaborates with women's oppression and restores the white patriarchal system that Doña Bárbara's agency had destroyed.

Marisela and Doña Bárbara are both beautiful in traditional terms, but the connotations and repercussions of their physical appearances diverge greatly because of Santos's intervention. Unlike Doña Bárbara's beauty, which is blamed for "instigating" her being raped by a gang of men when she is still young and innocent, Marisela's beauty does not mark her for tragedy. This is partly because Marisela does not know how to act beautiful. She only finds out she is beautiful when Santos discovers her and tells her so (76). At the time, Marisela is living in a hut with her poor father. She is poorly dressed and does not bathe or groom herself (74). Her beauty is described as "natural," like the beauty of the noble savage. Indeed, her beauty is so natural that Santos reprimands her for treating herself carelessly once they finally meet: "es pecado contra la Naturaleza, que te ha hecho hermosa, el que cometes con ese abandono de tu persona" (76–77). Santos claims that taking care of her personal appearance is in accord with nature, though she should not go so far as to enhance or alter her appearance artificially, as Doña Bárbara (and Pintada) does. Marisela only needs water to shine her beauty, which Santos demonstrates by washing her arms and face (76). Sommer sees that the way in which Santos meets and educates Marisela can be read as a morality play in which "Civilization conquers barbarism" (278). I agree with Sommer, but I also understand this scene as an initiation rite. From the beginning of their relationship, Santos intervenes in Marisela's life to subdue her agency. He baptizes her in water and teaches her the rules for fitting into patriarchal society. Marisela's physical beauty becomes a product of Santos's craftsmanship; it requires his white upper class heterocissexual "male gaze" to be recognized and given value.

Men also recognized Doña Bárbara's natural, youthful beauty. Her beauty, however, does not conform to social values of women's purity because of her gang rape. She projects the sensuality of the temptress. She manipulates her appearance to become a more artificial, sexualized beauty, which she does to please herself and seduce men. The narrator describes her sensual beauty at the rodeo as follows: "Brillantes los ojos turbadores de hembra sensual, recogidos, como para besar, los carnosos labios con un enigmático pliegue en las comisuras, la tez cálida, endrino y lacio el cabello abundante" (117). This type of femininity does not reproduce socially accepted ideals of women's beauty in all circles and avoids specific references to her origins. Doña Bárbara's visible sensuality is intended to win and subjugate men. Her adult beauty combines fury with sensuality: "Así en el alma de la mestiza tardaron varios años en confundirse la hirviente sensualidad y el tenebroso aborrecimiento al varón. La primera víctima de esta horrible mezcla de pasiones fue Lorenzo Barquero" (25). By joining hatred to sensuality, Doña Bárbara transforms her simple, innocent, decorative beauty into a weapon of revenge against men. Victorien Lavou Zoungbo argues that Doña Bárbara's beauty is associated with the devil because she uses it to tempt, corrupt, and dominate men (213), while I see it is associated with an uncontrolled sexuality that originates from her having been gang raped. Within the novel's economy, Doña Bárbara's trauma establishes a desire for revenge. Hers is a dangerous beauty that shifts her outside of patriarchal control.

Combining natural physical beauty with sensuality and sexual autonomy produces a weapon that repudiates the logic of traditional masculine power. Doña Bárbara can disempower and even symbolically castrate powerful men such as Lorenzo by seducing them with her sensuality. Even Santos is tempted when he sees Doña Bárbara dressed in feminine clothing for the first time (in the chapter "El rodeo"). He feels compelled to get to know her better even as he is repelled by her personality (120). Rosegreen-Williams similarly views her dualistic image—both beautiful and dangerous—as a projection of men's fear of being castrated by women (290). Gilbert and Gubar consider the battle between the sexes to be a trope for the conflict between women's uncontrolled, frenetic desire and socially acceptable feminine chastity (*No Man's* 5). In *Doña Bárbara*, the warrior woman character is not only depicted as evil and conniving, but as sexually rebellious, to provide a contrast to the virtuousness and sexual purity of the preferred femininity embodied in Marisela. Doña Bárbara's sexual transgressions and beauty function to emphasize Marisela's chastity and support the development of patriarchal society in the Plains, as Gallegos proposes. Marisela is not the gang-raped *cacica* who will subjugate men with her beauty.

Mestiza Mother and Daughter

Pejorative labels such as "monster" or "devil" are not only given to sexually rebellious women, but also to women who threaten one of the basic tenets of traditional femininity and kinship relationships, the maternal instinct. When Doña Bárbara acts against the naturalized feelings of motherhood by abandoning her newborn daughter, she becomes positioned as a non-conventional woman, a *mujerona* with "sinister intent." She does not participate in the reproduction of society. Although Doña Bárbara attempts to redeem herself later in the novel, she reverts to her former attitude of hatred toward her daughter as soon as she finds out that Marisela is going to marry Santos. Immediately upon hearing about the impending marriage, Doña Bárbara rides out intending to kill Marisela: "[r]eapareció por completo en doña Bárbara la mujerona de los ímpetus avasalladores y, sin decir una palabra, con un arrebato preñado de intenciones siniestras, volvió a montar a caballo y se encaminó a *Altamira*" (239). Every time she reacts in such "unnatural" ways to her daughter, it is evaluated in the negative as masculine behavior unsuitable for a woman.

Doña Bárbara plans to shoot Marisela with a gun, which like the knife is a phallic symbol associated with traditional masculine

Chapter Four

power. At the last moment, recalling when she herself was young and in love, she stays her intention to murder Marisela: "el arma bajó sin haber disparado y, lentamente, volvió a la cañonera de la montura" (240). Contrary to Pintada, who uses a knife to murder her rival, Doña Bárbara resists killing her daughter just to keep Santos for herself. Doña Bárbara chooses to relinquish the phallic element that contributed to putting her in a position of power. She disempowers herself because she identifies with Marisela. Her painful memory of lost love tames her ferocity (240).

After lowering the gun, Doña Bárbara contemplates Marisela for a long time and experiences the first stirring of maternal feeling (240). The resurrection of a maternal instinct is the only thing that manages to tame this rebellious warrior woman. I propose that Doña Bárbara's disempowerment is complete when she reproduces the traditional image of maternal self-sacrifice. By recognizing Marisela as her daughter, Doña Bárbara fills the maternal void, fixes a past mistake, and reconsecrates the victory of civilization (Lavou Zoungbo 214). The maternal feeling Doña Bárbara formerly lacked, once generated, guarantees Marisela's position in their society as daughter and heir. Doña Bárbara fulfills her proper kinship role by legally recognizing her daughter.

Two critics have viewed the mother-daughter relationship in this novel as representing progress or evolutionary change. Jorge J. Barrueto argues that Marisela survives, even thrives, because she represents a stage of development superior to that of Doña Bárbara, who disappears at the end of the novel (194). That is, Marisela improves upon Doña Bárbara's life story. Glenn A. Wilson believes that Marisela is a new Doña Bárbara because she represents the future, particularly the triumph of civilization over barbarity (488). Marisela is considered superior to Doña Bárbara in both of these analyses. From examining the intersections of gender, skin color, and ethnicity, I argue that Marisela is not actually better than her mother, but is constructed as such to contrast with the "inferior" and "undesirable" intersectional position Doña Bárbara embodies.

Javier Lasarte Valcárcel argues that Gallegos's novel represents José Martí's idea of populist *mestizaje* (172). A hero of the Cuban project of independence in the 19th century and a prominent intellectual figure, Martí called for a return to origins and invited all Americans to embrace the mixture of cultures represented on the continent in his well-known essay, "Nuestra América" (Our

America). The reference to populist *mestizaje* involves a racist ideology in Gallegos's work, however. The text discounts the mixing of cultures by disregarding Doña Bárbara's past and present while depicting a better form of *mestizaje* in Marisela. As made evident by most novels of *mestizaje*, the mixture implies a progressive whitening and the loss of non-European traits. While Marisela shares features with her mother such as physical beauty (in conventional European terms) and being *mestiza*, she is unlike her mother in not being culturally indigenous.

The intersections between gender, race (as skin color), and ethnicity contribute to Doña Bárbara's transgressions and disempowerment. The racist thought behind the nineteenth-century whitening project in Venezuela implied a hierarchy of color gradation. Any person with "lighter" skin tone was placed in a position of greater privilege compared to people whose skin colors were considered "darker." This division is known as "colorism," a term first coined by U.S. Black woman author Alice Walker in 1982. Colorism refers to the privileged position that lighter-skinned people have over darker-skinned people. Having a lighter skin color (perceived as approaching whiteness) better equips a person to achieve success in society. Even though the novel does not describe Marisela explicitly as having "lighter" skin color than her mother, she is the daughter of a *mestiza* (rather than an indigenous) woman and an educated, upper-class white man. Marisela thus represents a more "advanced" stage in the desired racial and cultural whitening project favored by the Venezuelan elites and her social context and family background give her advantages not possessed by her mother. Marisela is also better equipped than Doña Bárbara to be the best *mestiza* because she fulfills ideals of traditional femininity. She is docile, domestic, and naïve and even learns how to speak "correctly." Pablo Quintero suggests that the novel pushes forward its problematic modernization ideology through the character of Marisela because she belongs to the "good race" that is capable of being educated into civilized European traditions (178). Being malleable allows Marisela to fit into the progressive whitening project elites wanted for Venezuela. I see that through education and coaching by another educated upper-class white man who does not fall for Doña Bárbara (i.e., Santos), Marisela becomes part of the preferred Venezuela promoted in Gallegos's novel.

Race (as skin color) and gender were keystones of Gallegos's national project. The intersection of race and gender allow us to see that only one very specific type of *mestiza* is allowed into the new and desired Venezuela and it certainly does not include empowered, transgressive, indigenous warrior women. The ideal *mestiza* is one who can marry an upper-class, white, educated, and masculine cis man. Moreover, as Sommer notes, that *mestiza* happens to be related by blood to Santos (289).

Embodying National Femininities

Mary Louise Pratt compares Gallegos's novel to *Las memorias de Mamá Blanca* (Mama Blanca's Memoirs) (1929) by Venezuelan woman writer Teresa de la Parra. Pratt argues that the two novels register contrasting forms of feminism. She explains that while de la Parra aims to construct a lost oligarchic mother, Gallegos feminizes and barbarizes the traditional image of motherhood so that it can be removed from the nation's history ("Women" 58). For Pratt, Doña Bárbara is not an oligarchic matron who wants to be redeemed, but a feminized cacique who must be rejected in the logic of the narrative (by disappearing at the end of the novel). I agree with Pratt that the character has to be cast off, but, as I have already argued in Chapter 3, Doña Bárbara still represents a new type of cacique. She demonstrates that it is possible for a woman landowner, a *cacica,* to use diverse strategies and performances to rise socially and economically in the Araucan Plains of Venezuela. As a *mestiza llanera cacica* who refuses the role of motherhood, her character transgresses the values of the cacique and the matron, two roles which stand for the future of the nation in this novel.

While Doña Bárbara transgresses the national ideology, according to Emanuelle K. F. Oliveira, Marisela symbolizes the combination of classes, ethnicities, and moral values that constitute the Venezuelan people. She is poor, but will rise to wealth through marriage; she is a *mestiza*, simultaneously indigenous and white European; and she is depicted as both saint and sinner in the novel (101). Marisela embodies almost as much diversity as Doña Bárbara, but, unlike her mother, she does not fuse indigenous cultural traditions with those of the urban West (represented by Santos) nor does she perform any female masculinities. She is also subordinated to Santos: she is not the *cacica*, but the cacique's wife. She reproduces the image of *marianismo*. Considering the intersection of ethnicity, gender performance, race, and gender, I thus see that, because Marisela seems to represent a desired national citizenry through her marriage with Santos, neither female masculinity nor cultural nor religious diversities really have a place in Gallegos's ideology of nationhood.

Unlike Camila, who is murdered by Pintada in *Los de abajo,* the good woman character does not die at the hands of a warrior woman in *Doña Bárbara*. Instead, the warrior woman character permits the good woman she could not be herself to emerge under the tutelage of a patriarchal upper class white heterocissexual man figure. In this sense, the whitening project also implicates the disempowerment of *mestizo* women, since Marisela does not become self-empowered. Instead, she is dehumanized by being compared to an animal—the wild mare tamed by Carmelito (107). As critics have stated, Santos's ability to transform Marisela into a good woman stands for his capacity to civilize all that is wild while eradicating that which he considers barbarous. More than Doña Bárbara, I see that Marisela represents the wild Plains that cannot be civilized except through the outside agency of upper-class, white, heterocissexual man with a European (i.e., civilized) upbringing. Sommer considers Marisela's marriage to Santos to be Gallegos's way of repairing a history of appropriation and civil war (289). As I have discussed, by taking her to his house, he controls her present and future: he prevents Marisela from being raped, educates her, rationalizes her actions, and makes her his fiancée. Finally, he appropriates Marisela's sexuality through marriage to enhance his own social and economic standing. It is evident that he prevents her from becoming a *cacica* in her own right. Doña Bárbara's power meanwhile represents subaltern peoples who refuse traditional masculinities as well as European and white upper-class interventions. Similar to Pintada in Azuela's novel, the warrior woman character in Gallegos's work has an expiration date because she does not represent the ideal femininity and racial and ethnic nationality that uphold the traditional power of the cacique.

Sexuality in *Grande sertão: veredas*

Like *Los de abajo* and *Doña Bárbara*, the events related in *Grande sertão: veredas* occur in very traditional masculine settings. A lar-

Chapter Four

ger number of woman characters move in and out of the settings in João Guimarães Rosa's novel than in the previous two novels, however. The most significant ones include the sex workers (Nhorinhá, Maria-da-Luz, and Hortência) with whom Riobaldo relates; Riobaldo's ex-girlfriends, Miosótis and Rosa'uarda; Riobaldo's fiancée and wife, Otacília; and Hermógenes's wife. All of these characters are defined by their sexual roles with respect to men, whether as socially legitimate partners (i.e., potential or actual wives) or temporary partners (i.e., sex workers). None of these characters are shown wielding weapons or taking on the masculine *jagunço* role even though women did carry guns and were able to fight if necessary in the Brazilian Backlands.

Durval Muniz de Albuquerque Júnior states that women could not afford to be afraid or cowardly if they were to survive such a harsh environment (224). The history of the *cangaceiras* provides evidence of just how strong these women had to be. For example, researchers report that no less than forty and possibly up to eighty women were in Lampião's bands (Câmara et al. 207; Freitas 122; G. Nascimento 12). These women certainly carried weapons and knew how to shoot, but how much they participated in combat has been debated (Araújo, *Lampião* 251). Geraldo Maia do Nascimento argues that they were not soldiers and probably remained hidden during combat (19–20). They only learned to shoot guns in order to defend themselves or their group if they were ambushed (21). According to Antônio Amaury Correia de Araújo, who interviewed Dadá, women usually carried handguns, not rifles, although might have known how to wield a carabiner (*rifle, fuzil, mosquetão*) when necessary (*Lampião* 251). For instance, Dadá told Araújo that Cirillo's partner "Moça" knew how to use a rifle but would not participate in gunfights (251). In the documentary *A musa do cangaço* (The Cangaço's Muse) (1982), directed by José Umberto Dias, Dadá also states that many girls carried "pistolinha de brincadeira" (a toy gun). It is evident that women in the *cangaço* were familiar with guns and could have used them under special circumstances.

Sila is an example of a *cangaceira* who definitely used firearms. In her autobiography, *Angicos. Eu sobrevivi. Confissões de uma guerreira do cangaço* (Angicos. I Survived. Confessions of a Female Warrior in the Cangaço) (1997), she recounts two incidents in which she intervened in conflict. The first time occurs while she is pregnant, when she breaks the butt of a *mosquetão* on a soldier who is about to stab her husband, Zé Sereno, in the heart (*Angicos* 69). The second time she pulls out a gun she carries inside her shirt at her left breast and points it at another soldier while demanding that he let Zé Sereno go (92). According to her testimonial, Sila never shot firearms, but did use them as clubs or threats when she had to defend or rescue her husband. This is further evidence that *cangaceiras* carried guns and sometimes wielded them when it was strategic to do so.

Not all the *cangaceiras* in the Backlands were the same as Dadá and Sila. For example, Lampião's wife, Maria Bonita (Maria Gomes de Oliveira), has been historicized as a quite feminine figure because of the photographs of her taken by Abrahão Benjamim Boto (Freitas 144–48). According to Ana Paula Saraiva de Freitas, Maria Bonita seems to have been quite vain, while Dadá was a more courageous woman (161). Maria Bonita's importance as the wife and companion of the leader of the *cangaço* also suggests that historians, who prefer to see women in such roles, have downplayed the fighting skills of the *cangaceiras*. Despite this diminishment, *cangaceiras* could act as warriors when they so desired. For example, Dadá differentiates herself from other *cangaceiras* in her testimonial and her life history provides evidence that she was a warrior woman, albeit in feminine attire. First, she admits to having carried a 38 Colt revolver and a dagger and to using up lots of ammo ("A musa"). Freitas further notes that Dadá states that she had great aim and took pleasure in shooting (161). Second, according to Araújo, many of the *cangaceiros* recognized Dadá's bravery. He writes that Zé Rufino, one of the deadliest *cangaceiros*, tells Dadá that she should have been a man (*Gente* 37). Her warrior skills are so prominent that she is perceived as performing the masculinity of a most-desired position, even though she always wears a feminine outfit. Last, Dadá clearly knew how to fight. Araújo explains that when the *cangaceiro* Caixa de Fósforo provoked Dadá too much, she shot him, aimed well enough that the bullet only scratched him (*Gente* 89). Her fighting skills and resourcefulness are also visible when, having run out of ammunition during combat, she begins throwing stones at the enemy (*Gente* 117). Other events demonstrate her readiness to become involved in armed conflict. For example, when her husband, Corisco, is injured, Dadá takes up his rifle and points it at soldiers to force them to back off; she then takes over leadership of Corisco's group (*Gente* 118; *Lampião* 251). Such events showcase her ability to defend herself and others with firearms and reveal that such an ability was respected by others.

Although Dadá did not constantly perform as a warrior (Câmara et al. 214; Santos and Lima 11), she was more than just a wife and seamstress. In a way, her role as a warrior woman resembles that of many of her near contemporaries in the Mexican Revolution. For example, the character of Jesusa in Elena Poniatowska's *Hasta no verte, Jesús mío* (1967) is very like Dadá in that Jesusa supports her father and later her husband in the midst of combat. She even leads the troop after her husband dies. While I have chosen to focus my analysis on warrior woman and trans warrior characters who constantly perform as warriors, the Dadá case shows the porosity and complexity of warrior women's roles as they transform over time. Still, *cangaceiras* such as Dadá were not usually considered soldiers by the men with whom they interacted and they had to have husbands to render their position in the *cangaço* acceptable. As cis women who did not cross-dress and always appeared traditionally feminine, they differ from the trans warrior character, Diadorim.

Diadorim's masculine appearance has been related to the defenselessness of feminine women in rape situations. After hearing *jagunços* tell stories about how they raped women, Diadorim comments to Riobaldo that "[m]ulher é gente tão infeliz ... " (188; ellipsis in the original). While Diadorim is obviously criticizing the violent sexual subjugation of women by men, his comment has been interpreted as an explanation for not being open about his genitalia or sexuality. Some critics argue that he began cross-dressing to avoid being raped, although there is no other evidence for that in the novel. The compulsion to explain away his gender performance by reducing the identity of trans* man characters to the fear response perpetuates transphobia. I avoid that trap by reading Diadorim's comment as a way of making women's lack of freedom, vulnerability, and dependency on men in the Backlands obvious to the reader. The vulnerability of most women (that is, women other than the *cangaceiras*) is contrasted with Diadorim's strength as a trans warrior quite capable of protecting himself.

Diadorim's autonomy and empowerment in *Grande sertão: veredas* make it impossible for Riobaldo to establish a (heterosexual) romantic relationship with him, however. Although Riobaldo loves Diadorim, he looks for traditional feminine objects of love and sexual pleasure in order to construct and emphasize his own heterosexuality. In this final section of the chapter, I argue that Diadorim's presence and gender is contrasted with the feminine woman characters in order to emphasize Riobaldo's desire to be heterosexual. Daniel Balderston notes that Riobaldo constantly questions the nature of his affection for Diadorim, but never finds an answer to his dilemma (68), I see that Riobaldo's relationships to the feminine woman characters and his comparisons between them and Diadorim constitute a declaration of his sexual orientation. As narrator, he carefully weaves heterosexuality into his discourses in order to diminish his same-sex desire for Diadorim.

Sexually Active Women Characters

Nhorinhá is the first sex worker to appear by name in the narrative. Riobaldo often recalls their sexual relationship, as she "[r]ecebeu meu carinho no cetim do pêlo—alegria que foi, feito casamento, esponsal" (49). This fond memory implies that his relationship with Nhorinhá went beyond a simple sexual transaction. The word *casamento* (marriage) suggests their sexual relationship was nearly as profound as a marital union. Later, when Diadorim argues that Nhorinhá's mother, Ana Duzuza, should be executed for having revealed the identity of Medeiro Vaz, a *jagunço* leader, Riobaldo defends her because "essa Ana Duzuza fica sendo minha mãe!" (54), meaning she could become his mother-in-law. This comment further suggests that Riobaldo has more than a fleeting attachment to Nhorinhá. She represents the potential (although not the actualization) of a legitimate heterosexual romantic and sexual relationship.

Kathrin Holzermayr Rosenfield considers Nhorinhá to be similar to Diadorim in that both characters embody an androgyny marked by exuberant pleasure and happiness (*Desenveredando* 274). Explaining that the name Nhorinhá is composed of "Nhor" (*senhor* or mister) and "Nha" (*sinhá* or miss), she argues that the combination of feminine and masculine elements reiterates the totalizing androgynous fusion of opposites that often characterizes pagan virgins (274). While I do not consider Nhorinhá an androgyne, I agree with Rosenfield that Nhorinhá is characterized by

Chapter Four

her sexuality. Her sexual activity distinguishes her from Diadorim and gives her a space of her own in Riobaldo's desired emotional life. Riobaldo never rejects Nhorinhá for being a sex worker and actually considers her (in retrospect) a potential wife. He often says that if he had run into her again after he had become a better *jagunço*, his life would have changed.

Critic José Maurício Gomes de Almeida argues that Nhorinhá's sensual femininity represents the erotic phase of love, which Guimarães Rosa always describes lyrically ("Quem" 115). In general, Guimarães Rosa treats women sex workers positively in his texts. They are generous beings who help men and can become their wives. Even Riobaldo says that "*meretrixes*"—the word Guimarães Rosa uses—are sisters, and that men need their goodness (251–52). Prostitution is here treated as a vital profession that should be appreciated and respected. However, sex workers are only respected for their sexuality in service of heterocissexual men; they remain objects for these men to use in satiating their own sexual and social desires. The affects, desires, difficulties, preferences, and traumas experienced by sex workers as individuals seem to have no space in this limiting discourse. In fact, their perspective is nowhere present in the novel.

Riobaldo seems to avoid objectifying sex workers by never mentioning the economic transactions that would have been part of his relationship with them. Such neglect only further marginalizes the sex workers by rendering the heteropatriarchal system that oppresses them invisible and unimportant. Ignoring the economic exchange simultaneously emphasizes Riobaldo's heterosexuality and presents the *meretrixes* as fragile, submissive, and pleasing to men—that is, as performing an idealized femininity and sexuality. All the sex worker characters in the novel are depicted as good cis women who enable men to satisfy their needs for sex and affection. Within the novel's economy, these women help men maintain their heterosexuality while operating in a masculine world necessarily distant from their hometowns and families. At the same time, their presence seems to erase the possibility of homosexuality and/or same-sex intercourse or desire among *jagunços*. That is, it does not show the Backlands as a place where a person is or can be homosexual or where men who define themselves as heterosexual can desire and have sex with each other. The sex workers even reproduce legitimate heteropatriarchal relationships when

Warrior Women, Trans Warriors, and Traditional Femine Characters

they become the fiancées or wives of the *jagunços*. In Riobaldo's discourse, sex workers perform gender in compliance with the heterocispatriarchal system. They are the Angels in the Brothel.

The only other sex workers who are given names in the novel are Maria-da-Luz and Hortência, both of whom welcome Riobaldo to Verde-Alecrim after he has become a *jagunço* leader. They tell Riobaldo that Filiberto, the *jagunço* who protected him, has the right to have sex with them (545). The comment teaches Riobaldo a lesson about treating his subordinates as his equals. These two women are not poor sex workers, however. Since they live in the same house and own cultivable land in the area, Neitzel explains that they might better be termed "courtesans" (71). Their economic status displaces them from the traditional image of sex workers who must work hard to earn even a low standard of living. They are also different from other sex workers in that they are rumored to be more than friends (545); this implies that they might be bisexuals, pansexuals, or lesbians. That the discourse on their sexual relationship is public and refers to two sexually and economically autonomous women reveals that a non-traditional sexual relationship is possible in the Backlands. The sexual orientation of these two characters puts them outside the rules of their patriarchal society, as does Riobaldo's love for Diadorim, but their bisexual/pansexual/lesbian behavior and identity are not treated as something hidden and forbidden. They are still feminine woman characters that confirm Riobaldo's heterosexuality. Homosexuality is only disparaged when it applies to masculine characters such as Diadorim and Riobaldo, the macho *jagunços*.

Sex workers are not the only sexually active women characters in the novel. Riobaldo's girlfriends Miosótis and Rosa'uarda initiate him into sexual and romantic relationships while he is still a student living in Curralinho under the protection of his godfather (actually his father, although Riobaldo does not know it). Riobaldo has a relationship with Miosótis, but is more attracted to Rosa'uarda (139). The only time he misses Miosótis is when he wishes she could witness his rebellion against his godfather (139). Miosótis is treated as an object, a mirror intended to reflect Riobaldo's growing independence, maturity, and self-importance. Rosa'uarda, however, occupies a special place in Riobaldo's list of women to which he has been attached, because she is the first woman with whom he has sex (130). Because of her sexual role,

Riobaldo assigns her nearly as important a place in his memory as Nhorinhá. Both Rosa'uarda and Nhorinhá confirm Riobaldo's heterosexuality and displace his mixed feelings of love for Diadorim.

Diadorim does not interact with Riobaldo's girlfriends, Maria-da-Luz, or Hortência. He does not approve of Riobaldo having sex with sex workers and insists sex should not occur outside of marriage. He even makes Riobaldo promise to remain chaste when they go to war (207). It could be argued that Diadorim is trying to prevent Riobaldo from raping more women or he is jealous of Riobaldo's visits to sex workers, but the novel does not provide sufficient evidence to elaborate on Diadorim's motivations. Diadorim only justifies his moralizing discourse by arguing that sex makes men lose the courage to fight (208). He thus seems to provide Riobaldo with an education on a type of masculinity usually associated with a spirituality, mind, and body that Riobaldo does not have. Within this context, I suggest that Riobaldo's relationship with his fiancée, Otacília, is the only representation of traditional, socially legitimate, heterocissexual adult love in the novel.

The Feminine Fiancée

I analyze Riobaldo's interest in Otacília and desire to make her his fiancée as evidence of his anxiety about homosexuality and attempt to represent love in traditional terms. Otacília is the only daughter of the owner of the Santa Catarina ranch. He meets her when the *jagunço* group stops at the ranch. Otacília represents the upper class in the Backlands, far from the world of combat. Unlike the sex workers he meets elsewhere, Otacília lives with her family and is considered a valuable object within their heterocispatriarchal society. Marrying her will give Riobaldo access to the higher socioeconomic status denied to him by the refusal of his godfather to recognize him as his son and legal heir. Selecting her generates a triangle, composed of two white men and one white woman, in which one of the men uses the woman to counter his own homosexual panic. Both women and trans* men are manipulated in the triangles analyzed in this chapter; the major difference with the triangle that includes Diadorim is that his gender identity is sacrificed to avoid any challenge to normative sexual relationships. The Otacília—Diadorim—Riobaldo triangle not only reproduces heteronormativity, it perpetuates heterocisnormativity by treating the trans* man as a cis woman at the end of the novel.

That Riobaldo and Otacília's relationship is serious is hinted at during their first meeting, when Otacília points out a flower called a "casa-comigo" (206). Naming the flower with such a term establishes her role in the novel as potential wife. Despite their destined union, Riobaldo does not immediately fall for Otacília. Even after they become engaged, he tells his reader that their relationship is based on his "will to love" (213). These words suggest that he deliberately chose to fall in love with her, in contrast to his love for Diadorim, which is not his conscious choice. He even comments that "Diadorim pertencia a sina diferente. Eu vim, eu tinha escolhido para o meu amor o amor de Otacília" (444). Diadorim belongs to a different "sina" (fate, destiny), separate from Otacília. Meanwhile, it is Otacília's fate to become the woman who waits at home while her man is at war. She reproduces the culture of *marianismo*.

Neitzel considers the key difference between the Diadorim and Otacília to be largely metaphysical: Diadorim is associated with emotional chaos, while Otacília represents the hope of ending chaos (78). Neitzel does not take into account the homophobia underlying Riobaldo's emotional conundrum, however. As Balderston states, Riobaldo is concerned to avoid a homosexual panic (66). I see that his love relationships with his girlfriends occurred in his youth. As an adult, Riobaldo must establish a romantic relationship with Otacília as proof of his continuing heterosexuality and desire to have a family. Her character thus represents Riobaldo's struggle against his feelings for Diadorim. Although Otacília and Diadorim are not objective opposites, Riobaldo treats them as such. This opposition is demonstrated when Riobaldo gives Diadorim a topaz gemstone. Diadorim asks Riobaldo to keep it until after they have avenged the assassination of Joca Ramiro (390). Later on Riobaldo sends the topaz to Otacília, thereby changing the addressee of an object that symbolizes love (457). Riobaldo wants to demonstrate publicly and to himself and Diadorim that he loves Otacília. Giving Diadorim's gemstone to Otacília is his attempt to diminish his affection for Diadorim and transfer it to a socially legitimate recipient within his homophobic context.

Chapter Four

Since Riobaldo's love for Diadorim makes him question his identity as a masculine heterosexual man and *jagunço*, he selects Otacília, a woman whose class and emphasized femininity will guarantee his heterosexuality and with whom he can have a traditional, sanctified, and upper-class relationship and family. Recalling how he met Otacília, Riobaldo says: "ela eu conheci em conjuntos suaves, tudo dado e clareado, suspendendo, se diz: quando os anjos e o vôo em volta, quase, quase" (156). The reference to the angels belongs to a romantic tradition with which Riobaldo can justify his love for Otacília. He also idealizes her (Almeida, "Quem" 115). I see that this idealization arises in part because Riobaldo barely interacts with Otacília. Unlike Diadorim, she neither educates Riobaldo nor corrects his behavior. Her emphasized femininity remains intact in his memory, so she represents the peacefulness that comes from conforming to heterocispatriarchal parameters. In contrast, Riobaldo struggles to hide his passion for Diadorim, since it is a love for another man (Balderston 71). After recognizing that he has fallen in love with Diadorim, he says, "[a]certei minha idéia: eu não podia, por lei de rei, admitir o extrato daquilo. Ia, por paz de honra e tenência, sacar esquecimento daquilo de mim. Se não, pudesse não, ah, mas então eu devia de quebrar o morro: acabar comigo!" (308). Whereas Riobaldo associates Otacília with tranquility, loving Diadorim results in his questioning his identity and the rules of his world. This questioning even leads him to contemplate suicide.

Riobaldo's homophobic anxiety or panic can also be seen in that he is only at ease with his feelings of love for Diadorim when the latter is asleep or dead. Watching Diadorim sleep, Riobaldo describes him "De perto, senti a respiração dele, remissa e delicada. Eu aí gostava dele. Não fosse um, como eu, disse a Deus que esse ente eu abraçava e beijava" (213). Riobaldo prefers Diadorim at his most docile and vulnerable, because at such times Diadorim does not contradict or undermine his heterosexual masculinity. Describing Diadorim's breathing in conventional feminine terms allows him to admit his love for an otherwise apparently masculine man to himself. In the quote, he refers to Diadorim as an "ente" (being) in order to degenderize him and admit his love for him without constructing it as gay.

Only after Diadorim dies can Riobaldo idealize him much as he does Otacília. Once Riobaldo discovers Diadorim's genitalia, he considers "her" just as much of an Angel as Otacília. Alive, Diadorim represents the same-sex feelings that threaten Riobaldo's heterosexual manhood, but Diadorim asleep or dead sustains Riobaldo's heterosexuality. Riobaldo ceases to hide his love for Diadorim only after he no longer believes it will call his heterosexuality into question.

Riobaldo's homophobia is represented in his heterocisnormativity. The ways in which he discusses love puts further emphasis on both these discourses. Benedito Nunes contends that this character knows three types of love: 1) primitive passion for Diadorim; 2) sensual passion for Nhorinhá; and 3) spiritual love for Otacília (144–45). Although these three types can be interconnected, he ranks them hierarchically as a shift from the sensory to the intellectual or from the body to the soul. Nunes treats love as a spiritual aspiration superior to both asexual relationships (i.e., with Diadorim) and sexual pleasure (i.e., with Nhorinhá). Antonio Cândido presents a less hierarchical and more complex view of Riobaldo's romantic feelings than does Nunes. He positions Otacília and Nhorinhá as opposites, representing a dichotomy between sacred and profane love. He then treats Riobaldo's love for Diadorim as different, but does not engage with discourses on homosexuality ("O homem" 305). Rosenfield claims that Riobaldo's indecisiveness around choosing Diadorim over other women characters is not a hesitation between heterosexual and homosexual love (*Desenveredando* 281). Rather, the indecision is a poetic representation of the fundamental choice all human beings must make whether or not to accept life's challenges (281). While Rosenfield appreciates the diversity of experiences, loves, and types of human beings characterized within the novel, she still downplays Riobaldo's homophobia and same-sex desire.

None of these critics address the fact that Riobaldo himself does not distinguish women by whether he has experienced "carnal" or "spiritual" love with them. Having sex with Nhorinhá is enough for him to want to marry her. Furthermore, they do not consider the possibility that Riobaldo is only mimicking the idea of spiritual, sacred, or romantic love in becoming engaged to Otacília. Comparing Riobaldo's complex, close, and lasting relationship with Diadorim to his idealization of the distant, barely known Otacília actually highlights the artificiality of Riobaldo's love for her. I see that in asking her to marry him, he follows the social conventions of heterocisnormative romantic love that conveniently allows him to access a higher socioeconomic position. Traditional notions of love require that a masculine cis man obtain a virgin feminine cis woman as an object of exchange. Feminine cis women are meant to provide cis men with sexual relief and, as mothers, reproduce the conventional family. Any claim to love a feminine cis woman in this context is submerged within the kinship structures and power dynamics of heterocispatriarchal society. Considering how Diadorim resists this exchange of women, Riobaldo transforms both of their experiences after his death to fit his idea of heterosexuality. He establishes a relationship with Otacília that creates a triangle with Diadorim, a triangle that then allows him to diminish his homosexuality. With Diadorim's death, he is able to modify his own narrative to show that it has always been one of heterocissexuality.

The Feminine Object

Significantly, a woman without a name of her own is the person who discovers Diadorim's genitalia after he is dead. Referred to only as Hermógenes's wife, this woman resembles Otacília in coming from the landowning class. Neitzel suggests that her namelessness represents the sterile, secretive, feminine extreme of not being (108). I argue that in being defined solely by her relationship to a man, her presence in the novel reinforces the stability of the conventional family and the patriarchal notion that objectifies people—specially women—and treats them only as cis. Her own objectification is demonstrated by her being used as a pawn by Riobaldo, whose group kidnaps her in order to incite a battle with the enemy Hermógenes.

This character, along with the other objectified feminine characters in the novel (Otacília, sex workers, ex-girlfriends), reproduces a traditional culture and contributes to the oppression of women. Diadorim's performance opposes this culture. He avoids and even denigrates the treatment of women as objects of exchange (i.e., paying women for sex). He never appears as a conventional love object and refuses to emphasize femininity or reproduce the hegemonic rules of female-sexed people. Because of Diadorim's transgressions, Riobaldo aims to return him to a space protected by the norms of the heterocispatriarchy. This is

Warrior Women, Trans Warriors, and Traditional Femine Characters

what Hermógenes's wife accomplishes by uncovering Diadorim's sex and then cleaning and dressing the body of his corpse in her own feminine clothes. Neitzel argues that by shrouding Diadorim, thanks to the hands of Hermógenes's wife "se concretizará a cerimônia que reintegrará o homem ao Uno" (110). While she does prepare Diadorim for burial, I interpret her actions as positioning the masculine trans warrior character within the traditional category of feminine cis woman, thereby enabling Riobaldo to openly acknowledge his (now heterosexual) love for Diadorim.

Riobaldo nevertheless blames Diadorim for having kept his biological sex a secret from him. Toward the end of the novel, after Diadorim's death, Riobaldo comments sadly, "[p]orque eu, em tanto viver de tempo, tinha negado em mim aquele amor, e a amizade desde agora estava amargada falseada; e o amor, e *a pessoa dela*, mesma, ela tinha me negado" (621; emphasis mine). By having kept his sex a secret, Diadorim denied Riobaldo the chance to love "her" as a woman and take sexual pleasure in "her" female body. I suggest that Riobaldo's criticism of Diadorim for having prevented them from developing their sexuality as a couple in accordance with heterocisnormative standards provides further evidence that Riobaldo always avoids questioning either his own heterosexuality or Diadorim's. It is better to blame Diadorim than to assume same-sex attraction. Transphobia becomes obvious when the trans* person is blamed for being deceptive.

Riobaldo's rebuke implies a deeper critique of cis women and trans* men who refuse to be objectified by their reproductive systems. Riobaldo is never able to use or objectify Diadorim as he does the feminine woman characters in the novel. Rosenfield argues that Diadorim as a figure represents the impossibility of being a woman and the exclusion and disastrous marginalization of the feminine (272). Patriarchal society has no space for the feminine (272). To see Diadorim's performance as the impossibility of the empowered feminine is to reproduce Riobaldo's discourse, however. Masculinity and femininity are neither contradictory nor exclusionary. By performing masculinity and achieving a most-desired position as a trans* man, I propose that Diadorim retains agency and follows his own agenda throughout the novel. Instead of marginalizing the feminine, this character represents just one trans* identity out of many that contributes to emphasizing the fluidity of gender performances and the complexities of gender identities.

Chapter Four

Mexican man writer Fernando Zamora explores the trans* theme in the Mexican Revolution in the 2001 novel *Por debajo del agua* (Under the Water). One of the main characters in this novel is a *soldadera* named Isabel who takes care of children, tends wounded soldiers, and helps women in labor. Isabel is described as extremely feminine and beautiful; she is also trans*. With this character, Zamora opens up spaces of gender performance that are rarely explored in the literature of the Mexican Revolution. The novel emphasizes the diversity of gender identities and sexual orientations among the *soldaderas*, ordinary soldiers, and officers in the Revolution, a social context that has traditionally been treated as a heterosexual cis men's space. Isabel lives as the *soldadera* of General Pablo Aguirre, but he kills her once her sex is discovered because he cannot permit himself to be seen as "homosexual." This novel criticizes transphobia and gender violence and makes evident the precarious position trans* women hold in heterosexual men-dominated war environments. The heterocisnormativity of the Revolution is so transphobic and homophobic that the heterosexual trans* character must be sacrificed. By contrast, Guimarães Rosa's novel exemplifies a different trans* experience, in that the genitalia of the trans* character, his transness and identity, are not what provoke his death. Instead, Diadorim's courage and abilities are highlighted and he dies defending his own ideals and agenda.

By comparing Diadorim with the women characters (and Riobaldo's descriptions of them) in the novel, I have demonstrated his transgressive performance and trans* identity. I have also provided evidence of the heteronormativity of Riobaldo's sexual orientation and discourse on love, along with his homophobia, transphobia, and trans-ignorance. Despite Riobaldo's masculinist and homophobic perspective, the novel does introduce a variety of possibilities for relationships between Riobaldo and women characters that need not fall in line with upper–class white conventions. Still, the relationship between Riobaldo and Diadorim is the only one that challenges traditional notions of love.

Conclusion

Comparing the relationships between the trans warriors and warrior women with feminine cis women characters in three novels of the early twentieth century exposes the artificiality of hegemonic discourses on gender, women, beauty, love, and heterocissexuality. Warrior women's and trans warriors' performances of masculinity present a strong contrast to the emphasized femininity represented by other women characters. In *Los de abajo*, the differences between Pintada and Camila, Cervantes's fiancée, and Codorniz's girl show that Pintada refuses to become such an object and actually brings a halt to the exchange of women. In *Doña Bárbara*, comparing Doña Bárbara and Marisela demonstrates that the latter subordinates her emphasized femininity to Santos and his masculinist discourse, while Doña Bárbara's empowerment remains transgressive, autonomous, and permeated by indigenous and sexual elements. In *Grande sertão*, Riobaldo professes love for feminine cis women characters (representative of women's sexuality or emphasized femininity) in opposition to a love that undermines his heterosexual macho identity, that is, for a (trans*) man. Diadorim's performance of masculinities interrogates the artificiality of Riobaldo's hegemonic discourse on love and identity that is based on arbitrary binary divisions of gender and sexual desire. I see that it also exposes trans-ignorance and transphobia.

Warrior women's and trans warriors' transgressive autonomy may be compared to the lack of agency of conventional feminine cis women, whose actions are mediated by men protagonists in all three novels. Furthermore, cis men protagonists' privilege is visible when they intervene in and generate artificial antagonisms between lead women characters. Men characters place trans warrior and warrior woman characters in a triangle along with a woman character. With the help of Cervantes, Demetrio establishes the relationship between the main women characters by preferring Camila to Pintada; he also determines their interactions thereafter. Santos puts mother and daughter into an antagonistic relationship by educating and preferring Marisela. Riobaldo mediates the relationships among women characters by comparing them to each other. In attempting to recover his heterosexuality, which he views as having been "stolen" by his attraction for Diadorim, he claims to prefer a variety of feminine women over his true love, Diadorim. Thus, the presence of a masculine man character in each triangle forces feminine cis women into opposing warrior woman and trans warrior characters. This dynamic also implies that women and trans* men are exploitable, since they are ultimately made to support the man character's power. Camila dies

Chapter Four

and Pintada is expelled from the band, Doña Bárbara leaves and Marisela ends up embodying the ideal of *marianismo*, and Otacília becomes the wife once Riobaldo finds out Diadorim's baptismal name and mourns his death as "her" death. Analyzing the relationships between warrior woman and trans warrior characters with women and men characters thus shows the classism, homophobia, racism, sexism, and transphobia embedded in homosociality.

Masculine men protagonists never have to question the gender norms of their society because they already occupy positions of privilege. The main non-transgressive women characters in each novel (i.e., Camila, Marisela, Otacília) readily subordinate themselves to such privileged cis men without questioning their masculinity or challenging the structures of their society. When cis men characters deliberately select traditional feminine women, they reproduce the norms of their heterocispatriarchal societies regarding the exchange of women and their own roles in the transaction. At the same time, they reject trans warriors and warrior women because such characters undermine the system that they trust and represent, a complex discriminatory system that supports them as leaders in most-desired positions. In the next chapter, I examine other warrior women and trans warriors in the twentieth century in Latin America in order to analyze their performances of masculinity, empowerment, and leadership skills.

Chapter Five

Trans Warriors and Warrior Women in Twentieth-Century Latin America

Real flesh and bone trans warriors and warrior women populate Latin American history. For example, Maria Quitéria de Jesus (1792–1853) cut her hair short, put on men's clothes, and enlisted in the Brazilian War of Independence in 1822 (Schumaher and Brazil 406–07). Even though troop leader Major Castro realized she was a woman, he allowed her to enlist with his men because she was disciplined and good at handling guns. (He required that she wear a skirt over her military uniform, however.) (C. Oliveira 116). Maria was but one of the many Latin American women who throughout history have joined military forces. Native women such as Clara Camarão (in Brazil) and Eréndira (in Mexico) fought the Portuguese and Spanish invaders. Many enlisted in armies fighting for independence. In Mexico, Teodosea Rodríguez ("La Generala") along with Juana Guadalupe Barragán ("La Barragana") formed a platoon and joined Father Hidalgo, one of the leaders of Mexican independence (Herrera-Sobek 87–88). In Venezuela, Ecuador, Panamá, and Colombia, women such as Teresa Corneja, Manuela Tinoco, and Rosa Canelones fought in Vargas Swamp and Boyacá battles (Cherpak 222). In Brazil, Bárbara de Alencar joined the Pernambucan Revolt of 1817 and the revolutionary movement Confederation of Equator in 1824 (Schumaher and Brazil 96). In the next century, warrior women and trans warriors also participated in combat as bandits, guerrillas, even terrorists.

Their participation in diverse armed conflicts, anti-dictatorship movements, and criminal activities has been kept alive in the social imaginary of Latin America through a variety of fictional and historical media. In this chapter, I examine changing images and gender performances of warrior characters throughout the twentieth century by comparing *Los de abajo*, *Doña Bárbara*, and *Grande*

Chapter Five

sertão: veredas with other texts that portray fictional and historical trans warriors and warrior women. Strategies of empowerment such as transgressive use of clothes, playing with names and nicknames, and interactions and competition amongst men and women characters—the topics of previous chapters in this book—are represented in all these texts, although some strategies prevail over others in particular contexts. Cross-dressing becomes less important over time as being feminine ceases to prevent women from empowering themselves in men-dominated spaces of armed conflict. Meanwhile, issues of sexuality acquire more prominence as cis men and men characters attempt to retake control over warrior women's and trans warriors' identities, desires, and pleasures.

This chapter is divided into two sections, each of which examines trends I consider central to the development of characterizations of transgressive warriors of the twentieth century. The first section focuses on women and trans* men of the Mexican Revolution. Women, trans* men, warrior women, and trans warriors were increasingly portrayed in Mexican folk songs, films, and literary texts as the century progressed. The Mexican government even appropriated such figures to promote heterocispatriarchal notions of nationalism. From amongst the great quantity of texts that depict revolutionary times, I have chosen first to concentrate on the gender performance and identity of the historical Petra/Pedro Ruiz to highlight trans* narratives. I then examine two significant texts that simultaneously engage and reject governmental portrayals of warrior women: *Cartucho: Relatos de la lucha en el norte de México* (Cartucho: Tales of the Struggle in Northern Mexico) (1931) and *La negra Angustias* (The Black Woman Angustias) (1944). *Cartucho* is the first work by a Mexican woman writer to depict the Revolution. That *Cartucho* was written by a woman (Nellie Campobello) is key to comparing her warrior woman character, Colonel Nacha Ceniceros, with the Pintada character from Azuela's earlier text. In one short yet powerful vignette, Nellie Campobello reconsiders the figure of the warrior woman and challenges official discourses on the Revolution.

La negra Angustias is the first novel of the Mexican Revolution with a Black woman protagonist, who also happens to be a warrior woman. The racial issues I have previously addressed in discussing Pintada's and Doña Bárbara's performances are central to my examination of Angustias's clothing strategies. However, indigenous,

indigenous-descendent, mixed, or *mestiza* women characters such as Doña Bárbara and Pintada do not expose the same kinds of oppression and discrimination endured by Afro-descendent characters such as Angustias. The intersection of race, gender, and class in *La negra Angustias* provides evidence that, even though a man writer, Francisco Rojas González, attempted to rescue the contributions of Black Mexicans to the Revolution from oblivion in his portrayal of a strong Black warrior woman, he still ended up domesticating and sexualizing her empowerment.

The second section of this chapter moves forward in time to analyze a sample of fictional and non-fictional portrayals of women guerrillas and revolutionaries in Cuba, Brazil, and Nicaragua. Such warrior women played a vital role in Latin American revolutions and revolutionary movements. Although the guerrillas I discuss here were hardly the first warrior women to engage in combat in the region, their struggles to be allowed to fight and be considered equal to men are just as fraught. Despite the advances in women's rights of the later twentieth century, leftist revolutionary movements were not free of gender bias. Furthermore, if women were not vocal about their participation and contributions to revolutionary change, they were not included in combat, were misrepresented, or even written out of history altogether. National governmental agencies and popular media often manipulated depictions of women guerrillas in order to send specific messages about revolutionary movements and women's normative roles in heterocispatriarchal societies. The fight of warrior women to be heard and depicted accurately constitutes their gendered performances and strategies for accessing power. Moreover, their struggles confirm the lack of gender equality. Although they had to fight to be respected, warrior women of the twentieth century gradually obtained access to power that had historically been denied them. Their performances demonstrate that power need not only be associated with masculinities performed by cis men. Whether masculine or feminine in appearance, women accessing power is inherently transgressive. Their performances queer the hegemonic ideas about power and masculinity.

Unfortunately, the presence of trans* men guerrillas in most of the revolutionary movements of the mid-twentieth century has yet to be recorded. While both trans* and women guerrillas definitely participated in the Mexican Revolution, their existence has not been narrated for other revolutions. For example, portrayals of Brazilian, Cuban, and Sandinista revolutionary movements are dominated by images of cis men revolutionaries such as Carlos Marighella, Fernando Gabeira, Carlos Lamarca, Ernesto "Che" Guevara, Fidel and Raúl Castro, Carlos Fonseca, Daniel Ortega, and Tomás Borge. The experiences of women in Brazil, Cuba, and Nicaragua demonstrate that these groups were not only men-dominated, they were highly chauvinistic and *machista*. While the chaos that characterizes war allows spaces and opportunities to gender non-conforming people to enter and fight, homophobia and transphobia remained rampant in Latin American revolutionary movements. This discrimination made it very difficult for trans-identified people or *travestis* to out themselves in military contexts or even participate in militant movements. Moreover, class struggle was considered the only fight to be fought in the Latin American revolutionary movements of the 1950s through 1980s. Addressing the intersectional oppression of Black people, women, and the LGBTQAI+ community was seen as a distraction from the main goal. As a result, warrior women are more prominent than trans warriors throughout this chapter.

Warrior Women and Trans Warriors in the Mexican Revolution

With the exception of the Mexican folk ballads known as *corridos*, most texts written during the Mexican Revolution (1910-1920) lacked women characters. Famous men authors such as Martín Luis Guzmán and José Vasconcelos largely ignored women in their depictions of the Revolution. In *El águila y la serpiente*, Guzmán only mentions some upper-class women who accompanied high-ranking (men) military personnel and women sex workers looking for customers in street cafes. Luis A. Marentes argues that Guzmán and Vasconcelos were primarily interested in presenting the world of those from above rather than those from below, which is a strong contrast to the underdogs described in Azuela's novel. Such authors failed to notice the existence of *soldaderas* amongst the rank and file. Even men who wrote about underdogs in their novels of the revolution tended not to develop women characters. While the protagonists in Rafael Muñoz's ¡*Vámonos con Pancho Villa!* (Let's Join Pancho Villa!) (1931) are common soldiers, *soldaderas* only appear in the background. Azuela's 1915 warrior woman character Pintada is thus unique for the time.

It was not until after the Mexican Revolution was over that women and trans* characters began to appear in texts such as Baltasar Dromundo's *Francisco Villa y la 'Adelita'* (Francisco Villa and the 'Adelita') (1934), Agustín Yáñez's *Al filo del agua* (1947), Elena Poniatowska's *Hasta no verte, Jesús mío* (1967), Carlos Islas's *La Valentina* (1980), Laura Esquivel's *Como agua para chocolate* (1989), and Fernando Zamora's *Por debajo del agua* (2001). Warrior women were also depicted in Mexican films about the Revolution. They were usually portrayed by the actress María Félix, who had warrior women roles in films such as *La Cucaracha* (The Cockroach) (1959) and *Juana Gallo* (1961). Although Nellie Campobello's text was published earlier (in 1931), it was written in the same context of growing interest in recording the presence of women in the Revolution.

Before discussing Campobello's text, I want to call attention to the ways in which trans* men and cross-dressed women in the Mexican Revolution have been described or narrated, as I contend that they have been rendered invisible and/or complicit with heterocisnormativity. I have already described in Chapter 1 how the Zapatista Colonel Amelio Robles Ávila, who preferred the masculine name and lived as a man, has been recovered as a "woman" at several moments in recent history to emphasize the presence of women, but not trans* men, in the Revolution. This violent erasure of his gender identity makes me wonder if the same act has been committed against other trans* warriors/guerrillas and how many other trans* men and women have been rendered anonymous.

Petra or Pedro Ruiz is another historical figure whose gender transgression has been recorded. In *La mujer en la Revolución mexicana* (The Woman in the Mexican Revolution) (1961), Ángeles Mendieta Alatorre mentions Petra in a few paragraphs. She describes Petra/Pedro as reckless and bellicose and states that "she" was known as "echa bala." Petra cross-dressed, cut her hair, and masculinized herself with the name "Pedro Ruiz" so well that no one suspected her of being a woman (91). Mendieta Alatorre adds that "Pedro" disputed with the other revolutionary soldiers over women man soldiers had abducted. After brandishing his knife and gun to intimidate the soldiers, Pedro would wrest the women away, only to abandon them later on (91). The text makes it obvi-

Chapter Five

ous that Pedro was actually a heterocissexual woman (Petra) whose only interest in other women was to save them. Mendieta Alatorre's narration is another example of fear of homosexuality and how revolutionary histories are recovered in ways that provide no space for lesbianism, same-sex desire, or trans* identities. While many gender rules were broken and new roles and sexualities configured in the context of armed conflict, desire, sexual orientation, and gender identity remained heterocissexual and binary. The use of pronouns in Mendieta Alatorre's text indicates that Pedro is treated almost as a completely different person than Petra.

Mendieta Alatorre describes how Pedro/Petra came out as a woman in 1913. "She" stepped to the front of the assembled troops to ask the First Chief of the Constitutionalists, Venustiano Carranza, to discharge her, stating that "una mujer le ha servido como soldado" (91). Having quenched her thirst for adventure and been confirmed female, Pedro then returned to living as Petra (91). In this version of her biography, Petra/Pedro's military career becomes a sort of playful temporary escapade, not a serious commitment to the nation and the Revolution. Mendieta Alatorre never mentions Pedro/Petra's ethical engagement with revolutionary ideals, just the need for adventure. Mendieta Alatorre adds that Carranza was intensely interested in hearing about the life of such a colorful and beautiful "hembra" (female) (91). By referring to Petra's beauty through Carranza's eyes, Mendieta Alatorre uses the male gaze to make it very clear that Petra is neither butch nor masculine. Thus, "she" cannot be accused of having a suspect sexual orientation. The reference to her being aesthetically pleasurable to Carranza implies that Petra's femininity is recovered at the end of her adventure; "she" is once again available to the heterocissexual white male gaze/desire.

In *Las Soldaderas* (1999), Elena Poniatowska likewise recovers the images, stories, and histories of many women involved in the Mexican Revolution, whom she portrays as brave and fearless (Estrada *Troubled*, 159). Petra Ruiz is included in this book. Labeled "el Echa Balas," "she" is depicted as a skillful fighter with excellent aim (*Las soldaderas* 16). Poniatowska does not describe Petra as cross-dressed, however, but as "in disguise" (*disfrazada*) (16). Being disguised can imply deceit or playfulness, but either interpretation suggests only temporary posing or passing. The term "disguise" in no way welcomes the possibility of a gender identity that challenges binaries. In the same vein, Poniatowska always puts the name in quotation marks to indicate that "Pedro" is really "Petra," even in the description of an incident in which "Pedro" rescues a young woman from being raped. In doing so, Poniatowska seems to indirectly confirm Mendieta Alatorre's perspective while simultaneously suggesting that Petra is always behind "Pedro's" actions. The quotation marks around the name function as another disguise. As in *La mujer en la Revolución mexicana*, Petra's heterosexuality is never questioned in *Las Soldaderas*. Moreover, "her" cis status is confirmed when "Pedro" opens his shirt to show the young woman "he" rescued that they are physically the same in having breasts (16). Once again, any potential for queering Petra/Pedro seems to be dismissed.

Still, Poniatowska does mention that Petra was in charge of a battalion that defeated federal troops in Mexico City and that "she" obtained the rank of lieutenant (16). In recovering this episode, Poniatowska underscores Petra's prestigious position on the battlefield. "She" is not merely a woman in disguise concerned for the well-being of other women caught up in the Revolution as Mendieta Alatorre's narrative suggests. Poniatowska further adds that, after hearing a rumor that women were going to be expelled from the army, Petra resigns rather than be barred (16). Petra has an agenda. "She" decides when to cease her involvement in the Revolution and selects to whom "she" will declare her withdrawal from combat. Highlighting her intentions and her victory in the battlefield indicates that Petra has agency: "she" is not just the adventurer of Mendieta Alatorre's narrative. Outing herself in front of Carranza further underscores her autonomy. "She" confronts the highest authority by showing him the pervasiveness and importance of women on the battlefield.

The ways in which Petra/Pedro's biography is recovered implicate gender transgressions, but by the end of these texts, Pedro/Petra is returned to the category of cis woman. I argue that despite their transgression, the manner in which they are recovered in the texts prevents the possibility of a trans* identity and the continuation of any queer gender and sexuality following the armed combat. Rather, these discourses on Petra/Pedro do the opposite: they emphasize the strength of compulsory heterocisnormativity. Once it is confirmed that "she" is a cis woman or that "she" returned to live as Petra, Pedro/Petra and Pedro disappear from history.

Chapter Five

Changing Images of a Warrior Woman from 1931 to 1960

Published in 1931 by Campobello, *Cartucho* is structured as a series of short scenes, each one exploring events or people involved in the Revolution. Most of the women characters (including the narrator) in these stories merely witness the war or its consequences. For example, "Las mujeres del norte" (Women from the North) features women who watch their men leave them to go fight for independence. One vignette, "Nacha Ceniceros," introduces a feminine woman officer in the Pancho Villa army. This is Colonel Nacha Ceniceros, who "usaba pistola y tenía trenzas" (66). In achieving a most-desired position through strength and skill, Nacha most resembles Doña Bárbara. Unlike the *cacica* and Pintada, both of whom are driven to empower themselves so they can achieve personal wealth and status, obtaining profit and boosting her ego are not Nacha's goals. Nacha is an ethical warrior woman who does not take credit for others' work and is committed to the noble cause of the Revolution.

Unlike Diadorim, Nacha never cross-dresses. She is always identified as a "girl" and her unusual strength is explained away as the result of having been raised in the mountains. Although Nacha projects a feminine image with her hairstyle and does not wear gender-transgressive clothing, she occupies a position of military power and uses a gun. She is thus a warrior woman and, like the other warrior women and trans warrior characters I have analyzed in this book, she becomes disempowered by the end of the original version of Campobello's story (Campobello published three versions of her text, 1931, 1940, and 1960). While cleaning her gun, she accidentally kills Gallardo, the man she loves, and is then charged with murder and executed: "En otra tienda estaba sentado Gallardo junto a una mesa; platicaba con una mujer; el balazo que se le salió a Nacha en su tienda lo recibió Gallardo en la cabeza y cayó muerto" (66). This ending suggests that a woman who dares to perform men's tasks is not suited to them and hence must be punished. Indeed, she is penalized twice, first in losing her love object and second in losing her own life.

Emron Esplin suggests that Nacha deliberately killed Gallardo because he was cheating on her (95), but I do not find sufficient evidence to support that reading. First, although she was in love with him, the narrator never indicates they were a couple, so there is no infidelity implied. Second, the narrator states that she was cleaning her gun, so it was an accident, not a revenge killing (66). Nacha may have been heartbroken by his rejection—indeed, she cries just before she cleans her gun—but there is no suggestion that she plans to murder him. Not all rejected women are vindictive. The way in which the narrator describes how the bullet was fired, "se le salió un tiro" (66), also suggests Gallardo's death was an accident. The impersonal *se* structure in Spanish (*se le salió*) indicates that Nacha did not press the trigger on purpose. Moreover, Nacha is portrayed as an innocent who behaves like a child, not a soldier: "Se puso en su tienda a limpiar su pistola, estaba muy entretenida cuando se le salió un tiro" (66). The narrator's words suggest she treats the gun as a toy. She is "entertained" by cleaning it and does not take the task seriously. She seems to be playing carelessly with a deadly object. She pays for using an object that has not historically been assigned to women by being put to death. Within the logic of the story, her execution seems to be for the right reasons. Nacha is an incompetent officer, unable to use her most important tool properly. She must be eliminated for her ineptitude, even though she has managed to become a colonel. The way Nacha is represented during her execution is also written as a lesson to be learned. According to the narrator, those who witnessed her execution are left with the indelible image of a crying feminine woman (66). Nacha must be remembered as the penitent feminine woman, not as a Colonel.

This vignette is not about banning women altogether from the battlefield, since women participated in many tasks and roles during the Revolution. It is about controlling their presence in war and manipulating them into reproducing binary gender roles. Even though government ideology associated the figure of the warrior woman with progress in building the Mexican nation, official discourses often aimed to delimit women's performances during and after the Revolution. Indeed, Nacha's very outsider-ness suggests that many stories of women's revolutionary activities have been domesticated, ignored, or stepped over in the official discourses of the Revolution. As Debra Castillo observes, the role of women during the Revolution has mostly been erased (5). Castillo notes that most *corridos* emphasize the role of the nurturing woman who attends her brave man during the Revolution, but even popular *corridos* that depict woman fighters (e.g., "La Valentina," "La Cucaracha," "La Soldadita," and "Juana Gallo")

Chapter Five

promote gender conventions (5). According to Ela Molina Sevilla de Morelock, strong, independent women during and after the armed fight were inconvenient for the restructuration and respatialization of Mexico (46). The heteropatriarchal ideology had to control such excesses.

Films, *corridos*, and literary texts supported this ideology by pressuring women to return home to a traditional femininity. Susan Dever argues that post-revolutionary melodramas in Mexico pushed women who had been masculinized by taking on fighting roles or becoming heads of households during the war to return to more feminine pursuits after it was over (44). Women who existed outside the normative household were made aware that they would end up destroying themselves and their loved ones. As an unmarried orphan and autonomous woman, Nacha must be executed as a warning for women in similar situations.

The warning would be retained in the next edition of the book a decade later. When Campobello revised and edited *Cartucho* in 1940, she added twenty-four new vignettes, removed one, and changed the organization, structure, language, or narratorial subjectivity of many of the stories, but did not modify "Nacha Ceniceros" (B. Rodríguez 159–60). However, she did lengthen and change the storyline for a 1960 reprint of her collected works (160). Whereas the original 1931 vignette reduces Nacha's empowerment and skills, the 1960 version permits her to act autonomously and in accord with her own conscience and she is not punished for her violations of gender norms.

By 1960, the *Partido revolucionario institucional* (Institutional Revolutionary Party, PRI), the party that had been in power since 1929, had taken over the image of the Revolution and integrated it into its nationalist propaganda. The state has always been highly selective in promoting its ideology, as can be seen in its neglect of Pancho Villa for the first three decades following the Revolution. According to Friedrich Katz, Villa was only celebrated as a hero by the state after presidents were elected who had not fought against him during the Revolution. Since 1966, Mexican presidents have drawn on Villa's fame to strengthen their own status (Katz 790), but previously, his image was only widely known in popular culture and in the works of intellectuals (793). Campobello was one of the literati who favored Villa. In 1940, she published *Apuntes sobre la vida militar de Francisco Villa* (Notes on the Military Life of Francisco Villa), in which she reconstructs his life and battles based on interviews and research in his archive (203). Critics have suggested that Campobello also intended to restore Villa's reputation in the later edition of *Cartucho* (Avechuco Cabrera 72–73). Campobello admitted as much in an interview with Emmanuel Carballo (385). It seems that not having Villa order Nacha's execution was meant to present him in a more favorable light. This is a valid argument, but I am more interested in how the changes to the vignette oppose official manipulations of warrior women's images than in how they resurrect Pancho Villa as a hero. Whereas Victoria McCard suggests that Campobello only "*inadvertently* creates a female character who defies the *soldadera* stereotype of the novels and *corridos* of the Mexican Revolution" (46; emphasis mine) in the 1960 version, I see that Campobello intentionally rewrote the Nacha story to rectify history.

According to B. Christine Arce, by modifying the 1931 version of the story in 1960, Campobello invites her readers to challenge a variety of discursive genres, including gossip, oral traditions, journalism, and official history (*Mexico's* 130). In the 1960 prologue to her collected works, Campobello explains that the earlier version of "Nacha Ceniceros" had not been historically accurate, since the real Nacha on which the story is based was not in fact executed (353). Not only is Nacha not executed in the later version of the story, it is not even evident that she is responsible for killing Gallardo. Campobello thus rescues the autonomy of women warriors who fought in the Revolution and allows Nacha to have a future after participating in armed conflict. Nacha also acquires a past in the 1960 version, as Campobello added a laudatory description of her as a woman who "domaba potros y montaba a caballo mejor que muchos hombres; era lo que se dice una muchacha del campo, pero al estilo de la sierra; podía realizar con destreza increíble todo lo que un hombre puede hacer con su fuerza varonil" (66–67). The strong, agile Colonel Nacha is equal to men and even better that many of them. By emphasizing her physical strength and skills with horses, Campobello's additions reveal that Nacha performed a most-desired position as a very strong person and had even performed it before joining the Revolution.

I agree with Ignacio M. Sánchez-Prado that Campobello reinscribes women's combat experiences in the cultural memory with the 1960 edition ("La destrucción" 161). Whereas in the

Chapter Five

1931 version, Nacha loses control over the element (her gun) that symbolizes power and warrior skills, and consequently loses her life, the 1960 version depicts her prowess and ethics throughout the story. She remains a warrior woman even after she voluntarily relinquishes the desired position of colonel, quits the army, and returns home "seguramente desengañada de la actitud de los pocos que pretendieron repartirse los triunfos de la mayoría" (66). Other critics disagree on this point. Tabea Alexa Linhard reads Nacha's return home as representing the domestication of a formerly fearless woman (171) and Oswaldo Estrada argues that it reinforces the marginality, subordination, and silencing of women ("Trazos" 230). I argue the opposite. In returning home, Nacha is choosing not to become part of corrupt official history. She gains greater prominence through holding fast to her ethics and taking autonomous action. Nacha's home becomes another revolutionary space as she uses the masculine skills that were part of her mountain upbringing to fix the holes in the walls and skylights from which thousands of bullets had exited during the fight against the murderous Carrancistas (67). Returning even to the traditional space of a house does not domesticate her masculinity and rebuilding her house does not necessarily reproduce the subordination or silencing of women. Instead, her actions claim a different history, one that avoids official discourses, resists official representations of punished revolutionary women, and describes women having some forms of most-desired performances and fighting skills even before joining the Revolution. Nacha has been a warrior woman all along.

Controlling Images: The Black Warrior Woman

While the 1960 version of Nacha's story does not perpetuate the usual binary gender norms promoted after the Revolution, such discourses do appear in Francisco Rojas González's novel about another woman colonel of the Revolution, Angustias (introduced in Chapter 1). Angustias is said to have been modeled on Colonel Remedios Farrera and also to resemble Colonel María de la Luz Espinosa Barrera de Yautepec (Macías 42). As a warrior woman, Angustias's masculinity comprises leadership abilities, military rank, gun skills, and masculine attire. Unlike Pintada, Doña Bárbara, and Diadorim, her gender performance does not become a performativity that exposes the rules of the heteronormative society. Rather, her transgressive use of clothing reinforces misogynoirism and classism throughout the novel. Angustias is marginalized and disempowered like other warrior women characters, but the ways in which race (and skin color) intersects with class and gender differentiate her from Pintada, Doña Bárbara, and Diadorim.

Revisiting the representations of iconic women in Mexican history, among which he includes the *soldadera* type, Estrada argues that their commodification is evidence of social tensions and gender transgressions in the country's patriarchal culture (*Troubled* 2). *Soldaderas*, for example, are still mainly known as camp followers or *adelitas* (3, 146). It is important to keep this in mind when considering Angustias's transgressive use of clothing and intersectional identity. As Arce clarifies, the complete erasure of Black people from official history and national discourse makes Angustias's presence in the Revolution seem foreign and exotic (*México's* 9). She appears so unique that it makes all Black people seem exceptional and singular (9), when in reality their existence has been fundamental to Mexico and its history. As a "mulatto" and Black woman, Angustias's prominence in the novel also contradicts official representations of Mexico as a predominantly *mestizo* nation. After the Revolution, the Mexican government endorsed the idea that Mexico had resulted from an integration of white and indigenous peoples, a mixing known as *mestizaje*. This pervasive notion was well-established by the mid-1940s. By the time Rojas González published the novel in 1944, the government was already foregrounding the formerly neglected history of indigenous peoples. However, in doing so, the presence and histories of Afro-descendants and other ethnicities in Mexico were rendered invisible. In fact, it was not until 2015 that the national census questionnaire even included a box for Mexicans to identify themselves as Black (Arce, *México's* 20).

While Rojas González superficially seems to rescue the importance of Black Mexicans and their contributions to modern Mexico in the character of Angustias and her father, my analysis suggests otherwise. I agree with Arce that Angustias's blackness initially allows her to obtain power, but then later enervates her (*México's* 205). In marginalizing and disempowering Angustias, the text only replicates the same racist erasure as that which occurs in the official history of Mexican *mestizaje*. The changing descriptions of Angustias's masculine men's clothing throughout the novel illustrate the intersection of gender, race, class, and sexuality in the construction and ultimate disempowerment of this character. I argue that her clothed image as a *charro* is controlled from the beginning in order to keep her gender, class, and racial transgressions at the margins. Angustias's loneliness at the end of the novel also reinforces the misogynoirism and classism that dominated and survived the Revolution.

The first time Angustias dons masculine men's clothes is after she has been raised to the rank of colonel. She then commands one of her subordinates, Güitlacoche, to remove and hand over his outfit, a "hermoso traje de charro, de gamuza de venado con cachirulos de cabritilla blanca y botones de plata, un par de zapatos de vaqueta de esos llamados 'de dos riendas' y un gran sombrero de pelo con enormes alas arriscadas y alta copa" (99). The skilled traditional horsemen of early twentieth century Mexico known as *charros* usually exhibited wealth through their attire. By putting on this beautiful, expensive outfit, Angustias appropriates the characteristic image of the *charro*, which was one of the mostadmired positions for men in Mexico. (Apparently, Güitlacoche wants to possess this image for himself.) Her elegant suit, shoes, and sombrero locate her in a position of privilege that signals new socioeconomic advantages. Like other warrior women and trans warriors characters, she reinforces this masculine image with guns (a Colt or a 31) and a cartridge belt. Considering she is a Zapatista colonel, her donning of *charro* suits directly connects her to the revolutionary leader, Emiliano Zapata (1879–1919). After he was assassinated, he was mythologized and resurrected as a *charro* hero of the Revolution (Schell, Jr., 337). Angustias's entire outfit thereby confirms her performance in a most-desired position, that of revolutionary leader.

The character's appropriation of masculine attire is not an attempt to pass as a man nor is she a trans warrior like Diadorim. Rather, the detailed description of her attire can be related to the outfit of the dandy. Two details—the patches of white kidskin and the silver buttons—of Angustias's *charro* suit constitute the elegance of her outfit. As markers of wealth, they are indicative of Angustias's capacity to obtain and wear valuable goods. As I discussed in Chapter 1, such sartorial details have the performative power to differentiate and emphasize the dandy's presence and style. Angustias is not really a dandy, however, because she does not put much effort into modifying her attire. She does not personalize the outfit as Pintada did with the satin shoes and torn stockings. Her only modification to the suit is to replace the image of the Christ of Chalma with one of the Virgin of Guadalupe on her hat. Even though the suit itself is a man's outfit, she does not change the icons to improve her style as a dandy would because she does not want the image of a man attached to her attire.

Moreover, Angustias does not seem to be personalizing military men's attire, first because she does not really change the *charro* suit, and second because her body shape makes gender passing impossible. The narrator says that the tight fit of the suit, which accentuates her feminine curves, presents a "curioso" (curious) image (107). Angustias's body under the clothing is given more attention than her outer attire, as was the case for previous warrior women characters, but not the trans warrior Diadorim. The novel's narrator even describes Angustias as moving inside her masculine suit with "torpeza risible" (107), indicating that her performance of masculinity is peculiar and even funny. Angustias does not project a failed performance of a *charro* so much as her peculiarity and clumsiness challenges the notions of gender normativity embedded in clothing. That she can wear masculine attire and still be accepted by her society demonstrates the importance of breaking stereotypes about clothing and cisgender norms. Angustias can don men's attire to go with her position of power. Nevertheless, her "laughable clumsiness" suggests that such clothing is *obviously* not meant for her, not because of her gender transgression, but because of her "curvas desproporcionadas" (107). That is, despite the deconstruction embedded in her gender transgression, Angustias's performance does not reach the level of performativity, so does not render misogynoir stereotypes unnatural. While the author's interest in the cross-dressing colonel is made evident in descriptions of her clothing, Angustias's race and skin color displace and alter any meanings that arise from the gender transgression.

As discussed in previous chapters, Pintada was marginalized by the intersection of class, gender, and race/skin color, but Angustias's gender, class, and racial transgressions also involve stereotypes related to sexuality. Not only is she characterized as a Black woman, she is presented as a sexualized Black woman in men's attire. Laura Kanost suggests that the emphasis on Angustias's curves references

Chapter Five

the hypersexualized bodies of mulatto women throughout history ("Viewing" 559). Arce similarly notes that Rojas González prefers to depict Angustias as the sexual *mulata* instead of the "butch military hero" (*México's* 190). Indeed, the term "mulata" has historically reinforced the double oppression endured by Black women in Latin America. Labeling bodies of Afro-descendant women as "desirable *mulatas*" seeks to attach a positive valence to their blackness so that the term connotes that their bodies are considered beautiful by the traditional heterocissexual male gaze. Although individual women whose bodies correspond to the *mulata* stereotype may exploit their appearance to achieve upward socioeconomic mobility at the community and national levels in Latin America, the majority of such women continue to be disenfranchised.

Unlike Mexican *mulatas, mulatas* in the Caribbean are highly visible and frequently depicted in literary texts. According to Arce, however, they mainly appear as mistresses or mothers of "*mulatez*" (*México's* 148), never as characters with much agency. They are objectified when they are depicted as being sexually available to cis white men. Traditional discourses surrounding *mulatas* thus exploit the bodies and sexualities of women of African descent while reinforcing white hegemony. In the case of Angustias, being a *mulata* reinforces colorism and hegemonic discourses regarding Black women's sexuality. Even though she empowers herself through assuming the position of colonel, she is stripped of her military power soon after she has sex with a cis white man. Even though the bodies of *mulatas* may be considered desirable by cis white men, *mulatas* are still treated as the undesirable other in mainstream society. Such vilification overlooks the historical violence imposed on their bodies (Arce, *México's* 279). The stereotype of the voluptuous and sexually available *mulata* perpetuates ideologies related to slavery, in which Black women's bodies and sexuality belong to the cis white master and his gaze. The bodies of indigenous, indigenous-descendent, and *mestiza* women such as Doña Bárbara and Pintada have not accumulated the same sexual stereotypes as Afro-descendant women's bodies in Latin America. Whereas repulsion follows Doña Bárbara's adoption of man's attire because it hides her figure, the horror is turned into amusement and mockery in *La negra Angustias*. The depiction of her laughable clumsiness upon adopting men's clothing reveals the compulsive sexualization of Black women's bodies.

Analyzing the misogynoirism operating in depictions of Angustias's body demonstrates another hierarchy operating in the novel. The reaction to her wearing an elegant *charro* suit underscores the class hierarchy of her society. When the novel's narrator dismisses her masculine performance as clumsy and laughable, it suggests that poor or low-income Black women cannot represent authoritative figures in men-dominated spaces. Pintada is likewise rendered foolish by not wearing her white satin slippers. Women of color cannot pass as upper class by wearing stolen clothing because their bodies are not suited to a most-desired style. To be accepted as upper-class requires having a cis white body. Although Doña Bárbara is a *mestiza*, her performance is not mocked in the same way as Pintada's and Angustias's because she is already in a position of monetary power and her physical appearance falls in line with traditional European standards of beauty. Pintada and Angustias conduct the triple transgression of gender, race, and class. As warrior women, they are treated with derision in order to eliminate their three-fold questioning of hegemonic rules. By discounting the performance of these two non-white, poor warrior women, both novels make it clear that such transgressions need not be feared.

Another suit worn by Angustias seems to erase the absurdity of her appearance dressed as a man, yet also emphasizes the innocuousness of her transgressions: "Llevaba un traje de charro de paño negro con alamares y botonadura de plata; el corte del atavío, hecho a su medida, asentábale perfectamente; más que mujer antojábase un robusto rapaz" (121). There is no clumsiness to her movements because this suit has been custom-made to fit her perfectly while hiding her curves. There is nothing "curious" about her appearance and she now projects a coherent image as a robust young man. With this tailored outfit, Angustias performs not just any masculinity, but specifically that of a cis man colonel.

If Angustias's gender, racial, sexual, and class transgressions were visible with the first suit, her transgressions are disguised with the second suit. Not only is her gender transgression masked by the fit of the suit, she does not violate the class hierarchy when she wears it. Unlike her earlier *charro* outfit, none of the details of the second suit differentiate Angustias in terms of class or value. This outfit is not described as "hermoso" (beautiful) or accompanied by stylish shoes or hat, so it is more suitable to Angustias's new

Chapter Five

socioeconomic level. Instead of representing an appropriation of a class status that has been historically denied to her, the second suit shows her occupying an authorized (albeit temporary) class level. Dressing as a cis man colonel in the Revolution does not challenge the position of the upper classes.

Angustias's image in this second outfit can be related to the figure of the drag king in that her performance has become more aligned with masculine gender norms and she seems to have the intention of passing. However, while Angustias can be read as putting on a performance to emphasize her position of power in the Revolution, her performance is different from that of the drag king, since the suit is not intended to be theatrical and wearing it is not meant to call into question traditional gender rules. The clothing indicates rank and prestige and demonstrates her climb up the military hierarchy. In donning this *charro* outfit, she is only adopting an image coherent with the daily routine and activities of any colonel. That it has been tailored to allow Angustias to pass demonstrates that she is following social conventions as much as possible, not trying to disrupt them.

Her donning of *charro* suits also demonstrates that she can embody popular national symbols, albeit provisionally. The first suit is made of deer suede, most likely brown with patches of white kidskin. The second suit is described as black, which inserts her into the tradition of the black *charro*. In the decades following the Mexican Revolution, the state's nationalistic discourse appropriated the figure of the *charro* (Nájera-Ramírez 5–6). Additionally, as Christopher Conway explains, the image of a *charro* clothed in black became prevalent in Mexico thanks to a popular comic book of the 1930s titled *El charro negro* (Black Charro) and Raúl de Anda's films in the 1940s (70–71). By 1944, the year *La negra Angustias* was published, the actor, director, and screenwriter Raúl de Anda had played the leading role in *El charro negro* (1940), *La vuelta del charro negro* (The Return of the Black Charro) (1941), and *La venganza del charro negro* (The Revenge of the Black Charro) (1942). As with the clothing worn by trans warrior and warrior woman characters, Angustias donning a black *charro* suit signals that she can embody a popular, national symbol. Still, her clumsiness, transgressions, and eventual disempowerment suggest that this representation is only a temporary possibility fraught with misogynoirism.

As with previously analyzed trans warrior and warrior woman characters, Angustias's clothing functions as a sign of traditional masculinity, but she, more than the other characters, needs to combine it with a phallic weapon. Her performance is even more precarious than that of the other warrior woman and trans warrior characters. Arce explains that the vigorous sexuality characterization of the mulatto woman generates Angustias's problems ("La Negra" 1091). That is, the intersection of her race/skin color (she is considered both Black and *mulata* in the novel) and gender locates her in a sexually desired category. Whereas using weapons supported other warrior women characters' initial empowerment, Angustias needs the gun to reinforce her authority and protect herself even when she is able to pass as a young man. Although donning masculine attire reinforces her authority as a colonel, she still must carry a gun to deter men from harassing her (121). Like the knife she used to kill her harasser when her father's threats were insufficient, her gun is the phallic weapon that ultimately protects her from men's persecution. Her transgressive use of clothes, fighting skills, and leadership ability are not enough to secure her authority and physical integrity in her context.

Furthermore, the second suit establishes a connection with Afro-Mexicans while pointing out the ubiquity of racism in Mexico. It makes an association between Angustias's race (as skin color) and the ways in which Africans and Afro-descendants were treated in Mexican colonial past. While scholars such as Conway point out that the word "charro" (or *charros*) comes from Spain (68), Marco Polo Hernández Cuevas indicates that the *charro* originates in the Viceroyalty of New Spain, specifically among the poor classes, most of whom were "afromestizos" (77). In this sense, wearing *charro* suits also connects Angustias to the strong presence and vital contributions of Africans and their descendants in the Mexican colonial past. The connection remains permeated with racism, however, since, as Arce explains, blackness was commonly associated with witchcraft and pacts with the devil throughout the sixteenth and seventeenth centuries (*México's* 183). Wearing a black suit references this racist history and implicates the prevalence of racism since colonial times, since the popular legend of the black *charro* is still associated with the devil. Angustias's unsanctioned performance as a *charro* and Zapatista colonel suggests that she is an evil, unwanted, and untrustworthy Black woman.

Chapter Five

A more obviously discriminatory description of Angustias is provided with her appearance in a third *charro* suit, the "fieros ropajes y arreos del guerrillero: el pantalón de cuero de venado, la chaquetilla alamareada, el sombrerón que hacía pavoroso su rostro oscuro, las espuelas ... Tercióse dos cananas y volvió a lucir en su cintura su vieja compañera la 'cuarenta y y uno'" (180). This time, her "fierce" attire contrasts with the "delicada indumentaria mujeril" (180), she was just wearing. No references are made to this outfit's differentiating details, elegance or aesthetic value, and the description of the outfit does not relate to skin color or class. She is not a Colonel and is not passing as a young man. The description is a list of elements in a uniform—leather pants, jacket, hat, spurs, hat, cartridge belt, and gun—intended to demonstrate fierceness. Unlike the descriptions of the two other suits, this list lacks specificity. How she wears the suit is also neglected. She seems to have checked every box of items necessary for donning another image of masculinity. This is simply an outfit that includes all the accessories—especially the spurs, cartridge belt, and gun—of any man guerrilla fighter.

The hat has a new function, however; it makes Angustias's "rostro oscuro" (dark face) seem "pavoroso" (dreadful) (180). The adjective "dark" needlessly reminds the reader that Angustias is not white, while the addition of the adjective "dreadful" suggests she is also ugly and to be feared, even though the narrator previously described her as beautiful. The insistence on labeling her superficially as an Afro-descendent reveals the novel's compulsory reinforcement of misogynoir discourses. Her African or Afro-Mexican heritage and culture are not highlighted in the novel, only the blood connection with a father with whom she barely interacts. Hegemonic society aims to control Angustias by constantly labeling and demeaning her. Such a compulsion is based on dread of her transgressiveness and empowerment as challenges to naturalized racist, sexist, and classist rules. Arce explains that the body of the *mulata* has been the battlefield of many forces, such as colonial fetish, contested whiteness, and mythical blackness (*Mexico's* 186). In Rojas González's text, I see that Angustias must always be seen as a Black woman, so that she can be retained in her "right" place at the bottom of the socioeconomic ladder. The message is that Black warrior women are not aesthetically beautiful and cannot be permitted upward socioeconomic mobility—she is not even the desirable *mulata*.

I perceive a progression regarding the portrayal of Angustias's body in the descriptions of the three *charro* suits. The first time she dons masculine clothes, she has a curious, absurd aspect; the second time she looks like a robust young man; and the third time she seems ugly and dreadful. Her body shape—the presence or absence of curves—is the focus of the first two instances, but her face is the focus of the third instance. The comment on her face suggests that Angustias's clothes are not dreadful, she herself is. The novel invalidates Angustias's gender performance as clumsy, then goes to grant her an *authorized* position based on her skin color and class (black tailor-made suit), and finally erases her beautiful physical appearance. Thus, the second outfit was designed specifically to fit her curves and socioeconomic class, as well as overstate her skin color. This suit shows that her complex transgression must still be contained, even if it cannot be dismissed as absurd.

Patricia Hill Collins discusses the intricacies of oppression of Afro-descendants, and how traditional racist power relations are perpetuated through gender-specific portrayals of Black people, which she calls "controlling images" (69). Controlling images aim to be seen as natural (69). Angustias's transgressive use of clothing provides evidence of the presence of such controlling images, specifically the sexual *mulata* and the ugly Black woman. As the novel progresses, Angustias ceases to be the sensual mulatto woman and becomes the other misogynoir stereotype. Her clothed performance of a *charro* is thus manipulated to control and disempower her. While the social context of the Revolution allows her to conduct a transgressive gender performance, she cannot break with complex racist and classist rules; she and her body are constantly limited and permanently subordinated.

Class, gender, and race further intersect with other aspects of Angustias's sexuality to compound her oppression. So long as she remains a virgin, she is allowed to escape patriarchal control. As an armed military officer, she enjoys the respect of men and women. But once she has sex with Manuel, she becomes his puppet. Her lack of formal education and love for an educated white man undermine her empowerment and she becomes a traditional obedient wife; this is similar to the ways in which Dona Bárbara changes roles. The novel thus follows the model of theatrical works from the seventeenth century Iberian Golden Age, which required that the gender order always be restored by the end of the play. The

Chapter Five

ending of *La negra Angustias* falls in line with the state ideology of 1944, which encouraged the assumption that masculinized Mexican women had returned home to fulfill traditional roles after the end of the Revolution. It even goes a step further because it denies upward socioeconomic mobility for high-ranking Black warrior women and reinforces traditional racist hierarchies. Angustias ends up living in a low-income neighborhood, while her white husband takes over her job and paycheck.

Maria da Fé in João Ubaldo Ribeiro's *Viva o povo brasileiro* is another Black warrior woman character, but she comes from a very different background than Angustias. Whereas the only Black person Angustias knew was her father, Maria da Fé was raised in a context in which Black people were in the majority. This was also the context of slavery, as her Black mother was raped by the white slave owner, Barão de Pirapuama. Out of a commitment to social justice, Maria da Fé joins the *Milicianos do povo* brotherhood and then becomes the leader of the group. The Brazilian army with which her group fights dismisses Maria da Fé as a mere bandit (*"bandida," "bandoleira"*), but her commitment to racial equity is visible throughout the novel. Knowing that abolishing slavery will not be sufficient to promote Black people's position in society, she not only fights for their rights, she establishes schools at which racial and national pride will be taught (519).

With her feminine gender performance and altruistic goals, Maria da Fé exemplifies the classic "social bandit" figure. She is a warrior woman because she handles weapons and leads a revolutionary band, but she only cross-dresses once to avoid detection by the authorities so she can attend her grandfather's funeral. She does not need to don a military outfit to justify her position of command because she is obviously more intelligent than the men in the band and is driving their ideological agenda. Even as she seeks to prove herself equal to or even better than men in combat, she does not attempt to pass or pose as a man.

Maria da Fé's sexual mandate is different from Angustias's. She has a relationship with a cis white man, Patrício Macário, with whom she falls in love and has a son, but she ends the relationship so she can dedicate herself to the fight for social justice. Having already rejected her inheritance from her wealthy grandfather, she clarifies that does not break up with Patrício because he is rich and white (512). She tells Patrício that she does it because of her position of power, which prevents her from serving him as a traditional wife or allowing him to be her husband (512). Here, I emphasize that she is the one who makes the decision for herself (and Patrício) regarding the nature of her sexual relationships. Her resolution in this regard presents a stark contrast with Angustias, who just follows and obeys Manuel after they have had sex. Still, it must be noted that, as with Pintada, Doña Bárbara, and Diadorim, neither Maria da Fé nor Angustias have an active sex and fulfilling love life. Warrior women and trans warriors are not depicted as developing long-lasting, affective relationships with sexual partners. Their other transgressions prohibit them from maintaining amorous relationships and an ongoing sex life.

Maria da Fé's and Angustias's loneliness highlights the racism in Latin American societies. Their stories perpetuate the trope of the lonely Black woman, as both characters continue to be denied a fulfilling sex life because their sexuality often times must involve cis white men. Either cis white men objectify and use them for their sexuality (as Manuel does with Angustias) or Black women must deny them access (as Maria da Fé does with Patrício). The Black woman in both situations is also denied her own sexuality. She cannot have a loving partner and/or a fulfilling sexual life because she must either remain an object of abuse—Angustias—or subject of worship and sacrifice—Maria da Fé. This lack of affection and/or warm sexual relationships reproduces misogynorism. Black women are lonely because the racist system dictates that cis men prefer cis white women. Only cis white women (or *mestizas* like Marisela) are allowed to have affective relationships and sexual autonomy.

In 1949, director Matilde Landeta adapted *La negra Angustias* for film. One of the fundamental differences is that María Elena Márques, a white actor, plays the role of Angustias by performing a black face. Another major difference between the written work and the cinematographic adaptation is the ending. In Landeta's version, Angustias neither kidnaps Manuel nor submits to him; instead, she becomes an independent feminine person who continues fighting for the Revolution. In this way, the director shows a warrior woman femininizing herself and finding a true cause in the Revolution. As Dever suggests, Landeta's mid-century adaptation and direction subvert the original melodramatic image of women who joined the Revolution because here the feminine woman does not return to the domestic sphere (44). By the late 1950s, the transgressiveness of Landeta's character had become integrated into official government discourse. The success of the Mexican state's appropriation of the revolutionary warrior woman image is evident in other films such as *Juana Gallo* (1961) that starred María Félix. In these films, the warrior woman always decides to fight for the Revolution for altruistic, not personal, reasons. The state appropriation and rehabilitation of the warrior woman figure thus followed a different trajectory than that of Villa. When images of warrior women were first adopted into official discourse in the 1940s, they were feminized and asked to return home. It was only in the late 1950s that they were celebrated as strong national heroes, albeit still explicitly feminine ones. Campobello then challenged this state discourse in 1960 by foregrounding Nacha's ethical agenda and masculinity.

Throughout the twentieth century, more warrior women characters than trans warrior characters were featured in Mexican literary, musical, and cinematic works set during the Revolution. Initially depicted as eccentric or secondary characters, warrior women gradually developed into complex protagonists with their own agendas and ideological commitments. Their development reflects the gender, racial, sexual, political, and ideological struggles that were occurring in Mexico at the time. Similar struggles are seen in depictions of women who participated in other Latin American revolutions of the twentieth century.

Women Guerrillas in Latin American Revolutions

Whereas women had no assured place in the Mexican Revolution, they were officially permitted to participate in other revolutionary movements in Latin America. Such women were true guerrillas, following Raymond Williams's definition of a guerrilla as a person committed to a liberating fight that aims for independent social change; guerrillas usually seek to create a new social order by installing a new government (273). Women were still not considered fit to fight alongside men in guerrilla warfare, however, and warrior women and trans warriors continually struggled for their political rights. The guerillas of the Brazilian, Cuban, and Nicaraguan revolutions were hampered by systems of gender inequality that prevented them from developing military careers and slowed the progress of their full and equal incorporation into revolutionary armies. Sometimes depicted as true revolutionaries, but other times as mere "bandits" or sex objects, their struggles were prominently featured in a variety of Latin American novels, films, and testimonials of the second half of the twentieth century. Unlike the previously analyzed characters, women do not need to masculinize themselves physically in order to be part of guerrilla groups and they remain marked by their cis gender identity and performance.

In this section, I focus on women guerrillas involved in three major revolutionary movements of twentieth-century Latin America, two of which succeeded (in Cuba and Nicaragua) and one of which failed (in Brazil). I then discuss the erasure of trans warriors from nationalist discourses on revolutionary history despite increasing LGBTQAI+ activism throughout Latin America.

Cuban Women Guerrillas of the Late 1950s

Fulgencio Batista held power in Cuba from 1934 through 1952. Growing dissatisfaction with his regime prompted the development of oppositional political and revolutionary parties and led to the Cuban Revolution, which lasted from 1953 to 1959. Guerrilla warfare weakened the Cuban army and eventually forced Batista to flee the country on the 31st of December in 1958. Fidel Castro became the Prime Minister and held that position until 1976, then became President of Cuba until 2008. The image of the Cuban revolutionary promulgated by the state has almost always been of men, as represented by men such as Che Guevara or the brothers Fidel and Raúl Castro. Official discourses even mediate images of warrior women in their own "testimonials," a popular genre of biographical texts about women who participated in the Cuban Revolution.

One of the first texts to delineate women's complex experiences in the Cuban Revolution was U.S. woman activist Margaret Randall's book of interviews with Cuban women. Entitled *Mujeres en la revolución: Margaret Randall conversa con mujeres cubanas* and translated as *Cuban Women Now*, the book was published in Mexico in 1972. Acknowledging Cuba's extensive history of gender oppression, Randall recovers the historical presence of women in the Cuban Revolution. This is an important contribution because, even though the activities of women guerrillas were essential to the success of the Cuban Revolution, public perception of their roles has remained tied to gender (Shayne 121–22). This may partly have stemmed from the chauvinism of the original men leaders of the revolution. Julie D. Shayne claims that, although Che Guevara instructed women to participate in combat during the Cuban Revolution, he still took a *machista* attitude toward them, a tone that was adopted by many of his contemporaries (45). Women could be expected to act as nurses or messengers, but the image of a woman with a rifle fighting in the mountains alongside Fidel Castro or Che Guevara never achieved the same prominence as depictions of man guerrillas in Cuban revolutionary discourse.

Randall counters this ignorance of women's guerilla activities by presenting Haydée Santamaría and Melba Hernández, both of whom took part in the Moncada attack of 1953 and supported the revolutionary movement afterwards. Randall also describes the many women who helped unload the *Granma*, the boat on which revolutionaries traveled from Mexico to Cuba to join the 26th of July Movement instigated by Fidel Castro. These women transported messages, organized uprisings, coordinated logistics, provided medical attention, made uniforms, tended the troops, and taught peasants how to read and write. Vilma Espín, who married Raúl Castro in 1959, was another major woman figure of the Cuban Revolution. In her interview with Randall, Espín explains that women of all ages participated in the Revolution in diverse ways. Some placed bombs, transported guns, or hid guerrillas from the Cuban army. Women were particularly effective in carrying weapons to the guerrillas, since Batista's soldiers, assuming women could not be terrorists or carry weapons, did not search them (Randall, *Mujeres* 281; Waters 30). The hegemonic view of women in the 1950s and 1960s was that they were not rebellious and so were not objects of suspicion. As Shayne points out, femininity had the "ability to cloak women's subversive political activities" in Latin America at the time (115).

The figure of the woman guerrilla who used guns emerges more strongly in Randall's interviews with Teté Puebla (Delsa Ester Puebla Viltre) and Isabel Rielo. They were among thirteen women that formed the only women's platoon, the Mariana Grajales, which was founded by Fidel Castro on September 4, 1958. The women in this platoon integrated into the guerrilla army and participated in battles such as Cerro Pelado, Holguín, and Güiros. Puebla told another interviewer that Rielo became leader of the Mariana Grajales because she had the best aim (Waters 47). Even women who demonstrated excellent combat skills had to continually defend their right to fight to their men peers, however. Unlike man recruits, women were not allowed to fight until after they had demonstrated their abilities to resist the enemy.

In her interview with Randall, Rielo describes a 1950s discourse that was intended to prevent women from participating in actual combat on scientific or medical grounds (137). Randall notes that many men and even some women thought that men and women should not be expected to do the same tasks, even when women were physically capable of doing so (26). Gender conservative people perpetuated traditional discourses of reproduction and femininity to substantiate their assertions that women should not join combat (26). They argued that the maternal instinct in women was so strong, it would only lead them to pity any man they saw bleeding, even if he was an enemy soldier (137). Emphasizing that she never saw a woman guerrilla hesitate to kill an enemy combatant, Rielo dismisses this discourse as part of the psychological "complex" of Cuban men (137). Randall's book demonstrates that traditional cultural codes of gender behavior were still being perpetuated in Cuba in the early 1970s, long after the triumph of the Revolution.

In 2003, another U.S. woman activist named Mary-Alice Waters published *Marianas in Combat: Teté Puebla & the Mariana Grajales Women's Platoon in Cuba's Revolutionary War 1956–58*. This is a book-length biography of Teté Puebla, who in 1996 became the first woman to reach the rank of Brigadier General in Cuba. Puebla's oral history confirms that women guerrillas had to convince men guerrillas they could carry out the same tasks as men (46). Puebla mentions that she initially helped guerrillas by transporting bullets and dynamite to them in the mountains and organizing revolutionary meetings. When she and other women demanded to participate as equals, that is, fight alongside men guerrillas in the Sierra Maestra, the men questioned their bravery and aptitude. The reluctance of men to accept women into their ranks is further demonstrated by the fact that men leaders discussed the formation of a women's platoon for seven hours before approving the establishment of the Mariana Grajales in 1958, only four months before victory.

Chapter Five

In her testimonial, Puebla reinforces the image of Fidel Castro as a generous leader and far-seeing commander-in-chief. Puebla told Waters that Castro supported and trained the women in the platoon, even made them part of his personal guard. I contend that by training and keeping them close to him, he was constantly supervising them. Furthermore, he exploited the thirteen women who constituted the Mariana Grajales by using the existence of the platoon to claim that the Cuban Revolution had promoted gender equality even in armed conflict. His speech on the 1st of January 1959 in Céspedes Park in Santiago de Cuba erases their struggle to be allowed to fight. He does not address the sexist power imbalance. He only admits to having been biased against women, then puffs up his own importance by stating that he simply overcame this obstacle. Despite the actual presence of warrior women in the Cuban Revolution, it continues to be associated with men and, more specifically, with one man, Fidel Castro. While superficially glorifying warrior women in its nationalist discourse, as was done in Mexico, the Cuban government has always hidden their actual struggles to fight in the Revolution beneath a false ideology of gender equality.

Proportionally fewer women went into actual combat in the Cuban Revolution than in the Mexican Revolution, even though it took place about fifty years after the Mexican Revolution and implied a different kind of mobilization. As far as is currently known, Cuban women were not required to demonstrate physical masculinization as women had been in the Mexican Revolution, but they still struggled to be allowed to fight, to be treated as equals to man combatants, and to achieve military rank. After the revolutionaries won, the new Cuban government heavily regulated participation of women in the military forces. Puebla was the only woman guerrilla to develop a successful military career and it still took her thirty-eight years to become a Brigadier General. The Cuban government might not have sent women home after the Revolution, but it did keep pretending that its military had treated them as equal to men when it had not.

While official discourses in Cuba and Mexico manipulated images of women guerrillas to align with their post-revolutionary nationalist ideologies, at least they acknowledged that warrior women had made contributions to their revolutions. What happens to depictions of warrior women when a revolutionary movement fails? This question is addressed in the next section on the women guerrillas of Brazil.

Brazilian Women Guerrillas of the 1960s through 1970s

Guerrilla warfare appeared in Brazil in the 1960s in reaction to the intense, widespread repression of freedom and human rights that followed the right-wing military coup of 1964, but by the late 1970s, the right-wing military had completely quashed the nascent revolution. In the intervening years, Brazilian women provided logistical support to guerrillas and participated in armed guerrilla activities such as politically-motivated kidnappings and robberies (M. Ribeiro 175). Like their Cuban counterparts, women in Brazil struggled to be recognized by men for their contributions and fighting skills. Sexuality and gender had different connotations in Brazil than in Cuba, however.

One of the first major representations of a Brazilian woman guerrilla was in the 1969 film *Macunaíma*, by Brazilian director Joaquim Pedro de Andrade. This innovative, politically radical film was a major success in Brazil (R. Johnson 178). Dina Sfat plays an urban woman guerrilla character called Ci. Ci first appears in the film running through city streets, carrying a variety of weapons, and shooting at a police van full of officers. She then enters the police van and kills all the men inside. She is next shown holding one of the men's arms, which she has apparently cut off. She tosses it away as she exits the van.

This depiction of a courageous, dangerous woman associates Ci with the guerrilla movement of the 1960s in Brazil. However, the film was not based on reports of actual guerrilla action in Brazil at the time, but on a 1928 novel with the same title (*Macunaíma*) written by Mário de Andrade. Macunaíma is a character out of Brazilian folklore. He is usually depicted as a Black man from the jungle who whitened his skin by bathing in a magical fountain. In the novel, Ci appears as a wild woman of the jungle, a sort of Amazon warrior fully capable of killing men.

The Ci character in the 1928 novel is actually an adaptation of the fictional character named Iracema, an indigenous warrior woman described in José de Alencar's historical novel *Iracema*. Thus, the image of a warrior woman from the time of the conquest has been reimagined in three different periods. In Alencar's

Chapter Five

nineteenth-century imaginary, Iracema dies from lack of affection from her white Portuguese partner. In the third decade of the twentieth century, during Brazil's Modernism period, Ci dies after her son dies. Finally, during the 1960s aesthetic movement toward realism, known as *Cinema novo* (New Cinema) in Brazil, Ci is portrayed as an urban woman guerrilla who also dies with her son.

The figure of a native warrior woman is actualized in each of these works, but she is always imagined through a conservative gender filter. In the 1928 novel and 1969 film, Ci resists Macunaíma's attempts to catch her. Macunaíma enlists his brothers' help to overpower her and then rapes her. He and Ci go on to have consensual sex for the remainder of the story. These events misrepresent women's sexuality. Macunaíma and Ci's relationship in the novel and film not only diminishes the trauma and violence of Ci's rape, but suggests that women enjoy non-consensual sex. In the film, when they both live in her house, she uses money to entice him into having sex with her. When he refuses to have sex with her because he is tired, Ci coerces Macunaíma by poking him with a dagger and, later, beating him with a branch of poison ivy. Randal Johnson argues that the film subverts Brazilian social values by turning Macunaíma into Ci's object of desire. Macunaíma becomes an object that has to function according to Ci's desire in the same way that she became an object to give him pleasure. Johnson says that the myth of masculine domination is thereby unmasked in the film and 1928 novel (181). I disagree. By behaving like her rapist, Ci does not unmask the myth of masculine dominance, but perpetuates it. Ci's performance thus preserves the status quo of those in (monetary) positions of power rather than criticizing the system of sexual assault and prostitution.

Her sexy image and the events that conclude the film provide further evidence of the retention of the patriarchal perspective. She wears clothes made out of leather or denim and her breasts are constantly visible. Her scanty attire reflects a patronizing man attitude toward women's liberation that assumes advances in women's rights had more to do with the freedom to wear less clothing than the desire to gain socioeconomic and political power. Furthermore, while Ci is depicted initially as a strong, powerful revolutionary, by the end she seems to be nothing more than another weak woman who needs a man. Similar to the transformation of Doña Bárbara in Rómulo Gallegos's novel, Ci's desire for Macunaíma normalizes her and makes her appear less threatening, even a bit stupid. Distracted by thinking about having sex with Macunaíma, Ci fails to set the timer on a bomb properly, and she and her son (by Macunaíma) die in the explosion. Ci is killed off in the film and the novel on which it is based because her empowerment threatens Macunaíma's masculinity and sexuality. Empowered sexuality is further portrayed as weakening the resolve and effectiveness of women guerrillas in fighting oppression. Her son, whose blackness is a reminder that Macunaíma was originally Black before he magically whitened himself, also dies. Thus, although Ci superficially appears to be a modern, liberated, warrior woman in the 1960s film, the sexist and racist ideologies embedded in the earlier novels are retained.

Women guerillas have continued to be depicted in Brazil into the twenty-first century. Historical guerrillas have been featured in several Brazilian testimonial texts and films. One of the best known is Fernando Gabeira's testimonial novel, *O que é isso, companheiro?* (What's Wrong, Comrade?), published in 1979. In this book, Gabeira describes the events surrounding the 1969 kidnapping of a United States ambassador to Brazil by a group of student activists, as well as Gabeira's involvement with the guerrillas and subsequent incarceration. Gabeira rarely describes women participating in guerrilla activities in his memoir. The only non-sexualized woman guerrilla he mentions is Adamaris Lucena, who he hears screaming under torture while he is imprisoned in São Paulo (162). Gabeira does not explain that Adamaris and her husband had in fact hidden weapons and money for the *Vanguarda popular revolucionária* (Revolutionary Popular Vanguard, VPR). He does discuss one woman guerrilla called Márcia in more detail, however. Márcia is his pseudonym for the woman who later became his wife, Vera Sílvia Magalhães. According to Luiz Maklouf Carvalho, Vera was the only woman to participate in the kidnapping of the U.S. ambassador. In the text, Vera/Márcia poses as a domestic employee to obtain access to the ambassador's house (170). She succeeds in this subterfuge largely because, in Brazil as in Cuba, men were not suspicious of women and assumed they lacked courage and fighting skills.

In his testimonial, Gabeira acknowledges that this form of sexism operates in Brazilian culture, but does not refute it in his depiction of Vera/Márcia (98). He describes her simply as a femi-

Chapter Five

nine woman with traces of European origins. As young student activists, they share an apartment, but he is not permitted to see her. He depicts her as a mystery woman who leaves bras strewn around the apartment and evidence of sexual intercourse in her bed sheets (93). This very partial and sexualized portrayal of Vera/Márcia is only slightly ameliorated by Gabeira noting that she (like Pintada) hides weapons beneath her feminine garments and accessories: "[e]la tem uma metralhadora dentro da bolsa, um revólver dentro da liga e, possivelmente, uma navalha no sutiã" (92). Her feminine clothes veil weapons she could use to attack their enemies and defend herself. This suggests she is an empowered woman guerrilla. Nevertheless, by naming these garments, Gabeira personalizes and feminizes Vera/Márcia's political agenda. He traces her only through her gender and sexuality rather than describing her fighting prowess or actual participation in armed robberies.

Furthermore, by mentioning her European looks and hidden weapons, Gabeira associates her with the image of the *loira dos assaltos* (lit. "blonde of the assaults") or the blonde bandit figure that was popular in newspapers of the 1960s. Guerrillas in Brazil (and elsewhere in Latin America) indeed robbed banks and businesses to expropriate money to subsidize their revolutionary activities. Gabeira acknowledges that newspapers manipulated the images of the guerrillas: "Os jornais estimulavam nossas fantasias. Eram descrições mirabolantes; jovens com nervos de aço (ainda saíamos nas páginas de polícia); louras que tiravam uma metralhadora de suas capas coloridas" (80). By depicting women guerrillas in explicitly sexual and racial terms, the media's "blonde bandit" imaginary undermines their importance to the revolutionary movements of Brazil. Relatively few people in Brazil (or throughout Spanish America) are natural blondes. The hair color is considered exotic and highly attractive because Latin America has for the most part reproduced traditional European standards of beauty. Imagining and representing armed women guerrillas as "blondes" and depicting them in fashionable clothing makes them seem irrelevant as fighters, not real threats or committed revolutionaries.

Women guerrillas' testimonials suggest that gender binaries were also perpetuated in Brazil even after the earlier Latin American revolutions of Mexico and Cuba. Warrior women certainly struggled for a place and a voice in Brazil's revolutionary movements. For example, in *Mulheres que foram à luta armada* (Women Who Joined the Armed Fight) (1998), Carvalho published an interview with Renata Guerra de Andrade, a woman he claimed was the first "blonde bandit." In her account, Renata recalls participating in a robbery on August 1, 1968 to prove to the public that women had joined the VPR (37). She mentions that she had to convince her men peers to allow her to participate in the robbery, however. Carvalho also interviewed Vera Magalhães, who likewise emphasized that since she was the only woman working amongst seven men to plan the kidnapping, she had to put up with a great deal of chauvinism (172).

Despite these gender struggles, the Brazilian mass media of the late 1960s attached the image of the woman guerrilla to a dangerous and exotic sexuality. Women guerrillas were portrayed as belligerently transgressing gender and social barriers just as the women's liberation movement was gaining traction worldwide. The "blonde bandit" imaginary, Ci, and other depictions of sexy women guerrillas were set up in opposition to images of the traditional (angelic) women who stayed at home, married, and did not challenge the political system. The refusal of women guerrillas to obey gender norms resulted in their portrayal as dangerous, sexual beings. These portrayals were attempts to domesticate the rebelliousness of warrior women. While the Brazilian government condemned and demonized women guerrillas for their actions, the popular mass media simply trivialized them by treating them as sexy Hollywood heroes, rather than with respect as freedom fighters. The media also naturalized their transgressions by fitting them into existing woman depictions. The gender-conservative media avoided being censored by the government for reporting actual guerrilla warfare by exoticizing the image of warrior women as mere bandits. In doing so, the media severely limited the historical imaginary of their performances. The political failure of revolutionary movements in Brazil also impeded women guerrillas from autonomously representing themselves to the public. Even though Dilma Rousseff, a former woman guerrilla who does not at all resemble the sexy blonde bandit stereotype, became president of Brazil in 2011, the image of these revolutionary warrior women has yet to be revised in the mass media.

Chapter Five

Nicaraguan Women Guerrillas of the 1970s

The women's liberation movement that developed during the twenty years between the Cuban and Nicaraguan revolutions accounts for changes in warrior women's performances over time. Although, like their Brazilian and Cuban counterparts, Nicaraguan women struggled to be treated as equals to men in guerrilla groups, they participated in greater numbers and held a wider range of roles in the Sandinista Revolution than women did in the Brazilian and Cuban movements. Furthermore, the mass media and the government in Nicaragua did not appropriate the image of the woman revolutionary the same way that was done in Cuba and Brazil.

Revolution in Nicaragua was largely in reaction to the oppressive Somoza regime. The Somoza patriarch and two of his sons ruled Nicaragua throughout most of the twentieth century, during which time the Somoza family increased its wealth while impoverishing the Nicaraguan people. Started in 1961, the most active revolutionary group was the *Frente Sandinista para la liberación nacional* (Sandinista National Liberation Front, FSLN). The Sandinistas, as these Nicaraguan guerrillas were called, were strongly influenced by the Cuban Revolution and received support from the Cuban government. In March 1979, other guerrilla groups taking a variety of ideological positions joined the FSLN to overthrow the Somoza dictatorship. Unlike the Brazilian guerrillas, Nicaraguan revolutionaries triumphed in July 1979.

In her preface to *Sandino's Daughters: Testimonies of Nicaraguan Women in Struggle* (1981), Randall explains that women who joined the FSLN broke with past tradition to fight for equality. They became involved in every facet of the movement. Some women provided support to the revolutionaries, while others worked undercover as civil servants to bring down the regime from within. Many became soldiers and held important positions in the army. Major Dora María Téllez, interviewed in Randall's book, emphasizes that women participated not only as cooks but as combatants. She was involved in the Sandinista occupation of the National Palace in Managua on August 22, 1978 and there assumed responsibility for negotiations.

Sandinistas conducted intense warfare that lasted much longer than the Cuban Revolution. The Nicaraguan Revolution is more like the Mexican Revolution in having evolved over time, which allowed greater numbers of women to join combat. The high number of women who eventually participated in the Nicaraguan Revolution can be attributed to a variety of social factors including economic changes, increasing men's unemployment, transformations in family structure with more families headed by women, migration to cities, more women entering higher education, and the spread of liberation theology (Chinchilla, "Women in Revolutionary" 2–3; Kampwirth 25–37). The shift from a *foco* strategy, based on Che Guevara's theory of warfare, to mass mobilization also had an impact. Norma Stoltz Chinchilla argues that the change from a "'foquista' conception of guerrilla warfare in favor of a Vietnamese-inspired conception of Prolonged People's War" ("Women in Revolutionary" 12) permitted a larger incorporation of women to the armed fight. That is, the Sandinistas adopted a more inclusive strategy of revolt in which they no longer had to choose between rural or urban guerrilla warfare, political or military forms of resistance, developing a vanguard party or a mass organization, or conducting legal or clandestine activities (13).

Téllez's testimonial corroborates these trends. She states that peasant women joined the Sandinistas quite early, while urban women did not start getting actively involved until 1972, largely because politically inclined women were considered prostitutes at the time. Timothy P. Wickham-Crowley confirms that the number of women guerrillas who participated in armed combat greatly increased between 1965 and 1975 (216–17). Many of them joined the Sandinistas after Anastasio Somoza Debayle became president in 1967. Karen Kampwirth argues that even though Somoza pretended to favor women's rights in his campaign speeches, his oppressiveness in government provoked their uprising (23). A woman's organization known as *Asociación de mujeres ante la problemática nacional* (Association of Women Confronting the National Problem, AMPRONAC) particularly encouraged women to fight during the last two years of the Somoza regime (Chinchilla, "Revolutionary" 374) and by the time of the final offensive in 1979, women constituted almost thirty percent of the armed forces (Chinchilla, "Women in Revolutionary" 1). Kampwirth considers it likely that this figure is somewhat exaggerated (2–3), but she and other scholars acknowledge that a large number of women fought in the Nicaraguan Revolution and that they participated in greater numbers the longer the movement lasted.

Chapter Five

Despite their high numbers in the FSLN, their right to join active combat remained a hot issue in Nicaragua. Many Sandinista women still had to deal with men comrades who thought women were only good for sex. As Major Monica exclaims in another interview in Randall's book, "[i]t's been a long struggle! We won those battles through discussions and by women comrades demonstrating their ability and their resistance" (*Sandino's* 66). Monica's testimonial echoes the discussions that occurred in Cuba and Brazil. Although they certainly encountered sexism, these Nicaraguan warrior women do not seem to have had to undertake the struggle to be accepted as soldiers from scratch. In an interview by Randall, Víctor Perez Espinosa, a company leader who instructed women in combat, asserts that women soldiers can achieve everything men soldiers can (145). His testimonial suggests that gender biases had begun to change in Latin America by the mid- to late 1970s, at least ideologically. Despite the commitment to gender equality voiced by the Sandinistas, the national army that formed after the 1979 victory abandoned these ideals and began separating soldiers by gender for training purposes (Randall, *Sandino's* 138).

As in Mexico and Brazil (but unlike Cuba), a corpus of well-known literary texts about the Revolution developed in Nicaragua following the 1979 victory. One of the first Nicaraguan testimonials was Omar Cabezas's 1982 memoir *La montaña es algo más que una inmensa estepa verde* (Fire from the Mountain: The Making of a Sandinista). Cabezas mentions only two women guerrillas in his book and does not report interacting with them. Cabezas's emphasis on Che Guevara's idea of the *hombre nuevo* (new man) in the Revolution might explain the lack of women in the text (I. Rodríguez 45, 178; Barbas Rhoden 73). Their absence may also derive from Cabezas's desire to narrate his own experiences in becoming a man guerrilla fighter. In this masculinist and homosocial discourse, he has to learn to overcome the rough conditions of living in a guerrilla camp in the mountain. Woman guerrillas appear more frequently in his second testimonial, *Canción de amor para los hombres* (Love Song for Men) (1988), however.

The presence of women in the Sandinista Revolution is much more prominently depicted in the works of Nicaraguan woman author Gioconda Belli. Belli had also joined the Sandinistas, although not as a combatant. She only participated in the FSLN by attending meetings, reading revolutionary texts, recruiting new members, and transporting people in her car. Belli's novel *La mujer habitada* (The Inhabited Woman), published in 1988, centers on the story of Lavinia, a young, upper-class architect who joins the Sandinistas. She becomes involved in armed conflict because her body is inhabited by the soul of an indigenous woman named Itzá who had fought the Spanish during the Conquest. Itzá exemplifies a warrior woman who rebels against social norms that consider war only to be the work of men. She says: "[f]ui afortunada. Aunque mi madre se enfurecía, yo siempre tuve inclinación por los juegos de los muchachos, los arcos y las flechas. Ella no concebía que las mujeres pudieran guerrear, acompañar a los hombres" (115). Itzá implies that she is supposed to recruit soldiers for the revolutionary group, but men do not trust her and women think she is a *texoxe* (witch).

Itzá knows that she has to fight to be respected and valued and be involved in making decisions for the group, but she struggles to reconcile her desire to fight with the gendered norms of her social context. Recognizing that she is perceived as abnormal, she questions her gender identity, her value to society, and her position in the revolution. Yarince, a revolutionary leader (and her partner), tells her that she is a "mujer valiente" (brave woman), that is, a warrior woman. Itzá's position as an indigenous warrior woman in armed combat implies a double transgression because she not only transgresses the social norms of society at large, she also deals with biases from members of her revolutionary group. Just as the formation of the Mariana Grajales platoon had to be publicly supported by Fidel Castro, her performance can only be sanctioned by a man leader (Yarince).

Itzá makes Lavinia aware of oppression in Nicaraguan society and encourages her to join the fight against the dictatorship. Flor, a working-class woman nurse, then initiates Lavinia into the Sandinistas. Belli's novel thus shows how contemporary warrior women attempting to reshape society according to their ideals of justice and equality transgress gender and class borders. Like the women guerrillas who joined the Cuban and Nicaraguan Revolutions, but unlike the three novels analyzed in the first several chapters of this book, the warrior women characters in *La mujer* do not need to don men's clothing or project masculine images in order to negotiate spaces for themselves within the sphere of war,

Chapter Five

traditionally an environment of men. Their actions alone make them warrior women. Lavinia becomes a warrior woman when she joins an operation to take over General Vela's house.

Vinodh Venkatesh indicates that Lavinia acts out a female masculinity in changing from "a passive stance toward an active performativity within the rebel group" (151). While I see that Lavinia becomes a warrior woman by participating in hijacking General Vela's house, I am cautious in using words such as "passive" and "active" to describe Lavinia's changing attitude, as these words must be carefully contextualized to avoid reproducing gender binaries. Considering her family background and socioeconomic class, Lavinia is already a feminist (even if it is a bourgeois feminism) in that she lives alone and has a job. Additionally, the way in which Venkatesh uses "performativity" does not engage the Butlerian sense of the term as I have used it throughout this book. Lavinia's performance does not render as unnatural gender discourses that have been forced as natural. Lavinia does not conduct a performativity because her performance fails to uncover imposed rules.

The way in which the Sandinista group as a whole takes over General Vela's house does uncover gender hierarchies, however. All of the guerrillas wear stockings to hide their faces and refer to each other by numbers instead of names to hide their identities. Víctor de Currea-Lugo comments that using numbers instead of names negates the right to have a name and objectifies the subject (98). I suggest, however, that deliberately using numbers to make themselves anonymous enables the guerrillas to assert the right not to be labeled by the gender and class markers normatively embedded in names.

Venkatesh argues that the revolutionary masculinity depicted in Belli's novel does not change the system, but only aims to usurp the traditional position of power on the behalf of men revolutionaries. This is because revolutionary movements reproduce sexism and homophobia (150). While I agree with him that revolutionary movements generally sustain heterocisnormativity, I do not consider that the goal of masculinities as performed by trans warriors or warrior women is to replace other people in positions of power. That rationale in itself would perpetuate heterocispatriarchy. My standpoint comes from recognizing and valuing the diverse roles and performances that have hitherto been ignored or erased when only one performance of masculinity was considered legitimate. Warrior women and trans warriors break with a discourse that considers only one type of heterocissexual man as capable of embodying the most-desired position. Whether fictional or real, the trans warriors and warrior women I analyze demonstrate that gender performances are varied and that masculinities should be seen in the plural and are not exclusively connected to the male sex. The most-desired position varies from context to context and can be performed by anyone.

Belli's portrayal of warrior women protagonists contrasts sharply with Gabeira's and Cabezas's narratives. As a cis white woman in Latin America, Belli seems more attuned to gender issues within revolutionary movements. Furthermore, she wrote this novel in the mid-1980s, by which time the social context had changed greatly from when the two cis white men were writing. Her temporal distance from the events of the Revolution also allowed her to introduce greater complexity into her depiction of the guerrillas. In one respect, however, Belli follows a rather bourgeois discourse by having Lavinia die at the end of the novel. Lavinia is only presented as an equal to the men guerrillas when she finds and fights with General Vela, after which they both die. In becoming a martyr for the cause, Lavinia symbolizes a very specific type of Sandinista guerrilla, that of the upper-class hero. She does not represent the majority of women who joined the revolutionary movement, most of whom were rural working women. To use Che Guevara's term, she is not the "new woman."

This discourse is also evident in Belli's autobiography, *El país bajo mi piel. Memorias de amor y guerra* (The Country Under my Skin) (2002). Published fourteen years after the novel, *El país* has a tone of disillusionment. Belli introduces a different view of the Revolution from Randall's of the early 1980s and even from her own of 1988. Nicaragua had nearly been demolished by the Contras war that followed the Sandinista victory. Women were then displaced from the revolutionary movement soon after Violeta Chamorro was elected president of Nicaragua in 1990s. Even though Chamorro was the first woman head of any state to be democratically elected in the Americas and was responsible for ending the Contras war, she was a political conservative. Even upper-class women who had been guerrillas were prevented from taking high-ranking positions within the new government and many of them dropped out of politics altogether. Having heroically risked their lives to bring about a more just society, they found themselves again pushed to the side because they had transgressed gender, racial, and social borders to assert their right to fight. It bears mentioning that during Chamorro's presidential term, Sandinistas were in the opposition, which implied that their moving to high positions in the government was challenging even for men.

The discussions on women guerrillas of Brazil, Cuba, and Nicaragua and depictions and actual experiences of Latin American warrior women fighting in guerrilla wars have changed from the time of the Mexican Revolution to the Nicaraguan Revolution. While warrior women were not as prominent in the Cuban Revolution as in the Mexican Revolution, they did not have to cross-dress to join combat. Both Cuban and Nicaraguan warrior women became revolutionary leaders, but few remained in the armed forces after their revolutions were won. None of these warrior women found it easy to be included in revolutionary movements and all experienced gender biases. At the same time, their successes as warriors ironically led to manipulations of history by mass media and governments. Either their sexuality or their obedience to the revolutionary cause were accentuated so as to put women back in their place in the patriarchy. Still, their increasing visibility in nationalist discourses presents a strong contrast with the absence of trans warriors in other post-revolutionary imaginaries. This topic is discussed next.

Latin American Trans Warriors in Revolutionary History

The women's liberation movement of the mid to late twentieth century promoted women leaving the household, becoming involved in politics, and acquiring public lives. Women's gains lent support to the fight for equal rights for the LGBTQAI+ community. Despite such advances, trans warriors have yet to appear in literature depicting revolutionary movements in Cuba, Brazil, and Nicaragua. For example, neither trans* men nor non-heterosexual guerrillas are mentioned in testimonials of the Cuban Revolution. Instead, it seems to have been assumed that everyone involved was heterocissexual. This is probably because sexual orientation and desire were highly taboo topics in Cuba. Before the Revolution, homosexuality was associated with sex work, mafia, and criminals, and after 1959, it was seen as a form of U.S. imperialism (Stout 35–36). When Cuba turned to Soviet-style communism in 1961, homosexuality was criminalized (36). It was not until the 1990s that Cuban *travestis* achieved any public visibility, and even then they were still heavily discriminated against by the government. Because of homophobia, they struggled to find state employment and were often harassed by police on suspicion of being sex workers (79). Noelle M. Stout suggests that Cuba only began to include lesbians and gays in the national discourse after it began opening up to capitalist trade and foreign tourism in the 1990s (41). At the same time, the presence of capitalism implied that nationalist discourses had to be exaggerated in order to resist cultural contamination, and same-sex desire continued to be marginalized. Eventually, new discourses permitted lesbians and gays to belong to the nation if they supported the Cuban Revolution (41–42). Nevertheless, homophobia continued to be part of the state-sponsored ideology until at least 2010, when Fidel Castro finally apologized for having detained gays and lesbians in work camps in the 1960s (39).

Castro probably would not have apologized for the work camps if it were not for the efforts of various organizations that promoted inclusion and tolerance towards trans* people in Cuban after the revolution. Gender policies were first developed by the *Federación de mujeres cubanas* (Federation of Cuban Women, FMC), which was established in 1960 and led by Espín. This organization advanced several rights, such as having an abortion, accessing contraceptives, and establishing sexual education (Kirk, *The Normalization* 55). Under Espín's leadership at the FMC, the first organization to promote sex education in Cuba, *Grupo nacional de trabajo de educación sexual* (National Working Group on Sexual Education, GNTES), was established in 1972 and officially recognized in 1977. GNTES described same-sex desires as normal (Kirk, *The Normalization* 80; Stout 49). In 1979, at the request of FMC and GNTES, the Ministry of Public Health established a team to provide assistance to trans* peoples (Kirk, *The Normalization* 151). As a result, the first sex-correction surgery in Cuba took place in 1988 (151). In 1989, GNTES was renamed the *Centro Nacional de Educación Sexual* (Cuban National Center for Sex Education, CENESEX) (147–48). In the early 2000s, under the leadership of Mariela Castro Espín (Espín and Castro's daughter),

Chapter Five

CENESEX stated that homosexuality has a biological basis, so should not be considered a crime or a deviation. The organization has continued leading workshops on gender and sexuality issues (Stout 49; Kirk, *The Normalization* 117) and it held Cuba's first celebration of International Day Against Homophobia in 2007 (Kirk, *The Normalization* 150). Another major achievement occurred in 2012, when Adela Hernández became the first trans* person elected to public office in Cuba.

As in Cuba, trans* men's participation in Brazil's revolutionary movements has yet to be described despite the increasing trans* activism of the late twentieth century. According to James Green, the Brazilian dictatorship of the second half of the twentieth century did not persecute gay men from the privileged classes, but *travesti* sex workers were constantly harassed, beaten, incarcerated, and even murdered. Furthermore, sex reassignment surgeries became illegal in Brazil in the late 1970s. Roberto Farina, the first doctor to perform such surgeries in Brazil, was arrested and sentenced for having done so in 1978. His clients had included both *travestis* and trans* men such as João W. Nery. Nery wrote about having undergone sex-correction surgery in 1977 in his two autobiographies, first in *Erro de pessoa* (1984) (*Error of a Person*) and then in an updated version titled *Viagem solitária. Memórias de um transexual trinta anos depois* (2011) (Lonely Journey. Memoirs of a Transsexual Man Thirty Years Later) (Ávila, *FTM* 140).

Simone Ávila explains that *travesti* activist organizations first emerged in Brazil during the early 1990s as a response to the AIDS epidemic (*Transmasculinidades* 189). Soon after, Brazilian LGBT activists discussed whether they should add more initials to their collective acronym so as to include transsexuals, *travestis*, and transgenders (*transgêneros*)—resulting in LGBTTT—or unite all the Ts in order to have more presence (187). Trans* support groups only began developing in the early twenty-first century, including *Associação Nacional de Travestis e Transexuais* (National Association of Travestis and Transsexuals, ANTRA) founded in 2000 and *Coletivo nacional de transexuais* (National Collective of Transsexuals, CNT) in 2005 (191). Trans* men (*transhomens*) almost never joined these groups before 2010 (196) and it was only in 2012 that *Associação Brasileira de Homens Trans* (Brazilian Association of Trans Men, ABHT) was organized specifically to serve their needs (200).

In stark contrast to Cuba and Brazil, lesbian and gay Nicaraguans are known to have participated in many revolutionary activities and to have joined the Sandinistas (McGee and Kampwirth 64–65). Various gay and lesbian groups, and then LGBTQAI+ groups, were founded throughout the 1980s in Nicaragua. Their presence was not welcomed by the government, however. In 1987, the Nicaraguan government persecuted members of the gay-lesbian pride group *Grupo inicio* who had been meeting in private houses since 1985 (McGee and Kampwirth 65; Babb 308). Nevertheless, LGBTQAI+ organizations continued to gain prominence even after conservatives took power in 1990 (Babb 309). Between 1992 and 2008, when homosexuality was considered a crime, diverse NGOs focused on topics related to sexual diversity (*Diagnóstico* 186). Since regaining political power in Nicaragua, the FSLN party has shown more interest in supporting the LGBTQAI+ community both as a way to maintain social control and so it can export an image of Nicaragua as a welcoming country (McGee and Kampwirth 67). Still, until 2021, there was not a law in Nicaragua that supported the rights of transgender peoples, as evidenced by NGOs such as the *Asociación nicaragüense de trans* (Nicaraguan Association of Trans, ANIT) and *Organización de personas transgénero de Nicaragua* (Organization of Transgender People of Nicaragua, ODETRANS).

According to Héctor Domínguez-Ruvalcaba, the public presence of *travestis* in Latin America represents a denunciation of human rights violations (*Translating* 135). *Travestis* have also advanced tactics of resistance in the face of abuse by criminals and state institutions (137). Their activism then aided the trans* community throughout Latin America. While I have highlighted state politics and the efforts of activists, I realize that not all laws are intended to be inclusive and that inclusivity as a goal is not held by all *travestis*, transexuals, and trans* people. With regard to the works of Chilean Claudia Rodríguez and Argentine Susy Shock, Joseph Pierce states that neoliberal politics of inclusion can be problematic when they imply a normalization or categorization of trans issues. Pierce argues that the trans politics of resistance in both Rodríguez's and Shock's poetry not only explodes the gender binary, but also lays claim to the discourse of the monster as an affirmation of recognition (306, 308).

Chapter Five

I was initially reluctant to separate my discussion of trans* rights and the LGBTQAI+ community from the rest of my analysis because doing so creates an uncomfortable isolation of this topic. Still, I did so because considering different national experiences together allows me to highlight the history and fight of trans* rights in Latin America, which in turn emphasizes the importance of trans* peoples, *travestis*, and transsexuals. It is also my hope that this will also serve to call attention to the need of conducting more research on trans warriors in the twentieth century. At the time of this writing, countries such as Bolivia, Perú, and Chile, now allow trans* people to change their legal name and gender without undergoing surgery. The first countries to pass this kind of legislation nation-wide were Argentina, Brazil, Colombia, Ecuador, and Uruguay.

Despite such advances in gender rights for trans* peoples, trans warriors still have a long way to go before they will be considered respectable by everyone, appreciated for their contributions to society, and achieve equity. Perhaps future writers and filmmakers will discover and represent the histories of their involvement in the revolutionary movements and trans warriors will gain just as much a place in the public imagination as heroes of revolutions and revolutionary movements as have cis warriors.

Conclusion

By the late twentieth century, it has been recorded that warrior women could become soldiers, guerrillas, bandits, or criminals, and even achieve most-desired positions as military officers or political leaders without dressing in men's garb and today women are no longer required to adopt a masculine appearance if they want to participate in armed combat. Furthermore, their ability to own and wield weapons such as guns and rifles (whether for legal or illegal purposes) demonstrates that these phallic objects have ceased to be strictly linked to a specific gender. Weapons have become symbols of genderless power.

Warrior women's sexuality was also permitted to change in the latter part of the twentieth century. Although still regulated, representations of their sexuality have become more complex. Warrior women are no longer depicted as mere camp followers obeying men revolutionary leaders. Even though their sexuality has been appropriated by the government or the media, they have become increasingly autonomous. Nevertheless, the full range of warrior women's and especially trans warriors' sexualities, desires, and orientations has yet to be fully acknowledged and deheteronormativized in the public media and literature.

A third transformation has occurred in portrayals of warrior women from bandits to revolutionaries to terrorists. While Latin American revolutionaries of the 1960s and 1970s committed illegal acts such as robbing banks or kidnapping foreign diplomats for short periods of time, they always did so in order to support their revolutionary causes and gain leverage to free political prisoners. They were a kind of "social bandit" as defined by Eric Hobsbawm (17–18). A social bandit has two faces—the hero and the criminal. Which figure is seen depends on who is judging their actions. Warrior women who operate in illegal spaces often embody this dualism. This is seen in depictions of women guerrillas of the late twentieth and early twenty-first century. They became associated less with ideologically-driven revolutionary heroism and more with criminality as national governments led by political conservatives rejected revolution as a method of social change and condemned guerrillas for employing ethically unconscionable means for achieving their goals. For example, between 1980 and 1992, the Peruvian guerrilla group known as *Sendero luminoso* (Shining Path) kidnapped and held politicians and civilians for long periods of time and massacred civilian populations. In Colombia, groups such as the *Fuerzas armadas revolucionarias de Colombia* (Colombian Revolutionary Armed Forces, FARC) and *Ejército de liberación nacional* (National Liberation Army, ELN) committed similar crimes against humanity. Since such groups are corrupt and oppose democratically elected governments, their discourses of revolution and social altruism are often discredited. Indeed, these "guerrillas" might be better termed terrorists, since they attack the populations they claim to protect and adopt coercive strategies that resemble the very governments they are attempting to overthrow. When women join these groups, they soon enter the public imagination. For example, the 2003 film *Paloma de papel* (Paper Dove) directed by Peruvian Fabrizio Aguilar Boschetti depicts a woman guerilla terrorist character.

Literary characterizations of warrior women thus became more complex as increasing numbers of real warrior women and trans

Chapter Five

warriors participated in armed conflict and drug wars over the past century. The presence of women, *soldaderas*, women soldiers, and trans warriors in the Mexican Revolution facilitated multifaceted representations of warrior women and trans warrior characters in Mexican literature, music, and cinema. The triumph of the Revolution in Mexico and in other international revolutionary campaigns throughout the world then influenced revolutionary armies in Cuba and Nicaragua to officially incorporate women into their ranks. The incorporation of women and trans* individuals into political, military, and public spheres remains a slow process, however. Few warrior women have been able to obtain and remain in high-ranking positions in military (or criminal) organizations. It still makes the news when a woman is appointed Brigadier General or a woman crime boss is arrested. Meanwhile, news media do not cover trans* individuals achieving the rank of Brigadier General in any Latin American army, and some countries in the region do not even allow members of the LGBTQAI+ community to serve in their armed forces. Most-desired positions in these areas remain elusive.

Along with the obstacles to participation in combat that have been imposed by hegemonic patriarchal society, warrior women and trans warriors also face biased representations in the public media. Novelists, journalists, filmmakers, and politicians continue to mediate warrior women's and trans warriors' images and construct their figures for public consumption. As I have discussed throughout this book, this is done for a variety of reasons, including to confirm nationalist versions of history (especially following the success of a revolution), support sociopolitical ideologies (e.g., gender equality), mark revolutionary or criminal alliances, or call for a return to traditional, submissive femininity (i.e., by publicly condemning women fighting). The performances of women guerrillas of the late twentieth century combined with the absence of depictions of trans guerrillas demonstrate that sexism and transphobia prevail even as their images are appropriated and reappropriated by the government and the media to serve nationalistic agendas. Women and trans* men continue to face difficulties accessing the traditionally cis men spaces of war and crime.

Such manipulations of their images do not negate the particular identities, orientations, desires, struggles, and strategies of individual warrior women and trans warriors, however. In the

Trans Warriors and Warrior Women

twenty-first century, Latin American women and trans guerrillas, revolutionaries, and criminals alike have built on a history of struggle and the effective performances of previous trans warriors and warrior women to empower themselves in the spaces of war and revolution. They no longer have to imitate specific images of cis men in order to become combatants and achieved most-desired positions. They can have a wide array of gender performances and identities in their fight against tyranny and in their sexual relationships with their comrades-in-arms. Their ongoing struggles thus not only highlight the need for further change, but also how far Latin America has come since Pintada's Revolution.

Epilogue

The presence of women and trans* men in armed conflicts in Latin America demonstrates their capacity for fighting and transgressing traditional gender rules. In the first half of the twentieth century, woman and trans* characters in literature began to play important roles in the traditionally masculine spaces of warfare despite the fact that the actual presence of warrior women and trans* men in such spaces was still marginalized or ignored. Literary depictions of warrior women and trans warriors such as Pintada, Doña Bárbara, and Diadorim thus spoke to issues of inclusion and the need to recognize and fight intersectional oppression around gender, class, race, and ethnicity. As diverse performances became more visible, portraying trans* men and women in positions of leadership formerly only available to cis men also became more urgent. Thus, as the century progressed, more warrior woman and trans warrior characters such as Nacha, Angustias, Claire, Gertrudis, Itzá, Maria Moura, and Maria da Fé appeared in Latin American literature.

The gender performances of Pintada, Doña Bárbara, and Diadorim revealed the capacity for trans warriors and warrior women to be empowered in men-dominated spaces. These early characters achieved distinction by accessing phallic elements and projecting masculine images and behaviors. Their transgressive use of clothing and adoption of new names enabled them to compete with men characters to obtain most-admired positions within their social contexts. In doing so, warrior women and trans warriors simultaneously exposed the construction of emphasized femininity that was the social norm for women in their societies, while rendering visible the masculinity of men. Their effective use of the four strategies discussed in this book—manipulating clothed images, playing with names, occupying most-desired positions, and distinguishing themselves from men and traditional

Epilogue

feminine women characters—thus threatened the foundations of heterocispatriarchal society.

These warrior woman and trans warrior characters articulated their roles in society by manipulating their attire. Their use of clothing demonstrated the artificiality of gendered sartorial rules. Gendered binaries, especially the traditional categories of 'woman' and 'man', were thus interrogated. Furthermore, by projecting an image that was not normally available to women and trans* men in classist, sexist, transphobic, racist societies, these characters climbed the social ladder. Though poor and not white, Pintada demonstrates her ability to appropriate an upper-class aesthetic and improve her socioeconomic class by acquiring an elegant outfit. Doña Bárbara, a poor *mestiza* and indigenous woman, manipulates her clothing and ranching skills to appear more masculine; this enables her to hold power as a *cacica*. Finally, Diadorim constructs the complete image and performances of masculinity normally associated with cis men and thereby achieves prominence as a man warrior.

Such transgressive appropriations are furthered through naming. By refusing to be labeled with traditional gendered appellations, these trans warrior and warrior woman characters avoided being used as objects of exchange. Their names also confirmed their positions of power. However, the play with names and nicknames in the fictional works analyzed in this book provides evidence that women and trans* men who achieved positions of leadership were liable to be disempowered. Pejorative nicknames reinvoked hegemonic rules and categories to minimize these characters' transgressions. The nicknames applied to these characters reveal how heterocispatriarchal societies attempt to explain away the achievements of powerful trans warrior and warrior woman characters and pathologize their gender transgressions. Pintada is given animalistic nicknames because she refuses to become an object of exchange between men. Nicknames suggesting that Doña Bárbara is naïve and stupid undermine her actual intelligence and power as a *cacica*. Diadorim, who in life was the best of warriors, in death is diminished with the discovery of his sex and birth name. Warrior women and trans warriors are turned into caricatures because their presence inherently threatens the normative functioning of patriarchal societies.

Trans warrior and warrior woman characters successfully performed most-desired masculinities to empower themselves within

Epilogue

such masculine contexts as revolution in Mexico, ranches in the Venezuelan Plains, and war in the Brazilian Backlands, but their performances resulted in rivalry with men characters. The ability of characters such as Pintada, Doña Bárbara, and Diadorim to occupy most-admired positions not only threatened the masculinity of cis man characters, it demonstrated the artificiality of gendered hierarchies and challenged the stability of patriarchal social structures and national discourses. In early to mid-twentieth-century Latin American novels, warrior woman and trans warrior characters were invariably deposed from their positions of power, usually by being expelled from society, marginalized, or killed. Nonetheless, that they achieved these positions of privilege in the first place forces us to rethink the gender, class, religious, ethnic, and racial hierarchies operating in contexts of armed conflict. The performances of these warrior characters show that most-desired positions have never been exclusively "masculine" and "male" even within traditionally masculine social contexts.

The performances of warrior woman and trans warrior characters not only called into question traditional discourses on masculinity, they revealed and challenged discourses on femininity. They exposed by contrast the subjugation of other women characters to heterocispatriarchal rules. The powerful Pintada prevents men from exchanging women, while the feminine Camila accepts being treated as an object of exchange. Doña Bárbara empowers herself by transgressing barriers of skin color, ethnicity, gender, and class, whereas Marisela submits to the rules of heterocispatriarchy and thereby obtains the position of obedient wife. Diadorim's masculinity and independent agency also stand in stark contrast to the feminine sexuality and submissiveness of traditional women characters. The performances of trans warrior and warrior woman characters also point to the ways in which men characters perpetuate men's homosociality by making them compete with women characters.

In each case, the performances of these characters revealed the stress fractures in naturalizing discourses on gender and sexuality within the hegemonies of their times. According to Michel Foucault, nineteenth-century European bourgeoisie established rigid gender borders because they believed they could control society by regulating people's bodies and sexualities (19, 34). The attempt to regulate people's bodies was weaker in Latin America than in

Epilogue

Europe, however. Alternative cultural traditions maintained by subaltern or isolated groups also resisted bourgeois norms. Lack of state governance enabled subjects to escape legal and other regulatory discourses. The absence of strong governance, especially amongst low-income or poor populations, enabled subjects to transgress the rules of naturalizing gender discourses. Such transgressions become even more probable during periods of chaos, which suggests why real trans warriors and warrior women often emerge in history during times of conflict and war.

The strategic performances of the three analyzed characters in their respective contexts enrich understanding of the roles people can take during times of war. That is, I have taken an inclusive approach to rethinking each country and Latin America as a whole. For example, my analysis of Pintada's performance contributes to a non-romanticized view of the Mexican Revolution and rescues the complex roles and intersectional position of women in that armed conflict. The narrative of her empowerment and subsequent disempowerment can be read along with more contemporary texts to reclaim the stories and value of *soldaderas*, camp followers, and sex workers. Her performance highlights her agenda and the desire for greater socioeconomic mobility in the midst of the Revolution; it also shows how bands of men displace women's attempts to improve themselves. Doña Bárbara's performance challenges the masculinist image of *llaneros* in the Araucan Plains, by showing that their required skills can be genderless. Her performance also interrogates traditional views on *caciquismo* by demonstrating that subjects who are disenfranchised in terms of race, gender, ethnicity, religion, and class can still access most-desired positions. Diadorim's performance adds dimensions to the role of *jagunços* in the Brazilian Backlands while stressing the compulsoriness of their heterocissexual masculinity. He challenges the idea that only cis men participate in armed battles and underscores the importance of trans* warriors during times of conflict.

The publication dates of the three novels suggest that gender transgressions developed over time. In 1915, the warrior woman Pintada behaves in a masculine way, including occasionally as a leader. In 1929, Doña Bárbara sometimes dons masculine attire and can behave in a masculine manner when it suits her to do so; she then becomes the *cacica* of her region. Finally, in 1956, Diadorim is a powerful trans warrior. While all three novels include non-normative gender experiences, the destabilization of binary gender rules and identities becomes more prominent toward the 1960s. Even if *Grande sertão: veredas* is the most complex of the three novels with regard to gender identity and transgression, the performances of the warrior women characters in *Los de abajo* and *Doña Bárbara* must be emphasized because they go beyond gender to involve racial, cultural, ethnic, religious, and class transgressions. Both Pintada and Doña Bárbara manage to empower themselves in societies in which power traditionally had only been granted to upper-class white cis men. João Guimarães Rosa did not engage such complexities in the Brazilian context since his trans warrior character is upper class and white. Thus, the performances of Mariano Azuela's and Rómulo Gallegos's cis women characters more accurately reflect the socioeconomic, cultural, religious, and racial diversity of Latin American people than does Diadorim's. Still, all three novels problematize the ways in which warrior women's and trans warriors' struggles are permeated not only by sexism and transphobia, but also by racism, colorism, classism, and discrimination against non-European cultural, and religious practices.

These novels can be read in dialogue with the struggle for women's and trans' rights and the women's liberation movements in Latin America during the first part of the twentieth century. That is, the transgressive performances of the warrior woman and trans warrior characters reflect the fact that the roles of women and trans* men in society were changing and they were acquiring a more public presence. On the other hand, the disempowerment of the three characters in all three works suggests that the novels authored by white men writers were not proposing a future of gender equity or nonbinary gender identities. The disempowerment of the trans warrior and warrior woman characters demonstrates how hegemonic society constantly reinforces heterocispatriarchy to curb any challenges to traditional rules, be they concern gender identity, sexual orientation, race or skin color, class, culture, ethnicity, or religion. In attempting to domesticate, explain, and pathologize warrior women and trans warriors, society rendered their agentive strategies temporary during the early twentieth century.

Trans warriors and warrior women achieved permanent agency in the second part of the twentieth century, as they increasingly participated in war environments. Real warrior women (and trans warriors) were officially incorporated into many armed groups,

Epilogue

whether criminal gangs or legally sanctioned military forces. As they became actively involved in political and social conflicts, their presence has been officially recorded for posterity. Their participation released women and trans* men from other gender constraints in these spaces, including constraints on their sexuality. Sexuality had always been a key motif in the performances of warrior woman and trans warrior characters. Sometimes they manipulate their own sexuality as an empowerment strategy, but in other instances their sexuality has been exoticized for public consumption, especially in films. Their sexuality has also been ignored, erased, or manipulated by the government for propaganda purposes.

Socioeconomic changes, coupled with a transformation in the social status of women and trans* men thanks to sexual and feminist revolutions and LGBTQAI+ activism since the late twentieth century have resulted in modified strategies of empowerment for trans warriors and warrior women. Along with growing recognition of the achievements of historical warrior women and trans warriors, their public image changed. By the second decade of the twentieth-first century, trans warriors and warrior women are acquiring an official presence and public voice, yet it continues to be important to revise histories and imaginaries of their sexualities, gender performances, gender identities, embodiments, and positions of leadership in a variety of contexts. This is especially urgent for trans warriors, who did not occupy the same spaces as warrior women in the guerrilla movements of the second part of the twentieth century. As evidenced in Chapter 5, while many women and trans* people alike can enter the arena of combat as soldiers, revolutionaries, or bandits, and cis women, at least, are no longer required to cross-dress or adopt other forms of masculinization if they wish to become warriors, the presence and contributions of trans* people still need to be recovered and emphasized. Their representation in fictional and historical texts provides images in tune with Latin American diversity.

The women and trans* men who fought alongside cis men had to contend with many obstacles to being there and being treated as equals. Their resilience is key to rethinking non-traditional projects of Latin America. Just as Latin American women and trans* men have struggled for recognition within highly masculinized, hypervirile societies (Molloy 187), so have trans warriors and warrior women characters rarely been allowed to embody nationalist and regionalist discourses. For the most part, only traditional heterosexual (white) cis men heroes have been permitted to symbolize the region or nations within the region. Since heroic women and trans* men contest nationalist propaganda and representations of national identity, they are usually displaced or disempowered in the public sphere. While such displacements aim to invalidate trans warriors and warrior women as heroes of the nation, their ongoing presence, capabilities, and impact in fields of war cannot be denied. Fictional warrior women and trans warriors have thus come to represent revolutionary alternatives to traditional constructions of nationalism and Latin America.

At the end of his book, *Naciones intelectuales*, Ignacio Sánchez-Prado poses the question: What will be the consequences of rethinking Mexican traditions if the myths of virility perpetuated by some authors are replaced by other myths or critical approaches? (242). Sánchez-Prado argues that using Octavio Paz's *El laberinto de la soledad* as the only reference for Mexico implies that only very specific images and peoples are included in the nationalist project. Such a selection fails to reflect the entire Mexican nation and the heterogeneity of its population. In revisiting Latin American literature, especially in reviewing woman and trans* characters who had been ignored or read in binary terms for the most part, this book has proposed another possibility that questions the old myths of national virility. Pintada, Doña Bárbara, and Diadorim laid the ground for specific transgressive gender performances throughout Latin American literature of the first part of the twentieth century. By employing various strategies of empowerment, including posing, passing, cross-dressing, and defying traditional binary rules, these warrior women and trans warriors offer an alternative to the constructions of traditional masculinities in Latin America. Showing that trans warrior and warrior woman characters had a strong presence in canonical texts speaks to the ways in which even the most-desired positions were not exclusively occupied by heterocissexual men. To answer Sánchez-Prado's question, my reading of these characters reclaims a Latin America that is not necessarily predicated on myths of virility. I thus expose and challenge the sexism, transphobia, racism, classism, colorism, and discrimination against indigenous communities that have formerly been taken for granted. Although

Epilogue

trans warriors and warrior women are barred from fully embodying the heroic figures required in the regionalist and nationalist discourses of the twentieth-century, their performances reveal that these masculinist discourses were less dominant than originally believed. My analysis foregrounds the increasing importance of warrior women and trans warriors to diverse national projects in twentieth century Latin America. As their contributions to revolutionary movements have been uncovered, their public imaginaries have also changed. Pintada's rebellion against class and gender norms, Doña Bárbara's movement from the lower to upper class as indigenous *mestiza cacica*, and Diadorim's performance as a great trans warrior represent part of the desires, resiliencies, and empowerment of oppressed races, ethnicities, classes, gender identities, embodiments, and genders throughout Latin America.

Sánchez-Prado proposes to find other texts that provide nontraditional images on which may be built new national and regional traditions and references. This book has likewise demonstrated the importance of reading canonical texts against the grain in order to queer hegemonic discourses on gender, gender identity, and sexuality. I have strategically dialogued with theories and critiques that were originally developed and applied in other regions in order to illustrate the complexities of empowerment and disempowerment in Latin America. Similar to the work done by B. Christine Arce and Emily Hind, I incorporated an intersectional framework and conducted close readings of important Latin American texts to move marginalized subjects such as women and trans* people to the center of the discussion.

One of my goals in this book has been to show critics and consumers of literature the potential for shifting perspectives on the canon. Although I recognize the importance of acknowledging women and trans* writers and quoting women and trans*critics, I have chosen to analyze well-known novels authored by white men writers in order to reread and recover woman and trans* characters that had been either ignored or treated in stereotypical ways by some literary critics. The works of Azuela, Gallegos, and Guimarães Rosa can be read as products of their time while still embracing other possibilities and points of view, in this case, that of (feared) empowered warrior women and trans warriors. Considering the importance of representation, revisiting how these characters have been depicted and appropriated in mainstream li-

Epilogue

terature allows us as critics to understand how traditional discourses were perpetuated even as challenges to these discourses were being crafted. The trans*/queer/gender readings of the canon that I have conducted in this book enable us to see how transgressive performances were able to persist despite the marginalization of the transgressors. By emphasizing an intersectional trans*feminist and queer framework and conducting a close-reading analysis of historical and fictional trans warriors and warrior women, this book has broadened the discussions on gender, gender identity, embodiments, femininities, masculinities, and sexualities in Latin America.

Notes

Introduction

1. In the Seville and Madrid versions of the manuscript on Eraúso's life, Sherry Velasco discusses how Eraúso discovered his sex (4).

2. Jack Halberstam's theory on female masculinity is an important reference here.

3. As I explain in another section, I propose to use the term "most-desirable position" to replace "hegemonic masculinity."

4. These actors have played more roles as expert fighters. Even though Hollywood films feminize and sexualize their appearance, their performances are similar to the masculinities I analyze here.

5. For more information, please refer to Carsten/Carla LaGata Balzer and Lukas Berredo's report and Bruna G. Benevides e Sayonara Naider Bomfim Nogueira's 2018 and 2019 Dossiers.

6. All trans* peoples, especially those who are non-white, low-income sex workers, must be recognized because how trans* peoples and travestis are seen and understood is critical to avoiding future violence and transphobia. I am not defining LGBTQAI+ activists' goals and range of action here, but simply pointing out that certain social causes take priority for Latin American transsexuals, transgenders, and travestis.

7. One thinks of Aurélia in *Senhora* (1875), Santa in *Santa* (1903), Lúzia in *Luzia-homem* (1903), Joana in *Perto do coração selvagem* (1944), Ana Maria in *Uma mulher diferente* (1968), and L. Iluminada in *Lumpérica* (1983).

8. In *Women Warriors* (1997), Jones used the word "warriors" to refer to "women wielders of military weapons, leaders of armies, planners of strategy, directors of generals, commanders in chief, military empire builders" (8). His term does not capture sex and gender differences between cis and trans warriors, however.

9. In Brazil, the term "cangaceira" refers to women bandits in the Backlands. I do not adopt this term because it denotes a very specific sociohistorical-geographic context. (Cangaceiras are discussed further in Chapter One and Four)

10. Linda Grant De Pauw discusses other roles, such as viragos and androgynous warriors depicted in military history (17–18). A *virago*, often defined

Notes

as a maiden who is like a man, is a term insufficient for showing how gender performances expose and challenge traditional rules. The androgynous is problematic because it combines two gender categories into one inflexible third category without destabilizing the original two categories.

11. By "sex" I refer to genitalia, hormones, internal reproductive organs, gonads, and chromosomes.

12. "Cucaracha" (cockroach) and "galleta" (cookie) were also used to refer to women involved in the Revolution. I do not adopt them because their meanings have varied throughout history and they objectify women's sexuality.

13. Arce argues that the term *soldadera* shows how women's participation in war has been marked as unacceptable (65). For her, it is a word that highlights the ways in which women's presence has been demeaned so that they were not recognized and treated as soldiers (65).

14. Alicia Arrizón argues that eventually the term became synonymous with *soldadera* to designate all women soldiers (90).

15. Louise O. Vasvári discusses the ballad "La donçella guerrera" and how the protagonist's gender transgression challenges the gender binary. She proposes to see the maid's warrior performance as the real identity and their passivity as a masquerade (111).

16. According to Carmen Bravo-Villasante, the topic of the woman crossdressed as a man arrived to the Iberian Peninsula from Italy and in texts such as Ludovico Ariosto's *Orlando Furioso* (14–15).

17. Daphne Patai explains that a testimonio is an eyewitness account from a person who has suffered oppression, usually obtained in an interview with an academic researcher (191). The scholar tapes, edits, sometimes translates, and publishes the interview (191). Testimonios have a leftist political inflection (191).

18. The reference to the fierce woman comes from Debra Castillo's book *Easy Women: Sex and Gender in Modern Mexican Fiction*. This woman is the one "who combines a masculine arrogance with sexual aggressivity and feminine allure" (162).

19. Queer theory in Latin America has been criticized, welcomed, rejected, misinterpreted, and/or reused/reappropriated. Postcolonial-informed scholars and activists as well as those emphasizing the importance of the context and the identity of minority groups have criticized it for its global North bias and poststructuralist approach. According to María Amelia Viteri et al., some of the first responses to queer theory from Latin America were produced in the scholarly journals *Debate feminista* in Mexico (1997), *Nómadas* in Colombia (1999), and *Cadernos Pagú* in Brazil (2007) (51–54). I must also acknowledge the work conducted by scholars and activists in Latin America, as well as discussions and theorizations on sexual dissidence in twentieth century Latin American literature.

20. For instance, Berenice Bento refers to queer studies as "estudos transviad@s," and Héctor Miguel Salinas Hernández chooses the term *disidencias sexuales* (sexual dissidences) for analyzing Latin American sexualities.

Notes

Poet, writer, and scholar Tatiana Nascimento uses "queerlombismo" and "cuíerlombismo." For more information, see Foster's book *Ensayos sobre culturas homoeróticas latinoamericanas* (2009) and *Nascimento* (2018).

21. I do not identify individual trans* critics' gender identity or preferred pronouns, as not all of them have made them explicit or discussed their experiences in their academic work.

22. Shimizu Akiko criticizes Butler's performativity concept by suggesting that performances can simultaneously oppose and affirm dominant systems (48). I argue that the warrior women's and trans warriors' empowerment and disempowerment present critiques of hegemonic structures.

23. Her position is reminiscent of Louis Althusser's rituals of ideological recognition, discussed in Chapter One.

24. Intersectionality is critical to trans theory because, as reese simpkins points out, examining "trans* as separate from 'other' categories fundamentally misconstrues the operation of power and paints a simplistic picture of identification" (232).

25. I have used this term before in an article published in *Latin American Research Review*.

26. I am aware that "gay" identity as understood today developed in Brazil and other Spanish American countries in the late twentieth century. I use the word "gay" to avoid overusing the word "homosexual" with its pathological connotations.

27. Sánchez-Prado questions how Octavio Paz's *El laberinto de la soledad* became central to the idea of the Mexican nation, achieving prominence despite other projects of the *naciones intelectuales*. Sifuentes-Jáuregui's *Avowal of Difference: Queer Latino American Narratives* (2014) revisits Paz's *El laberinto* to establish a critical framework for discussing Latin American literature while avoiding U.S. theory and criticism on gender.

28. Azuela, a medical doctor, was originally a follower of the Mexican president Francisco Madero until he was assassinated in 1913. Azuela then joined the armed fight against Victoriano Huerta's government. His experience in the Mexican Revolution inspired *Los de abajo*. The novel was first published as a serial in an El Paso, Texas newspaper (*El Paso del Norte*), then as a book in 1915.

29. Pintada appears in only 38 out of 134 pages.

30. Gallegos thought that Venezuela needed to be modernized and leave behind the backward state created during nearly three decades of Juan Vicente Gómez's dictatorship (1908–1935).

31. Guimarães Rosa was born and lived in the state of Minas Gerais. He was familiar with the Backlands and its armed conflicts. In the 1932, he voluntarily participated in the Constitutionalist Revolution by joining the Public Force. He was also a medical doctor with Barbacena's Ninth Platoon of Infantry.

32. For instance, conservative people dismissed the proactive rebelliousness of women characters in Hollywood films as bad habits (Bassanezi 610).

33. According to James N. Green, police only tolerated cross-dressing during Carnival (Beyond 22).

Notes

34. Other terms for describing genres of literature related to Latin American Regionalism include "criollismo" (creoleism), "mundonovismo" (newworldism), "posmodernismo" (postmodernism), "escritura autóctona" (autochthonous writing), "novela rural" (rural novel), and "novela costumbrista" (costumbrist novel). Because the three novels analyzed here might be classified differently according to any of these terms and to avoid using Spanish words to discuss texts written in Portuguese, I prefer the more general term "Regionalism."

Chapter One

1. Susan B. Kaiser argues that fashion is based on contradiction and ambivalence. Ambivalence refers to conflicting emotions, which are a way of feeling and knowing (2).

2. Here I am taking into consideration Mark Johnson's critique of Garber for failing to make the connection between dress and power (24).

3. In the novel Pintada is described as "de cuello y brazos muy trigueños" (146), "pelo hirsuto" (146), and "tinte aceitunado de su rostro y las manchas cobrizas de la avería" (160). I highlight that Pintada can be indigenous, *mestiza*, or Black in order to avoid contributing to the erasure of Afrodescendants' presence in Mexico.

4. Feminism needs not be antagonistic to trans studies, since both fields share the ultimate goal of gender equity.

5. Despite this deception, Camila decides to stay with Demetrio. She believes her mother would not accept her returning back home and she has begun to find him attractive.

6. Lavou Zoungbo argues that the pervasive symbolism in the novel preceded its writing (216), since Gallegos decided to write the novel using certain ideas and ideology.

7. *The Histories* were written in the 450s BC. Jones adds that this outfit is "still worn by nomadic pastoral groups in the area" (6). Phrygia was an ancient Anatolian kingdom.

8. For example, according to José Quiroga, gay men in Latin America have been seen as inverts (13). As Domínguez-Ruvalcaba states, the crossdressed man in Latin America is a repellant body in normative men's imaginaries because it questions discourses on masculinities. It threatens to undo heteronormativity and become a desirable body (Modernity 37). The fear of being gay is thus highly emphasized in the social contexts of Latin American heterocissexual men.

9. Diadorim goes to war by his own choice, not at the behest of his father. When his father is murdered, he decides to avenge his death. Diadorim also passes as a man throughout his adult life, and he cannot be considered an archetypal warrior maid considering one of the key aspects of a warrior maid is that her sex is discovered before her death (Galvão, "Ciclo" 9).

10. This technique of a character influencing the narration can be seen in other Brazilian novels, including those written by Joaquim Maria Machado

de Assis, who had a great influence on Guimarães Rosa. In Machado de Assis's *Dom Casmurro* (1899), Bento is another protagonist-narrator; he structures the story to reveal how his wife came to cheat on him with his best friend.

11. According to Jack Halberstam, "trans* can be a name for expansive forms of difference, haptic relations to knowing, uncertain modes of being, and the disaggregation of identity politics predicated upon the separating out of many kinds of experience that actually blend together, intersect, and mix" (Trans* 4–5). Transitioning is a complex experience that cannot be reduced to certain types of surgeries. According to this logic, instead of being understood as inflexible categories, both gender and body are understood as fluid constructs.

12. "Trans" is preferred over the terms "transvestite," "transgender," and "transsexual."

13. Balderston acknowledges Diadorim's connections to other cross-dressers, but does not elaborate on their transgressive performances (59).

14. In the novel, she was almost not forgiven for her crossdressing (208).

15. This musical was shown in the Teatro do Sesi-SP, from April 25 to August 4, 2019.

Chapter Two

1. In "Of Names" (1843), the Englishman John Stuart Mill divided names into two types: connotatives and non-connotatives. A connotative name denotes a subject and implies an attribution, while a non-connotative name signifies only a subject or attribution. According to Mill's division, proper names are non-connotative, since once a name has been given, its meaning no longer depends on the reason for which it was given. A half century later, another English philosopher, Bertrand Russell, argued that proper nouns are denotative, that is, they express something about the objects they name. Denotative phrases are not the object itself, but refer to it. In "On Denoting" (1905), he wrote, "A proposition about Apollo means what we get by substituting what the classical dictionary tells us is meant by Apollo, say 'the sun-god'" (491). Published posthumously in the early 1930s, the works of the U.S. philosopher, C. S. Peirce, supported Russell's ideas by arguing that the first time one encounters a name, the name is an accurate index of the object being named, but later, "[t]he habitual acquaintance with it having been acquired, it becomes a Symbol whose Interpretant represents it as an Icon of an Index of the Individual named" (286). That is, through repetition, a proper name gains a referential function, but does not have any inherent meaning.

2. Butler largely drew upon the work of Jacques Lacan, Slavoj Žižek, Louis Althusser, and Michel Foucault.

3. According to Butler, what Austin calls the failure of the statement—that is, when a statement is not capable of communicating—generates the possibility of agency (Excitable 44).

Notes

4. According to Richard Corson, the Sears Roebuck's catalogue was "a reliable barometer of what Americans were buying" (369). By 1897, it was already offering a wide selection of cosmetics.

5. In Brazil, this type of system is called coronelismo.

6. She is described as such a dozen times over the course of the novel, on pages 46, 103, 117, 126, 127, 128, 129, 173, 223, 225, 234, 239.

7. Davidiva implies a word play with Diadorim, diva, the verb *dar* (to give); Dindurinh represents phonetic variations; and Deodorina is a woman's name. Traditionally, names than end in -a are considered feminine, and in -o masculine.

8. Machado points out that the resonance is connected to the names' origins—both are derivations from Germanic words.

9. Within the novel's economy, it is only when Reinaldo reveals that his name is Diadorim that it becomes evident to the reader that they are the same character. Previously, they seemed to be two different characters.

10. Tatarana denotes someone very courageous, and Urutú-Branco refers to a type of white snake.

Chapter Three

1. By contrast, the protagonist of Queiroz's novel *Memorial de Maria Moura* (1992) is a warrior woman.

2. Although I discuss twentieth-century novels, I must add that using a knife or a dagger is considered ignoble compared to wielding a sword, mainly because a knife is not as long as a sword (so not as masculine a phallic symbol). It is associated more with dishonorable in-fighting rather than with the gentlemanly art of fencing by members of the privileged socioeconomic classes (Anglo 144). Knives and daggers also have fewer spiritual connotations than swords (Cirlot 95, 163).

3. Max Parra contends that Pintada is a complex figure because she sometimes depends on Güero Margarito as "her man," but other times does whatever she wants (28). I do not consider Margarito to be "her man," but just one amongst the characters she interacts with.

4. Derrida analyzes Jacques Lacan's study of Edgar Alan Poe's short story, "The Purloined Letter." Lacan first argues that the role of the Queen is to protect the King's legitimacy, which she does by hiding a letter ("Seminar" 42). The person who obtains the purloined letter must then hide it from the King, so essentially adopts the role of the Queen (44). The owner of the purloined letter thus acquires the Queen's attributes of femininity and shadow in order to confirm the King's power (44). Derrida argues that the person who has the purloined letter becomes a castrated queen, however (183). The stolen letter represents the power of the phallus (King), but the power is maintained by the queen's disempowerment—her castration of power—and subjection. According to Derrida, then, the purloined letter and the person that owns it represent the phallus's place because the letter's location is the place in which power confirms women's castration within the dominant cul-

Notes

ture (183). Derrida, thus, critiques Lacan's traditional view of power based on kinship and not castration. He also argues that Lacan is mistaken in considering that the purloined letter always arrives at its addressee (the King). For Derrida, the possibility of the letter not arriving is plausible because the phallus does not always remain in the same place (187).

5. Porfirio Sánchez sees these criminal behaviors as part of human nature, so not limited to a decadent period of the Revolution.

6. These soldiers are members of the band. By using the word "soldier," Azuela's novel speaks to different perspectives and how fighters sometimes changed sides during the Revolution.

7. While Carlos Alonso refers to the allegoric structure that is central to Gallegos's novel, he makes evident that constant references to the gang rape make it a theme for *Doña Bárbara* ("Otra" 434–35). He argues that the character is unable to reconcile past and present because her present is dominated by the gang rape (434). I see that her past makes her a strong woman in her context.

8. Santos, who represents European rational culture in the novel, also remains unimpressed by her supposed witch's skills.

9. Doña Bárbara kills the Colonel to empower herself. She assassinates him before Santos returns to the Araucan Plains.

10. Magnarelli notes that "the power of the word rests not in the term itself but rather in the supplementation which inevitably accompanies it" ("Woman" 15). By supplementation, she means use and context.

11. In Latin America, most of Europeans and European-descendants are considered white. Although there is colorism, there is not a clear marked distinction between different European nations in terms of skin color and their biracial/multiracial descendants.

12. Henighan argues that Doña Bárbara's femininity is constructed in order to consolidate Santos's masculinity (44), but I read her gender performance differently.

13. In Brazil, a Colonel represents the government and the law in the area he controls.

14. I do not examine Diadorim's interactions with the jagunço leaders Joca Ramiro and Medeiro Vaz, however, because Riobaldo prioritizes his own relationship with them.

15. See Serra, Neitzel, Filho, Olivieri, and Payne and Fitz.

16. Just as the owner of the purloined letter is disempowered when the letter is taken away in Poe's short story.

17. I also analyze the death of Maria da Fé and argue that the absence of a corpse implies that Maria da Fé becomes a saint ("Mulheres" 125). Maria da Fé is the revolutionary that transcends her gender and physical body. The body/corpse of another warrior woman character is the topic of Duerme by Carmen Boullosa, which I discussed in Chapter One.

Chapter Four

1. Lévi-Strauss also argues that, as symbols of the social body, women represent the cultural evolution of the human being. Their exchange therefore represents the transformation of humankind from nature to culture (Las estructuras 102–03).

2. In *The Creation of Patriarchy* (1986), Gerda Lerner also revisits Lévi-Strauss to argue that the reification of women's sexuality is another consequence of the exchange of women (213). Lerner suggests that patriarchy uses women's sexuality to reproduce itself (213).

3. In the English translation of the novel, this woman character is referred to as "Quail's little companion" because Codorniz means 'quail' (144).

4. Baker concludes her chapter asserting that Pintada is a foil to Demetrio (Revolutionaries 104).

5. Chauvinist stereotypes regarding Malinche are found in the essay *El laberinto de la soledad* (The Labyrinth of Solitude) (1950), in which Octavio Paz argues that Malinche represents the raped mother, a symbol of a fucked up (*chingado*) aspect of Mexican culture.

6. Azuela explained this selection at a conference given in the Colegio de Mexico in 1945; his speech is transcribed in ALLCA XX's edition of *Los de abajo* (324–38).

7. As I explained in Chapter One with regard to Pintada, I do not limit characters to one ethnic or racial category partly because of the lack of descriptors in the novel and partly to avoid erasing the presence of Black Mexicans.

8. The only other woman characters that appear (infrequently) in Doña Bárbara are the granddaughters of an old llanero named Melesio, who works for Altamira. One of the granddaughters, Genoveva, is Marisela's confidante in the chapter entitled "La pasión sin nombre" (The Nameless Passion); she has no other role in the narrative.

9. The novel *Os desvalidos* (Wretched People) (1993) by Francisco J. C. Dantas depicts a warrior woman who dresses in male clothing and fights in Lampião's group. Unlike Diadorim, she is only a secondary character and she is not a trans* man.

10. A clear reference can be found in Corpo de baile (1956), specifically in "Dão-lalalão."

11. While some sex workers such as high-income escorts may feel empowered and appreciate their profession, most are exploited.

12. Riobaldo mentions other sex workers he has known, but does not seem to develop relationships with them and ends up forgetting them.

Chapter Five

1. As Miriam Cooke explains, popular media have increasingly influenced the articulation of heroic myths in war texts (181–82).

2. In featuring cross-dressing women that go to war, corridos are similar to Brazilian texts known as *literatura de cordel* (literature on a string), a writ-

Notes

ten tradition that originated in European ballads.
3. The woman revolutionary character, Guadalupe, is only developed superficially in Salvador Quevedo y Zubieta's book *Mexico marimacho* (1933?).
4. María Félix played Doña Bárbara in a 1943 adaptation of the novel.
5. Mendieta Alatorre also mentions Encarnación Mares, known as Chonita, who "vestía de hombre, engrosaba la voz para hablar y llevaba el pelo corto" (90). Men soldiers respected Chonita because she was not afraid of gunfire. She reached the rank of second lieutenant (her husband made it to first captain) before Venustiano Carranza reorganized the army in 1916, during which time he got rid of all the women soldiers and soldaderas (90; Reséndez Fuentes 550).
6. Kristine Vanden Berghe has analyzed the ludic aspect of Cartucho.
7. Coined by Moya Bailey and disseminated by Trudy, the term "misogynoir" refers to the double oppression Black women endure because of their gender and racial status ("On Misogynoir" 762–63).
8. In Spanish, the word *mestizaje* often does not have the same connotations as the term "miscegenation" in English or mestiçagem in Portuguese. Mexico represents a case of "Mexicanizing" indigenous populations to make them fit the nationalist discourse.
9. Although I am well aware of the offensive connotations of the term "mulata," I use it to highlight the sexualization of women of mixed African and European descent in the Americas. As Jasmine Mitchell explains, using this term can emphasize the historical weight of such oppression as well as the intersection of gender and race (18).
10. Lisa Ze Winters indicates that discourses that portray free(d) mulatto women as concubines with agency are reductive and limiting (5–6). They also perpetuate traditional rules (11–12).
11. According to Zuzana M. Pick, Raúl de Anda got his nickname "black charro" after the 1935 film Juan Pistolas (225).
12. When Angustias falls in love with Manuel, she changes her clothes and wears feminine attire. I do not analyze those attires.
13. Arce compares Angustias to the narrative figure of the tragic *mulata* (México's 190).
14. In 2015, Randall published Haydée Santamaría, Cuban Revolutionary: She Led by Transgression.
15. In the *Grupo de alzados de Las Piedras* (Rebel Group from Las Piedras), Gladys Marel García-Pérez states that 28 people took arms and rose up against Batista's regime. Leonor Arestuche, known as Sobrina (niece), was the only woman in the group (20, 35–36).
16. The other members of the platoon were Lilia Rielo, Olga Guevara, Angelina Antolín, Rita García, Ada Bella Acosta, Normita Ferrer, Flor Pérez, Eva Palma, Orosia Soto, Juana Peña, and Edemis Tamayo.
17. Filmmakers such as Glauber Rocha, Nelson Pereira dos Santos, Joaquim Pedro de Andrade, and Carlos Diegues were all committed to emphasizing Brazilian realities in their films of the 1960s.
18. Other testimonial Brazilian works that feature women guerrillas inclu-

Notes

de the film *Que bom te ver viva* (How Nice to See you Alive) (1989) and *A memória que me contam* (Memories They Told Me) (2012) by Lucia Murat and testimonials and memoirs such as *Guerrilheira* (Woman Guerrilla) (2003) by Antonio Nascimento, *O baú do guerrilheiro: Memórias da luta armada urbana no Brasil* (The Guerrilla's Trunk: Memoirs of the Armed Fight in Brazil) (2004) by Ottoni Fernandes Júnior, *Náufrago de utopia: Vencer ou morrer na guerrilha. Aos 18 anos* (The Sinking of Utopia: Win or Die in the Guerrillas at 18 Years Old) (2005) by Celso Lungaretti, and *Helenira Resende e a guerrilha do Araguaia* (Helenira Resende and the Araguaia Guerrilla) (2007) by Bruno Ribeiro.

19. Vera Sílvia Magalhães was depicted later in a film by Bruno Barreto, *O que é isso, companheiro?* (Four Days in September) (1997). Two characters named Maria and Renée represent her in the film. Neither character is portrayed as particularly sexy, although Renée seduces a man employee of the embassy and Maria has a romantic-sexual relationship with a man character named Fernando.

20. The U.S.-sponsored contras war, started in 1981, interrupted their triumph.

21. The foco theory or foquismo is based on three lessons of the Cuban Revolution: a popular force capable of defeating the army, the conditions for the revolution will be created by the insurrection, and the armed fight will take place in the countryside (Childs 604).

22. The sandinitos, or Little Sandinos, youths around twelve or thirteen years old, who had joined the guerrillas to bring down the Somoza regime, were not separated by gender however.

23. Venkatesh sees that revolutionary masculinity "hovers over the sociocultural model, gun in hand, waiting to usurp traditional hierarchies of power" (153).

24. The disillusionment with how the Sandinista Revolution took shape after the victory and the divisions between the revolutionaries can also be seen in Sergio Ramírez's 1999 novel *Adiós muchachos*.

25. One of the goals of the revolutionary government was to eradicate the sex trade.

26. The *Sociedad cubana multidisciplinaria para el estudio de la sexualidad* (Cuban Multidisciplinary Society for the Study of Sexuality, SOCUMES) was created in 1985. It was created by the GNTES with the goal of conducting research related to sexuality (Kirk, The Normalization 84).

27. She became a delegate to the municipal government of Caibarién in the Province of Villa Clara.

28. Other Peruvian guerrilla groups of the late twentieth century claimed to be different from the Shining Path, as seen in the testimonials of members of the *Movimiento revolucionario Tupac Amaru* (Revolutionary Movement Tupac Amaru, MRTA) published in *Fuga de Canto Grande* (Tunnel to Canto Grande) (1992) by Claribel Alegría and D. J. Flakoll.

Bibliography

Adler, Freda. *Sisters in Crime. The Rise of the New Female Criminal.* With Herbert M. Adler, McGraw-Hill, 1975.

Ahmed, Sara. *The Cultural Politics of Emotion.* Routledge, 2004.

Alarcón, Norma. "Traddutora, Traditora: A Paradigmatic Figure of Chicana Feminism." *Cultural Critique*, no. 13, 1989, pp. 57–87.

Albuquerque Júnior, Durval Muniz de. *Nordestino: invenção do 'falo'. Uma história do gênero masculino (1920–1940).* 2003. Intermeios, 2013.

Alegría, Claribel, and Darwin Flakoll. *Death of Somoza. The First Person Story of the Guerrillas Who Assassinated the Nicaraguan Dictator.* Curbstone P, 1996.

———. *Fuga de Canto grande.* UCA, 1992.

Alencar, José de. *Iracema.* 1865. Luso-Brazilian Books, 2004.

Allen, Prudence. *The Concept of Woman. The Aristotelian Revolution. 750 BC–AD 1250.* Eden, 1985.

Almeida, José Maurício Gomes de. *A tradição regionalista no romance brasileiro (1857–1945).* 2nd ed., Topbooks, 1999.

———. "Quem tem medo de Guimarães Rosa? (Introdução à leitura de Grande sertão: Veredas)." Secchin et al., pp. 104–27.

Alonso, Carlos J. "La novela criollista." *Historia de la literatura hispanoamericana. II. El siglo XX*, edited by Roberto González Echeverría and Enrique Pupo-Walker. Gredos, 2006, pp. 214–30.

———. "'Otra seria mi historia:' Allegorical Exhaustion in *Dona Barbara.*" *MLN*, vol. 104, no. 2, 1989, pp. 418–38.

———. *The Spanish American Regional Novel. Modernity and Autochthony.* Cambridge UP, 1990.

Althusser, Louis. "Ideología y aparatos ideológicos del estado." *La filosofía como arma de la revolución.* 1968. Translated by Oscar del Barco et al. Siglo XXI, 1997, pp. 102–51.

Alvarez, Sonia E. *Engendering Democracy in Brazil. Women's Movements in Transition Politics.* Princeton UP, 1990.

Bibliography

Anderson-Imbert, Enrique. *Spanish-American Literature: A History*, vol. 2, Wayne State UP, 1969.

Andrade, Mário de. *Macunaíma. O herói sem nenhum caráter.* 1928. Coordinated by Telê Porto Ancona Lopez. ALLCA, 1996.

Andrade, Vera Lúcia. "Conceituação de jagunço e jagunçagem em *Grande sertão: veredas.*" Coutinho, pp. 491–99.

Angeloglou, Maggie. *A History of Make-Up.* Macmillan, 1970.

Anglo, Sydney. *The Martial Arts of Renaissance Europe.* Yale UP, 2000.

Araújo, Antônio Amaury Correia de. *Gente de Lampião: Dada e Corisco.* Traço, 1982.

———. *Lampião: as mulheres e o cangaço.* Traço, 1985.

Arce, B. Christine. "La Negra Angustias: The Mulata in Mexican Literature." *Callaloo*, vol. 35, no. 4, 2012, pp. 1085–102.

———. *México's Nobodies. The Cultural Legacy of the Soldadera and Afro-Mexican Women.* State U of New York, 2017.

Aristotle. *Metaphysics. The Complete Works of Aristotle*, vol. 2, edited by Jonathan Barnes, Princeton UP, 1984, pp. 1552–728.

———. *Poética.* Edited by Escuela de Filosofía Universidad ARCIS. Web. www.ddooss.org/articulos/textos/aristoteles_poetica.pdf. Accessed 27 Aug. 2009.

———. *The Poetics of Aristotle.* 3rd ed, edited by S. H. Butcher, Macmillan, 1902. Google digitized. www.stmarysca.edu/sites/default/files/attachments/files/Poetics.pdf. Accessed 17 June 2015.

Arrington Jr., Melvin S. "Doña Bárbara. Novel by Rómulo Gallegos." Smith, pp. 340–41.

———. "Spanish America." In "Regionalism." Smith, pp. 704–05.

Arrizón, Alicia. "'Soldaderas' and the Staging of the Mexican Revolution." *The Drama Review*, vol. 42, no. 1, 1998, pp. 90–112.

Atencio, Rebecca J. *Memory's Turn: Reckoning with Dictatorship in Brazil.* U of Wisconsin P, 2014.

Avechuco Cabrera, Daniel. "La Revolución narrada desde los márgenes: representaciones anónimas de la violencia en Cartucho, de Nellie Campobello." *Literatura Mexicana*, vol. XXVIII, no. 1, 2017, pp. 69–98.

Ávila, Simone Nunes. *FTM, transhomem, homem, trans, homem: A emergência de transmasculinidades no Brasil contemporâneo.* 2015. Universidade Federal de Santa Catarina, PhD Dissertation.

———. *Transmasculinidades. A emergência de novas identidades políticas e sociais.* Multifoco, 2014.

Bibliography

Azuela, Mariano. *Los de abajo*, coordinated by Jorge Ruffinelli. ALLCA XX, 1988.

———. *Los de abajo*. 1915. Cátedra, 1999.

Babb, Florence E. "Out in Nicaragua: Local and Transnational Desires after the Revolution." *Cultural Anthropology*, vol. 18, no. 3, 2003, pp. 304–28.

Bailey, Moya. "New Terms of Resistance. A Response to Zenzele Isoke." *Souls. A Critical Journal of Black Politics, Culture, and Society*, vol. 15, no. 4, 2014, pp. 341–43.

Bailey, Moya and Trudy. "On Misogynoir: Citation, Erasure, and Plagiarism." *Feminist Media Studies*, vol. 18, no. 4, 2018, pp. 762–68.

Baker, Pascale. "In Search of the Female Bandit in the Novel of the Mexican Revolution: The Case of la Pintada." *Bulletin of Hispanic Studies*, vol. 89, no. 7, 2012, pp. 721–36.

———. *Revolutionaries, Rebels and Robbers. The Golden Age of Banditry in Mexico, Latin America and the Chicano American Southwest, 1850–1950*. U of Wales P, 2015.

Balderston, Daniel. "El narrador dislocado y desplumado: los deseos de Riobaldo en *Grande sertão: veredas*." *El deseo, enorme cicatriz luminosa: ensayos sobre homosexualidades latinoamericanas*. Viterbo, 2004, pp. 85–101.

Balzán, Andrea, et al. "Viabilidad jurídica de inclusión de las minorías transgénero en el ordenamiento jurídico venezolano." *Cuestiones jurídicas*, vol. IX, no. 1, 2015, pp. 9–30.

Balzer, Carsten/Carla LaGata and Lukas Berredo. "TMM Annual Report 2016." *TvT Publication Series*, vol. 14, 2016, transrespect.org, transrespect.org/wpcontent/uploads/2016/11/TvT-PS-Vol14-2016.pdf.

Bandeira, Arkley Marques. "A teoria queer em uma perspectiva brasileira: escritos para tempos de incertezas." *Revista de arqueologia pública*, vol. 13, no. 1, 2019, pp. 34–53.

Bar On, Bat-Ami. "Why Terrorism Is Morally Problematic." *Feminist Ethics*, edited by Claudia Card, UP Kansas, 1991, pp. 107–25.

Barbas Rhoden, Laura H. "Cabezas y el discurso revolucionario en Nicaragua." *Confluencia*, vol. 14, no. 2, 1999, pp. 63–75.

Bardsley, Sandy. "Introduction: Medieval Women." *Women's Roles in the Middle Ages*. Greenwood P, 2007, pp. 1–26.

Barrueto, Jorge J. "The Othering of Women in the Twentieth-Century Latin American Canon: Misogyny in Rómulo Gallegos' *Doña Bárbara*." *Misogynism in Literature. Any Place, Any Time*, edited by Britta Zangen, Lang, 2004, pp. 181–99.

Bibliography

Barthes, Roland. *The Language of Fashion*. Translated by Andy Stafford, Berg, 2006.

Bartra, Eli. "How Black is *La Negra Angustias*?" *Third Text*, vol. 26, no. 3, 2012, pp. 275–83.

Bassanezi, Carla. "Mulheres dos anos dourados." *História das mulheres no Brasil*, organized by Mary del Priore, coordinated by Carla Bassanezi, Contexto / UNESP, 1997, pp. 607–39.

Beard, Mary. *Woman as Force in History. A Study in Traditions and Realities*. Macmillan, 1946.

Beasley, Chris. *Gender & Sexuality. Critical Theories, Critical Thinkers*. Sage, 2005.

Bederman, Gail. "Remaking Manhood through Race and 'Civilization.'" *Manliness & Civilization. A Cultural History of Gender and Race in the United States, 1880–1917*. U of Chicago P, 1995, pp. 1–44.

Belli, Gioconda. *El país bajo mi piel. Memorias de amor y guerra*. 2002. Vintage, 2003.

———. *La mujer habitada*. 1988. Emecé, 1999.

Benevides, Bruna G. e Sayonara Naider Bomfim Nogueira. *Dossiê. Assassinatose violência contra travestis e transexuais no Brasil em 2018*. ANTRA e IBTE, 2019, antrabrasil.files.wordpress.com/2019/01/dossie-dos-assassinatos-e-violencia-contra-pessoas-trans-em-2018.pdf

———. *Dossiê. Assassinatos e violência contra travestis e transexuais no Brasil em 2019*. ANTRA e IBTE, 2020. antrabrasil.org/2020/01/29/lancado-dossie-sobre-assassinatos-e-violencia-contra-pessoas-trans-em-2019/.

Bento, Berenice. *O que é transexualidade*. 2008. Brasiliense, 2012.

———. *Transviad@s: gênero, sexualidade e direitos humanos*. EDUFBA, 2017.

Besse, Susan K. *Restructuring Patriarchy. The Modernization of Gender Inequality in Brazil, 1914–1940*. U of North Carolina P, 1996.

Betancourt, Alfredo. *Doña Bárbara y don Juan ante el espejo de la conducta sexual*. Ediciones del ministerio del interior, 1976.

Beverly, John. "Algunos apuntes sobre la relación literatura-revolución en el caso nicaragüense." *La literatura centroamericana como arma cultura*, vol. 1, compiled by Jorge Román-Lagunas and Rick McCallister, León Palacios, 1999, pp. 13–27.

Bezerra de Meneses, Adélia. *Cores de Rosa*. Ateliê, 2010.

Bhabha, Homi K. "La otra pregunta. El estereotipo, la discriminación y el discurso del Colonialismo." *El lugar de la cultura*. Translated by

Bibliography

César Aira, Manantial, 2002, pp. 91–109.

Biron, Rebecca E. *Murder and Masculinity: Violent Fictions of Twentieth Century Latin America*. Vanderbilt UP, 2000.

Blanco, Fernando A. "Queer Latinoamérica: ¿Cuenta regresiva?" *Resentir lo queer en América Latina: diálogos desde/con el Sur*, edited by Diego Falconí Trávez et al., Egales, 2013, pp. 27–43.

Blasi, Alberto. "Doña Bárbara como ícono verbal." Rodríguez-Alcalá, pp. 59–81.

Boullosa, Carmen. *Duerme*. 1994. Alfaguara, 1995.

Bradley, D. "Patterns of Myth in *Los de abajo*." *The Modern Language Review*, vol. 75, no.1, 1980, pp. 94–104.

Bravo-Villasante, Carmen. *La mujer vestida de hombre en el teatro español (Siglos XVI-XVII)*. Sociedad general española de librería, 1976.

Brickell, Chris. "Masculinities, Performativity, and Subversion. A Sociological Reappraisal." *Men and Masculinities*, vol. 8, no. 1, 2005, pp. 24–43.

Brown, Monica. "American She: Gendering Gangs." *Gang Nation. Delinquent Citizens in Puerto Rican, Chicano, and Chicana Narratives*. U of Minnesota P, 2002, pp. 81–123.

Brownmiller, Susan. "Prologue." *Femininity*, by Brownmiller, Linden P / Simon & Schuster, 1984, pp. 13–19.

Brushwood, John S. *La novela hispanoamericana del siglo XX. Una vista panorámica*. 1975. Translated by Raymond L. Williams, Fondo de cultura, 2001.

Bruyas, Jean-Paul. "Técnicas, estruturas e visão em *Grande sertão: veredas*." Coutinho, pp. 458–77.

Bullough, Vern L. *The Subordinate Sex. A History of Attitudes Toward Women*. U of Illinois P, 1973.

Bullough, Vern L., and Bonnie Bullough. *Cross Dressing, Sex, and Gender*. U of Pennsylvania P, 1993.

Butler, Judith. *Bodies that Matter. On the Discursive Limits of "Sex."* Routledge, 1993.

———. *Excitable Speech. A Politics of the Performative*. Routledge, 1997.

———. *Gender Trouble. Feminism and the Subversion of Identity*. 1990. Routledge, 1999.

———. *Undoing Gender*. Routledge, 2004.

———. "Performative Agency." *Journal of Cultural Economy*, vol. 3, no. 2, 2010, pp. 147–61.

———. "Speaking Up, Talking Back. Joan Scott's Critical Feminism." *Ques-*

Bibliography

tion of Gender: Joan W. Scott's Critical Feminism, edited by Elizabeth Weed and Butler, Indiana UP, 2011, pp. 11–28.

Butler, Judith, and Elizabeth Weed. Introduction. *Question of Gender: Joan W. Scott's Critical Feminism*, edited by Weed and Butler, Indiana UP, 2011, pp. 1–8.

Cabezas, Omar. *Canción de amor para los hombres*. Nueva Nicaragua, 1988.

———. *La montaña es algo más que una inmensa estepa verde*. 1982. Nueva Nicaragua, 1983.

Caesar, Gabriela. "Quase 300 transgêneros esperam cirurgia na rede pública 10 anos após portaria do SUS." *Globo.com*, 19 Aug. 2018, g1.globo.com/ciencia-e- saude/noticia/2018/08/19/quase-300-transgeneros-esperam-cirurgia-na-rede-publica-10-anos--apos-portaria-do-sus.ghtml. Accessed 20 Aug. 2019.

Caldwell, Kia Lilly. *Negras in Brazil. Re-envisioning Black Women, Citizenship, and the Politics of Identity*. Rutgers UP, 2007.

Câmara, Yls Rabelo, et al. "Maria Bonita e Dadá revisitadas: a análise de sua importância para o cangaço e seu registro na literatura brasileira como um testemunho de sua prática cultural." *Raído*, vol. 9, no. 20, 2015, pp. 203–18.

Campobello, Nelli. *Cartucho*. 1931. Era, 2000.

———. "Nellie Campobello. 1909." *Protagonistas de la literatura mexicana*, with Emmanuel

Carballo, 4th ed., Porrúa, 1994, pp. 377–87.

———. "Prólogo a 'Mis libros.'" 1960. *Obra reunida*. Fce, 2007, pp. 333–72.

———. *Apuntes sobre la vida militar de Francisco Villa* (1940). *Obra reunida*, Fce, 2007, pp. 199–314.

Cândido, Antonio. "Literatura e subdesenvolvimento." *América Latina em sua literatura*, coordinated by César Fernández Moreno, Perspectiva, 1972, pp. 343–62.

———. "O homem dos avessos." Coutinho, pp. 294–309.

———. "Ser jagunço em Guimarães Rosa." *Revista iberoamericana de literatura*, vol. 2, no. 2, 1970, pp. 61–71.

———. *Tese e antítese. Ensaios*. 5th ed., Ouro sobre Azul, 2006.

Cândido, Antonio, e José Aderaldo Castelo. *Presença da literatura brasileira. História e antologia. II Modernismo*. 1964. 10th ed., Bertrand Brasil, 1997.

Cano, Gabriela. "Amélio Robes, andar de soldado velho: fotografia e masculinidade na Revolução Mexicana." *Cadernos Pagu*, no. 22, 2004, pp. 115–50.

Bibliography

———. "¿Es posible hacer la historia de las mujeres en la Revolución mexicana?" *Mexico's Unfinished Revolutions*, edited by Charles B. Faulhaber, U of California P, pp. 11–24.

———. "Unconcealable Realities of Desire. Amelio Robles's (Transgender) Masculinity in the Mexican Revolution." Olcott et al., pp. 35–56.

Card, Claudia. "The Feistiness of Feminism." *Feminist Ethics*, edited by Card, UP Kansas, 1991, pp. 3–31.

Cárdenas Trueba, Olga. "Amelia Robles y la revolución zapatista en Guerrero." *Estudios sobre el zapatismo*, edited by Laura Espejel López, Instituto Nacional de Antropología e Historia, 2002. *Bibliotecas virtuales de México*.

Carpentier, Alejo. *El siglo de las luces*. 1962. Alianza, 2003.

Carrera, Magali M. "Fabricating Specimen Citizens: Nation Building in Nineteenth-Century Mexico." *The Politics of Dress in Asia and the Americas*, edited by Mina Roces and Louise Edwards, Sussex Academic P, 2007, pp. 215–35.

Carvalho, Flávia Paula. *A natureza na literatura brasileira: regionalismo pré-modernista*. Hucitec / Terceira Margem, 2005.

Carvalho, Luiz Maklouf. *Mulheres que foram à luta armada*. Globo, 1998.

Casasola, Gustavo. "La mujer en la Revolución." *Historia gráfica de la Revolución Mexicana 1900–1960*, vol. 1, Trillas, 1960, pp. 262–63.

———. "La soldadera." *Historia gráfica de la Revolución Mexicana 1900–1960*, vol. 1, Trillas, 1960, pp. 720–23.

Castellanos, Gabriela, et al. "Mujeres y conflicto armado: representaciones, practicas sociales y propuestas para la negociación." *Sujetos femeninos y masculinos*, compiled by Castellanos and Simone Accorsi, La manzana de la discordia y Centro de estudios de género, mujer y sociedad de la Universidad del Valle, 2001, pp. 167–84.

Castellanos Gonella, Carolina. "Mulheres guerreiras: *Viva o povo brasileiro* e *Memorial de Maria Moura*." *Letras femeninas*, vol. XXXIX, no. 2, 2013, pp. 113–27.

———. "*Por debajo del agua*: transgenerismo como performatividad de la Revolución." *Revista de literatura mexicana contemporánea*, vol. 67, no. 22, 2016, pp. 73–88.

———. "The Most Desired Positions: Brazilian Female Traffickers in *Inferno* and *Falcão: mulheres e o tráfico*." *Latin American Research Review*, vol. 52, no. 3, 2017, pp. 405–17.

Castillo, Debra. *Easy Women: Sex and Gender in Modern Mexican Fiction*. U of Minnesota P, 1998.

Castro, Fidel. "Discurso pronunciado por el Comandante Fidel Castro

Bibliography

Ruiz." Parque Céspedes, Santiago de Cuba, 1 Jan. 1959. Speech. Web.

Castro, Manuel Antônio. "Grande Ser-Tao: diálogos amorosos." Secchin et al., pp. 142–77.

Castro Leal, Antonio. Introduction. *La novela de la Revolución Mexicana*, by Castro Leal, Aguilar, 1958, pp. xv-xxx.

Cavallaro, Dani, and Alexandra Warwick. *Fashioning the Frame. Boundaries, Dress and Body.* Berg, 1998.

Chang-Rodríguez, Raquel. "Trayectoria y símbolo de una revolucionaria: 'La negra Angustias' de Francisco Rojas González." *Revista de crítica literaria latinoamericana*, vol. 7, no. 13, 1981, pp. 99–104.

Chant, Sylvia and Nikki Craske. *Gender in Latin America*. Rutgers UP, 2003.

Charlebois, Justin. "Geographies of Femininities." *Gender and the Construction of Hegemonic and Oppositional Femininities*. Lexington, 2011, pp. 21–42.

Chaves, Flávio Loureiro. "Perfil de Riobaldo." Coutinho, pp. 446–57.

Cherpak, Evelyn. "The Participation of Women in the Independence Movement in Gran Colombia, 1780–1830." *Latin American Women. Historical Perspectives*, edited by Asunción Lavrin, Greenwood, 1978, pp. 219–34.

Childs, Matt D. "A Historical Critique of the Emergence and Evolution of Ernesto Che Guevara's Foco Theory." *Journal of Latin American Studies*, vol. 27, no. 3, 1995, pp. 593–624.

Chinchilla, Norma Stoltz. "Revolutionary Popular feminism in Nicaragua: Articulating Class, Gender, and National Sovereignty." *Gender & Society*, vol. 4, no. 3, 1990, pp. 370–97.

———. "Women in Revolutionary Movements: The Case of Nicaragua." June 1983. pdf.usaid.gov/pdf_docs/PNAAX120.pdf.

———. "Women in the Nicaraguan Revolution." *Nicaraguan Perspectives*, no.11, 1985–1986, pp. 18–26.

Cirlot, Juan Eduardo. *Diccionario de símbolos*. 1958. Siruela, 2004.

Clack, Robert J. *Bertrand Russell's Philosophy of Language*. Mijhoff, 1969.

Cleusa, Maria. "Assim falou Riobaldo." *Jornal do Brasil online*, 10 Feb. 2005, Caderno B.

Cnossen, Christine. "Demystifying Women Warriors: An Historical Overview." *Women in Uniform & the Changing World Order. Conference proceedings from the WREI's Fifth Biennial Conference on Women in Uniform, Arlington, VA, 30 Nov.–1 Dec. 2000*, Women's Research and Education Institution, 2000, pp. 0–13.

Coelho, Nelly Novaes. "Guimarães Rosa e o 'homo ludens.'" Coutinho, pp. 256–70.

Bibliography

Collins, Patricia Hill. "Mammies, Matriarchs, and Other Controlling Images." *Black Feminist Thought*, Routledge, 2000, pp. 69–96.

Connell, R. W. *Gender and Power. Society, the Person and Sexual Politics*. Stanford UP, 1987.

———. *Masculinities*. U of California P, 1995.

———. *The Men and the Boys*. U of California P, 2000.

Connell, R. W., and James W. Messerschmidt. "Hegemonic Masculinity. Rethinking the Concept." *Gender and Society*, vol. 19, no. 6, 2005, pp. 829–59.

Connell, Raewyn. "Change among the Gatekeepers: Men, Masculinities and Gender Equality." *Confronting Equality. Gender, Knowledge and Global Change*. Polity, 2011, pp. 7–24.

Conway, Christopher. "Charros: A Critical Introduction." *Modern Mexican Culture: Critical Foundations*, edited by Stuart A. Day, U of Arizona P, 2017, pp. 66–83.

Cooke, Miriam. *Women and the War Story*. U of California P, 1996.

Cooke, Miriam, and Angela Woollacott. Introduction. *Gendering War Talk*, edited by Cooke and

Woollacott, Princeton UP, 1993, pp. ix-xiii.

Corson, Richard. "The Late Victorians 1880–1900." *Fashions in Makeup. From Ancient to Modern Times*. Universe, 1972, pp. 361–91.

Cortés, Jason. *Macho Ethics: Masculinity and Self-Representation in Latino-Caribbean Narrative*. Bucknell UP, 2015.

Costa, Ana Luiza Martins. "Diadorim belo feroz." *Vozes femininas: gêneros, mediações e práticas da escrita*, organized by Flora Süssekind et al., 7letras, 2003, pp. 146–64.

Costigan, Lucia e Leopoldo M. Bernucci. "Introdução." *Revista Iberoamericana*, vol. LXIV, no. 182–83, 1998, pp. 11–14.

Coutinho, Afrânio. "Duas anotações." Coutinho, pp. 291–93.

Coutinho, Eduardo F., organizer. *Guimarães Rosa*. Civilização brasileira, 1983.

———. "Guimarães Rosa e o processo de revitalização da linguagem." Coutinho, pp. 202–34.

———. *The "Synthesis" Novel in Latin America. A Study on João Guimarães Rosa's Grande Sertão: Veredas*. U of North Carolina P, 1991.

Creighton, Margaret S., and Lisa Norling. Introduction. *Iron Men, Wooden Women. Gender and Seafaring in the Atlantic World, 1700–1920*, edited by Creighton and Norling, The John Hopkins UP, 1996, pp. vii–xiii.

Bibliography

Crenshaw, Kimberlé. "Mapping the Margins: Intersectionality, Identity Politics, and Violence Against Women of Color." *Stanford Law Review*, vol. 43, no. 6, 1991, pp. 1241–99.

Cunha, Maria Lourdes da Conceição. "Diadonzela Guerrerim." *Convivendo com Guimarães Rosa: Grande sertão veredas*, organized by Beatriz Berrini, Educ, 2004, pp. 115–31.

Currea-Lugo, Víctor de. *Poder y guerrillas en América Latina. Una mirada a la historia del guerrillero de a pie*. SEPHA, 2007.

Da Costa, Francisco Augusto Pereira. *Cronologia histórica do estado do Piauí*. 1909, vol 2, Artenova, 1974.

Daniel, Mary L. "Brazilian Fiction from 1900 to 1945." *The Cambridge History of Latin American Literature*, vol. 3, edited by Roberto González Echevarría and Enrique Pupo-Walker, Cambridge UP, 2008, pp. 157–87.

———. "João Guimarães Rosa 1908–1967. Brazilian Prose Writer." Smith, pp. 398–400.

———. *João Guimarães Rosa: Travessia literária*. Olympio, 1968.

———. "Redemptive Analogy in the Fiction of João Guimarães Rosa." *Romance Notes*, vol. 27, no. 2, 1986, pp. 127–34.

Dantas, Francisco J. C. *Os desvalidos*. Companhia das letras, 1993.

Daydi, Santiago. "Characterization in *Los de abajo*." *The American Hispanist*, vol. 2, no.11, 1976, pp. 9–11.

De Campos, Augusto. "Um lance de "dês" do grande sertão." *Guimarães Rosa em três dimensões*, Conselho estadual de cultura / Comissão de literatura, 1970, pp. 41–70.

De Castro, Nei Leandro. *Universo e vocabulário do Grande Sertão*. Olympio, 1970.

De Jesus, Jacqueline Gomes et al. *Transfeminismo: teorias e práticas*. Metanoia, 2014.

De Nemes, Graciela Palau. "La doña Bárbara de Gallegos: transparencia onomástica y opacidad histórica." Rodríguez-Alcalá, pp. 156–82.

De Pauw, Linda Grant. *Battle Cries and Lullabies. Women in War from Prehistory to the Present*. U of Oklahoma P, 1998.

Derrida, Jacques. "The Purveyor of Truth." *The Purloined Poe. Lacan, Derrida & Psychoanalytic Reading*, edited by John P. Muller and William J. Richardson, The Johns Hopkins UP, 1988, pp. 173–212.

Dever, Susan. "Las de abajo: la Revolución Mexicana de Matilde Landeta." *Archivos de la Filmoteca*, no. 16, 1994, pp. 36–49.

Diagnóstico sobre los crímenes de odio motivados por la orientación sexual e identidad de género en Costa Rica, Honduras y Nicaragua. CEJIL,

2013, www.cejil.org/es/diagnostico-crimenes-odio-motivados-orientacion-sexual-e-identidad-genero-costa-rica-honduras-y.

Dias, José Umberto. "A musa do cangaço." 1982. *YouTube*, uploaded by Luciana Medeiros, 3 Nov. 2010, www.youtube.com/watch?v=w1t4q4FGE3o#t=234.332297815

Díaz, Arlene J. *Female Citizens, Patriarchs, and the Law in Venezuela, 1786–1904*. U of Nebraska P, 2004.

———. "Vicenta Ochoa, Dead Many Times: Gender, Politics, and a Death Sentence in Early Republican Caracas, Venezuela." French and Bliss, pp. 31–51.

Díaz del Castillo, Bernal. *Historia verdadera de la conquista de la Nueva España*. Linkgua, 2011.

Díaz Marcos, Ana María. *El triunfo de lo efímero: visiones de la moda en la literatura peninsular moderna (1728–1926)*. 2003. University of Massachusetts Amherst, PhD dissertation.

———. "Un ángel con espada de raso: moda y literatura." *La edad de seda: representaciones de la moda en la literatura española (1728–1926)*. Servicio de publicaciones U de Cádiz, 2006, pp. 17–53.

Díaz Sánchez, Ramón. "Evolución social de Venezuela (hasta 1960)." *Venezuela independiente 1810–1960*, edited by Mariano Picón-Salas et al., Eugenio Mendoza, 1962, pp. 157–342.

Dietz, Mary G. "Current Controversies in Feminist Theory." *Annual Review of Political Science*, vol. 6, 2003, pp. 399–431.

Dijkstra, Bram. "Metamorphoses of the Vampire; Dracula and his Daughters." *Idols of Perversity: Fantasies of Feminine Evil in Fin-de-Siècle Culture*, Oxford UP, 1986, pp. 333–51.

Dixon, Paul B. "Transverse and Universe in *Grande sertão: veredas*." *Reversible Readings. Ambiguity in Four Latin American Novels*, U of Alabama P, 1985, pp. 125–50.

Doan, Laura. "Passing Fashions: Reading Female Masculinities in the 1920s." *Feminist Studies*, vol. 24, no. 3, 1998, pp. 663–700.

Domínguez-Ruvalcaba, Héctor. *Modernity and the Nation in Mexican Representations of Masculinity. From Sensuality to Bloodshed*. Palgrave, 2007.

———. *Translating the Queer. Body Politics and Transnational Conversations*. Zed, 2016.

Doña Bárbara. Directed by Fernando de Fuentes and Miguel M. Delgado, performances by María Félix and Julián Soler, Clasa film mundiales, 1943.

Dor, Joël. "La metáfora paterna – El nombre del padre. La metonimia del de-

Bibliography

seo." *Introducción a la lectura de Lacan. El inconsciente estructurado como lenguaje*, Gedisa, 1994, pp. 103–109.

Doremus, Anne. "Indigenism, Mestizaje, and National Identity in Mexico During the 1940s and the 1950s." *Mexican Studies/Estudios Mexicanos*, vol. 17, no. 2, 2001, pp. 375–402.

Dowsett, G. W. "Wusses and Willies; Masculinity and Contemporary Sexual Politics." *Journal of Interdisciplinary Gender Studies (JIGS)*, vol. 3, no. 2, 1999, pp. 9–22.

Dudink, Stefan, and Karen Hagemann. "Masculinity in Politics and War in the Age of Democratic Revolutions, 1750–1850." *Masculinities in Politics and War. Gendering Modern History*, edited by Dudink et al., Manchester UP, 2004, pp. 3–21.

Duffey, J. Patrick. "A War of Words: Orality and Literacy in Mariano Azuela's *Los de abajo*." *Romance Notes*, vol. 38, no. 2, 1998, pp. 173–78.

Dugaw, Dianne. *Warrior Women and Popular Balladry, 1650–1850. With a New Preface*. 1989. U of Chicago P, 1996.

Eakin, Marshall C. *Brazil. The Once and Future Country*. St. Martin, 1997.

———. *The History of Latin America. Collision of Cultures*. Palgrave, 2007.

Ekins, Richard. *Male Femaling. A grounded Theory Approach to Cross-Dressing and Sex-Changing*. Routledge, 1997.

Eltit, Diamela. "Las batallas del Coronel Robles." *Debate feminista*, vol. 4, 1991, pp. 171–77.

Entwistle, Joanne. "The Dressed Body." *Body Dressing*, edited by Entwistle and Elizabeth Wilson, Berg, 2001, pp. 33–58.

———. *The Fashioned Body. Fashion, Dress and Modern Social Theory*. Polity Press, 2000.

Entwistle, Joanne, and Elizabeth Wilson. "Introduction: Body Dressing." *Body Dressing*, edited by Entwistle and Wilson, Berg, 2001, pp. 1–9.

Esplin, Emron. "The Profane Saint *vs.* the Revolutionary Child: Portrayals of Pancho Villa in the Writings of Nellie Campobello and Jack Conway's Viva Villa!" *Studies in Latin American Popular Culture*, vol. 24, 2005, pp. 83–100.

Esquivel, Laura. *Como agua para chocolate*. 1989. Random, 1992.

Estrada, Oswaldo. "Trazos y retazos de mujer en la obra revolucionaria de Nellie Campobello." *Independencias, revoluciones y revelaciones: doscientos años de literatura mexicana*, coordinated by Alicia Rueda Acedo et al., U Veracruzana, U of Texas Arlington, 2010, pp. 217–37.

———. *Troubled Memories: Iconic Mexican Women and the Traps of Representation*. State U of New York, 2018.

Bibliography

Falce, Juliet Alison. *Underlying Gender Structures in the Latin American Regionalist Novel.* 1997. University of California Irving, PhD dissertation.

Fanon, Frantz. *A Dying Colonialism.* 1959. Translated by Haakon Chevalier, Grove, 1965.

Feinberg, Leslie. *Trans Gender Warriors. Making History from Joan of Arc to Dennis Rodman.* Beacon, 1996.

Ferreira, João. "Algunas congeminações sobre o mito de Diadorim do *Grande Sertão: Veredas.*" *Minas Gerais,* 5 Mar. 1983, Suplemento literário, 4.

Ferris, Suzanne. Foreword. *Styling Texts. Dress and Fashion in Literature,* edited by Cynthia Kuhn and Cindy Carlson, Cambria, 2007, pp. xiii–xv.

Filho, Ormindo Pires. "A frustração amorosa feminina em *Grande sertão: veredas.*" *Revista de cultura vozes,* vol. 84, no. 2, 1990, pp. 227–33.

Fitz, Earl E. "Spanish American and Brazilian Literature in an Inter-American Perspective: The Comparative Approach." *Comparative Cultural Studies and Latin America,* edited by Sophia A. McClennen and Fitz, Purdue UP, 2004, pp. 69–88.

———. "Regionalism as a Shaping Force." *Rediscovering the New World. Inter-American Literature in a Comparative Context,* U of Iowa P, 1991, pp. 169–90.

Foster, David William. *Ensayos sobre culturas homoeróticas latinoamericanas.* U Autónoma de Ciudad Juárez, 2009.

———. Introduction. *Gay and Lesbian Themes in Latin American Writing,* by Foster, U of Texas P, 1991, pp. 1–8.

———. "Is Luis Cervantes Queer in Mariano Azuela's 'Los de abajo?'" *Romance Notes,* vol. 50, no. 1, pp. 61–66.

Foucault, Michel. *Historia de la sexualidad. 1-la voluntad de saber.* 1976. Translated by Ulises Guiñazú. Siglo XXI, 2005.

Franco, Adolfo M. "Opresión e identidad en *Los de abajo.*" *Secolas,* vol. 17, 1987, pp. 63–72.

Franco, Jean. *An Introduction to Spanish-American Literature.* 1969. 3rd ed., Cambridge UP, 2000.

———. *Plotting Women. Gender and Representation in Mexico.* Columbia UP, 1989.

Freitas, Ana Paula Saraiva de. "A presença feminina no cangaço: práticas e representações (1930–1940)." 2005. Universidade Estadual Paulista, MA thesis. *Repositório institucional UNESP.*

French, Katherine L., and Alyson M. Poska. *Women and Gender in the Western Past.* Houghton, 2007. 2 vols.

Bibliography

French, William E., and Katherine Elaine Bliss, editors. *Gender, Sexuality, and Power in Latin America Since Independence*. Rowman, 2007.

———. "Introduction: Gender, Sexuality, and Power in Latin America since Independence." French and Bliss, pp. 1–30.

Fuentes, Carlos. *La muerte de Artemio Cruz*. 1962. Aguilar, 2001.

Gabeira, Fernando. *O que é isso, companheiro?* 1979. Companhia das letras, 2009.

Galaos, José Antonio. "Rómulo Gallegos o el duelo entre civilización y barbarie." *Cuadernos hispanoamericanos*, vol. LV, no. 163–64, 1963, pp. 299–309.

Gallagher, Catherine, and Thomas Laqueur. Introduction. *The Making of the Modern Body*, edited by Gallagher and Laqueur, U of California P, 1987, pp. vii-xv.

Gallegos, Rómulo. *Doña Bárbara*. 1929. Ayacucho, 1985.

———. "La pura mujer sobre la tierra." *Cuadernos hispanoamericanos*, no. 675, 2006, pp. 63–77.

Gallegos Ortiz, Rafael. *La historia política de Venezuela. De Cipriano Castro a Pérez Jiménez*. Imprenta universitaria, 1960.

Galvão, Walnice Nogueira. *A donzela-guerreira. Um estudo de gênero*. Senac, 1998.

———. "Ciclo da donzela-guerreira." *Gatos de outro saco. Ensaios críticos*, Brasiliense, 1981, pp. 8–59.

———. "O certo no incerto: o pactário." Coutinho, pp. 408–21.

Garber, Marjorie B. *Vested Interests: Transvestim and Cultural Anxiety*. Routledge, 1992.

García-Pérez, Gladys Marel. *Crónicas guerrilleras de Occidente*. Editorial de ciencias sociales, 2005.

Gardiner, Judith Kegan. "Masculinity's Interior: Men, Transmen, and Theories of Masculinity." *The Journal of Men's Studies*, vol. 21, no. 2, 2013, pp. 112–26.

Gargallo, Francesca. "A propósito de lo queer en América Latina." *Francesca Gargallo*, francescagargallo.wordpress.com/ensayos/feminismo/feminismo-genero/a-proposito-de-lo-queer-en-america-latina/. Accessed 11 Sept. 2020.

Garro, Elena. *Los recuerdos del porvenir*. 1963. Mortiz, 1987.

Geczy, Adam, and Vicki Karaminas. *Queer Style*. Bloomsbury, 2013.

Gerdes, Dick. "Point of View in *Los de Abajo*." *Hispania*, vol. 64, no. 4, 1981, pp. 557–63.

Gibbs, Virginia. "Erauso, Catalina de (1592–1635)." *Women in World His-*

tory. A Biographical Encyclopedia, vol. 5, edited by Anne Commire and Deborah Klezmer, Yorkin, 2000, pp. 241–44.

Gilbert, Sandra M., and Susan Gubar. *No Man's Land. The Place of the Woman Writer in the Twentieth Century.* Yale UP, 1988. 3 vols.

———. "Toward a Feminist Poetics." *The Mad Woman in the Attic. The Woman Writer and the Nineteenth-Century Literary Imagination*, 1979, Yale UP, 1984, pp. 3–104.

Gilio, María Esther. *La guerrilla tupamara*. La Flor, 1970.

Girman, Chris. *Mucho Macho. Seduction, Desire, and the Homoerotic Lives of Latin Men.* Harrington Park, 2004.

Glantz, Margo. "Vigencia de Nellie Campobello." *Fulgor*, vol. 3, no. 1, 2006, pp. 37–50.

Gonzales, Michael J. *The Mexican Revolution, 1910–1940*. U of New Mexico P, 2002.

González, Alfonso. "Onomastics and Creativity in *Doña Bárbara* y *Pedro Páramo*." *Names. Journal of the American Name Society*, vol. 21, no.1, 1973, pp. 40–45.

González Echevarría, Roberto. "*Doña Bárbara* escribe la ley del llano." *La voz de los maestros. Escritura y autoridad en la literatura latinoamericana moderna*, 1985, translated by González Echevarría, Verbum, 2001, pp. 71–109.

———. "*Doña Bárbara, Mamá grande* y *Cobra*: notas para una relectura de Gallegos." Rodríguez-Alcalá, pp. 82–98.

González Ortuño, Gabriela. "Teorías de la disidencia sexual: de contextos populares a usos elitistas. La teoría *queer* en América latina [sic] frente a las y los pensadores de disidencia sexogenérica." *De raíz diversa*, vol. 3, no. 5, 2016, pp. 179–200.

Grases, Pedro. *Escritos selectos*. Ayacucho, 1989.

Green, Adam Isaiah. "Queer Theory and Sociology: Locating the Subject and the Self in Sexuality Studies." *Sociological Theory*, vol. 25, no. 1, 2007, pp. 26–45.

Green, James N. *Beyond Carnival. Male Homosexuality in Twentieth-Century Brazil.* U of Chicago P, 1999.

———. "Doctoring the National Body: Gender, Race, Eugenics, and the "Invert" in Urban Brazil, ca. 1920–1945." French and Bliss, pp. 187–211.

Green, James, and Florence E. Babb. "Gender and Same-Sex Desire in Latin America." *Latin American Perspectives*, vol. 29, no. 2, 2002, pp. 3–23.

Griffin, Clive. *Azuela: Los de abajo*. Grant & Cutler, 1993.

Bibliography

Güiraldes, Ricardo. *Don Segundo Sombra.* 1926. Archivo, 1991.

Gutiérrez, Natividad. "Mujeres patria-nación. México: 1810–1920." *Revista de estudios de género. La ventana,* no. 12, 2000, pp. 209–43.

Gutiérrez Chong, Natividad. "Symbolic Violence and Sexualities in the Myth Making of Mexican National Identity." *Ethnic and Racial Studies,* vol. 31, no. 3, 2008, pp. 524–42.

Gutiérrez Cham, Gerardo. "Periferias de silencio, culpa y transgresión, en *Los de abajo* y *Al filo del agua.*" *Literatura mexicana,* vol. 14, no.1, 2003, pp. 113–37.

Gutmann, Matthew C. Introduction. *Changing Men and Masculinities in Latin America,* by Gutmann, Duke UP, 2003, pp. 1–26.

———. *The Meanings of Macho. Being a Man in Mexico City.* U of California P, 1996.

Guzmán, Martín Luis. *El águila y la serpiente.* 1928. Compañía general de ediciones, 1971.

———. *La sombra del caudillo.* 1929. Compañía general de ediciones, 1962.

Hahner, June E. "Feminism, Women's Rights, and the Suffrage Movement in Brazil, 1850–1932." *Latin American Research Review,* vol. 15, no. 1, 1980, pp. 65–111.

———. Introduction. *Women through Women's Eyes. Latin American Women in Nineteenth-Century Travel Accounts,* by Hahner, Scholarly Resources, 1998, pp. xi-xxvi.

Halberstam, Jack. *Female Masculinity.* Duke UP, 1998.

———. "Female Masculinity." *Men & Masculinities. A Social, Cultural, and HistoricalEncyclopedia,* vol. 1, edited by Michael Kimmel and Amy Aronson, ABC CLIO, 2004, pp. 294–95.

———. "The Good, the Bad, and the Ugly: Men, Women, and Masculinity." *Masculine Studies & Feminist Theory. New Directions,* edited by Judith Kegan Gardiner, Columbia UP, 2002, pp. 344–67.

———. *Trans*. A Quick and Quirky Account of Gender Variability.* U of California P, 2018.

Hall, Donald E. *Fixing Patriarchy. Feminism and Mid-Victorian Male Novelists.* New York UP, 1996.

Hampton, Janet J. "La negra Angustias: Flawed Hero or Tragic Victim?: A Feminist Reading." *Afro-Hispanic Review,* vol. 10, no. 3, 1991, pp. 27–32.

Hancock, Joseph, et al. Introduction. *Fashion in Popular Culture: Literature, Media and Contemporary Studies,* edited by Hancok et al., Intellect, 2013, pp. ix–xvi.

Hansen, João Adolfo. "Forma, indeterminação e funcionalidade das imagens

Bibliography

de Guimarães Rosa." Secchin et al., pp. 29–49.

Harris, Chris. "Mariano Azuela's *Los de abajo*: Patriarchal Masculinity and Mexican Gender Regimes under Fire." *Bulletin of Hispanic Studies*, vol. 87, no. 6, 2010, pp. 645–66.

Hart, Lynda. "The Paradox of Prohibition." *Fatal Women. Lesbian Sexuality and the Mark of Aggression*, Princeton UP, 1994, pp. 3–28.

Henighan, Stephen. "The Reconstruction of Femininity in Gallegos's *Doña Bárbara*." *Latin American Literary Review*, vol. 32, no. 64, 2004, pp. 29–45.

Hernández Carmona, Luis Javier. "Los conjuros de la fe y al amor en *Doña Bárbara* de Rómulo Gallegos." *Cuadernos americanos*, no. 97, 2003, pp. 126–36.

Hernández Cuevas, Marco Polo. "Las raíces africanas del charro y la china mexicanos." *Afro-Hispanic Review*, vol. 23, no. 2, 2004, pp. 77–86.

Hernández González, Manuel. "Raza, inmigración e identidad nacional en la Venezuela Finisecular." *Contrastes. Revista de historia*, no. 9–10, 1994–1996, pp. 35–48.

Herodotus. *The Histories*. Translated by Robin Waterfield, introduced by Carolyn Dewald, Oxford UP, 1998.

Herrera-Sobek, María. "The Soldier Archetype." *The Mexican Corrido. A Feminist Analysis*, Indiana UP, 1990, pp. 84–116.

Hind, Emily. *Dude Lit: Mexican Men Writing and Performing Competence, 1955–2012*. U of Arizona P, 2019.

Hirschon, Renée. "Introduction: Property, Power and Gender Relations." *Women and Property—Women as Property*, edited by Hirschon, St. Martin, 1984, pp. 1–15.

Historia de la Monja Alférez, Catalina de Erauso, escrita por ella misma, edited by Ángel Esteban, Cátedra, 2006.

Hobsbawm, Eric J. *Bandits*. 1969. Pantheon, 1981.

Hoisel, Evelina de C. de Sá. "Elementos dramáticos da estrutura de *Grande sertão: veredas*." Coutinho, pp. 478–90.

Horn, Maja. "Introduction: The Politics of Gender in the Caribbean." *Masculinity after Trujillo: The Politics of Gender in Dominican Literature*. UP of Florida, 2014, pp. 1–22.

Horne, John. "Masculinity in Politics and War in the Age of Nation-States and World Wars, 1850–1950." *Masculinities in Politics and War. Gendering Modern History*, edited by Stefan Dudink et al., Manchester UP, 2004, pp. 22–40.

Huaco-Nuzum, Carmen. "Matilde Landeta. An Introduction to the Work of a Pioneer Mexican Film-Maker." *Screen*, vol. 28, no. 4, 1987, pp. 96–105.

Bibliography

Hughes, Clair. *Dressed in Fiction*. Berg, 2006.

Hughes, Sarah Shaver, and Brady Hughes. *Women in World History*, vol. 1, Readings from Prehistory to 1500, Sharpe, 1995.

Huston, Nancy. "Tales of War and Tears of Women." *Women and Men's Wars*, edited by Judith Stiehm, Pergamon, 1983, pp. 271–82.

Iglesias, Francisco. *Breve historia contemporánea del Brasil*. Fondo de cultura económica, 1994.

IHU On-Line. "Nós fazemos gênero dia a dia." *Transviad@s: gênero, sexualidade e direitos humanos*, by Berenice Bento, EDUFBA, 2017, pp. 107–11.

Irigaray, Luce. "This Sex Which Is Not One." *This Sex Which Is Not One*. Translated by Catherine Porter, Cornell UP, 1985, pp. 23–33.

Irwin, Robert. "*Los de abajo* y los debates sobre la identidad masculina nacional." *La otredad: los discursos de la cultura hoy*: 1995, coordinated by Silvia Elguea Véjar, Fideicomiso para la cultura México-USA, 1997, pp. 71–81.

———. *Mexican Masculinities*. U of Minnesota P, 2003.

Islas, Carlos. *La Adelita*. Fontamara, 2006.

Jaen, Didier. "Realidad ideal y realidad antagónica en *Los de abajo*." *Cuadernos americanos*, vol. 183, no. 4, 1972, pp. 231–43.

Jaquette, Jane S. "Women in Revolutionary Movements in Latin America." *Journal of Marriage and Family*, vol. 35, no. 2, 1973, pp. 344–53.

Jones, David E. *Women Warriors. A History*. Brassey's, 1997.

Jones, Gareth A., and Dennis Rodgers. *Youth Violence in Latin America. Gangs and Juvenile Justice in Perspective*. Palgrave, 2009.

Johnson, Ernest A. Jr. "The Meaning of *Civilización* and *Barbarie* in Doña Bárbara." *Hispania*, vol. 39, no. 4, 1956, pp. 456–61.

Johnson, Maria Amália. "A Paixão de Diadorim segundo Riobaldo." *Coloquio/Letras*, no. 76, 1983, pp. 10–17.

Johnson, Mark. "On Location(s): Cultural Crossings and Transformational Genders." *Beauty and Power. Transgendering and Cultural Transformation in the Southern Philippines*. Berg, 1997, pp. 16–42.

Johnson, Randal. "Cinema Novo and Cannibalism: *Macunaíma*." *Brazilian Cinema*, edited by Johnson and Robert Stam, Columbia UP, 1995, pp. 178–90.

Jordan, David M. *New World Regionalism. Literature in the Americas*. U of Toronto P, 1994.

Juana Gallo. Directed by Miguel Zacarías, performances by María Félix, Jorge Mistral, and Luis Aguilar, Producciones Zacarías, 1960.

Bibliography

Kaas, Hailey. "Birth of Transfeminism in Brazil. Between Alliances and Backlashes." *TSQ: Transgender Studies Quarterly*, vol. 3, no. 1–2, 2016, pp. 146–49.

Kaiser, Susan B. *Fashion and Cultural Studies*. Berg, 2012.

Kampwirth, Karen. *Women & Guerrilla Movements: Nicaragua, El Salvador, Chiapas, Cuba*. The Pennsylvania State UP, 2002.

Kanost, Laura. "'Por camino torcido.' Liminal Identities in the Novel, Screenplay, and Film Versions of *La Negra Angustias*." *Bilingual Review/La revista bilingüe*, vol. 29, no. 2–3, 2008, pp. 81–88.

———. "Viewing the Afro-Mexican Female Revolutionary: Francisco Rojas González's 'La negra Angustias.'" *Hispania*, vol. 93, no. 4, 2010, pp. 555–62.

Katz, Friedrich. "The End and the Survival of Villa." *The Life and Times of Pancho Villa*, Stanford UP, 1998, pp. 761–94.

Kendrigan, Mary Lou. "Gender and the Warrior Ethic." *Women in Uniform & the Changing World Order. Conference proceedings from the WREI's Fifth Biennial Conference on Women in Uniform, Arlington, VA, 30 Nov.–1 Dec. 2000*, Women's Research and Education Inst, 2000, pp. 0–20.

Kimmel, Michael. "Masculinities." *Men & Masculinities. A Social, Cultural, and Historical Encyclopedia*, vol. 1, edited by Kimmel and Amy Aronson, ABC CLIO, 2004, pp. 503–07.

———. "Masculinity as Homophobia: Fear, Shame, and Silence in The Construction of Gender Identity." *The Masculinities Reader*, edited by Stephen M. Whitehead and Frank J. Barrett, Polity, 2001, pp. 266–87.

Kirk, Emily J. "Setting the Agenda for Cuban Sexuality: The Role of Cuba's CENESEX." *Canadian Journal of Latin American and Caribbean Studies*, vol. 36, no. 72, 2011, pp. 143–63.

———. *The Normalization of Sexual Diversity in Revolutionary Cuba*. 2015. University of Nottingham, PhD Dissertation. *Semantic Scholar*.

Kristeva, Julia. "About Chinese Women." *The Kristeva Reader*, Columbia UP, 1986, pp. 138–59.

Kripke, Saul A. *Naming and Necessity*. Harvard UP, 1980.

Kuhn, Cynthia, and Cindy Carlson. Introduction. *Styling Texts. Dress and Fashion in Literature*, edited by Kuhn and Carlson, Cambria P, 2007, pp. 1–10.

La negra Angustias. Directed by Matilde Landeta, performances by María Elena Márquez, Agustín Isunza, and Ramón Gay, Tacma, 1950.

Lacan, Jacques. "Seminar on 'The Purloined Letter.'" *The Purloined Poe.*

Bibliography

Lacan, Derrida & Psychoanalytic Reading, edited by John P. Muller and William J. Richardson, The Johns Hopkins UP, 1988, pp. 28–54.

Laqueur, Thomas. *Making Sex. Body and Gender from the Greeks to Freud.* Harvard UP, 1990.

Lasarte Valcárcel, Javier. "Mestizaje y populismo en 'Doña Bárbara': de Sarmiento a Martí." *Iberoamericana*, vol. 24, no. 78–79, 2000, pp. 164–86.

Latham, JR. "Trans Men's Sexual Narrative-Practices: Introducing STS to Trans and Sexuality Studies." *Sexualities*, vol. 19, no. 3, 2016, pp. 347–68.

Lavou Zoungbo, Victorien. "Discurso burgués y legitimación machista en *Doña Bárbara* de Rómulo Gallegos." *Revista de crítica literaria latinoamericana*, vol. 22, no. 43–44, 1996, pp. 211–25.

Lavrin, Asunción. "In Search of the Colonial Woman in Mexico: The Seventeenth and Eighteenth Centuries." *Latin American Women. Historical Perspectives*, edited by Lavrin, Greenwood, 1978, pp. 23–59.

Leal, Luis. "La hija de los ríos." Rodríguez-Alcalá, pp. 99–117.

Leavitt, Sturgies E. "Sex and Symbolism in *Doña Bárbara*." *Revista de estudios hispánicos*, vol. 1, no. 1, 1967, pp. 117–20.

Lefebvre, Henri. "The Social Text." *The Routledge Critical and Cultural Theory Reader*, edited by Neil Badmington and Julia Thomas, Routledge, 2008, pp. 95–99.

León Ortiz, Miguel Ángel. "Avances en el reconocimiento del derecho humano a la identidad de género auto-percibida en México." *Ciencia jurídica*, vol. 8, no. 16, 2019, pp. 119–38.

Lerner, Gerda. *The Creation of Patriarchy.* Oxford UP, 1986.

Lévi-Strauss, Claude. *Las estructuras elementales del parentesco.* 1949. Translated by Marie Thérèse Cevasco, Paidós, 1998.

———. *The Savage Mind.* 1962. Translated by George Weidenfeld and Nicolson Ltd, U of Chicago P, 1973.

Levy, Kurt L. "*Doña Bárbara*: The Human Dimension." *The Internacional Fiction Review*, vol. 7, no. 2, 1980, pp. 118–22.

———. "En torno al regionalismo en su sentido más amplio." *Studies in Honor of DONALD W. BLEZNICK*, edited by Delia V. Galván et al., Juan de la Cuesta, 1995, pp. 85–93.

Lewis, Paul. "Attaining Masculinity. Charles Brockden Brown and Woman Warriors of the 1790s." *Early American Literature*, vol. 40, no. 1, 2005, pp. 37–55.

Lima, Caroline de Araújo. "Mulheres em movimento e sua invisibilidade: a memória e o esquecimento das cangaceiras." *Universidade e sociedade*, vol. XXVI, no. 58, 2016, pp. 92–103.

Linhard, Tabea Alexa. *Fearless Women in the Mexican Revolution and the Spanish Civil War*. U of Missouri P, 2005.

Liscano, Juan. "Otra doña Bárbara" *Doña Bárbara ante la crítica*, organized by Manuel Bermúdez, Monte Ávila, 1991, pp. 153–60.

———. *Rómulo Gallegos y su tiempo*. Monte Ávila, 1969.

———. "Tema mítico de *Doña Bárbara*." 1976. *Doña Bárbara*, Ayacucho, 1977, pp. ix-xxix.

List Reyes, Mauricio. "El trabajo académico y la teoría queer en México." *Mirada antropológica*, vol. 13, no. 14, 2018, pp. 72–85.

Lobao, Linda. "Women in Revolutionary Movements: Changing Patterns of Latin American Guerrilla Struggle." *Women and Social Protest*, edited by Guida West and Rhoda Louis Blumberg, Oxford UP, 1990, pp. 180–204.

Lloyd, Moya. "Performativity, Parody, Politics." *Theory, Culture & Society*, vol. 16, no. 2, 1999, pp. 195–213.

Locke, John. *Two Treatises of Government*. 1698. Cambridge UP, 2005, pp. 141–263.

Lombardi, John V. *Venezuela. The Search for Order, The Dream of Progress*. Oxford UP, 1982.

Long Chu, Andrea. *Females*. Verso, 2019.

Lopes, Denilson. *O homem que amava rapazes e outros ensaios*. Aeroplano, 2002.

López López, Margarita. "*La negra Angustias*, preámbulo a una revolución trunca. El elemento afromexicano en la narrativa de la revolución." *Bilingual Review/La revista bilingüe*, vol. 29, no. 2–3, 2008, pp. 113–26.

Lungaretti, Celso. *Náufrago da utopia. Vencer ou morrer na guerrilha aos 18 anos*. Geração, 2005.

Lynch, Margaret E. "Joan of Arc (c. 1412–1431)." *Women in World History. A Biographical Encyclopedia*, vol. 8, edited by Anne Commire and Deborah Klezmer, Yorkin, 2000, pp. 185–93.

Mac Adam, Alfred J. "João Guimarães Rosa *Honneur des Hommes*." *Modern Latin American Narratives: The Dreams of Reason*, U of Chicago P, 1977, pp. 69–77.

Machado, Ana Maria. *Recado do nome. Leitura de Guimarães Rosa à luz do nome de seus personagens*. 1976. Martins Fontes, 1991.

Macías, Anna. *Against All Odds. The Feminist Movement in Mexico to 1940*. Greenwood, 1982.

Bibliography

Macunaíma. Directed by Joaquim Pedro de Andrade, performances by Grande Otelo, Paulo José, Jardel Filho, Milton Gonçalves, and Dina Sfat, Filmes do Sêrro, Grupo Filmes, and Condor Filmes, 1969.

Magnarelli, Sharon. "Woman and Nature in *Doña Bárbara* by Rómulo Gallegos." *Revista de estudios hispánicos*, vol. XIX, no. 2, 1985, pp. 3–20.

———. "Women and Nature: In Man's Image Created." *The Lost Rib. Female Characters in the Spanish-American Novel*, Bucknell UP / Associated UP, 1985, pp. 38–58.

Marentes, Luis A. *José Vasconcelos and the Writing of the Mexican Revolution*. Twayne, 2000.

Martínez Herrarte, Antonio. "La creación del personaje en *Doña Bárbara*: un juego de espejos." *Pacific Northwest Conference on Foreign Languages*, vol. 28, no. 1, 1977, pp. 145–48.

Martins, Cyro. *A criação artística e a psicanálise*. Sulina, 1970.

Masiello, Francine. Introduction. *Between Civilization & Barbarism. Women, Nation, and Literary Culture in Modern Argentina*, by Masiello, U of Nebraska P, 1992, pp. 1–14.

McCard, Victoria. "*Soldaderas* of the Mexican Revolution." *West Virginia University Philological Papers*, vol. 51, 2004, pp. 43–51.

McGee, Marcus J., and Karen Kampwirth. "The Co-optation of LGBT Movements in Mexico and Nicaragua: Modernizing Clientelism?" *Latin American Politics and Society*, vol. 57, no. 4, 2015, pp. 51–73.

McMurray, George R. "*Los de abajo*. Novel by Mariano Azuela." Smith, pp. 91–92.

———. "Mariano Azuela 1873–1952. Mexican Prose Writer, Dramatist and Critic." Smith, pp. 89–91.

McQueen, Paddy. Introduction. *Subjectivity, Gender and the Struggle for Recognition*, by Paddy. Palgrave, 2014, pp. 1–17.

Medina, Fabiana Grazioli. "Diadorim: um amor em suspenso." *Convivendo com Guimarães Rosa: Grande sertão veredas*, organized by Beatriz Berrini, Educ, 2004, pp. 167–82.

Melhuus, Marit, and Kristi Anne Stølen. Introduction. *Machos, Mistresses, Madonnas. Contesting the Power of Latin American Gender Imagery*, edited by Melhuus and Stølen, Verso, 1996, pp. 1–33.

Méndez Rodenas, Adriana. "From the Margins of History. Gender and Nationalism in Spanish American Literature." *Gender and Nationalism in Colonial Cuba. The Travels of Santa Cruz y Montalvo, Condesa de Merlin*, Vanderbilt UP, 1998, pp. 3–16.

Bibliography

Mendieta Alatorre, Ángeles. *La mujer en la revolución mexicana*. Biblioteca del instituto nacional de estudios históricos de la revolución mexicana, 1961.

Menton, Seymour. "La estructura épica de *Los de abajo* y un prólogo especulativo." *Hispania*, vol. 50, no. 4, 1967, pp. 1001–011.

———. "*La negra Angustias*, una *Doña Bárbara* mexicana." *Revista Iberoamericana*, vol. XIX, no. 38, 1954, pp. 299–308.

Merrim, Stephanie. *Logos and the Word. The Novel of Language and Linguistic Motivation in Grande sertão: veredas and Tres tristes tigres*. Lang, 1983.

Miguel-Pereira, Lúcia. "Regionalismo." *Prosa de ficção: de 1870 a 1920*, 3rd ed., Olympio, 1973, pp. 177–238.

Mijares, Augusto. "La evolución política (1810–1960)." *Venezuela independiente 1810–1960*, edited by Mariano Picón-Salas et al., Mendoza, 1962, pp. 21–156.

Miliani de Mazzei, Marina. "Los proyectos de inmigración y colonización en Venezuela como política de poblamiento en el siglo XIX." *Tiempo y espacio*, vol. 21, no. 56, 2011, pp. 30–49.

Mill, John Stuart. "Of Names." *A system of Logic. Ratiocinative and Inductive. Being a Connected View of the Principles of Evidence and the Methods of Scientific Investigation*, 7th ed., vol. 1, Logmans, 1868. *Internet Archive*. www.archive.org/details/asystemoflogic01milluoft. Accessed 15 Sept. 2009.

———. *The Subjection of Women*. 1869. *On Liberty and Other Writings*. Cambridge UP, 2005, pp. 117–217.

Miller, Elizabeth Carolyn. *Framed. The New Woman Criminal in British Culture at the Fin de Siècle*. U of Michigan P / U of Michigan Library, 2008.

Miller, Francesca. *Latin American Women and the Search for Social Justice*. UP of New England, 1991.

Mitchell, Jasmine. Introduction. *Imagining the Mulatta: Blackness in U.S. and Brazilian Media*, by Mitchell, U of Illinois P, 2020, pp. 14–35.

Moghadam, Valentine M. "Gender and Revolutions." *Theorizing Revolutions*, edited by John Foran, Routledge, 1997, pp. 133–62.

Molina Sevilla de Morelock, Ela. "Nellie Campobello, cuando madre naturaleza y madre cultura son una." *Relecturas y narraciones femeninas de la Revolución Mexicana. Campobello, Garro, Esquivel y Mastretta*, Tamesis, 2013, pp. 22–64.

Molloy, Sylvia. "The Politics of Posing: Translating Decadence in Fin-de-Siècle Latin America." *Perennial Decay: On the Aesthetics and Politics of Decadence*, edited by Liz Constable et al., U of Pennsylvania

Bibliography

P, 1999, pp. 183–97.

Monsiváis, Carlos. "La aparición del subsuelo (sobre la cultura de la Revolución Mexicana)." *La cultura en México*, 14 Dec. 1983, pp. 36–42.

———. "Sexismo en la literatura mexicana." *Imagen y realidad de la mujer*, compiled by Elena Urrutia, Secretaría de educación pública, 1975.

———. "When Gender Can't Be Seen amid the Symbols: Women and the Mexican Revolution." Olcott et al., pp. 1–20.

Moreno Figueroa, Mónica G. "Distributed Intensities: Whiteness, Mestizaje and the Logics of Mexican Racism." *Ethnicities*, vol. 10, no. 3, 2010, pp. 387–401.

Morínigo, Mariano. "Civilización y barbarie en *Facundo* y *Doña Bárbara*." *Revista nacional de cultura*, vol. 26, 1963, pp. 91–117.

Morón, Guillermo. *Breve historia contemporánea de Venezuela*. Fondo de cultura, 1994.

Mudarra, Miguel Ángel. *Aproximación a la mujer venezolana*. Corporación gráfica industrial, 1986.

Muller, John P., and William J. Richardson. *The Purloined Poe. Lacan, Derrida & Psychoanalytic Reading*. The Johns Hopkins UP, 1988.

Muñoz, Rafael F. ¡*Vámonos con Pancho Villa!* Espasa-Calpe, 1935.

Murad, Timothy. "Foreshadowing, Duplication, and Structural Unity in Mariano Azuela's *Los de Abajo*." *Hispania*, vol. 64, no. 4, 1981, pp. 550–56.

Nájera-Ramírez, Olga. "Engendering Nationalism: Identity, Discourse, and the Mexican Charro." *Anthropological Quarterly*, vol. 67, no. 1, 1994, pp. 1–14.

Nascimento, Antonio. *Guerrilheira*. 7Letras, 2003.

Nascimento, Geraldo Maia do. *Amantes guerreiras. A presença da mulher no Cangaço*. 2nd ed., Sebo vermelho, 2015.

Nascimento, Tatiana. "Da palavra queerlombo ao cuíerlombo da palavra." *Palavra, preta! Poesia di dendê*, 12 Mar. 2018, palavrapreta.wordpress.com/2018/03/12/cuierlombismo#comments. Accessed 31 Mar. 2022.

Neitzel, Adair de Aguiar. *Mulheres rosianas. Percursos pelo Grande sertão: veredas*. UFSC / UNIVALI, 2004.

Nery, João W. *Viagem solitária. Memórias de um transexual trinta anos depois*. Leya, 2011.

Norwood, Kimberly Jade, and Violeta Solonova Foreman. "The Ubiquitousness of Colorism. Then and Now." *Color Matters. Skin tone Bias and the Myth of a Post-Racial America*, Routledge, 2014, pp. 9–28.

Bibliography

Nunes, Benedito. "O amor na obra de Guimarães Rosa." Coutinho, pp. 144–69.

Núñez Noriega, Guillermo. *Masculinidad e intimidad: identidad, sexualidad y sida*. U Nacional Autónoma de México / El Colegio de Sonora / Porrúa, 2007.

Nye, Robert A. "Locating Masculinity: Some Recent Work on Men." *Signs*, vol. 30, no. 3, 2005, pp. 1937–1962.

O que é isso, companheiro? Directed by Bruno Barreto, performances by Pedro Cardoso, Fernanda Torres, and Alan Arkin, Columbia, 1997.

O'Toole, Laura L., Jessica R. Schiffman, and Margie L. Kiter Edwards, editors. *Gender Violence. Interdisciplinary Perspectives*. 2nd ed., New York UP, 2007.

Olcott, Jocelyn et al., editors. *Sex in Revolution. Gender, Politics, and Power in Modern Mexico*. Duke UP, 2006.

Oliveira, Carolina Rennó Ribeiro de. *Biografias de personalidades célebres. Para uso escolar nos diversos níveis do ensino e dos estudiosos de história do Brasil*. Mestre, 1966.

Oliveira, Emanuelle K. F. "La República y las Letras – literatura y carácter nacional en Brasil y Venezuela." *Mester*, vol. 24, no. 2, 1995, pp. 81–114.

Oliveira, Valdeci Batista de Melo. *Figurações da donzela-guerreira: Luzia-Homem e Dona Guidinha do Poço*. Annablume, 2005.

Oliver, Kelly. *Women as Weapons of War. Iraq, Sex, and the Media*. Columbia UP, 2007.

Olivieri, Rita. "Reelaboração do mito da androginia em *Grande sertão: veredas*." *Lusorama*, no. 29, 1996, pp. 42–47.

Osorio, Nelson. "Doña Bárbara y el fantasma de Sarmiento." *Escritura*, vol. 8, no. 15, 1983, pp. 19–35.

Paloma de papel. Directed by Fabrizio Aguilar Boschetti, performances by Antonio Callirgos, Melania Urbina, and Tatiana Astengo, Luna llena films, 2003.

París, Marta de. *Amantes, cautivas y guerreras*. Vol. 2, Almagesto, 1996.

Parra, Max. "Villa and Popular Political Subjectivity in Mariano Azuela's *Los de abajo*." *Writing Pancho Villa's Revolution. Rebels in the Literary Imagination of Mexico*, U of Texas P, 2005, pp. 22–47.

Pascal, Maria Aparecida Macedo. "As mulheres e a guerra do Paraguai." *Scribd*, 15 maio 2009, www.scribd.com/doc/4893635/guerra-do--paraguay.

Patai, Daphne. "We, Rigoberta's Excuse-Makers." *Academic Questions*, vol. 25, no. 2, 2012, pp. 190–208.

Bibliography

Payne, Judith A., and Earl E. Fitz. *Ambiguity and Gender in the New Novel of Brazil and Spanish America*. U of Iowa P, 1993.

Paz, Octavio. *El laberinto de la soledad*. 1950, edited by Enrico Mario Santí, Cátedra, 2003.

Pécora, Antonio Alcir Bernárdez. "Aspectos da revelação em *Grande sertão: veredas*." *Remate de males*, vol. 7, 1987, pp. 69–73.

Peirce, Charles Sanders. "Sundry Logical Conceptions." *The Essential Peirce. Selected Philosophical Writings*, vol. 2, edited by the Peirce Edition Project, Indiana UP, 1998, pp. 267–88.

Peluffo, Ana, and Ignacio M. Sánchez Prado. Introduction. *Entre hombres: masculinidades del siglo XIX en América Latina*, edited by Peluffo and Sánchez Prado. Iberoamericana / Vervuert, 2010, pp. 7–20.

Pennington, Eric. "Beyond Realism and Allegory: Myth and Psyche in *Doña Bárbara*." *Crítica Hispánica*, vol. 9, no. 1–2, 1987, pp. 87–99.

Perdomo Escalona, Carmen. *Heroínas y mártires venezolanas*. Destino, 1994.

Perez, Hakim. "You Can Have My Brown Body and Eat It, Too!" *Social Text*, vol. 23, no. 3–4, 2005, pp. 171–91.

Perlongher, Néstor. "Los devenires minoritarios." *Los devenires minoritarios*, Diaclasa, 2016, pp. 121–49.

Perrone, Charles. "Lyrical Passage(s): Verse, Song and Sense in *Grande Sertão: Veredas*." *Luso-Brazilian Review*, vol. 27, no. 1, 1990, pp. 47–61.

Pick, Zuzana M. "Pancho Villa on Two Sides of the Border." *Constructing the Image of the Mexican Revolution: Cinema and the Archive*, U of Texas P, 2010, pp. 69–96.

Pickering, Michael. "The Concept of the Stereotype." *Stereotyping. The Politics of Representation*, Palgrave, 2001, pp. 1–21.

Pierce, Joseph M. "I Monster: Embodying Trans and *Travesti* Resistance in Latin America." *Latin American Research Review*, vol. 55, no. 2, 2020, pp. 305–21.

Platón. *Crátilo*. www.edu.mec.gub.uy/biblioteca_digital/libros/P/Platon%20-%20Cratilo.pdf.

Poniatowska, Elena. *Hasta no verte, Jesús mío*. 1969. Era, 2006.

———. *Las Soldaderas*. 1999. Era / INAH, 2000.

Portal, Marta. Introduction. *Los de abajo*, by Mariano Azuela, Cátedra, 1999, pp. 9–68.

———. *Proceso narrativo de la Revolución Mexicana*. Espasa-Calpe, 1980.

Potthast, Barbara. "Protagonists, Victims, and Heroes. Paraguayan Women during the 'Great War.'" *I Die with My Country. Perspectives on the Paraguayan War, 1864–1870*, edited by Hendrik Kraay and Tho-

Bibliography

mas L. Whigham, U of Nebraska P, 2004, pp. 44–60.

Pratt, Mary Louise. "Mi cigarro, mi singer, y la revolución mexicana: la danza ciudadana de Nellie Campobello." *Cadernos Pagu*, no. 22, 2004, pp. 151–84.

———. "Women, Literature, and National Brotherhood." *Women, Culture, and Politics in Latin America. Seminar on Feminism and Culture in Latin America*, U of California P, 1990, pp. 48–73.

Prince, Gerald. *A Dictionary of Narratology*. U of Nebraska P, 1987.

Proença, Manoel Cavalcanti. *Trilhas no Grande sertão*. Ministério de educação e cultura, 1958.

Puar, Jasbir. "'I would rather be a cyborg than a goddess.' Intersectionality, Assemblage, and Affective Politics." *Transversal Texts*, Jan. 2011, transversal.at/transversal/0811/puar/en. Accessed 19 June 2020.

Pulido Herráez, Begoña. "*Cartucho*, de Nellie Campobello: la percepción dislocada de la Revolución Mexicana." *Latinoamérica*, vol. 52, no. 1, 2011, pp. 31–51.

Pupo-Walker, Enrique. "Algo más sobre la creación de personajes en *Los de abajo*." *Romance Notes*, vol. 12, no. 1, 1970, pp. 50–54.

———. "*Los de abajo* y la pintura de Orozco: un caso de correspondencias estéticas." *Cuadernos Americanos*, vol. 154, no. 5, 1967, pp. 237–54.

Queiroz, Rachel de. *Memorial de Maria Moura*. Siciliano, 1992.

———. *O quinze*. 1930. José Olympio, 1985.

Quevedo y Zubieta, Salvador. *México marimacho*. 2nd ed., Botas, 1933.

Quintero, Pablo. "La invención de la democracia racial en Venezuela." *Tabula rasa*, no. 16, 2012, pp. 161–85.

Quiroga, José. *Tropics of Desire. Interventions from Queer Latino America*. New York UP, 2000.

Ramírez, Sergio. *Adiós muchachos*. 1999. Alfaguara, 2007.

Randall, Margaret. *Inside the Nicaraguan Revolution. As Told to Margaret Randall*. Translated by Elinor Randall, New Star, 1978.

———. *Mujeres en la revolución. Margaret Randall conversa con mujeres cubanas*. 1972. Siglo veintiuno, 1978.

———. *Sandino's Daughters. Testimonies of Nicaraguan Women in Struggle*. 1981. Rutgers UP, 1995.

———. "Una brasileña en la lucha: Adamaris Oliveira Lucena." *Casa de las Américas*, vol. 11, no. 65–66, 1971, pp. 75–82.

Reis, Roberto. "Brazil." In "Regionalism." Smith, pp. 703–04.

Bibliography

———. "*Grande Sertão: Veredas.* Novel by João Guimarães Rosa." Smith, pp. 400–01.

Reséndez Fuentes, Andrés. "Battleground Women: Soldaderas and Female Soldiers in the Mexican Revolution." *The Americas*, vol. 51, no. 4, 1995, pp. 525–53.

Retter, Yolanda. "Amelia Robles Fights in the Mexican Revolution." *LGBT History, 1855–1955*, 2005, pp. 3–5.

Ribeiro, Bruno. *Helenira Resende e a guerrilha do Araguaia.* Expressão popular, 2007.

Ribeiro, João Ubaldo. *Viva o povo brasileiro.* Nova Fronteira, 1984.

Ribeiro, Maria Claudia Badan. "As mulheres da Ação libertadora nacional." *Guerrilha e revolução. A luta armada contra a ditadura militar no Brasil*, organized by Jean Rodrigues Sales, Lamparina, FAPERJ, 2015, pp. 173–97.

Rios, Cassandra. *Uma mulher diferente.* 1968. Record, 1980.

Robe, Stanley L. *Azuela and the Mexican Underdogs.* U of California P, 1979.

Rocha, Carolina. Introduction. *Modern Argentine Masculinities*, edited by Rocha, Intellect, 2013, pp. 3–16.

Rocha, Karina Bersan. "Veredas do Amor no Grande sertão." *Veredas de Rosa II*, organized by Lélia Pariera Duarte et al., PUC Minas, 2003, pp. 383–88.

Rocha, Martha Eva. "Las mexicanas en el siglo XX." *Mujeres mexicanas del siglo XX. La otra revolución*, edited by Francisco Blanco Figueroa, vol. 4, Edicol, 2001, pp. 89–159.

Roche, Daniel. *The Culture of Clothing. Dress and Fashion in the 'Ancien Régime.'* Translated by Jean Birrell, 1989, Cambridge UP, 1994.

Rodríguez, Blanca. *Nellie Campobello: eros y violencia.* U nacional autónoma de México, 1998.

Rodríguez, Ileana. *Women Guerrillas & Love. Understanding War in Central America.* Translated by Ileana Rodríguez with Robert Carr. U of Minnesota P, 1996.

Rodríguez Monegal, Emir. Introduction. *The Borzoi Anthology of Latin American Literature*, edited by Monegal, vol. 1, Knopf, 1977, pp. xiii-iv.

Rodríguez-Alcalá, Hugo, editor. *Nine Essays on Rómulo Gallegos.* Latin American Studies Program of the U of California Riverside, 1979.

Rojas González, Francisco. *La negra angustias.* EDIAPSA, 1944.

Romero, José Rubén. *Apuntes de un lugareño.* 1932. *Obras completas.* Porrúa, 1986, pp. 19–147.

Root, Regina A. Introduction. *The Latin American Fashion Reader*, edited by Root, Berg, 2005, pp. 1–13.

Rosa, João Guimarães. *Corpo de baile*. Vol. 2. Nova Fronteira, 2006.

———. *Grande sertão: veredas*. 1956. Nova Fronteira, 2001.

Rose, Mary Beth. "Women in Men's Clothing: Apparel and Social Stability in *The Roaring Girl*." *English Literary Renaissance*, vol. 14, no. 3, 1984, pp. 367–91.

Rosegreen-Williams, Claudette. "Rómulo Gallegos's *Doña Bárbara*: Toward a Radical Rereading." *Symposium*, vol. 46, no. 4, 1993, pp. 279–96.

Rosenfield, Kathrin Holzermayr. *Desveredando Rosa. A obra de J. G. Rosa e outros ensaios rosianos*. Topbooks, 2006.

———. *Grande Sertão: Veredas. Roteiro de Leitura*. Ática, 1992.

———. *Os Descaminhos do Demo. Tradição e Ruptura em Grande Sertão: Veredas*. EDUSP, 1993.

———. "Rosa e a invenção de uma aura poética para as 'raízes do Brasil.'" Secchin et al., pp. 128–41.

Rubin, Gayle. "The Traffic in Women: Notes on the 'Political Economy of Sex.'" *Toward an Anthropology of Women*, edited by Rayna R. Reiter, Monthly Review P, 1975, pp. 157–210.

Rufinelli, Jorge. "Nellie Campobello: pólvora en palabras." *La palabra y el hombre*, no. 113, 2000, pp. 63–72.

Russell, Bertrand. "On Denoting." *Mind New Series*, vol. 14, no. 46, 1905, pp. 479–93.

Russell-Wood, A. J. R. "Female and Family in the Economy and Society of Colonial Brazil." *Latin American Women. Historical Perspectives*, edited by Asunción Lavrin, Greenwood, 1978, pp. 60–100.

Rutherford, John. "La novela de la revolución mexicana." *Historia de la literatura hispanoamericana. II. El siglo XX*, edited by Roberto González Echeverría and Enrique Pupo-Walker, Gredos, 2006, pp. 231–43.

Sacks, Karen. "Engels Revisited: Women, the Organization of Production, and Private Property." *Toward an Anthropology of Women*, edited by Rayna R. Reiter, Monthly Review P, 1975, pp. 211–34.

Salas, Elizabeth. *Soldaderas in the Mexican Military. Myth and History*. U of Texas P, 1990.

Salinas Hernández, Héctor Miguel. *Políticas de disidencia sexual en América Latina. Sujetos sociales, gobierno y mercado en México, Bogotá y Buenos Aires*. Eón, 2010.

Sánchez, Porfirio. "La deshumanización del hombre en *Los de abajo*." *Cuadernos americanos*, vol. 192, no. 1, 1974, pp. 179–91.

Bibliography

Sánchez-Prado, Ignacio M. "La destrucción de la escritura viril y el ingreso de la mujer al discurso literario: El libro vacío y Los recuerdos del Porvenir." *Revista de crítica literaria latinoamericana*, vol. 32, no. 63–64, 2006, pp. 149–67.

———. *Naciones intelectuales: las fundaciones de la modernidad literaria mexicana (1917–1959)*. Purdue UP, 2009.

Santana, Dora Silva. "Mais Viva! Reassembling Transness, Blackness, and Feminism." *TSQ: Transgender Studies Quarterly*, vol. 6, no. 2, 2019, pp. 210–22.

Santos, Julia Conceição Fonseca. *Nomes de personagens em Guimarães Rosa*. Instituto nacional do livro, 1971.

Santos, Michele Soares, and Caroline de Araújo Lima. "Cangaceiras em cena: uma análise das Marias na produção cinematográfica e literária." *XXVII simpósio nacional de história, Natal, RN, 22–26 July 2013*, Anpuh, 2013.

Schell, Jr., William. "Emiliano Zapata and the Old Regime: Myth, Memory, and Method." *Mexican Studies/Estudios Mexicanos*, vol. 25, no. 2, 2009, pp. 327–65.

Schneider, Jane. "The Anthropology of Cloth." *Annual Review of Anthropology*, vol. 16, 1987, pp. 409–48.

Schüler, Donaldo. "Grande sertão: veredas – Estudos." Coutinho, pp. 360–77.

Schumaher, Schuma, e Érico Vital Brazil, editores. *Dicionário mulheres do Brasil. De 1500 até a atualidade*. Zahar, 2000.

Schwarz, Roberto. "*Grande sertão*: estudos." Coutinho, pp. 378–89.

Scott, Joan Wallach. *Gender and the Politics of History*. Rev. ed., Columbia UP, 1999.

Secchin, Antonio Carlos, et al., organizers. *Veredas no sertão rosiano*. 7letras, 2007.

Segal, Lynne. *Slow Motion. Changing Masculinities, Changing Men*. Rutgers UP, 1990.

Sedgwick, Eve Kosofsky. "Introduction: Axiomatic." *Epistemology of the Closet*, U of California P, 1990, pp. 1–63.

———. *Between Men. English Literature and Male Homosocial Desire*. Columbia UP, 1985.

Serano, Julia. *Whipping Girl. A Transsexual Woman on Sexism and the Scapegoat of Femininity*. 2nd. ed., Seal P, 2016.

Serra, Tânia Rebelo Costa. "A Donzela Guerreira de Homero a Guimarães Rosa." *Revista do Instituto de estudos brasileiros*, no. 41, 1996, pp. 181–88.

Shayne, Julie D. *Revolution Question: Feminisms in el Salvador, Chile, and Cuba Compared.* Rutgers UP, 2004.

Shaw, D. L. *Gallegos: Doña Bárbara.* Grant / Tamesis, 1972.

———. "Gallegos' Revision of *Doña Bárbara* 1929–1930." *Hispanic Review,* vol. 42, no. 3, 1974, pp. 265–78.

———. "More About the Making of *Doña Bárbara.*" *Nine Essays on Rómulo Gallegos.* Rodríguez-Alcalá, pp. 198–215.

———. "Rómulo Gallegos 1884–1969. Venezuelan Prose Writer." Smith, pp. 338–40.

Shimizu, Akiko. *Lying Bodies. Survival and Subversion in the Field of Vision.* Lang, 2008.

Showalter, Elaine. *Sexual Anarchy. Gender and Culture at the Fin de Siècle.* Penguin, 1990.

Sifuentes-Jáuregui, Ben. *The Avowal of Difference: Queer Latino American Narratives.* State U of New York, 2014.

———. *Transvestism, Masculinity, and Latin American Literature. Genders Share Flesh.* Palgrave, 2002.

Silva, Aguinaldo. *A história de Lili Carabina. Um romance da Baixada Fluminense.* Codecri, 1983.

Silva, Geysa. "Mujeres de ojos grandes: una relectura de los géneros en Latinoamérica." *Espéculo. Revista de estudios literarios,* no. 28, 2004–2005, www.ucm.es/info/especulo/numero28/ojosgran.html.

Silva, Joseli Maria Silva, and Marcio Jose Ornat. "Transfeminism and Decolonial Thought. The Contribution of Brazilian *Travestis.*" *TSQ,* vol. 3, no. 1–2, 2016, pp. 220–27.

Silverman, Debra. "Making a Spectacle, or Is There a Female Drag?" *Critical Matrix,* vol. 7, no. 2, 1993, pp. 69–89.

simpkins, reese. "Trans*feminist Intersections." *TSQ: Transgender Studies Quarterly,* vol. 3, no. 1–2, 2016, pp. 228–34.

Simpson, Amelia. *Xuxa. The Mega-Marketing of Gender, Race and Modernity.* Temple UP, 1993.

Sinclair-Webb, Emma. Preface. *Imagined Masculinities. Male Identity and Culture in the Modern Middle East,* edited by Mai Ghoussoub and Sinclair-Webb, Saqi, 2000, pp. 7–16.

Smith, Paul. *Discerning the Subject.* U of Minnesota P, 1988.

Smith, Verity, editor. *Encyclopedia of Latin American Literature.* Dearborn, 1997.

Socolow, Susan Migden. "Women and Social Deviance: Crime, Witchcraft, and Rebellion." *The Women of Colonial Latin America,* Cambridge

Bibliography

UP, 2000, pp. 147–64. FIQUEI

Solt, Mary Ellen. "A World Look at Concrete Poetry." *Concrete Poetry: A World View*, edited by Solt, translated by Augusto de Campos et al., Indiana UP, 1970, pp. 6–66.

Sommer, Doris. "Love of Country: Populism's Revised Romance in *La Vorágine* and *Doña Bárbara*." *Foundational Fictions: The National Romances of Latin America*, 1991. U of California P, 1993, pp. 257–89.

Souza, Ilda Ribeiro de (Sila). *Angicos. Eu sobrevivi. Confissões de uma guerreira do cangaço*. Oficina Cultural Monica Buonfiglio, 1997.

Spencer, Herbert. "Manners and Fashion." *Essays, Scientific, Political, and Speculative*, vol. 3, 1892, pp. 1–51, 10 Oct. 2008, files.libertyfund.org/files/337/062003_Bk.pdf.

Spivak, Gayatri Chakravorty. "The Rani of Sirmur: An Essay in Reading the Archives." *History and Theory*, vol. 24, no. 3, 1985, pp. 247–72.

Stallybrass, Peter, and Allon White. *The Politics and Poetics of Transgression*. Methuen, 1986.

Starling, Heloisa Maria Murgel. *Lembranças do Brasil. Teoria, política, história e ficção em Grande sertão: veredas*. Revan, 1999.

Stavans, Ilán. Introduction. *The Underdogs. A Novel of the Mexican Revolution*, by Mariano Azuela, The Modern Library, 2002, pp. vii-xv.

Steele, Cynthia. *Politics, Gender, and the Mexican Novel, 1968–1988: Beyond the Pyramid*. U of Texas P, 1992.

Stern, Steve J. *The Secret History of Gender. Women, Men, and Power in Late Colonial Mexico*. U of North Carolina P, 1995.

Stevens, Evelyn P. "Marianismo: The Other Face of íhismo in Latin America." *Female and Male in Latin America*, edited by Ann Pescatello, U of Pittsburgh P, 1973, pp. 89–101.

Stout, Noelle M. *After Love: Queer Intimacy and Erotic Economies in Post-Soviet Cuba*. Duke UP, 2014.

Stryker, Susan. "(De)Subjugated Knowledges. An Introduction to Transgender Studies." *The Transgender Studies Reader*, edited by Stryker and Stephen Whittle, Routledge, 2006, pp. 1–17.

Stryker, Susan, and Talia M. Bettcher. "Introduction. Trans/Feminisms." *TSQ: Transgender Studies Quarterly*, vol. 3, no. 1–2, 2016, pp. 5–14.

Suthrell, Charlotte. *Unzipping Gender. Sex, Cross-Dressing and Culture*. Berg, 2004.

Summerell, Orrin F. "Philosophy of Proper Names." *Namenforschung/Name Studies/Les noms propres*, vol. 1, Walter de Gruyter, 1995, pp.

368–72.

"TDoR 2016 Press Release." *Transgender Europe*, 9 Nov. 2016, tgeu.org/tdor-2016-press-release/.

Thompson, Carol B. "Women in the National Liberation Struggle in Zimbabwe. An Interview of Naomi Nhiwatiwa." *Women and Men's Wars*, edited by Judith Stiehm, Pergamon, 1983, pp. 247–52.

Thornton, Niamh. *Women and the War Story in Mexico. La novela de la Revolución*. Mellen P, 2006.

Torres-Ríoseco, Arturo. *Historia de la literatura iberoamericana*. Las Americas, 1965.

———. *The Epic of Latin American Literature*. U of California P, 1964.

Troconis de Veracoechea, Ermila. *Gobernadoras, cimarronas, conspiradoras y barraganas*. Alfadil, 1998.

Tseëlon, Efrat. "From Fashion to Masquerade: Towards an Ungendered Paradigm." *Body Dressing*, edited by Joanne Entwistle and Elizabeth Wilson, Berg, 2001, pp. 103–17.

Tuñón Pablos, Julia. "Las mexicanas del siglo XIX. Entre el cuerpo y el ángel." *Mujeres mexicanas del siglo XX. La otra revolución*, edited by Francisco Blanco Figueroa, vol. 4, Edicol, 2001, pp. 60–88.

Urioste, José Castro. "Poder y resistencia en la escritura de *Doña Bárbara*." *Explicación de textos literarios*, vol. 25, no.1, 1996–1997, pp. 41–49.

Usandizaga, Aranzazu, and Andrew Monnickendam, editors. *Dressing Up for War. Transformations of Gender and Genre in the Discourse and Literature of War*. Rodopi, 2001.

Utéza, Francis. *JGR: Metafísica do Grande sertão*. Translated by José Carlo Garbuglio, Edusp, 1994.

Valente, Luiz Fernando. "Affective Response in *Granda* [sic] *Sertão: Veredas*." *Luso-Brazilian Review*, vol. 23, no. 1, 1986, pp. 77–88.

Vanden Berghe, Kristine. "Alegría en la revolución y tristeza en tiempos de paz. El juego en *Cartucho* y *Las manos de mamá* de Nellie Campobello." *Literatura mexicana*, vol. XXI, no. 2, 2010, pp. 151–70.

Vasconcelos, José. *La tormenta*. In *Memorias I*. Fondo de cultura económica, 1983.

Vasvári, Louise O. "Queering the *Donçella Guerrera*." *Calíope*, vol. 12, no. 2, 2006, pp. 93–117.

Vaughan, Mary Kay. "Pancho Villa, the Daughters of Mary, and the Modern Woman: Gender in the Long Mexican Revolution." Olcott et al., pp. 21–32.

Velasco, Sherry. *Liutenant Nun: Transgenderism, Lesbian Desire, and Catalina*

Bibliography

de Erauso. U of Texas P, 2000.

Venkatesh, Vinodh. *The Body as Capital. Masculinities in Contemporary Latin American Fiction.* U of Arizona P, 2015.

Vianna, Lúcia Helena. *Escenas de amor y muerte en la ficción brasileña. El juego dramático de la relación hombre-mujer en la literatura.* Translated by Julia Calzadilla Núñez, Casa de las Américas, 1996.

Viggiano, Alan. *Diadorim-Deodorina. Hermes versus Afrodite em Grande sertão: veredas.* Quicé, 1987.

Vilalva, Walnice Aparecida Matos. *Marias: estudo sobre a donzela-guerreira no romance brasileiro.* 2004. UNICAMP, PhD Dissertation.

Villalobos Graillet, José Eduardo. "Las paradojas de la mexicanidad sobre el género y el mestizaje en la adaptación cinematográfica *La negra Angustias* de Matilde Landeta y en la novela de Francisco Rojas González." *Cincinnati Romance Review*, vol. 41, 2016, pp. 78–92.

Vincent, Jon S. "Grande sertão: veredas: The Critical Imperative." *João Guimarães Rosa.* Twayne, 1978, pp. 63–88.

Viteri, María Amelia, et al. "¿Cómo se piensa lo 'queer' en América Latina?" *Íconos. Revista de ciencias sociales*, no. 39, 2011, pp. 47–60.

Viveros Vigoya, Mara. "Contemporary Latin American Perspectives on Masculinity." *Changing Men and Masculinities in Latin America*, edited by Matthew C. Gutmann, Duke UP, 2003, pp. 27–57.

Von Hartenthal, Mariana. "The *Cangaceiros*: Bandits Covered in Stars and Flowers." *La Habana elegante*, no. 57, 2015, www.habanaelegante.com/November_2015/Invitation_vonHartenthal.html.

Ward Souto, Teresinha. *O discurso oral em Grande sertão: veredas.* Duas cidades, 1984.

Warhol, Robyn, and Susan S. Lanser. Introduction. *Narrative Theory Unbound. Queer and Feminist Interventions*, edited by Warhol and Lanser, Ohio State UP, 2015, pp. 1–20.

Waters, Mary-Alice. *Marianas in Combat. Teté Puebla & the Mariana Grajales Women's Platoon in Cuba's Revolutionary War.* Pathfinder, 2003.

Weiner, Annette B., and Jane Schneider. Introduction. *Cloth and Human Experience*, edited by Weiner and Schneider, Smithsonian, 1989, pp. 1–29.

Weinhardt, Marilene. "Fronteiras e margens." *Ficção histórica e regionalismo: (estudo sobre romances do Sul).* UFPR, 2004, pp. 15–27.

Whigham, Thomas L., and Hendrik Kraay. "War, Politics, and Society in South America, 1820s–60s." *I Die with My Country. Perspectives on the Paraguayan War, 1864–1870*, edited by Hendrik Kraay and Thomas L. Whigham, U of Nebraska P, 2004, pp. 1–22.

Bibliography

White, Michele. "Introduction. The Technologies of Producing Women: Femininity, Queerness, and the Crafted Monster." *Producing Women: The Internet, Traditional Femininity, Queerness, and Creativity*, Routledge, 2015, pp. 1–32.

Whittle, Stephen. Foreword. *The Transgender Studies Reader*, edited by Susan Stryker and

Whittle, Routledge, 2006, pp. xi-xvi.

Wickham-Crowley, Timothy P. "The Origins of the Second Wave." *Guerrillas and Revolution in Latin America. A comparative Study of Insurgents and Regimes since 1956*, Princeton UP, 1992, pp. 209–30.

Wilde, Lyn Webster. *On the Trail of the Women Warriors*. Constable, 1999.

Williams, Raymond. "Revolution." *Keywords: A Vocabulary of Culture and Science*, Oxford UP, 1983, pp. 270–74.

Wilson, Elizabeth. *Adorned in Dreams. Fashion and Modernity*. 1985. I.B. Tauris, 2003.

Wilson, Elizabeth, and Amy de la Haye. Introduction. *Defining Dress. Dress as Object, Meaning and Identity*, edited by De la Haye and Wilson, Manchester UP, 1999, pp. 1–9.

Wilson, Glenn A. "La tierra, protagonista de *Doña Bárbara*." *The Georgetown Journal of Languages & Linguistics*, vol. 1, no. 4, 1990, pp. 483–88.

Windler, Erica M. "Madame Durocher's Performance: Cross-Dressing, Midwifery, and Authority in Nineteenth-Century Rio de Janeiro." French and Bliss, pp. 52–70.

Winters, Lisa Ze. Introduction. *The Mulatta Concubine: Terror, Intimacy, Freedom, and Desire in the Black Transatlantic*, by Winters, U of Georgia P, 2016, pp. 1–24.

Woolf, Virginia. "Professions for Women." *Collected Essays*. 1925, vol. 2, Harcourt / Brace, 1967, pp. 284–89.

Wright, Winthrop R. *Café con leche. Race, Class, and National Image in Venezuela*. U of Texas P, 1990.

Yáñez, Agustín. *Al filo del agua*. 1947, edited by Arturo Azuela, ALLCA XX, 1996.

Yarrington, Doug. "Populist Anxiety: Race and Social Change in the Thought of Romulo

Gallegos." *The Americas*, vol. 56, no. 1, 1999, pp. 65–90.

Zamora, Fernando. *Por debajo del agua*. 2001. Plaza, 2002.

Zimmerman, Marc. *Literature and Resistance in Guatemala: Textual Modes and Cultural Politics from El señor Presidente to Rigoberta Menchú*, vol. 2, Center for Intern Stud Ohio U, 1995.

Index

access to power 1–3, 32–33, 70, 84, 89, 109, 117, 122, 135, 183, 229, 232
adelita 3, 4, 8–10, 82, 151, 193
agency 18, 60, 67, 69, 73, 77, 100, 103, 155, 157, 160, 165, 179, 187, 196, 233, 243–44n3, 247n10; of Diadorim 67, 135–36, 140, 143, 177, 231; of Doña Bárbara 159; of Pintada 40, 47–49, 80, 85, 150
Aguilar Boschetti, Fabrizio 225
Ahmed, Sara 123
Akiko, Shimizu 30, 241n22
Alarcón, Norma 150
Albuquerque Júnior, Durval Muniz de 134, 166
Alencar, Bárbara de 181
Alencar, José de 84, 209
Almeida, José Maurício Gomes de 170, 174
Alonso, Carlos 2, 50, 245n7
Althusser, Louis 30, 35, 77, 241n23, 243n2
Alvarez, Sonia E. 28
Amazon 52–53; Doña Bárbara as 52–55, 71, 103; Pintada as 148; Ci as 209
Ana Maria (*Uma mulher diferente*) 69
Anda, Raúl de 198, 247n11
Andrade, Joaquim Pedro de 209, 247n17
Andrade, Mário de 209
Andrade, Renata Guerra de 213
Andrade, Vera Lúcia 133, 139
androgyny 2, 13, 37, 59, 94–95, 169, 240n10
angel in the House 6, 149, 171
Angeloglou, Maggie 79
Angustias 31, 45, 182–83, 203, 229; and class 194, 197; and empowerment 193, 196, 198; and Güitlacoche 194; and lack of authority 199; and Manuel 201–02, 247n12; and nationalism 193, 198, 202; and passing 195, 198; and racism 195, 199–201; clothing of 45, 193–201; masculinity of 192, 194, 197, 199–200; race of 183, 193, 195–98, 247n13; sexuality of 195–96, 199–201
animalization 81–84, 99, 165, 230
appellations 73–74, 153, 230; of Diadorim 94, 96–97, 100–01; of Doña Bárbara 85, 89, 91, 93; of Pintada 78, 82, 84. *See also* nickname
Araújo, Antônio Amaury Correia de 62, 166–67
Arce, B. Christine 2, 4, 9–10, 12–13, 16, 40, 43, 45, 78, 80, 117, 119, 148, 191, 193, 196, 199–200, 236, 240n13, 247n13
Aristotle 74
Asociación de mujeres ante la problemática nacional (AMPRONAC) 215
Asociación nicaragüense de trans (ANIT) 223
assemblage (concept of) 20
Associação brasileira de homens trans (ABHT) 222
Associação nacional de travestis e transexuais (ANTRA) 222
attire 12, 33, 109, 230; as second skin 30, 34–35, 49, 70; of Angustias 192, 194–201, 247n12; of cangaceiras 62–63, 167; of Ci 210; of Diadorim 33, 58–70, 135, 140; of Doña Bárbara 24, 33, 39, 50–58, 70, 232; of Pintada 33, 36, 38–45, 47–50, 70, 195, 212, 230. *See also* sartorial transgressions

285

Index

authority 109; of Angustias 197, 199, 201; of Camila 148, 150; of Doña Bárbara 86, 90, 123–24; of Marisela 156, 159; of Pedro/Petra Ruiz 187; of Pintada 78, 112, 117
autonomy 25, 35, 108, 119, 142, 171, 179, 213; of Camila 150; of Diadorim 168; of Doña Bárbara 160, 179; of Maria Moura 89, 126; of Marisela 158, 203; of Nacha 190–91; of Petra/Pedro Ruiz 187; of Pintada 48, 113
Avechuco Cabrera, Daniel 191
Ávila, Simone 28, 222
Azuela, Mariano 4, 23, 40, 79, 81–82, 150–51, 185, 233, 236, 241n28, 246n6

Babb, Florence E. 223
Backlands (of Brazil) 24, 29, 62–64, 88, 98, 100, 111, 132–33, 136–38, 142, 166–68, 170–72, 231–32, 241n31
backward 11, 13, 50, 71, 85, 127, 241n30
Baker, Pascale 2, 12–13, 40, 81, 113, 117, 121, 148, 246n4
Balbino 51, 54, 91, 124–26
Balderston, Daniel 14, 64–65, 67, 169, 173–74, 243n13
Balzán, Andrea 29
Balzer, Carsten/Carla LaGata 7, 239n5
barbarous (*Doña Bárbara*) 2, 24, 50, 85–88, 90, 92–93, 127–28, 130–31, 160, 162, 164–65
Barbas Rhoden, Pedro 216
Barragán, Juana Guadalupe 181
Barreto, Bruno 248n19
Barrueto, Jorge J. 50, 162
Barthes, Roland 30, 34, 39, 55, 57
Bassanezi, Carla 28, 241n32

beauty 53, 82, 89, 153–54, 163, 178–79, 212; in Porfiriato 79–80; of Angustias 196–97, 200–01; of Cervantes's fiancée 153–54; of Diadorim 61, 64, 68, 100; of Doña Bárbara 51–52, 54, 91, 125, 127–28, 130, 159–61, 163; of Marisela 159–61, 163; of Petra/Pedro Ruiz 186
bedbug 77, 82, 84
Belli, Gioconda 17, 216–17, 219,
Benevides, Bruna G. 239n5
Bento, Berenice 20, 240n20
Bergmann, Emilie 14
Berredo, Lukas 7, 239n5
Besse, Susan K. 27
Bezerra de Meneses, Adélia 67
biological sex 5, 33–34, 58, 60, 65, 67, 70–71, 137, 146, 177
Biron, Rebecca E. 15, 105
Black ancestry 41, 128
Blasi, Alberto 89, 92–93
blonde bandit 212–13
Boullosa, Carmen 65, 245n17
bourgeoisie control 71, 231–32
Bradley, D. 116, 152
Brazil 129, 241n26, 244n5, 145n13, 247n17; cangaço in 61–64, 166–68, 239n9; LGBTQAI+ movement 32, 223, 240n19, 240–41n20; literature of 16, 69, 84, 88, 202, 243n10, 246–47n2, 248n18; Northeast 61, 134; revolutionary movements 3, 31, 183–84, 204–05, 209–14, 216, 220, 222–23, 248n18; trans people's murders 6–7, 37–38; trans people's history and rights 222, 224; women's history and rights 8, 25–29, 181. *See also* Backlands
Brownmiller, Susan 146
Bustamante, Nao 43

Index

butch 9, 45, 51, 54, 56–57, 70, 89–90, 128, 131, 186, 196
Butler, Judith 5, 14, 18–19, 30, 34–35, 54, 61, 69, 75–77, 84, 95, 241n22, 243n2, 243–44n3

Cabezas, Omar 216, 219
cacica 13, 24, 51, 53, 56, 70, 85, 87–90, 92, 102–03, 111, 122–23, 126, 130–32, 157, 161, 164–65, 188, 230, 232, 236
cacique 3, 13, 23, 51, 70, 86, 89, 103, 122–24, 130, 164–65. *See also* cacica
Câmara, Yls Rabelo 62, 166
Camila 23, 26, 40, 47, 49, 81, 121, 147–56, 165, 242n5; as camp follower 83, 148, 150, 156; and Pintada 40–41, 49, 80–81, 119–21, 147–52, 154–57, 179–80; appearance and racism 154; as an object 154, 231. *See also* authority; autonomy
camp follower 4, 8–10, 116, 159–151, 156, 193, 224, 232; and cook 9, 11, 214; and Gertrudis 151; and Pintada 83, 113, 116; Camila as 148, 150, 156
Campobello, Nelli 17, 31, 182, 185, 188, 190–91, 204
Campos, Augusto de 94–95
Cândido, Antonio 12, 94–95, 132, 175
Canelones, Rosa 181
cangaceira 8, 61–63, 166–68, 239n9; attire 62–63, 167; participation in fights 166–67
cangaceirxs 61–63. *See also* cangaceira
Cano, Gabriela 3, 10, 45–46, 82, 110

capanga 88, 126, 132
Carballo, Emmanuel 191
Carmelito 122, 125, 165
Carvalho, Luiz Maklouf 211, 213
Casasola, Gustavo 44, 47
Castillo, Debra 189, 240n18
castration 24, 54, 122, 131, 138, 140, 160–61, 244n4
Castro, Fidel 184, 205–06, 208, 217, 221
Cavallaro, Dani 38, 49
Centro nacional de educación sexual (CENESEX) 221–22
Cervantes's fiancée 47, 82, 115, 147, 150–51, 153–55, 179
Charlebois, Justin 146
charro 45, 194; black charro 198–99, 247n11; suit 45, 195, 197–201. *See also* attire of Angustias
Chinchilla, Norma Stoltz 215
Chu, Andrea Long 18–19
Ci (*Macunaíma*) 209–11, 213
Cirlot, Juan Eduardo 244n2
cisgenderism 46, 110
civilization (and barbarity/savagery) 13, 50, 85, 87–88, 93, 107–08, 127–28, 162
Claire Fleurcy (*Duerme*) 65–66, 229
class 70, 77, 105, 109, 143–44, 146, 180, 184, 222, 229, 231–33; and clothing 34–36, 39, 43, 61, 66; and gender 25–28, 52, 70, 77, 108, 142; and masculinity 105, 142–43; and names 75, 94, 97, 100, 102; and race 13, 30, 52, 61, 70, 75, 77, 142; in *Doña Bárbara* 52, 55, 57, 74, 86, 89, 126, 128, 130, 159–60, 163–65, 233, 236; in *Grande sertão: veredas* 68, 70, 94, 97, 100, 172, 174, 176, 178, 236; in *La mujer habitada* 217–19; in *La negra*

287

Index

Angustias 183, 193–95, 197–98, 200–01; in *Los de abajo* 33, 38, 40–44, 48–49, 113, 116, 154, 197 230, 233, 236; in *Memorial de Maria Moura* 88; in *O quinze* 108; mobility 26, 43, 113, 143, 196, 200, 202, 232
classism 20, 42, 48, 58, 90, 148, 154–56, 180, 193–94, 197, 200–01, 230, 233, 235
clothing. *See* attire
Codorniz 81–82
Codorniz's girl 147, 150–51, 153, 179, 246n3
Coletivo nacional de transexuais (CNT) 222
Collins, Patricia Hill 201
colorism 163, 196, 233, 235, 245n11
combat 5–9, 11–12, 58, 70, 98, 106–07, 109, 140, 145, 168, 183, 187, 191, 202, 206; armed
combat 1, 14, 16, 102, 107, 109, 132, 217, 224; gender inequalities in 208, 216, 226; hand-to-hand combat 138, 140; participation in 4, 6–8, 58, 70, 109, 166, 172, 181, 183, 206–08, 214–16, 220, 226–27, 234; skills in 58, 98, 140, 166, 202, 207, 216
combatant. *See* combat; fight
competition 31, 38, 106, 111, 113, 118, 134, 139, 147, 152–53, 182, 229, 231
Connell, Raewyn 6, 14–15, 21–22, 36, 156,
controlling images 201
Conway, Christopher 198–99
Cooke, Miriam 7, 246n1
Corisco 62, 167–68
Corneja, Teresa 109, 181

corpse 24–25, 58, 60, 66–70, 99, 140–41, 177, 245n17
corrido 9–10, 119, 184, 189–91, 246n2
corruption 2, 13, 48, 80, 82, 90, 117, 149–50, 155, 160, 192, 225
Cortés, Jason 15, 105, 107
cosmetics 79–80, 244n4
courage 109, 113–15, 117, 120–21, 132–33, 135–36, 138, 167, 172, 178, 202, 209, 211, 244n10
Crenshaw, Kimberlé 20
cross-dressing 2, 10, 15, 28, 36–40, 45, 48, 53, 56, 59, 61, 66, 71, 109, 135, 143, 168, 182, 185–86, 188, 195, 202, 234–35, 242n33, 246n2
Cuba 28, 32, 205; LGBTQAI+ rights 220–22
Cuban Revolution 12, 31, 184, 204–06, 226, 248n21, 248n26; and women guerrillas 183, 205–09; inequality in the 204–05, 207–09, 211–12, 214, 216–17, 220
cucaracha 40, 80, 119, 185, 189, 240n12
cuíerlombismo 240–41n20
cuir 20
Currea-Lugo, Víctor de 218

Dadá (Sérgia Ribeiro da Silva) 62, 166–68
dagger 2, 62–63, 111, 121–22, 138, 140, 142, 167, 210, 244n2
dandy, technique of 36, 39, 55, 57, 62, 71, 194–95
Dantas, Francisco J. C. 63, 246n9
De Pauw, Linda Grant 239n10
dehumanization 81–84, 102, 165
Demetrio Macías 13, 23, 47, 49,

Index

79–84, 113–15, 119–21,
  149–50, 152–57, 179,
  242n5, 246n4
Demetrio's wife 80, 147–48, 153
Deodorina 95–96, 98–99, 103,
  244n7
Derrida, Jacques 116, 244–45n4
Dever, Susan 190, 203
devil 58–59, 65, 77, 82–84,
  94–95, 102, 160–61, 199
Diadorim 1–3, 5–7, 13–14, 18,
  21–22, 24–25, 28, 33,
  37–40, 71, 109, 143–44,
  147, 188, 192–95, 203,
  229–33, 235, 242n9,
  243n13, 244n9, 245n14,
  246n9; and clothing 58–70;
  and Riobaldo 168–80; as
  best warrior 111, 132–33,
  236; assertion of masculinity
  134–40; heroism 141–42;
  pronouns 64, 67. *See also*
  name; nickname
Dias, José Umberto 166
Díaz Marcos, Ana María 34
Díaz, Arlene J. 25–27, 90
discrimination 16, 137, 154–55,
  180, 183–84, 200, 221, 235
disempowerment 2–4, 6, 30–31,
  47, 50, 73–74, 76, 85,
  92, 99, 103, 111–12, 116,
  119–21, 125, 140–43, 158,
  160, 162, 188, 193–94, 198,
  201, 230, 232–33, 235–36,
  241n22, 244n4
diversity 1, 3, 6–7, 21, 32–33, 37,
  61, 106, 112, 122, 129, 132,
  141–42, 164–65, 175, 178,
  218, 223, 229, 233–34, 236
Dixon, Paul B. 14
Domínguez-Ruvalcaba, Héctor
  15, 17, 20–23, 36, 59, 65,
  107–09, 133, 139, 223,
  242n8
Doña Bárbara 1–4, 7, 13, 18,
  21–22, 24, 27, 33, 36–37,

39–40, 50–58, 70–71, 74,
  85–94, 99, 101–03, 108,
  111, 121–33, 135, 137,
  141–44, 147, 156–65,
  179–80, 182–83, 188,
  192–93, 196–97, 203, 210,
  229–33, 235–36, 245n7,
  245n9; and Marisela 24, 57,
  126, 130–31, 147, 156–65,
  179–80, 231; and Santos
  24, 50–51, 54–57, 86–87,
  90–93, 102–03, 122, 126,
  127–28, 130–32, 143,
  156–59, 161–65, 245n12;
  at the rodeo 54–57, 161;
  demystification of 85–86,
  89, 92–93. *See also* Amazon;
  attire; name; nickname
Donoso, José 15, 143
donzela guerreira 2, 10–12, 59
drag 37, 61; drag king 61, 198
dressing. *See* attire
Dromundo, Baltasar 185
Dudink, Stefan 31, 106

Eakin, Marshall 27
Ejército de liberación nacional
  (ELN) 225
Eltit, Diamela 46–47
emphasized femininity see
  femininity
empowerment 1–4, 7–9, 12–13,
  26, 30, 32, 38, 73, 84, 88,
  99, 103, 112–13, 118, 131,
  140, 142, 144, 146, 153,
  165, 180, 182–83, 211–12,
  227, 229–30, 234–36,
  241n22, 245n9; of Angustias
  183, 193, 196, 199–201; of
  Diadorim 33, 38, 65, 94,
  96, 140, 168, 177, 236; of
  Doña Bárbara 13, 51, 58,
  74, 87–88, 93–94, 125, 131,
  179, 188, 231, 233, 236; of
  Maria Moura 88–89, 126; of
  Pintada 26, 48, 74, 80–81,

289

Index

111–15, 117–21, 148, 150, 155–56, 188, 231–33, 236; self-empowerment 2, 26, 87–88, 94, 119, 150, 165, 196, 227, 231, 233, 245n16; strategies of 2, 7, 13, 30, 32, 38, 51, 71, 76, 109, 111, 113–15, 117, 182, 234–35
Entwistle, Joanne 30, 34, 53, 70
eponym 76, 95, 97, 100
Eraúso, Catalina de 1, 239n1
Espín, Vilma 206
Esplin, Emron 188
Esquivel, Laura 151, 185
estória 76
Estrada, Oswaldo 2, 9, 16, 40, 78, 186, 192–93
ethics 15, 82, 120, 133, 186, 188, 192, 204, 225
ethnicity 13, 30, 34–35, 74, 76, 105, 128–30, 142–44, 162–65, 193, 229, 231–33, 236, 246n7
evil 11, 13, 22, 40, 49, 64–65, 71, 85, 92–93, 119–20, 155, 157, 161, 199
exchange of women 84, 100, 146–49, 153, 155–56, 176, 179–180, 230–31, 246n1
explanation (of transgressions) 70–71, 73, 96–97, 99, 103, 127, 168, 188, 230, 233

Fabio (*Don Segundo* Sombra) 107–08
fashion theory 30, 33–35, 41, 49, 50, 242n1
Federación de mujeres cubanas (FMC) 221
Félix, María 185, 204, 247n4
female masculinity 14, 21, 36, 112, 122, 164–65, 218, 239n2
feminicide 13
femininity 9, 11–12, 15, 26–27, 31, 33, 35–37, 40, 44–45, 60–62, 73, 77, 80, 84, 108–09, 119, 142, 144, 145–47, 150, 153, 155–156, 167, 169–72, 177, 179, 180, 182–83, 186, 188–90, 195, 202–04, 206, 212, 226, 229–231, 237, 247n12; and Diadorim 61, 64, 67, 94–95, 100–01, 133–35, 138–40, 168–69, 174, 176–77, 231; and Doña Bárbara 50–59, 85, 89–91, 123, 157–61, 163, 165, 245n12; and masculinities 21–22, 35–37, 44, 47, 50, 52, 53–55, 59, 73, 94–95, 100–01, 109, 114, 133–35, 138, 142, 177, 183, 245n12; and Pintada 41–42, 44, 47–49, 77, 80, 84, 112–14, 147–48, 151, 155; as accomplice femininities 145, 159, 231; as emphasized femininity 6, 26, 153, 156, 161, 170, 174, 179, 190, 226, 229; feminine roles 2, 85, 123, 148, 150
fight 2–3, 5–10, 12–14, 16, 25–26, 41, 51, 58–59, 61, 64–66, 78, 81–82, 98, 106, 109, 111, 115, 119–21, 132–33, 137–43, 151, 155, 157, 166–67, 172, 181, 183–84, 186, 188–90, 192, 199–200, 202–04, 206–09, 211–13, 215–17, 220, 226–27, 229, 239n4, 241n28, 244n2, 245n6, 246n9, 248n21. *See also* combat; Diadorim and best warrior
Filho, Ormindo Pires 59
Fitz, Earl E. 2, 29, 245n15
Foster, David William 14, 241n20
Foucault, Michel 71, 243n2
Franco, Adolfo 1
Franco, Jean 2
Freitas, Ana Paula Saraiva de 166–67

290

Index

Frente Sandinista para la liberación nacional (FSLN) 214, 216, 223
Fuerzas armadas revolucionarias de Colombia (FARC) 225

Gabeira, Fernando 184, 211–12, 219
Galaos, José Antonio 85
Gallegos Ortiz, Rafael 27
Gallegos, Rómulo 4, 24, 50–51, 85, 93, 128, 164–65, 241n30, 242n6
galleta 240n12
Galvão, Walnice Nogueira 2, 10–11, 59, 242n9
gang rape 13, 87, 90, 123, 125, 158–61, 245n7
Garber, Marjorie 13, 34, 36, 53, 61, 242n2
garment. *See* attire
Garro, Elena 119
Gaucho 108
gay 15–16, 22, 35, 37, 64–65, 69, 97, 105, 112, 133–35, 137, 174, 221–23, 241n26, 242n8; anxieties about being 64–65, 242n8
gaze 56–57, 160, 186, 196
Geczy, Adam 34–35
gender 1–3, 12, 14, 17–19, 21–22, 32, 33, 36–37, 39–40, 46, 49–50, 52, 58–60, 67–69, 71, 74–75, 89, 94–95, 97, 101–03, 105, 107, 109–10, 113–14, 118, 120–21, 127–28, 132–33, 135–36, 142, 146, 169, 183–84, 187, 195, 199, 201, 205, 207–09, 212–13, 216, 218–19, 221–22, 224, 231, 234, 236–37, 239n8, 239–40n10, 241n27, 245n17, 247n7, 247n9, 248n22; and clothing 28, 30, 33–36, 55, 60, 70, 188, 195, 230; and misgender 66, 70; equality and equity 59, 127, 183, 204, 207–08, 214, 216, 220, 226, 242n4; fluidity 11, 56, 96, 177, 243n11; identity 1, 3–4, 6, 12, 18–19, 29, 38, 46–47, 60, 65, 74, 96, 110, 126, 135, 137, 147, 172, 178, 185–86, 205, 217, 233–34, 236–37, 241n21; intersection with 1, 13, 33, 35, 47, 70, 74, 77, 109, 137, 162–65, 179, 183, 194–95, 197, 201, 204, 220, 229, 231–33, 236; performance 2–3, 6, 16, 18–20, 22, 25, 33, 37, 39, 45, 51, 54, 58–60, 67, 70–71, 73–74, 78, 84, 94, 96, 99, 101, 103, 109–10, 112, 133, 136, 146, 165, 168, 171, 177–78, 182–83, 192, 201–02, 219, 227, 229, 234, 239–40n10, 245n12; performance theory 5, 18–20, 69; roles 26, 51, 54, 58–59, 63, 68, 76, 93, 107, 134, 151, 154–56, 189, 206; subversion 40, 51, 110, 123, 125; traditional rules of 2–4, 6–7, 9, 11–13, 16–17, 22, 25–26, 28, 30–31, 34–39, 46, 48, 52–53, 55–56, 58–60, 65, 68–71, 76–77, 79, 85, 87, 90–91, 95, 101, 103, 107, 110, 112–13, 120–21, 125, 127–28, 134–35, 144, 147, 179, 183, 189–90, 192, 198, 210, 212, 217–18, 223, 229–33, 236, 240n15; transgression 4, 11–13, 17, 28, 30, 48, 58, 63, 68, 127–28, 143, 156–57, 185, 187, 193–95, 197, 213, 230, 232, 235, 240n15. *See also* race and gender

Index

genitalia 1, 24, 34, 65–67, 69, 96, 99, 141, 145, 168, 174–76, 178, 240n11
Gertrudis (*Como agua para chocolate*) 151
Gilbert, Sandra 161
Gómez, Juan Vicente 27, 85, 241n30
González Echevarría, Roberto 2, 50
González, Alfonso 86
gossip 119, 191
Green, James 28, 222, 242n33
Griffin, Clive 2, 49, 112, 116–18, 149
Grupo inicio 223
Gubar, Susan 161
guerrilla 17, 31, 183, 185, 200, 204–20, 224–27, 234, 248n18, 248n22, 248n28; guerrilla warfare 3, 12, 204–05, 209, 213–215
Guevara, Ernesto 184, 205–06, 215–16, 219
Güiraldes, Ricardo 107
Gutmann, Matthew C. 105
Guy, Donna 14
Guzmán, Martín Luis 108, 184

Hagemann, Karen 31, 106
Hahner, June E. 26–28
Halberstam, Jack 6, 14, 18–19, 21, 30, 38–39, 61, 63, 102, 239n2, 243n11
Harris, Chris 121, 156
hate speech 76
hatred 122–23, 160–61
Henighan, Stephen 50–51, 57, 89, 126, 157, 245n12
Hermógenes 24, 98, 140, 176
Hermógenes's wife 166, 176–77
Hernández, Adela 222
Hernández Cuevas, Marco Polo 199
hero 3, 7, 13, 21–23, 32, 79, 82, 90, 98–99, 101, 106–09, 111, 132, 140–43, 190–91, 194, 196, 204, 213, 219–20, 224–25, 235–36, 246n1
heterocisnormativity 6, 18, 34–35, 60, 65, 67–69, 99, 110, 146, 173, 175–78, 187, 218
heterocispatriarchy 4, 8, 11, 74–76, 78, 80–81, 83–84, 86–87, 89–94, 98, 100, 106, 112, 117, 128, 146–49, 153, 158, 171–72, 174, 176, 180, 182–83, 218, 230–31, 233
heteronormativity 18, 33, 35, 99, 107, 110, 173, 178, 192–93, 225, 242n8
heteropatriarchy 11, 68, 70, 136, 170, 190
heterosexism 99, 110. *See also* sexism
Hind, Emily 16–17, 236
Hollywood 5, 213, 239n4, 241n32
homoeroticism 60, 65, 67, 97, 105, 112, 136
homophobia 16, 20, 22, 64–65, 136–37, 173–75, 178, 180, 184, 218, 221–22
homosexuality 15, 24, 64–65, 110, 134–35, 139, 170–72, 175–76, 178, 186, 220–223, 241n26;
fear of homosexuality 31, 53, 64, 94, 172–73, 175, 178, 186. *See also* gay
homosociality 15, 31, 84, 112, 152, 156, 180, 216, 231
Horn, Maja 105
Horne, John 31, 106
Hortência 166, 171–72
hypervirility 234

identity politics 6, 15, 20, 39, 243n11
ideology 9, 26, 35–36, 50, 71, 86, 92, 94, 106, 108, 128, 130, 155, 157, 163–65, 189, 190,

Index

202, 208, 221, 242n6
imperialism 116, 125, 221
indigenous 41, 43, 47, 49, 53,
  66, 71, 84, 86–87, 90, 124,
  129–31, 149, 154, 158,
  163–64, 179, 182–83, 193,
  196, 209, 217, 230, 235–36,
  242n3, 247n8
information (control of) 41,
  112–13, 115–117, 142, 155
insult 76–77, 82, 85, 100–02, 112,
  119, 134, 136–38
intellectual nations (concept of) 23
intellectual region 23, 107
interchangeability (in literature)
  95, 101
interpellation 30, 35, 71, 77,
  84–85, 102
intersectionality 2, 5, 13, 20–22,
  36, 40, 61, 105, 128, 142,
  148, 154, 162–65, 183–84,
  193–95, 199, 201, 229, 232,
  236–37, 241n24. *See also*
  class; ethnicity; gender; race
Irigaray, Luce 31, 145
Irwin, Robert McKee 15, 105, 112,
  152
Isabel (*Por debajo del agua*) 178
Islas, Carlos 185
Itzá 217, 229

jagunço 7, 24, 39, 58–59, 61, 64,
  68, 70, 96–101, 107–08,
  111, 132–33, 136–39,
  141–43, 166, 168–72, 174,
  232, 245n14
Jesusa 8–9, 168
João Goanhá (*Grande sertão:
  veredas*) 139
Joca Ramiro 97, 137, 173, 245n14
Johnson, Maria Amália 68
Johnson, Mark 242n2
Johnson, Randal 209–10
Jones, David E. 3, 52, 239n8,
  242n7
Juana Gallo 185, 189, 204

Kaiser, Susan B. 6, 36, 242n1
Kampwirth, Karen 215, 223
Kanost, Laura 195–96
Karaminas, Vicki 34–35
Katz, Friedrich 190
kinship 9–10, 31, 75, 80, 83,
  87, 100, 142, 146, 149,
  153, 158, 161–62, 176,
  244–45n4
Kirk, Emily J. 221–22, 248n26
knife 2–3, 111, 121, 123, 134–
  136, 138, 140, 142, 161–62,
  185, 199, 244n2
Kripke, Saul 74–75
kuir 20

Lacan, Jacques 75, 243n2,
  244–45n4
Lampião (Virgulino Ferreira da
  Silva) 61–63, 166–68
Landeta, Matilde 203–04
Latham, J.R. 18–19
Latin America 1, 4, 6–8, 10–11,
  13–17, 19–23, 26, 28–29,
  34, 36, 65, 70, 85–86, 110,
  125, 128, 133, 143, 145–47,
  180, 181, 183–84, 196, 203,
  204–05, 206, 212, 216,
  219–20, 225–27, 232–37,
  240–41n20, 241n26,
  245n11; and trans* rights in
  223–24; literature in 4–5,
  7, 11–12, 14–17, 20, 24,
  29–30, 32, 69, 73, 77, 84,
  107–08, 112, 144, 203, 205,
  229, 231, 235–36, 240n19,
  241n27; masculinities in
  105, 107–08, 110, 143;
  regionalism in 19, 242n34;
  queer theory in 14, 16–17,
  20, 36, 105, 240n19,
  240–41n20
Lavinia 217–19
Lavou Zoungbo, Victorien 50, 86,
  124, 160, 162, 242n6
Law of the Father 75

293

Index

leader 3, 9, 11, 13, 24, 40–41, 59, 66, 68, 80, 86, 88, 93, 96–99, 108, 115–16, 118, 120, 126, 132, 137, 139–42, 149, 156, 167, 169, 171, 180, 181, 194, 202, 206–08, 216–17, 220, 224, 232, 239n8, 245n14
leadership 2–3, 9, 28, 62, 112–13, 117–18, 120, 122, 168, 180, 192, 199, 221, 229–30, 234
Leavitt, Sturgis E. 50, 93
Lefebvre, Henri 57, 67
León Ortiz, Iván 29
Lerner, Gerda 246n2
Lévi-Strauss, Claude 30, 74–75, 146, 246n1
LGBTQAI+ community 4, 14, 20, 29, 32, 65, 184, 220, 222–24, 226; LGBTQAI+ activism 205, 222–23, 234, 239n6
Lima, Caroline de Araújo 168
Linhard, Tabea Alexa 192
llanero 7, 51–57, 70, 90, 94, 102, 107–08, 111, 122, 124, 126–27, 131, 133, 138, 141–42, 156, 232, 246n8; llanera 51, 86, 164
love 25, 57, 60, 64–68, 76, 80, 96, 106, 127, 130, 136, 152, 157, 159, 162, 169–79, 188, 190, 201, 203, 247n12
lover 8, 10, 23, 40–41, 45, 47, 49, 51, 54, 80–81, 118, 124–27, 131, 148–51, 154–56
Lucía (*Hasta no verte, Jesús mío*) 9
Luis Cervantes 43, 47, 82–83, 114, 116, 120, 148–50, 152–55, 179

Mac Adam, Alfred 14, 58–59
Machado de Assis, Joaquim Maria 243n10
Machado, Ana Maria 76, 86, 97, 100–01, 244n8

machismo 13, 15, 22, 64, 109, 127, 133, 137, 139, 143, 171, 179, 184, 206
machorra 9. *See also* butch; mannish; marimacho
Macías, Anna 25–26, 192
Magnarelli, Sharon 50, 87, 90, 126–27, 157–58, 245n10
Malinche (Malintzi) 149, 246n5
manipulation 13, 27, 55–57, 67, 71, 97, 112–13, 115–16, 120–21, 124, 136, 138, 141–42, 189, 191, 220, 226, 229–30
mannish 52–54, 56–57, 70, 89–91, 93, 102, 157
Manteca 81–82, 153
Márcia. *See* Vera/Márcia
Marentes, Luis 184
Mares, Encarnación (Chonita) 247n5
María (*Al filo del agua*) 119
Maria Bonita 167
Maria da Fé 141, 202–03, 229, 245n17
Maria Deodorina da Fé Bettancourt Marins. *See* Deodorina
Maria Melona (*Os desvalidos*) 63
Maria Moura 88–89, 126, 229, 244n1
Maria-da-Luz 166, 171
Mariana Grajales platoon 207–08, 217
marianismo 145, 148, 165, 173, 180
marimacho 56, 89, 127–28
Marisela 24, 126, 130–31, 158–65, 179–80, 203, 231, 246n8. *See also* Doña Bárbara and Marisela
marriage 25–26, 62, 87–88, 119, 129, 151–53, 155, 161, 164–65, 169, 172, 175, 190, 213
Martí, José 162

Index

masculinity 3, 6, 15–16, 21, 31, 35–36, 38, 45, 53, 56, 59, 64, 68, 93, 100, 107, 109–10, 112, 122, 127, 131, 133, 137–38, 142, 158, 172, 180, 183, 192, 195, 197, 204, 218, 229, 237, 239n4, 242n8, 248n23; and age 39, 136–38, 234; and clothing 61, 65, 200; and heterosexuality 101, 135–36, 139, 174, 232; and nationalism 106–07; and sexuality 211; as fluid 21, 110, 112; as hegemonic 21–22, 52, 143, 156, 239n3; assertion of 133, 135, 137–40; hierarchies of 125, 127; ideal of 52, 126, 130–31, 143; performance of 11–12, 18, 39, 59–61, 70, 74 , 95, 101–02, 105–06, 108, 111–12, 118, 120, 122–25, 127–28, 131–32, 134, 164, 177, 179–80, 183, 230; plurality of 122, 125–26, 131–32, 143, 165, 219; studies 2, 5, 105–07, 110; subordinated 110, 125; theory 14, 20–21, 30; traditional masculinity 46–47, 83, 94, 100, 105, 132, 136, 138, 142, 199, 219, 235, 242n8; trans* masculinity 6, 21, 45, 105, 110, 137. *See also* female masculinity; femininities
masculinization 3, 30, 38, 44, 88, 156, 185, 190, 202, 205, 208, 234
maternity 122–23, 148, 161–62, 207; hatred of 122–23, 161–62
McCard, Victoria 191
McGee, Marcus J. 223
McQueen, Paddy 105

Meco 81–84, 153
Medeiro Vaz 139, 169, 245n14
media 7, 181, 183, 212–14, 220, 225–26, 246n1
Melquíades 124–26, 159
men authors/writers 16–17, 107, 178, 183–84, 233, 236
Mendieta Alatorre, Ángeles 185–87, 247n5
menino 96–98, 101–02, 134, 136
meretrixes 170. *See also* sex work
Merrim, Stephanie 95, 101,
Messerschmidt, James W. 156
mestiçagem. *See* miscegenation
mestiza/o 13, 41, 43, 45, 47, 49, 53, 58, 74, 89–90, 108, 122, 128–231, 154, 156–57, 161–65, 183, 193, 196–97, 199, 203, 230, 236, 242n3, 247n8
mestizaje. *See* miscegenation; mestiza/o
Mexican Revolution 3, 9, 10, 12–13, 23–26, 29, 40–47, 70, 78–84, 102, 108–110, 112, 114–117, 119, 142, 148, 150–51, 153, 155–56, 168, 178, 182–94, 198, 204, 208, 214–15, 220, 226–27, 231–32, 240n12, 241n28, 245n5–6
Mexico 1, 7–9, 21, 23, 43, 45, 107–08, 111, 149, 181, 194, 204; and Afro-descendants 41, 43, 45, 47, 49, 154, 201–04, 193–96, 199, 242n3; and cosmetics 79–80; during the Revolution 7–9, 40, 81, 84, 109, 149, 190, 208, 216; gender dynamics in 25–26, 151, 212, 226, 230–31, 235; human rights in 6, 13, 29
Miguel-Pereira, Lúcia 29
Mijares, Augusto 27
Mill, John Stuart 243n1

295

Index

Miller, Francesca 27
Miosótis 166, 171
miscegenation (mestiçagem/
  mestizaje) 129–30, 247n8
misogynoirism 31, 193–95, 197–
  98, 200–01, 203, 247n7
Mister Danger 124–25, 158
Mitchell, Jasmine 247n9
modernization 24, 134, 163,
  241n30
Molina Sevilla de Morelock, Ela
  190
Molloy, Sylvia 15, 30, 39, 42, 56,
  105, 135, 234
Mondragones brothers 86
Monsiváis, Carlos 13, 79, 81
Morínigo, Mariano 85
most-desired position 2, 22, 31,
  39, 54, 103, 107, 110–11,
  115, 117–18, 120–23, 126,
  130, 132–33, 135, 137, 139,
  142–44, 146, 167, 177, 180,
  188, 191–92, 194, 219, 224,
  226–27, 229–32, 235
mujerona 51, 89, 92–93, 103, 161
mulatta/o (mulata/o) 134, 136–37,
  193, 196, 199–201, 247n10,
  247n13
Muñoz, Rafael 184
murder 15, 24, 40–41, 45, 49, 69,
  85, 120–21, 125–26, 130,
  140–41, 156, 158, 162, 165,
  173–74, 188–89, 241n28,
  242n9, 245n9; of trans*
  people 6–7, 37, 69, 222

Nacha Ceniceros 182, 188–92,
  204, 229
Nájera-Ramirez, Olga 198
name 24, 30, 73–80, 85, 176,
  182, 218, 229; Diadorim's
  74, 94–103, 180, 244, n7,
  244n9; Doña
  Bárbara's 85–94, 102; family name
  75–76, 82, 88–89, 99–100,
  137, 147; history of 74–75,

243n1; legal name 29, 80–
  81, 87–88, 99, 224; nameless
  102, 150, 153, 155, 176;
  Nhorinhá's 169; Petra/Pedro's
  185–187; Pintada's 78–83,
  84–85, 102; proper nouns as
  74, 81, 88, 95, 99–100. *See
  also* nickname; patronym
Nascimento, Geraldo Maia do 166
Nascimento, Tatiana 240–41n20
national project 3, 23, 107, 164,
  235–36
Neitzel, Adair de Aguiar 2, 136,
  171, 173, 176–77, 245n15
Nery, João W. 222
Nhorinhá 169–70, 172, 175
Nicaragua 12, 28, 184, 204–
  205, 214–20, 223, 226;
  LGBTQAI+ Community
  32, 223. *See also* Sandinista
  Revolution
nickname 30, 73–74, 76,
  81–82, 102–03, 153;
  and disempowerment 74,
  77–78, 81, 95, 102, 230;
  as negative 80, 82, 93, 102,
  230; Diadorim's 74, 94–103,
  244n7; Doña Bárbara's 74,
  85–94, 102; Pintada's 74,
  78–85, 102
nobody 4, 9, 11, 43, 45, 80–81,
  113, 118
Nogueira, Sayonara Naider
  Bomfim 239n5
Nunes, Benedito 136, 175
Núñez Noriega, Guillermo 105

objectification 11, 49, 153, 170,
  176–77, 196, 203, 218,
  240n12
Oliveira, Emanuelle K. F. 164
Olivieri, Rita 2, 245n15
Organización de personas
  transgénero de Nicaragua
  (ODETRANS) 223
orphan 13, 53, 58, 64–65, 86, 88,

Index

108, 156, 190
Osorio, Nelson 85
Otacília 147, 166, 172, 180; feminine fiancée 172–76

Pancracio 84, 113–14
Parra, Max 78, 118, 244n3
Partido institucional revolucionario (PRI) 190
passing (gender) 4, 25, 30, 36, 38–39, 41–42, 44, 64, 139, 186, 195, 198, 200, 235; Halberstam's definition of 38–39, 63–64, 110, 135
Patai, Daphne 240n17
patriarchy 3, 6–7, 12, 17, 22, 31, 33, 47, 49–50, 53, 58, 59, 68–69, 110–11, 121, 123–24, 128, 130–31, 134–35, 138, 140, 142, 144, 145, 150–51, 153, 158–60, 165, 177, 193, 201, 210, 220, 226, 231, 246n2. *See also* heterocispatriarchy; heteropatriarchy
patronym 75–76, 80–82, 87–88, 97, 100. *See also* name
Payne, Judith 2, 245n15
Paz, Octavio 133, 235, 241n27, 246n5
Peirce, C.S. 243n1
performativity 18, 30, 42, 54, 193, 195, 218, 241n2
Petra/Pedro Ruiz 31, 109, 182, 185–87
Pierce, Joseph 223
Pintada 1–4, 7, 12–13, 18, 21–24, 26, 37, 71, 87, 108, 111, 131, 135, 137, 142–43, 159, 162, 182–83, 185, 203, 227, 229, 231–33, 236, 241n29, 242n3, 246n7; attire of 33, 36, 38–45, 47–50, 70, 195, 212, 230; and Angustias 192–93, 195–97; and Camila 147–53, 155–57,

165, 179–80; and Demetrio Macías 113–14, 119, 121, 156–57, 246n4; and Güero Margarito 114–15, 244n3; cultural revolution of 79, 81; dehumanization of 81–84, 99, 102; female masculinity of 112–123; gender performance of 58, 84, 103, 112, 192–93, 235. *See also* name; nickname
Plato 74
Poniatowska, Elena 8–9, 168, 185–87
Porfiriato 79–80, 119
posing 30, 36, 39, 42, 49, 56–57, 70–71, 115, 121, 134–36, 138–39, 141, 143, 186, 202, 235
power 1–3, 5–6, 16–17, 22, 25–27, 32, 33, 43, 51–52, 56–57, 60, 71, 83–86, 89–90, 92–93, 111, 117–128, 130, 139–41, 145–46, 157, 183, 190, 196–98, 201, 203, 205, 210, 223–24, 230–32, 241n24, 244–45n4, 245n10; access to 1–3, 6, 32, 36, 38, 40, 51, 56–57, 70, 84–86, 89, 93–94, 109, 116, 121–23, 135–36, 138, 142, 159, 165, 183, 188, 192–93, 230; in clothing 30, 33, 41, 45, 49, 53, 55, 57, 70, 194–95, 242n2; in naming 73, 76–77, 88–89, 91, 93, 99, 102–03; power dynamics 37, 112, 142, 147, 152, 176; traditional power 3, 6, 33, 46–47, 70, 83, 86, 92, 116, 124, 135, 138, 142–43, 154–55, 159–62, 165, 180, 183, 208, 218, 233, 248n23. *See also* empowerment; disempowerment
Pratt, Mary Louis 164

Index

progress. *See* civilization
pronouns 64, 67, 186, 241n21
Puar, Jasbir 20
Puebla, Teté 206–08
Puig, Manuel 15

queer 14, 16–17, 20, 35–36, 65, 105, 110, 137, 183, 187, 236–37
queer theory 12, 14, 17, 20, 33, 50, 59, 240n19, 240–41n20
Queiroz, Rachel de 88, 108, 126, 244n1
Quintero, Pablo 163
Quiroga, José 19, 31, 242n8
Quitéria de Jesus, Maria 181

race 13, 20, 30, 33–34, 36, 40, 49, 61, 70, 74, 77, 89, 109, 128–29, 137, 142–44, 154, 163–65, 193–95, 197, 199, 201, 229, 232–33, 236, 247n9; and gender 13, 33–34, 36, 40, 47, 50, 61, 70, 74, 77, 109, 127, 137, 142–43, 154, 156, 163–65, 183, 193–95, 197, 199, 201, 204, 220, 230–33, 236, 247n9. *See also* class
racism 20, 37, 42, 48, 58, 128–30, 136, 148, 154–57, 163–65, 180, 193–95, 199–203, 211, 229–30, 232–33
Randall, Margaret 205–07, 214, 216, 219, 247n14
rape 87, 123, 129, 153–55, 165, 168, 172, 187, 202, 210, 246n5. *See also* gang rape
Regionalism 29, 107, 235–36, 242n34
Reinaldo 96–98, 100–01, 133, 244n9
Reséndez Fuentes, Andrés 247n5
revenge 119, 123, 160, 189
revolutionaries 3, 8, 10–11, 23, 44, 47, 66, 80, 82, 115–16, 119, 142, 149–53, 155, 183–85, 192, 205–06, 208, 210, 212, 214, 217, 220, 224–25, 227, 234, 245n17, 247n3, 248n24–25
Ribeiro, João Ubaldo 141, 202
Rielo, Isabel 206–07, 247n16
Riobaldo 14, 24–25, 37, 60–61, 64–69, 74, 94–103, 108, 132–41, 166, 168–80, 245n14, 246n12; and Ana Duzuza 169; as narrator 14, 24, 60, 67–68, 94, 98, 102; heteronormativity 98–99, 101, 168–171, 175–76; homophobia of 64–65, 99, 136, 173–74, 177–78. *See also* Diadorim; Nhorinhá; Otacília
Rios, Cassandra 69
rituals of ideological recognition 35–36, 52, 66–67, 69, 95, 106, 241n23
Robles Ávila, Amelio 10, 45–47, 109–110, 113, 185
Roche, Daniel 34
Rodríguez, Blanca 190
Rodríguez, Ileana 216
Rodríguez, Teodosea 181
Rojas González, Francisco 45, 183, 192–93, 196, 200
"Romance of the Warrior Maiden" 12
Root, Regina A. 30
Rosa, João Guimarães 24, 76, 94, 97, 101, 132, 170, 233, 236, 241n31, 243n10
Rosa'uarda 166, 171–72
Rosegreen-Williams, Claudette 127–28, 159, 161
Rosenfield, Kathrin Holzermayr 100, 135, 138, 169–70, 175, 177
rouge 79
Rousseff, Dilma 213
Rubin, Gayle 31, 146–47

298

Index

Russell, Bertrand 243n1

Salas, Elizabeth 8, 81, 148, 150
Salinas Hernández, Héctor Miguel 240–41n20
Sánchez-Prado, Ignacio M. 23, 191, 235–36, 241n27
Sánchez, Porfirio 116, 245n5
Sandinista Revolution 31, 184, 214–17, 219–20, 243, 248n22, 248n24
Santana, Dora Silva 37
Santos Luzardo 13, 24, 50–51, 54–57, 86–87, 90–93, 103, 108, 122, 124–28, 130–32, 143, 156–65, 179, 245n8–9, 245n12. *See also* Doña Bárbara; Marisela; masculinity ideal of
Santos, Julia Conceição Fonseca 97, 100
Santos, Michele Soares 168
sartorial transgression 30, 33, 35–36, 39–40, 42, 45, 48–50, 52, 55, 58, 61, 70–71, 182, 188, 193-94, 199, 201, 229–30
Sedgwick, Eve Kosofsky 14, 31, 64, 147, 152
Segal, Lynne 35
Sendero luminoso 225
Serano, Julia 6, 38
Serra, Tânia Rebelo Costa 2, 245n15
sex work 1, 8, 12, 25–26, 40, 48, 77, 79–80, 89, 118–19, 151, 166, 169–172, 176, 184, 210, 215, 220–22, 232, 239n6, 246n11–12
sex-correction surgery 6, 28–29, 221–22, 224, 243n11
sexism 13, 16, 20, 46, 58, 110, 148, 154–55, 180, 200, 208, 211, 216, 218, 230, 233, 235
sexual assault. *See* rape

sexuality 9, 11, 54, 58, 75, 90, 112, 155–56, 160, 168–70, 179, 182, 194, 210, 224–25, 231, 234, 237, 240–41n20, 248n26; and gender 14, 32, 58, 112, 186, 209, 212, 222, 231, 236; repression and control of 9, 71, 109, 119, 135, 137, 145, 153, 165, 170, 177, 187, 195–96, 199, 201, 203, 211, 213, 220, 224, 231, 234, 246n2; studies 4–5, 14, 38, 105; use of 80, 90, 125, 135, 155–56, 234
Shaw, Donald L. 51, 57, 91, 93
Shayne, Julie D. 206
Sifuentes-Jáuregui, Ben 15, 22, 30–31, 37, 40, 48, 52–53, 105, 133, 137, 143, 241n27
Sila (Ilda Ribeiro de Souza) 63, 166–67
Silva, Sérgia Ribeiro da. *See* Dadá
Silva, Virgulino Ferreira da. *See* Lampião
Smith, Paul Julian 14
soldadera 4, 7–10, 16, 22, 43–44, 47, 79, 148, 178, 184–85, 191, 193, 226, 232, 240n13, 247n5
soldier 1, 3, 7–10, 24–25, 38, 66, 70, 107, 109, 112, 116, 151, 166–68, 178, 184–85, 189, 206–07, 214, 216–17, 224, 226, 234, 240n13–14, 245n6, 247n5
Sommer, Doris 2, 13, 50, 85, 158, 160, 164–65
Souza, Ilda Ribeiro de. *See* Sila
Spencer, Herbert 41
Spivak, Gayatri 42
Stallybrass, Peter 17
Stevens, Evelyn P. 145
stockings 41–42, 44–45, 47–49, 70, 114, 195, 218
Stout, Noelle M. 221–22

Index

strength 13, 18, 40, 53, 77–78, 91–94, 100, 102, 113, 115, 117, 120, 123–24, 127, 134, 140, 145, 156, 168, 188, 191
Stryker, Susan 59
subaltern 110, 113, 141, 165, 232
subversion 3, 27, 39, 40, 42, 49, 51, 55–58, 77, 86, 88, 110, 123, 125, 131, 135, 137, 203, 206, 210
sword 111, 138, 244n2. *See also* dagger; knife

Téllez, Dora Maria 214–15
Tinoco, Manuela 109, 181
tomboy 14
trans identity 4, 6, 11–12, 19, 28, 33, 37–38, 45–47, 59–60, 63, 65–66, 68–69, 70, 74, 96, 143, 168, 177–78, 182, 184–87, 241n21
trans theory 2, 5, 14, 18–20, 46, 60, 241n24
trans warrior (definition) 2–11; strategies of 30, 32, 38, 71, 76, 139, 142, 182, 226, 299–30, 232-35. *See also* Diadorim; disempowerment; empowerment; Petra/Pedro
trans-ignorance 178–79
trans* masculinities 6, 11–12, 15–16, 21, 36, 39, 45–46, 59–61, 65, 70, 95, 105–06, 109–11, 132-34, 137, 142, 177, 179, 229–30, 232, 235, 237
trans* people in war 3–4, 6, 7–9, 11–12, 21–23, 31–32, 38, 45–46, 58–59, 63, 65–66, 105, 109–10, 132, 178, 181–87, 204–05, 224, 226–27, 229, 231–236
transgender 28, 45, 59, 222–23, 239n6, 243n12
transgenderism 39

transgression 1, 4–8, 11–13, 17–18, 31, 37, 41, 46–47, 50, 59, 71, 73, 77, 88, 99, 101–03, 113, 163, 176, 185, 187, 195, 197–98, 201, 203, 213, 217, 230, 233; definition of 17. *See also* gender transgression; sartorial transgression
transphobia 16, 20, 46, 99, 168, 177–80, 184, 226, 230, 233, 235, 239n6; trans murders 6–7, 69, 140, 222
transsexual 45, 222–24, 239n6, 243n12
travesti 7, 15, 28, 36–38, 40, 56, 69, 135, 137, 184, 221–24, 239n6, 243n12
travestismo 15, 69
triangle (erotic) 31, 147, 152–53, 156–57, 172, 176, 179

underdogs 43, 48, 81, 116, 184
unwriting (Doña Bárbara) 92–93, 99, 143, 159
usurper 38, 92, 131, 159, 218, 248n23

Valcárcel, Javier Lasarte 162
Vallenilla Lanz, Laureano 129
Vanguarda popular revolucionária (VPR) 211, 213
Vargas, Getúlio 28
Vasvári, Louise O. 12, 240n15
Velasco, Sherry 239n1
Venezuela 3, 6–7, 24, 29, 50, 53–54, 85, 111, 122–23, 125, 142–43, 158, 231, 241n30; immigration politics 128–31, 163; trans* rights 29; whitening project 158, 163–64; women's history in 25–27, 90, 181
Venkatesh, Vinodh 15, 17, 21–22, 105, 110, 218, 248n23
Vera/Márcia (*O que é isso,*

300

Index

companheiro?) 211–212
Villa, Pancho 44, 188, 190–91, 204
Vincent, Jon S 98
viper 82–84, 102–03
virago 8, 239–40n10
Virgin of Guadalupe 45, 149, 195
virginity 10–11, 22, 90, 153, 157, 169, 176, 201
visibility 16, 19–20, 34, 46, 53, 56, 108, 135, 220–21
Viveros Vigoya, Mara 105

Walker, Alice 163
warrior 3–5, 7–8, 12, 31, 39, 41, 44, 48, 53, 58, 70, 96, 98, 100, 102, 107, 132, 138, 141–42, 167-68, 181, 192, 209, 224, 234, 239n8, 239–40n10; best warrior 14, 39, 65, 74, 99, 103, 111, 133, 139–40, 142, 230. *See also* trans warrior; warrior women
warrior maid 2, 8, 10–13, 59, 64, 240n15, 242n9
warrior women (definition) 2–11; strategies of 2, 7, 30, 32, 39, 40, 47–48, 53, 71, 76, 111, 113, 115, 117, 142, 164, 182–83, 226, 229, 232–35. *See also* Angustias; Ci; Claire; empowerment; disempowerment; Doña Bárbara; Gertrudis; Iracema; Itzá; Maria da Fé; Maria Moura; Nacha Ceniceros; Pintada
Warwick, Alexandra 38, 49
Waters, Mary-Alice 206–08
weapons 2–3, 61–62, 111, 142, 166, 199, 206, 211–12, 239n8; beauty as 160; use of 2–3, 44, 49, 111, 121–22, 135, 140, 166, 199, 202, 209, 224

White, Allon 17
whitening project. *See* Venezuela
Whittle, Stephen 60
Wickham-Crowley, Timothy P. 215
Williams, Raymond 204
Wilson, Elizabeth 30, 34, 53
Wilson, Glenn A. 162
Winters, Lisa Ze 247n10
women in war 4, 7, 9–12, 38, 43–46, 58–59, 79, 81, 89, 109–10, 113, 181, 184, 188–89, 206, 217, 220, 224–26, 230–35, 240n13; as messengers 11, 206; as nurses 10–11, 206. *See also* guerrilla; warrior women
Woolf, Virginia 6
Wright, Winthrop R. 129

Yáñez, Agustín 119, 185

Zamora, Fernando 178, 185
Zapata, Emiliano 194
Zé Sereno (José Ribeiro Filho) 63, 167

301

About the book

Carolina Castellanos Gonella
Warrior Women and Trans Warriors: Performing Masculinities in Twentieth-Century Latin American Literature
PSRL 92

Latin American literature has depicted warrior woman and trans warrior characters in armed conflicts, but literary critics have not paid much attention to their empowerment. They have also critiqued these characters using traditional gender binary concepts or have viewed their access to power as evil or abnormal. *Warrior Women and Trans Warriors: Performing Masculinities in Twentieth-Century Latin American Literature* introduces a new perspective as it analyzes how one trans warrior and two warrior women from three canonical novels contest traditional codes of behavior and appearance. It examines Pintada in the Mexican novel *Los de abajo* (1915); Doña Bárbara, in the Venezuelan novel *Doña Bárbara* (1929); and Diadorim in the Brazilian novel *Grande sertão: veredas* (1956). *Warrior Women and Trans Warriors* focuses on how these three characters challenge conventional norms and empower themselves by giving orders, using weapons, fighting, competing with male characters, exposing traditional gender ideologies, and transgressing sartorial gender rules. Drawing on trans theory, intersectionality, gender performance theory, and masculinities studies, the book argues that performing masculinities allows these characters to occupy the place of the most-desired position of their contexts.

About the author

Carolina Castellanos Gonella is a Professor of Spanish and Portuguese at Dickinson College. She has a B.A. in Literature from the Universidad de los Andes in Bogotá, Colombia, an M.A. in Hispanic Languages and Literatures from the University of Massachusetts Amherst, and an M.A. in Portuguese from Vanderbilt University. Her Ph.D., also from Vanderbilt, is a double major in both Spanish and Portuguese. Her main areas of research are Brazilian and Mexican literatures and cultures. She has published articles in journals such as *Latin American Research Review, Luso-Brazilian Review, Revista canadiense de estudios hispánicos, Chasqui, Literatura mexicana, Revista de estudios de género y sexualidades,* and *Journal of Lusophone Studies.* She is currently researching how Latin American women drug traffickers are represented in literature and newspapers.

www.ingramcontent.com/pod-product-compliance
Lightning Source LLC
Chambersburg PA
CBHW061429300426
44114CB00014B/1612